DANISH   GREENLAND

No. 1. Seal-hunting from the kayaks with harpoon and bladder.

DANISH GREENLAND
ITS PEOPLE AND PRODUCTS

BY

HENRIK RINK
Translated from the Danish by the Author

With a New Introduction by
HELGE LARSEN

Montreal
McGILL–QUEEN'S UNIVERSITY PRESS
1974

First published 1877 by
Henry S. King & Co., London

Reprinted by offset-lithography 1974
© 1974, C. Hurst & Co. (Publishers) Ltd., London

New Introduction © 1974 by Helge Larsen

ISBN 0 7735 0217 3

Library of Congress Catalog Card No. 74–81690
Legal Deposit 3rd Quarter 1974
Bibliothèque Nationale de Québec

Printed in Great Britain

INTRODUCTION.

In the present book we meet Hinrich Johannes Rink—these were the author's actual Christian names—as a natural scientist and as a humanitarian. It was in the first capacity that he arrived in Greenland in 1848 to prospect for mineral deposits, primarily graphite, with a view to mining. Though attempts at mining in the Umanaq District proved unsuccessful he continued his geological investigations in North Greenland until 1851. He also accomplished the first survey of the coal deposits there and made the first geological map of a part of Greenland. Based on an earlier sketch map and with the aid of a compass, a pocket sextant, a mercury barometer, and a length of rope for measuring a base line, he made a map of North Greenland.

It was, however, as a geographer rather than as a geologist that he made a name for himself in the scientific world. One of the problems that occupied his mind during his first years in Greenland was the connection between the huge ice sheet that covers the interior of Greenland and the wonders of the arctic waters, the floating icebergs. He asked himself whether the snow and rain falling on the "inland ice" (as he called it) was accumulating and would cover ever larger areas, and in the end also the coast land, or whether these deposits would vanish—but, if so, how? The answer to this question was, according to Rink, that in certain areas of the inland ice there exist ice-flows in which the ice, faster than the surroundings, moves in the direction of one of a number of so-called ice fiords. At the head of these fiords the ice-flows converge,

Introduction.

forming one large glacier which, sliding along the bottom, slowly moves out into the fiord until, at a certain depth, the ice is lifted by the water and floats. Occasionally, tensions cause part of the glacier front to break off, and icebergs are formed. The results of Rink's observations obtained recognition in wide scientific circles and contributed to universal acceptance of the so-called ice age theory, which at the time was the subject of much discussion. It was said about Rink's treatise on the inland ice and the icebergs that his name would be preserved for the future even if he never set pen on paper again. Fortunately he did write more, and advanced other new ideas.

Rink returned to Denmark in 1851, but the following year he was back in Greenland, this time as a member of a governmental commission set up to look into "Greenland affairs", among them the questions of trade monopoly and the admission to Greenland of private people. Upon his return to Denmark he wrote a paper on "The Trade Monopoly in Greenland", declaring himself for the monopoly and against the free admission of private people. One already notices Rink's desire to protect the Greenlanders—a desire that was behind all his doings during his many years of service in the Greenland administration. Rink joined the administration in 1853 as manager of the Julianehåb District; in 1855 he moved to Godthåb, at first as manager and acting inspector and 1858–68 as Royal Inspector of South Greenland. The ability he had shown as a natural scientist he now applied to the benefit of the Greenlanders. It was during these years that he wrote and published the major part of the Danish version of *Greenland* which forms the basis of the present book. This work was duly recognized as the best description of Greenland and its people since Hans Egede's classical work of 1741, and it became known abroad through a German edition in 1860. The English version is not just a translation from the Danish; it is a book of its own, and in some respects superior to its

Introduction.

Danish counterpart. It is better planned, and the twenty years that had passed had added to Rink's understanding of the Greenlanders and their problems. A serious problem was the decrease in population since 1855. In eight years 200 people had died from cold and famine during the winters and from chest epidemics during the summers. In addition, the relations between the Greenlanders and the Danes had created problems. Rink had taken it upon himself to try and find the cause of the bad conditions, and as a result of his studies, which are comparable with those of present-day social anthropologists, he published a paper in 1862 entitled *The reason why Greenlanders and similar people living by hunting decline materially through contact with the Europeans.* Though he does not specifically mention it, Rink uses the conclusions of this paper in the present book. Searching for the cause of the gradual impoverishment of the Greenland people, he advances the hypothesis that "the real reason can be found in the disturbance of their original social conditions, caused by the influence of the foreigners. Their original customs and laws were closely connected with their worship of religious ceremonies and thus consequently abolished when Christianity was introduced." Hans Egede, "Greenland's Apostle", said that "the heathen Greenlanders had no authority, no laws, no order, and no kind of discipline". The early missionaries did not understand that the shamans or *angakoks*, as they were called in Greenland, were highly respected members of the community, that they were consulted in all questions of importance and, therefore, possessed authority. Instead of making friends with the *angakoks* and attempting to christianize them as their first step, the missionaries did everything to combat them and to abolish their authority. It was among the duties of the *angakok* to see to it that people obeyed the customs and unwritten laws, and without him, these gradually lost their significance and were forgotten. The missionaries banned the song contests where two opponents mocked each other in songs accompanied by the beating of a drum until one of them had to give in. They did not understand that the people gathered at such an occasion actually acted as judges in the contest, and that the punishment of the loser usually consisted of public disgrace. In a small community, disgrace is a serious penalty, and it sometimes had the result that the person thus punished left the community.

In addition to losing their authorities, their laws and legal proceedings, the traditional economic system of the Greenlanders was also in danger as a result of the trade with the Danes—all in all a very serious situation for the Greenlanders, "Having arrived at the conclusion", Rink wrote, "that the decline is due to the changes inflicted on the social life, the consequence must be to introduce improvements along the same line". His idea was to replace the lost institutions with new ones in which the Greenlanders themselves had influence. "First of all", he said, "we ought to have native clergymen. or the native catechists should be given the greatest possible authority. These clerical people should also be dominant in the secular authority, consisting of the most capable sealers preferably elected by their own countrymen. The Europeans, who after all are indispensable in the country, should merely act as supervisors, abstaining from any direct or casual interference, which might weaken the authority of the natives." Rink was not only a man with advanced ideas; he was also in the lucky position that he could put them into practice. In collaboration with good friends in Godthåb, among them the famous linguist Samuel Kleinschmidt, he made out the rules for the so-called Board of Guardians which was introduced in South Greenland in 1862 and in North Greenland the following year. They were local councils consisting of the Danish civil servants and representatives of the Greenlanders elected by the leaders of their districts. The Board of Guardians administered social welfare, acted as the legal authority in settling disputes among the Green-

Introduction.

landers, and had some police authority. At the meetings of
the Board, the Greenland members made their statements
first and their decisions were rarely overruled. The setting up
of the Board of Guardians marked a new era in Greenland,
being the first attempt to give the Greenlanders influence in
the management of their own affairs. For this alone Rink
deserves a place of honour in the history of Greenland.

HELGE LARSEN

DANISH GREENLAND

ITS PEOPLE AND ITS PRODUCTS

BY

DR HENRY RINK

KNIGHT OF THE ORDER OF DANNEBROG
DIRECTOR OF THE ROYAL GREENLAND BOARD OF TRADE
FORMERLY INSPECTOR OF SOUTH GREENLAND
AUTHOR OF 'TALES AND TRADITIONS OF THE ESKIMO' ETC.

EDITED BY

DR ROBERT BROWN, F.L.S. F.R.G.S.

AUTHOR OF 'THE RACES OF MANKIND' ETC.

WITH ILLUSTRATIONS BY THE ESKIMO, AND A MAP

HENRY S. KING & CO., LONDON

1877

PREFACE.

————•◦•————

SEVERAL REASONS have led the author to believe that this work might have claims to other than Danish readers, and that an English edition might be desirable. Long ago the series of expeditions in search of a North-west passage and of Sir John Franklin and his companions drew some public attention to Greenland. The Danish establishments along the coast of Davis Strait, on the very threshold of the extensive polar regions explored and surveyed on these occasions, were frequently visited by the English vessels. But of late years expeditions aiming at a more general investigation of the regions around the North Pole have given rise to several grand and bold undertakings more or less connected with the extensive coasts of Greenland. What can be more adventurous than spending an Arctic winter in navigating the ocean on a piece of ice? And yet this has of late been achieved, once along the east and once along the west coast of Greenland.

For very important special explorations of the remotest part of this country we have to thank the renowned American pioneers, *Kane, Hayes,* and *Hall.* On its desolate eastern shores a *German expedition* has made valuable discoveries. And now we are able to close the chronicle of daring adventure in the vicinity of Greenland with an exploit which in all probability has finally determined its vast outlines. It was a party of the last *expedition under Captain Sir George Nares*, consisting of Lieutenants *Beaumont* and *Rawson* and Dr. *Coppinger*, who brought back news from the far-off and, we may add, terrible outskirts of Greenland. Two of their gallant companions, *James Hand* and *Charles Paul*, came back no more—a fresh proof of the dangers and hardships such heroes have to meet in the service of science and in honour of their country.

For a century and a half Denmark has maintained stationary establishments over a large sweep of the Greenland coast. The scientific world is therefore entitled to expect from us such details as may throw light upon the Arctic regions in general, and which only long experience can give. It is a compendious account of the knowledge gained in this way which I have tried to draw up in these pages.

I am well aware that due attention has already been given to Danish sources in English works on this subject. In 'Arctic Geography and Ethnography' and the 'Manual and Instructions,' both published in 1875 in behalf of the Arctic Expedition, I have not only found my own contributions made use of in a way which I highly appreciate, but these books have also in several instances been of use to myself while composing the present essay. But my Danish description of Greenland, published at intervals from the years 1851 to 1857, required a new arrangement, with additions and improvements, to make it more suitable for a wider circle, and more abreast of what we now know of Greenland.

In this way my Danish original in this its English dress

has been so much altered that it must be considered a new book. Its compendious form has not allowed references to the earlier literature on Greenland ; and only in a few cases, especially as to the latest explorations, will our sources of information be quoted. My own share of the statements here given is based on the fact that I have been intimately connected with affairs of Greenland for twenty-eight years, of which sixteen winters and twenty-two summers have been spent in the country itself.

This immense land has peculiarities the study of which can throw light on geographical science in general. In the first place, although stretching several degrees south of the polar circle, it is thoroughly an Arctic country. This, in connection with its wide area and continental character, has produced the remarkable icy covering of its interior, un-equalled elsewhere. It exhibits the only regions where real icebergs have been observed in formation, and where the movements which have constituted the glacial epoch of the geologists are still going on, and may be studied by actual experience. At the same time we find ordinary Alpine glaciers of enormous size spread over the summits of its lofty headlands. The latest explorations have furnished most valuable information. A Norwegian geologist who visited Greenland in 1875 for the purpose of studying its glaciers discovered the extraordinary velocity with which the inland ice-covering is propelled towards the sea, and which proves its essential difference from the ordinary Alpine or high-land glaciers. And the finding of musk-oxen in the farthest north on both sides of Greenland, while there is no trace of them over the rest of its extensive outskirts, corroborates the opinion that the continent-like mainland with its peculiar frozen upland does not extend much farther towards the north-east than the extreme points indicated by the explorers despatched from the 'Discovery.'

Secondly, the population of Greenland furnishes an example of a nation in the age of stone which, though subject to the influence of modern culture for 150 years, has at the same time maintained its chief features, and still subsists by means of its own ancient contrivances, whose loss will in all likelihood cause its destruction.

Lastly, although almost without any history of its own, Greenland is remarkable for having sent out the ships which first made known American territory.

As regards Greenland life, no one will deny that it would be very interesting to see it pictured by the Greenlanders themselves. In a journal published among them in the Eskimo language, articles have been now and then inserted written by natives, chiefly on adventures in their hunting and travelling life. A selection from these is inserted in the present book, literally translated, and only abridged in some places. Notwithstanding their imperfection and rudeness, they give the direct impression of the scenes they describe, and I think will be found to possess a freshness and genuineness which will make them an appropriate supplement to the more systematic account of the same objects in the book.

To these little papers written by themselves I have been able to add some pictorial illustrations from the same source. The lithographs are exact copies of pictures made by natives. An explanation of each is given in Chapter XIV.

The coast of Greenland has of course been only imperfectly surveyed. In 1866 Mr. S. Kleinschmidt compiled a map from earlier plans and from information acquired in the country by himself. He added geographical names in the Eskimo language. Thinking it would be useful, I have sketched the outlines of the coast from this map of Kleinschmidt, which seems very neatly and carefully made. But I have appended some marginal maps illustrating the chief features of the ice-formations, as well as of the ancient colonisation, the whole sketch being merely intended for practical help in reading the book.

I should never have ventured to publish the present translation without having secured the assistance of some one who would take upon himself the responsibility of its descriptions, being in intelligible English, and its style tolerably correct. I was happy enough to find this assistance in my friend Dr. *Robert Brown*, who has already rendered me the same service with regard to my collection of the 'Eskimo Tales and Traditions,' published in 1875. The appreciation which this essay has met in English reviews still more confirmed my opinion that I could find no better editor than Dr. Brown, not only on account of his experience in literary work, but also on account of his familiarity with the subjects of the present book.

In numerical statements, care has been taken to give them in corresponding English standards. For length, English inches, feet, yards, and miles ; for volume, gallons and tuns (252 gallons) ; for weight, English ounces, pounds, hundredweights, and tons ; for money, £1 at the rate of 9 Danish rigsdalers or 18 Danish crowns ; for thermometrical observations, the scale of Fahrenheit.

Bits of the Eskimo language as spoken in Greenland,

when inserted in this book, are printed in bolder type and spelled according to the orthography now adopted for school instruction in Greenland. A brief outline of the construction of this tongue, its pronunciation, and especially the etymology and correct spelling of geographical names, will be found in the Appendix. It will be seen that only a few characters or signs differing from English are used in it. In Eskimo words and names wholly embodied in the English text, and printed in ordinary Roman type, these peculiarities are avoided by using the nearest corresponding common letters, and by omitting accents.

I cannot close these prefatory remarks without thanking our highly esteemed Professor of English here, the eminent archæologist, *George Stephens*, for the readiness with which he has always assisted me whenever I have applied to him in connection with this work, as well as the 'Tales and Traditions' lately published.

HENRY RINK.

Copenhagen : *May* 1877.

CONTENTS.

CHAPTER V.

PRODUCTS AND RESOURCES OF THE LAND.

CHAPTER VI.

THE CAPTURE OF SEALS AND WHALES.

CHAPTER VII.

THE FISHES AND FISHERIES OF GREENLAND.

CHAPTER VIII.

HISTORICAL REMARKS ON THE GREENLANDERS.

CHAPTER IX.

THE INHABITANTS : THEIR MEANS OF SUBSISTENCE.

CHAPTER X.

THE INHABITANTS : THEIR DOMESTIC LIFE AND HABITS.

CHAPTER XI.

KNOWLEDGE AND ENLIGHTENMENT.

APPENDIX.

ILLUSTRATIONS

ADDITIONS AND CORRECTIONS.

With reference to this List of Errata, the Publishers consider it to be due to themselves to say that they have supplied numerous proofs and revises to the Author, and have in no case printed off a sheet until it had been returned to them with instructions to print.

Page 43, line 21, *for* quite unknown *read* somewhat doubtful

  ,,   50, ,,   17, *for* twenty *read* between sixteen and twenty

  ,,   59, ,,   22, *for* 44' *read* 43'

  ,,   70, ,,   10, *read* the *oily* substances

  ,,   85, ,,   12, *read* willows (Salix arctica and S. glauca) and dwarf birches
                                  (Betula nana) . . . juniper (Juniperus nana)

Page 93, *after* line 4, *insert* :

To the species of phanerogamic plants mentioned in this chapter we might add the following as giving an idea of the *chief features* of the Greenland vegetation; the asterisks especially indicate *the bulk* of the sod or prevailing parts of the *common vegetable covering*; (S), (N) signify south, north :— Equisetum arvense ; E. silvaticum, Polypodium phegopteris (S), Aspidium fragrans, Woodsia ilvensis ; W. hyperborea (N), Lycopodium selago ; L. annotinum, Alopecurus alpinus * (N), Hierochloa alpina,* Calamagrostis purpurescens (N) ; C. neglecta. Aria alpina (S). Catabrosa algida, Poa alpina ; P. pratensis ;* P. cenisia (N). Festuca ovina ; F. brevifolia,* Elymus arenarius, Carex Wormskjoldii ;* C. rupestris (N) ; C. capitata ; * C. nardina ;* C. glareosa ;* C. Vahlii ;* C. hyperborea ;* C. rariflora ;* C. supina,* Eriophorum Scheuchzeri ;* E. angustifolium.* Luzula spicata ; * L. arcuata ; L. multiflora ;* L. parviflora,* Juncus arcticus ; J. castaneus ; J. biglumis.* Tofjeldia borealis, Habenaria albida (S). Salix herbacea.* Rumex acetosella ; R. acetosa (S). Polygonum viviparum, Armeria labradorica, Erigeron compositus; E. alpinus ; E. uniflorus, Artemisia borealis, Gnaphalium norvegicum (S) ; G. supinum, Antennaria dioica ; A. alpina, Taraxacum palustre, Hieracium alpinum (S) ; H. vulgatum (S), Campanula uniflora, Thymus serpyllum * (S), Veronica alpina, Pedicularis hirsuta (N) ; Pedicularis Langsdorffii (N) ; P. euphrasioides ; P. lapponica ; P. flammea, Bartsia alpina, Pinguicula vulgaris, Diapensia lapponica,* Azalea procumbens,* Rhododendron lapponicum. Ledum groenlandicum* (S); L. palustre. Phyllodoce coerulea,* Andromeda tetragona * (N), Oxycoccos palustris (S),

Cornus suecica (S), Saxifraga stellaris;* S. nivalis;* S. rivularis;* S. cæspitosa;* S. tricuspidata*(N); S. oppositifolia.* Ranunculus pygmæus; R. hyperboreus; R. nivalis; R. lapponicus; R. acris (S), Papaver nudicaulis, Vesicaria arctica (N), Cochlearia officinalis; C. fenestrata (N), Draba arctica (N); D. nivalis; D. hirta, Cardamine bellidifolia, Arabis alpina, Turritis mollis, Pyrola grandiflora, Alsine rubella, Stellaria Edwardsi, Cerastium alpinum, Silene acaulis, Epilobium latifolium; E. angustifolium (S). Dryas integrifolia,* Sibbaldia procumbens,* Potentilla anserina; P. Vahliana; P. nivea;* P. emarginata;* P. maculata;* P. tridentata,* Alchemilla vulgaris.

Rare or characteristic of certain localities are the following species:—

Blitum glaucum (60°-61°), Taraxacum phymatocarpum (70° 45'), Primula stricta (N); P. sibirica (61°); Arctostaphylos uva ursi; A. alpinus, Platypetalum purpurescens (70° 45'), Viola canina (60°); V. palustris (61°), Rubus saxatilis (60° 8'), Lathyrus maritimus (60°-61°), Vicia cracca (60°-61°).

Page 108, line 17, *read* pounds of raw eiderdown

,, 112, ,, 19, *for* the boat *read* the bladder or boat

,, 119, ,, 34, *for* atluk *read* agdlo

,, 158, ,, 23, *for* wall *read* hill

,, 174, ,, 12, *for* fifty *read* forty

,, 174, ,, 32, *for* 339 *read* about 370

,, 218, ,, 25, *for* womankind *read* mankind

,, 226, ,, 7, *for* without *read* within

,, 244, ,, 18, *put in parentheses* by the Almighty.

,, 269, ,, 14, *for* 7 (2) *read* 9 (2).

,, 277, ,, 12, *for* 1869 *read* 1864.

,, 279, ,, 4, *for* angákok *read* angákoκ.

,, 315, ,, 18, *for* Ikerasarsuk *read* Ikerasak.

,, 318, ,, 19, *for* walls *read* hills.

,, ,, ,, 22, *for* of *read* called.

,, 319, ,, 17, *for* Ikersak *read* Ikerasak.

,, 329, ,, 35, *insert* Kornok, 60; Kanginguak, 13.

,, 334, ,, 22, *for* S.E. *read* S.E., and 40 miles from N.E. to S.W.

,, ,, ,, 23, *for* Between *read* In between.

,, 338, ,, 34, *for* Igilorsuatsiak *read* Igdlorsuatsiak.

,, 341, ,, 10, *for* Itiudlermiut *read* Itivdlermiut

,, 344, ,, 17, *for* cliff *read* cleft.

,, 347, ,, 18, *for* originates *read* was met with.

,, 349, ,, 8, *for* 2,000 and 2,200 *read* 2,060 and 2,265.

Page 350, line 15, *insert* : On the north side of the Ingnerit-Fjord, Helland
    found one top (Agpatsiait) measuring 6,670 feet.

,, 351, ,, 13, *for* 6,000 *read* 4,000 to 6,000.

,, 363, ,, 5 and line 20, *for* Sermiliarsuk *read* Sermiligaitsiak.

,, 368, ,, 10, *for* discovered *read* described.

,, 371, at the end *insert* :

 Finally, it might be remarked, that if the Greenland inland-ice is said to
differ from ordinary glaciers only as regards their extent and the degree of their
action, this assertion might give rise to misapprehension.   The lowest and
foremost edge of an ordinary glacier essentially differs from its upper part on
the mountain top.   But all that has hitherto been seen or discovered of the
Greenland inland-ice, although we have called it a *mer de glace*, is to be considered merely the foremost part or seaward edge of enormous glaciers which,
on their way towards the coast, have flown together and coalesced.   Instituting
a comparison between this *mer de glace* and that on mountain tops in temperate
climates will be the same as comparing the lower and foremost part of extensive glaciers with the upper part of inconsiderable ones.

Page 395, line 28, *for* for *read* to.

,, 398, *after* line 15 *insert* : **eкaluk,** salmon trout ; **eкalugssuaк,** shark ;
      erкaк, neighbourhood, environs; **erкardleк,** relative,
      kinsman ; **erneк,** son.

,, 400, line 27, *for* nárporpoк *read* náparpoк.

,, 404, ,, 4, *for* Holgrimson *read* Kolgrimson.

,, 433, ,, 28, *for* Tornavi Arsuk *read* Tornaviarsuk.

 In several places, *for* Arsut or Arsuit *read* Arsuk ; *for* Sakak *read* Sarkak ;
for Sermiar*sut* *read* Sermiar*suit*.

Copenhagen, June, 1877.   THE AUTHOR.

DANISH GREENLAND.

——•◦•——

CHAPTER I.

INTRODUCTORY HISTORICAL REMARKS.

VERY DOUBTFUL and scanty remains have hitherto been found on the North American continent itself, which bear witness to its having been visited by voyagers from this side of the ocean, and even to its having been inhabited by European settlers several hundred years before the discovery of America by Columbus. Our sole knowledge of these ancient enterprises has been derived from the Icelandic sagas, or popular tales. These sources of inestimable value, on account of their having been written down at so early a period, when the events related in them were still in fresh remembrance, though historical, exist of course only in a fragmentary condition, and bear the general character of popular traditions to such a degree that they stand much in need of being corroborated by collateral proofs if we are wholly to rely upon them in such a question as an ancient colonisation of America. In Greenland several ruins are still to be found throwing light upon the story of its having been colonised at the same time and by the same race of seafaring people. These early settlers undoubtedly carried on a rough and frugal existence, and for that reason their habitations and other buildings were insignificant in size and almost without the application of

ornamental art, but at the same time the barrenness of the
Greenland soil has been more than usually favourable for
preserving the traces of their rustic dwellings throughout
the whole land. In a country where no tree can grow, the
growth of luxuriant vegetation cannot have concealed the
remains of human work, and the Eskimo people, who took
possession of the country after the disappearance of the
ancient settlers, have never possessed dwellings more pre-
tentious than small huts, the remains of which are always
situated just above the limits of high-water mark, and, in
most cases, easily distinguished from the former. For this
reason even the faintest traces of any former building may
be discerned on the ground, which is merely covered with
a vegetation the growth of which seldom exceeds some
inches, and only exceptionally attains a few feet in height,
and which has never afterwards been disturbed by any
kind of cultivation or any subsequent work of the hand of
man.

From the southernmost of the present chief stations,
an excursion of about twelve miles leads us to the most
remarkable of these ruins, viz. the Kakortok church,
situated on a small and pleasing flat at the foot of a lofty
jagged mountain ridge. It is constructed out of large
stones carefully selected from among the numerous blocks
found in the vicinity, but bearing only slight traces of having
been artificially formed or hewn. They are most skilfully
adapted to one another, and fitted together so as to leave
no open spaces or inequalities of the surface. From the
outside, moreover, no sort of cement is visible ; only by
lifting the stones may a little sand and some indications of
mortar be discovered. The church contains three separate
entrances ; the principal one is covered with a very large
regular flat stone, measuring about twelve feet in length.
In the opposite or Eastern wall is a window most skilfully

arched, but apparently likewise constructed from rough stones. In the vicinity of the church several other ruins of houses or fences are found, but only one of the walls can still boast of an entrance, being also covered with a stone. As to the others, they are all very low, and partly over-grown with creeping juniper and willows, a description which, in fact, applies to all the other places where Norse ruins have been found. In most cases the walls have mouldered away into stone heaps more or less covered with luxuriant tufts of grass, the general indication of any spot in Greenland having been occupied by human inhabitants. About a hundred of such places have been found scattered along the coast of Greenland, and by a careful comparison of these localities with the ancient nar-ratives it has been possible to lay down with the utmost degree of probability the old geographical names of the sagas on our present maps.

Red Erik and his followers.—An Icelander named Erik Rauthi, or Erik the Red, who was declared an outlaw in consequence of disputes and murderous frays, made ready his ship in order to find out for himself a new country where he could go and take up his abode. On the eve of departure he made known to his friends, who accompanied him beyond the islands, that his intention was to set out in search of the land which had some years before been sighted by Gunbjörn, son of Ulf Kraku, another Icelander, who at that time had been driven westward by fierce storms. Having happily found the land, Erik set out to the south-ward in order to see whether it might be there inhabitable. He made a two winters' stay in the new country, which he explored, and where he gave many places names. The third summer he again returned to Iceland, calling the land he had thus discovered Greenland, 'because,' said he, ' people would sooner be induced to go thither in case it had a good name.' And thus it happened that twenty-five ships were equipped, and followed him on his next voyage to Greenland, of which, however, fourteen only arrived, the rest being either lost or compelled to go back. The new comers settled down in the country, which they divided amongst them, each of the chiefs taking his 'fjord,' or inlet, most of them choosing the eastern settlement, whilst some also went to the western part. This colonisation of Greenland took place as nearly as possible in the year 986. When it is said that Erik, after having crossed the channel between Iceland and Greenland, sailed southward to see where the land might be found inhabitable, it appears not unreasonable to suppose that 'inhabitable' in the first place implies 'not inaccessible on account of its being encumbered with a belt of drift-ice,' and, secondly, 'yielding sufficient means for the subsistence of settlers.' It is to be taken for granted that the ancient records perfectly agree with the situation of the ruins which are now most generally assumed to be those of the so-called eastern and western 'bygds,' or settlements, as also with the present features of the country on the whole.

The only thing that calls forth our amazement is the fact that Erik and his followers in the course of three or four years should be able to find out what in modern times only repeated exploring expeditions, extending over more than a hundred years, at length succeeded in rediscovering, notwithstanding the enormous advantages furnished by science and new inventions, and the assistance rendered by governments to the later explorers. The first obstacle encountered by the voyagers to Greenland is the border of drift-ice that commonly guards the coast, which is generally so narrow that the vessels outside can sight the land across it, but yet so thick and dense that it becomes more or less impossible to force a way through it.

Secondly, if we succeed in reaching the shore we meet with labyrinths of rocks, islands, and bluff headlands, all of them barren and desolate, offering at first sight nothing that would seem to secure the necessary means of subsistence for human inhabitants. Numerous inlets are found between these islands and peninsulas leading further into the inner country, and here, at no less than thirty to forty miles' distance, or even further away from the outer islands, small tracts of flat land will be found, which might well have appeared inhabitable to the ancient discoverers. How they ever found out these spots, far apart from one another and totally hidden behind the craggy and ice-covered headlands, is a matter of surprise. When Erik had first sighted the land opposite to the coast of Iceland, he found it encumbered with the same barrier of drift-ice which in modern times has frustrated so many hazardous attempts to reach the coast. We may also conclude that he attempted to force his way through it in many places before he sailed four hundred miles to the south-west and rounded Cape Farewell, and, having finally succeeded in landing, he must afterwards be supposed to have tried hundreds of sounds, deceptive inlets and creeks, or *culs de sac*, on the coast bordering Davis Strait at a stretch of four hundred miles.

With all the detailed knowledge which has now been acquired regarding the same coast, the Danes having had establishments there for more than a century, no better localities for settlers have yet been found than those which Erik of old pointed out to his followers in the fourteen ships which succeeded in reaching the country. Some of them settled in the eastern, others went to the western 'bygds,' it is said. This gives rise to a belief that the eastern and western settlements were separated from each other by Cape Farewell, but it has been almost with certainty proved that both were situated on the west side of Greenland. This coast having a direction from south-east to north-west, the southernmost settlement might very properly be called the eastern one. They were separated by a coast-line of about two hundred and fifty miles in length, which has not been quite uninhabited, but where the ruins still existing bear evidence of only a few isolated houses or hamlets having been scattered here and there.

If we wonder how the ancient Norsemen were enabled to detect the localities best adapted for colonisation, it is also a striking fact that the first discoverer should have happened to fix upon the prettiest of them for his abode. For really, to settlers of another race than the Eskimo, no spot in Greenland could be more inviting, or, we may say, less discouraging, than the one which is now conjectured to have been the ancient residence of Erik the Red, and by whom it was called Brattelid, at Erik's-tjord. This is the present Eskimo station called Igaliko, situated on an isthmus between two tjords, the supposed Erik's and Einar's-fjords.

The ruins or foundation walls of about seventeen buildings have here been traced on a pleasant grass-covered plain. There is even reason to believe that one of these ruins still bears evidence of having been the very house in which Erik took up his first abode. At a distance of 400 feet from the shore, we find the remains of a building, one side and both ends consisting of huge piled-up stones, while a low perpendicular and smooth rock has been used for the other side, so that one of the inner walls of the house has been formed by a natural cliff between ten and twelve feet high. The name Brattelid signifies 'steep side of a rock,' and considering that among all the ruins of ancient habitations this seemed to be the only one of this kind of construction, and that this ruin is the most important one in that place as regards the solidity of the walls, and finally that the en-

virons of the houses present no other feature likely to have
given rise to the name, there is no small probability as to
the correctness of the conjecture. The walls of this remarkable house are more than four feet thick, and built up
with blocks of red sandstone, probably with interposed clay,
of which, however, now only the intermixed coarser parts
or gravel remain. Somewhat more than twenty years ago
the entrance was still well preserved, measuring about
six feet in height and four feet in breadth, but now since
the covering stones have fallen down it is hardly recognisable. The stones of these walls are of an astonishing size, some of them measuring four to six feet in
length, as well as in breadth and thickness, and we are
rather at a loss to imagine how they could possibly have
been transferred, lifted up, arranged and fitted so nicely
to one another, the inequalities having been carefully filled
up with wedges of smaller stones. One of the end walls
is now totally overturned, and the interior of the house,
measuring forty feet in length by twenty in breadth, is
filled up by a mass of the fallen stones.

One of the other ruins appears to have been a church,
and fragments of runic stones, indicating Christian sepul-
chres, have likewise been found thereabout. The surrounding plain gently rises into green hills, beyond which, at a
distance of scarcely two miles, lies Erik's-fjord, the opposite side of which is particularly rich in ruins of the old
settlement, and possesses a comparatively luxuriant vegetation. Although Erik, according to the sagas, is said to have
taken up his abode at the Erik's-fjord, and we, nevertheless,
find Igaliko to be situated on the banks of Einar's-fjord,
this does not necessarily invalidate our hypothesis that
Igaliko is the same as Brattelid. The distance being likewise so short to Erik's-fjord, there is some reason to believe
that the place may well have been considered as environs

of the latter, and that Erik might have been induced to fix on this spot nearer to the shore of the other fjord on account of its being earlier open to navigation in spring, and of its situation in the very centre of the regions around the interior inlets occupied by the eastern settlement offering the best means for communicating with most of them.

Bjarni Herjulfsson's Discovery of America.—Among the Icelanders who settled in Greenland in company with Erik was Herjulf, who took possession of Herjulf's-fjord, and put up his abode on a point called Herjulf's-ness. He had a son called Bjarni, a promising youth, who was fond of travelling abroad. Early he earned both riches and esteem, and fitted out a ship, intending to sail every second winter, whilst every other he would stay with his father in Iceland. It so happened that Bjarni returned home in the same year in which his father had left with Erik for Greenland. Bjarni instantly took a fancy to follow him. He intended, he said, to continue his old habit of spending every other winter with his father, drinking the Yule-tide ale with his father as had been his wont since a boy. Consequently, he now wished to bear for Greenland, and asked his crew whether they would join him, although his task might seem somewhat imprudent, seeing that none of them had ever been in the Greenland Ocean before. His companions having consented, they sailed for Greenland, and had a favourable wind ; but soon a dense fog arose, and they could see neither sun nor stars, and did not know whither they went, and continued thus for many days. At length they sighted land, but Bjarni said it could not be Greenland. They sailed close up to it, and found it to be without mountains, only exhibiting small heights covered with wood. And steering onwards for two days more they came in sight of another land, which was flat and also

covered with trees. Here Bjarni had a dispute with his
sailors, who insisted upon landing, which, however, he
would not agree to, but turned his prow and sailed on with
a fair south-westerly breeze for three days, when they
beheld the third land. But this appeared to be mountainous and covered with glaciers. Bjarni thought it but
little inviting, so he again turned about and put to sea as
before. The wind again favoured, but freshened anon, and
Bjarni ordered his men to shorten sail, and venture no
more than their ship could stand. They continued to sail for
four days, and when land was again seen, and the crew
asked Bjarni whether he believed this to be Greenland,
' It appears most like Greenland,' he answered, ' according to
what I was told concerning it, and here we will try to land.'
They did so, and at eventide landed on a promontory,
which they found was the very spot where Bjarni's father
lived, and there he took up his abode with him.

These are the words of the saga, but it appears somewhat
doubtful that the voyagers after such a cruise should happen
to find just that particular point of the vast Greenland coast
where Herjulf lived. We cannot but believe that they had
to roam about for a time in search of people, and did not
find their goal until they had got information in the country.
However, it seems conformable to the nature of traditional
stories, that details which would have been too onerous to
the memory of the story-tellers and no less tiresome to the
auditors, should during the lapse of years have been done
away with. This mode of condensing the narrative need
in no way shake our confidence in the trustworthiness
of the old tales with regard to their principal details.
A careful study of the saga has led to the conclusion,
that the coast discovered, but not visited by Bjarni, was
the tract stretching from Connecticut to Newfoundland,
and the investigations of the ruins in Greenland have

enabled us to point out the probable situation of Herjulf's-ness. The seat of Bjarni's father was an exception to the general rule in being situated on a promontory at the mouth of a fjord, and not at the innermost part of its shores. Opposite to the Moravian station of Frederiksdal, some remarkable ruins are found on a promontory facing the open sea, and presently called Ikigait. One of them appears to have been surrounded by a fence, the enclosed ground consisting of alluvial soil, and having been washed and undermined by the sea. Numerous remains have been revealed which prove it to have been the churchyard of the old Christian Norsemen. Wooden coffins have been found with skeletons, and entire shrouds made of coarse hairy cloth. In some of them were small wooden crosses, which had apparently been enclosed in the folded hands of the dead; and in one of these the name of Maria was carved in runes. A Christian tombstone with a runic inscription has also been found here. This place has probably been Herjulf's-ness.

The news of Bjarni's adventurous voyages soon reached Iceland and Norway, creating a great stir, though people wondered that he could have been so devoid of curiosity as to have omitted to put his foot on any of the new countries he had discovered, and that he had nothing at all to relate about them. The first voyage in search of these new countries issued from Greenland, and was planned at the seat of Erik the Red at Brattelid. His son Leif bought Bjarni's ship, and his crew consisted of thirty-five men all told. Erik reluctantly consented, on Leif's request, that he should accompany him as the leader of the expedition. But when Erik rode down from his house in order to go on board, his horse stumbled with him and he had a fall. The old man taking this as a bad omen said : ' It will never be my lot to discover any other land than the one we are now in possession of, and we shall henceforth make no more voyages together.' He then went back to his house, but Leif sailed with his men, and they first arrived at the coast which Bjarni had seen last. They moored the vessel and went ashore, but found the land a plain covered with flat stones without any grass, and up the country icy mountains. This country they called Helluland. Again they made sail till they came to another coast, where they also landed, but the country was flat and covered with wood. They called it Markland. But making no further stay there, they continued their voyage with a wind from the north-east for two days more, whereupon they made the third land.

Here they found an inlet, and took their ship up a river, and further into a lake, where they found the country so pleasant that they resolved to take up their winter quarters. They built large houses, and Leif then arranged their time, so that some of them remained at home while others explored the surrounding country, always using great circumspection, and without separating from one another or going out a greater distance than enabled them to reach the house at nightfall. They found an abundance of large salmon, an exuberant vegetation, and even discovered wild grapes—no doubt what are now called in New England 'fox-grapes'—which induced Leif to call the country Vinland. The next year they returned to Greenland with a cargo of timber and grapes. In the following winter Vinland was all the talk, and Leif's brother Thorvald thought that it had been too little explored, and was seized with an ardent desire to go thither. He borrowed the ship from Leif, and having consulted with him, put to sea with thirty men, reached his goal and spent the winter in Leif's house. In the following spring he refitted his ships in order further to explore the country, but returned to the house without having seen any sign of inhabitants. After having spent one winter more in this place, they again set out on a cruise and came to a flat promontory which looked very beautiful and was all over covered with wood. Down on the sandy beach they discovered three skin boats, and three men under each of them. They at once resolved to give chase to the strangers, and succeeded in catching and killing eight of them ; one, however, escaped and disappeared in the interior of the firth. Soon after an immense crowd of skin canoes appeared from that side, and began a battle with the ship, in which Thorvald was killed with an arrow. But his companions passed one more winter in Vinland, and next year returned to Greenland.

This voyage of Thorvald's is supposed to have taken place in the years 1002 to 1005. But another still more remarkable expedition was undertaken two years later, and, likewise from Brattelid, by a rich and active man named Torfin Karlsefne, who came to Greenland from Norway, and, stopping the winter over, was married there to a relation of Erik. He sailed with 160 men in all, and they likewise came to Helluland, Markland, and Vinland, and made many discoveries, but here we will only mention their encounter with the natives. It is told that whilst they were building their houses, they one morning early perceived a number of canoes making towards them. The crew were an ugly lot, with black coarse hair, large eyes, and broad cheeks, and after having stared for a while at the foreign settlers, they rowed away. But later on they again returned in greater numbers, and Karlsefne and his people hoisted a white shield as a sign of peace, and succeeded in persuading them to approach and began bartering with them. They preferred scarlet to any other article, and offered furs in exchange for it. They also wanted weapons, but Karlsefne—prudent man—would not allow them to have any. The natives would give an entire fur skin for a scrap of red cloth to tie round their heads. Thus the traffic was carried on for some time, till the cloth began to grow scarce. Then Karlsefne and his people cut it into small strips no wider than the breadth of a finger, and still the natives gave as much for it as before. It is also told that the Norsemen had milk from the cattle which they had brought along with them, and their women set boiled groats or porridge with milk before the natives, who relished the dish, and gave away their skins in exchange for it. But at the same time it so happened that a bull coming out of the forest gave a loud roar, on hearing which the natives all took to their canoes and fled the place. After a while they again made their appearance, but this time they showed hostile intentions, and an encounter ensued, ending in a murderous fight. Karlsefne returned from Vinland to Greenland in 1011 ; the Norse settlers in Greenland continued to have outlying colonies in Vinland, and occasionally visited them on their trading voyages, but they never acquired any possessions there for the same length of time as in Greenland.

In the sagas interesting details are found about what the ancient explorers saw in the mysterious countries which they had discovered. We will only add that a careful examination of the records as well as of the localities in question has suggested the opinion that Vinland, Markland, and Helluland are the present Massachusetts, the environs of Halifax, Nova Scotia, Newfoundland, or perhaps some coast tract further north, such as Labrador, and that the indigenous people have been Eskimo, who, in those remote ages, may have extended their migrations further south than they are known to have done in modern times. That the aboriginal hunting nations of America could have deterred the hardy and daring Northmen from taking

permanent possession of any part of their country is hardly
to be wondered at if we duly consider the scanty number of the latter, their isolation from their fellow countrymen, and their want of many of the means, particularly
of firearms, which have given subsequent European discoverers so great an advantage over the indigenous races
in other parts of the globe.

A Journey along the East Coast.—We have already stated
that the ancient Greenland colonies, although they were
termed the eastern and western settlements, both, in all
probability, were situated to the west of Cape Farewell.
An occurrence dating from the time of Erik the Red, the
history of which has been brought down by a saga, corroborates this opinion in a remarkable way. The simple and
unaffected account in the old record gives us a picture of
the ice-bound shores of Greenland to the east of Cape
Farewell, and opposite to Iceland, exactly agreeing with
the aspect of those desolate regions at the present day.

A man called Thorgils Orrabeinsfostre, although young
in years, proved himself a distinguished seaman, and commanded a ship in the service of Hakon Jarl, of Norway, at
whose house he made the acquaintance of the young Erik
the Red, with whom he contracted a cordial friendship.
Later on, when he had settled down in Iceland, his former
fancy for sea adventures was roused anew by an invitation
from Erik, who then resided in Greenland. Thorgils accordingly sold his estates, and engaged several companions to go
with him, besides his wife Thorey, his head man Thorarin,
and his thralls — or 'housecarls' — as he intended to
establish a farm in Greenland. They put to sea and sailed
westward, but had no sooner lost sight of land than they
met with headwinds and gales, and in this manner they
drifted about the whole summer till in the month of October
they were driven ashore on a sandy beach in Greenland,

probably in a high latitude and amidst numerous icebergs, so that the ship was a total wreck, whereas the boat escaped destruction. They now built a large winter hut, divided by screens made out of boards. The greater part of their cattle had perished, but they had still a supply of meal, and besides succeeded in catching some seals and went out fishing in their boat ; but notwithstanding, as winter wore on, their provisions grew scarcer. At this time it so happened that Thorey gave birth to a boy, whom she had great difficulty in nursing. It is told that Thorgils had adopted the Christian faith, but that the thralls of his companions were still heathens. At the time of the ' Yule ' or Christmas festival, the thralls carried on their usual heathenish games, when all of a sudden they passed into a state of frantic fury, and shortly after a severe sickness broke out amongst them. First, six men died, and afterwards more, until all of the accompanying party had been carried off by the beginning of March. On seeing so many deaths, the survivors in this desolate place were seized by a superstitious horror. They continually fancied that they saw ghosts—or wraiths, as they called them—and especially in that part of the hut where the heathens had revelled in their games.

These visions did not cease to torment Thorgils until he had gathered all the corpses and burnt them on a pile. Spring had now set in, but the drift-ice encumbering the coast rendered departure impossible. In the course of summer, however, they managed to gather a store of provisions which enabled them to get through the next winter. The second spring came, but still the ice did not give way. Then the wife of Thorgils was seized with strange apprehensions. She dreamt of seeing a charming country where lived people clothed in shining white garments, and this she considered a foreboding of death and delivery from all her troubles. One day, when the weather was fine, Thorgils resolved to ascend the glaciers and look out over the ocean to see whether the ice had begun to move. Three of his companions followed him, while the other thralls had to go out fishing, and Thorarin promised to attend to the sick wife, after having assisted them in pushing the boat into the water. In the afternoon Thorgils descended from the hills, and as it had commenced snowing, he walked in front making the way for them. But he was nearly stunned on finding that the boat was missing, and when he entered the hut he perceived that his men and chests had disappeared. 'There is something wrong here,' he cried, and advancing, they heard a rattling noise, and found Thorey in a dying state in her bed and the baby still sucking her. On a closer examination, they found that she had been stabbed to death by the thralls and the faithless Thorarin, who had afterwards taken flight in the boat, carrying off all the provisions. This sight caused Thorgils the greatest heart-ache he had yet suffered. The thought how he could preserve the life of his child was almost bringing him to despair. He then had recourse to a strange experiment by opening his own nipple and allowing the infant to suck it. The result, it is said, was that first blood appeared, and afterwards a mixed fluid, but he desisted not till milk was brought forth, and in this wise the boy was nursed.

He and his three men then took heart again, pursuing their fishery and building a boat, which was done by first making a frame work, over which was expanded a skin cover. One morning Thorgils went out by himself on the ice, and discovered the carcase of a whale in an opening, and beside two 'witches' (or 'goblins,' evidently Eskimo women), who were tying large bundles of flesh together. Thorgils instantly rushed upon one of them with his sword and cut off one of her hands, whereupon both of them took to their heels. They now procured a supply of provisions from the carcase, and when finally the ice had opened along the shore, they departed in their frail skiff from this dreadful place of sojourn. They travelled throughout the summer, and again put up a hut for their winter quarters. Next summer they started again, and though suffering frightfully from hunger, they still struggled on, forcing their way along glaciers and precipitous coasts. In a place where they had put up their tent, it once happened that their boat suddenly disappeared, at which Thorgils, in a fit of despair, was on the point of killing the child and himself, but his companions restrained him from so doing ; and again he had dreams and visions, which he interpreted to mean that all would turn out well in the end. Some time after, the boat, which appears to have been stolen by natives, was restored to them, and Thorgils had the luck to kill a bear, whose flesh was shared out with the utmost care and economy. Having passed by many fjords and creeks, they saw a tent of linen cloth pitched on a beach. Here they found Thorarin, who tried to excuse himself, saying that he had been compelled to do the deed by the thralls, who had threatened him with death. But Thorgils answered : 'Indeed I do not know what punishment such conduct of thine might deserve, but thy talk seems very improbable to me, and thou shalt live no longer.' Upon which they killed and buried him then and there. They once more continued their journey southward whilst autumn again was approaching. By this time they had passed about three years on the coast. They then quite unexpectedly came to an inhabited place, where lived a man named Rolf, who having been banished from the eastern settlement, had established a small farm in this deserted region. He treated the distressed travellers well ; they stayed with him through the winter, and the child was taken care of by the women. Next spring they got a ship from Rolf, and reached the residence of Erik the Red in the same summer.

The Introduction of Christianity.—It is said that Leif, the son of Erik the Red, spent one winter with King Olaf in Norway, and on this occasion was converted to Christianity. When Leif sailed for Greenland, the king ordered a priest and some other clerks to follow him, thinking this would be a favourable opportunity for propagating the new faith in Greenland. On arriving here, he went to dwell with his father at Brattelid, but Erik showed no disposition at all to embrace Christianity, and said that Leif had only brought evil men to Greenland, namely, the priests. But his wife Thiodhilda consented to being baptised, and she built a church at Brattelid where she often went to repeat her prayers. It is not ascertained whether Erik died as a heathen, but the people of Greenland soon adopted the Christian faith, although they remained very rude and ignorant. From the first century we have still very interesting records in the sagas of some distinguished chiefs, giving detailed accounts of the life then carried on by the settlers in Greenland. But subsequent to the death of the illustrious chief and bard, Helge of Brattelid, in 1070, the tidings from these colonies suddenly become rare.

It is said that the Pope resolved to give the Greenlanders a bishop to themselves, not on account of their number, but because of their country being situated at such a far-off place. Arnold was the first bishop, who took his abode at Garde on the shore of Einar's-fjord in 1126. The remains of this see, the church, and the adjoining monastery have been pointed out with great probability, opposite to the ruins of Brattelid above described. The Greenland settlement had a republican organisation like that of Iceland until the year 1261, when a new bishop came out from Norway, and, instigated by King Hakon Hakonsen, persuaded the Greenlanders to swear allegiance to him. From this time, forthwith Greenland was subject to the Norwegian government, and specially made one of the queen's domains. This dependency in great measure acted as a check upon the home communication, and tended to promote the decay of the colonies. From this very period, however, we have an interesting account of an exploring expedition undertaken by the Greenlanders to the farthest north, chiefly for the purpose of discovering the abodes of the Eskimo.

The Northern Discoveries of the Colonists.—The colonies did not extend further to the north than 65° N. lat., but in summer-time the inhabitants used to carry on seal hunting in the northern regions, and a runic stone found in a cairn upon a small island in about 73° N. lat., most strikingly confirms the old records as regards this statement. The runic inscription on this stone, which was presented to the Museum of Northern Antiquities in Copenhagen, contained the names of three Northmen, and a date which has been referred to the year 1235. The above-mentioned expedition is related to have been made in the year 1266, and the detailed statements and records have led to the conclusion that the explorers had passed through Lancaster Sound into the inlets of the Arctic archipelago, and reached a latitude of 75° 46′, or in other words have only been surpassed by the most renowned of modern explorers in penetrating into these ice-bound regions. Of course the observations upon which this calculation has been based are very rude ; but considering that the ancient explorers belonged to a seafaring race, having had their home in

Greenland, and their ordinary hunting grounds in 73° N. lat., the fact seems in no way improbable. The use of oars for propelling their vessels may especially have tended to facilitate their navigation in the icy seas.

The Decay of the Colonies.—During the lapse of the next century, periods of several years often seem to have passed by in which no ships at all came from Greenland to Norway. In the year 1347 one ship arrived which had also visited Markland ; this is the last trace of an ancient communication between Scandinavia and the American continent. During the period subsequent to the year 1349, when the plague or 'black death' broke out in Norway, the far-off colony was still more neglected. In 1379 (or 1349) it is said that the western settlement was attacked and destroyed by the Eskimo, and from that time the Norse were confined to the southernmost part of the country. From the year 1409 a remarkable document has been preserved, containing a wedding contract of a young Icelander, who was married on a visit to Greenland. This 'marriage settlement' was drawn up at Garde in Greenland, and signed by the officialis or vicar of the bishop. In all likelihood none of the bishops appointed to Greenland after that time ever set foot in the country ; the last one died in Denmark about the year 1540.

After the year 1409 the tidings grow more and more rare and obscure. In 1432 a treaty was made between England and Denmark, according to which the English king promised that such people as had been carried off from Iceland and other northern countries should be sent home again on having been duly paid. A brief written in 1448 by the Pope to a bishop in Norway treats of the pitiful condition of the inhabitants of Greenland, who thirty years before had been attacked by a hostile fleet. The invaders had laid waste the land and carried off people of both sexes into captivity. Now many of the prisoners had come back and rebuilt their houses, but being without churches and priests, they had to perform long and troublesome wanderings in order to repair to those amongst their countrymen whom the barbarians had spared. This writ, the very last official document from the time of the ancient colonies, has, by collating the contents with the treaty formerly mentioned, given rise to the conjecture that the invaders mentioned by the Pope had come from the British Islands, where the pestilence had caused a great decrease in the population, and people were sought for from those northern countries that had escaped the general calamity. This supposition, however, does not account for the final fate of the remaining colonists, in behalf of whom the Pope applied to the bishop in Norway. Between the years 1400 and 1448 some communication at long intervals still seems to have existed, but in the last half of that century it is known for certain to have perfectly ceased, and henceforward the sailing route to Greenland actually passed into oblivion. When the country had been rediscovered by John Davis in the year 1585, and the whole coast had been afterwards thoroughly searched, no others than the present Eskimo people were found there, who have only preserved two or three traditional tales about the ancient Europeans in their country.

According to the most popular one of these apparently trifling stories, an Eskimo who lived upon one of the islands visited the Europeans whose settlement was at the interior of a fjord, and wantonly killed one of them. From this murder a warfare arose between both parties. Winter having set in and the sea being frozen over, the Europeans attacked the islanders. While all the rest were put to death, two brothers fled away, persecuted by the chief of the enemies, called Ungortok, who overtook and killed one of them, whereas the other, called Kaissapee, escaped. Kaissapee travelled about to his countrymen, engaged companions, and procured an enchanted arrow, and a boat of a peculiar construction, enabling him to make it assume the appearance of a piece of ice. By means of this stratagem they made a stolen attack upon the Norse, put fire to their house, and killed the whole of them excepting Ungortok, who made his escape, and afterwards wandered from one place to another in search of a safe refuge. Kaissapee, however, continued the pursuit until he succeeded in killing him with the enchanted arrow.

The question concerning the decay and mysterious disappearance of the ancient European race in Greenland has also given rise to the conjecture that its climate had changed, the drift-ice from the North Atlantic Ocean having increased and encumbered its shores, and the snow accumulated on the top of the mountains. A careful examination, however, of everything tending to elucidate this problem leaves no sufficient reason to believe that the climate has deteriorated or the fertility of the soil decreased ; or on the other hand that snow and glaciers have accumulated to such a degree as to make the country less inhabitable and productive of the necessaries of life.

There might more likely be some grounds for supposing that the land in the course of time has become more difficult of access because of the greater accumulation of drift-ice from the ocean, but even this supposition has not been proved by sufficient evidence. Conjectures have also been made as to the possibility of the last Norse inhabitants having become intermixed with the Eskimo intruders, and consequently that their descendants are still to be found among the present natives of South Greenland. The author of this book is in favour of this last opinion, and adding it to some of the other causes of decay above touched upon, we shall be able to explain the utter decline of the settlements without being reduced to ascribe it to a single one among them. Regarding their means of subsistence, the settlers derived them more from the sea than from exclusively terrestrial resources, and as regards their marine undertakings, boats did not suffice, but ships were necessary for the prosecution of their hunting and fishery. The first cause of their decay was, here as in Iceland, internal feuds, concerning which the sagas of the first century give us a lively picture. The next must be attributed to the restricted intercourse with Iceland and Norway. Being deprived of the necessary means of building ships, they were cut off from one of their principal sources of wealth. The settlers, confined to small scattered establishments at the shores of the interior inlets, may besides, successively, have been subjected to many other privations, and even have come short of boats, which were requisite for their internal communication and their chief occupations. Then perhaps came the hostile invasions, of which we will here—omitting the other very dubious one—only consider that which was made by the Eskimo, who finally came into possession of the country.

The sudden attack reported in the sagas to have been made in 1379 by the Eskimo, whom the Norse were in the habit of calling Skrellings, makes it seem probable that an uncommonly numerous tribe of this people from the western regions had migrated to Greenland somewhat previous to that particular time. It may be considered a fact that they did not cross Davis Strait, but went over to Greenland in the farthest north, and it is also quite possible that during the period in question the Eskimo may have migrated or spread more speedily and in greater companies than their present habits denote. But a closer examination will also soon prove that the Skrellings not only existed in Greenland before the Norse, but also that their numbers may have increased more gradually in the remoter parts of its vast shores extending beyond 80° north latitude, whilst the Norse only maintained possession of the tract south of 65° on the west side. The renowned Icelandic author Are Torgilsson, who lived from 1068 to 1148, in his book 'On the Icelanders,' writes as follows:—'The land called Greenland was discovered and peopled from Iceland. . . . They (viz. Erik the Red and his companions) found there in the eastern as well as in the western tracts human dwellings, as well as fragments of boats and articles wrought of stone, giving evidence that the same race of people as those who inhabited Vinland, and whom the Greenlanders (viz. the settlers) called Skrellings, must have roamed about there.' The author adds that his information has been gained from Thorkel Gellerson, a distinguished Icelander, who on a visit to Greenland happened to meet and have some conversation with one of the very companions of Erik the Red. We have mentioned that Thorgils probably fell in with the natives on the east coast, and that a discovering expedition in 1266 was sent for the purpose of tracing out the dwelling-places of the Skrellings. When it was made known at Garde in the eastern settlement that the western one had been attacked by the Skrellings, who had killed eighteen men and carried off two boys as prisoners, a man named Iver Bere was despatched thither, but he found the colony deserted and only a few head of cattle left, which he carried along with him on returning.

This is the last time that mention is made of the western settlement, and the records neither speak of the Skrellings as having dwelt in the neighbourhood during the years before nor after the said attack, although it might seem probable that then they had been advancing towards the eastern settlement. This seems to prove that the appearance of Skrellings on the shores of the Arctic Seas was not so extraordinary to the settlers that it need be dwelt upon as a matter of moment in the scanty records we have of their deeds. It moreover becomes evident from the said last account that the western settlement must have been for a long time declining, and almost depopulated when the Skrellings came to make war upon it, and that they only had to vanquish a few remnants of the inhabitants. The traditions of the present natives evidently allude to a time when their ancestors and the ancient Europeans inhabited the country in fellowship, the former being stationed upon the islands on the outer coast, whilst the latter had their dwellings along the shores of the inlets. Both parties carried on a friendly intercourse before the last feuds began. We have reason to believe that the tale of Ungortok and Kaissapee is representative of similar conflicts and frays that occurred in different places, ending in the total destruction of the Europeans with the exception of those who amalgamated with the conquerors. An ancient and not untrustworthy account makes mention of certain Christian Greenlanders who, in the year 1342, fell off from their own religion, consorted with the Skrellings and adopted their mode of life.

If we picture to ourselves the small communities mentioned in the papal brief, scattered here and there in the fjords, the trade with their fellow-countrymen in Europe having been totally discontinued, their incorporation into the Eskimo nation seems the most probable consequence of their condition. Isolation and privations must necessarily in time have got the better of their national pride, whilst at the same time, witnessing those other people out upon the islands enabled by means of their skin-boats and peculiar contrivances to procure abundance, they must, at last, have had great inducement to adopt their mode of life. When, subsequent to the rediscovery of Greenland, the southern districts were again visited by European travellers, many individuals were found amongst the natives exhibiting a complexion, and also a frame of body, which seemed greatly to indicate an intermixture with European blood—a fact which also has been observed with regard to the natives east of Cape Farewell. The last supposition might also yield a clue to explain the fact that the same district which is now considered to have been the last ancient settlement, and has consequently been latest peopled by the Eskimo, is now the most populous part of the country, perhaps owing to the intermixture of the races having proved favourable to propagation. Before leaving the last historical glimpse of the ancient settlements we will only add a few words more about the numbers, stage of culture, and mode of life of their inhabitants during their period of prosperity.

State of the Old Greenland Settlements.—The eastern colony is reported to have had eleven or twelve churches, and 190 villages or farms. In the present southernmost district, comprising the most genial fjord-tracts, between eighty and ninety places have been discovered containing ruins of habitations, and eight of them, moreover, indicating remains of churches. In the western colony three or four churches and ninety farms are spoken of in the records, and at present two churches and many inhabited places have been traced on the fjords supposed to have been this inhabited tract. If we consider the usual size of the ruins, measuring scarcely more than from twelve to sixteen feet in breadth, and forty feet in length, they will appear most likely to have been inhabited by less than twenty to thirty souls, and in such places where the number of ruins indicate the largest villages to have stood, the inhabitants have hardly exceeded a few hundreds. According to these statements the whole population of the ancient settlements cannot be supposed to have amounted to 10,000 souls. A remarkable, and in all likelihood a contemporaneous, record written in Norway, runs thus: 'The people of Greenland are obliged to import a great many things from other countries, such as timber for their houses, as well as iron, whereas they on the other hand export sheep-wares, ox-wares, sealskins, tusks of walrus, and ropes cut out of their hides. Some of the richest persons have made the experiment of sowing corn, but people in general have no idea of bread, and have as yet never had the sight of it. There are, however, to be found pretty good pastures, and there are also fine large farms on which the owners keep plenty of cows and sheep, and prepare a good deal of butter and cheese; from this produce a great part of their means of sustenance is derived, as well as from all manner of game, such as the flesh of reindeer, whales, seals, and bears.' These words of the old record may be said to agree very well with the present physical features of the country, and there is no reason to assume that they should have deteriorated to any essential degree.

The soil could hardly have been submitted to any manner of cultivation without some trace of this being still visible. The fine grass plains, however, about the Igaliko ruins are almost the only spots exhibiting such an appearance. It must be admitted that our present attempts in the way of farming in Greenland are always attended by such a struggle for providing sufficient in winter, that at first glance they might seem to be wholly at variance with the old record, without supposing some extraordinary deterioration of the pastures of the olden times to have taken place; but on closer investigation we shall find the apparent contradiction to be sufficiently explained by the fact that the ancient colonists have surpassed the present European residents in Greenland both as regards their skill in finding out the indigenous plants best adapted for fodder, and in their mode of husbanding and preserving them.

As regards seal-catching, the Northmen had nothing like the kayaks of the Eskimo. They mostly seem to have practised it upon the ice, and as the sea off the coast where they lived is generally open, even in winter, it is to be observed as a remarkable fact how, in many instances, the situation of the ruins denotes that the sites of their dwelling-places have been chosen in the neighbourhood of inlets sufficiently sheltered to be covered with fixed ice in winter. There is, however, reason to believe that they may have made use either of harpoons or other tools similar to those of the Eskimo, though unknown in Iceland. Their summer expeditions into Baffin's Bay were undoubtedly chiefly undertaken with the aim of pursuing the seal upon the ice. This agrees with some notes in the ancient records referring to a remarkable walrus-hunt having been carried on by the Greenlanders. The tusks of the animal were the most precious article of export. They paid their tribute to the Crusades in the shape of walrus-tusks, delivered at Bergen in 1327, and their weight is noted on a receipt which is still in existence.

The size of the ruins, as well as the scanty remains of household and manufactured articles which have been found, demonstrate the very frugal, and generally speaking even poor and rough, mode of life carried on by the ancient Greenland colonists. That these colonies, comprising a population of only a few thousand souls, should have produced any considerable amount of wares for export cannot be expected. It nevertheless remains somewhat inexplicable that the commercial interest attached to them has been so insignificant; that the intercourse with the parent country gradually ceased, after having been repeatedly interrupted during periods of several years, and during almost a century apparently had only been continued by means of a single vessel occasionally arriving in Norway from Greenland. There has been found an old historical notice which tells us that in the year 1484 there still lived forty men in Bergen who were acquainted with the Greenland navigation, and used annually to bring home precious cargoes from that country. On returning in that year they were asked by some German merchants who stayed at Bergen, to sell some of the wares, but they declined to let them have any of them. The Germans then took revenge by murdering them in an assault committed during a banquet to which they had invited them. From this moment, it is said, it became impossible to sail for Greenland, because nobody knew the road thither. We are not able to test the truth of this account, but at all events it is the very last one relating to the old Greenland navigation.

Searching for the Lost Settlements.—In 1579 and 1581, the first expeditions were despatched from Denmark for the rediscovery of Greenland, and the resumption of the trade with its inhabitants. It seemed to have been a firm belief that people of Norse descent still lived there ; but so totally had the knowledge of the colony been neglected, that these expeditions only tried to reach the east coast opposite to Iceland. They did not even, like Erik the Red, sail southwards to learn whether the coast might be inhabited there. The pack-ice bordering the east coast proved impenetrable, the result of their attempts consequently was a total failure, and the rediscovery of the sailing route to the deserted settlements became the achievement of a foreign nation, and the accidental result of explorations undertaken with a very different object in view.

It was John Davis who, in the year 1585, in search of the north-west passage around America, discovered the strait named after him, and, following the west coast of Greenland, succeeded in landing there in about 64° N. lat., where he entered a fjord and bartered with the natives. It is a well-known fact that in this and the following voyages he penetrated into Baffin's Bay to upwards the latitude of our present northmost settlement, surveying the coasts on both sides. These discoveries in Denmark revived the thought of the long-neglected and given-up settlement, and even led to the opposite extreme in giving rise to the most sanguine expectations with regard to its significance and riches. In 1605, Christian IV. of Denmark sent out three ships under the command of two Englishmen and one Dane, named Lindenow, who were accompanied by one James Hall, who, having been in Greenland before, was appointed pilot or sailing-master. Shortly after they had got sight of Greenland, the commanders fell out, and the ships separated. Lindenow succeeded in getting through the ice, and finding a harbour somewhere about 62° or 63° N. lat. Here they met with a great number of natives, and began to barter with them for furs and narwhal-horns. The natives proved to be very thievish, snatching away everything they could lay hold on, and the Europeans, *per contra*, availed themselves of the favourable state of the market by giving a single nail, it is told, in cash for wares worth two to three Danish dollars.

Having carried on the traffic for a sufficiently long time, they secured two of the native merchants themselves, their skin-canoes into the bargain, and threw them into the ship's hold along with the other articles going for show to Denmark. The two poor wretches fell into a state of fury, so that the crew were obliged to have them tied to the mast, and with gun-shots to frighten away their countrymen who were coming out to their rescue. Meanwhile, the other ships had gone much further north, and landed somewhere south of 67° N. lat. They likewise met with many natives, and commenced bartering with them for skins, whalebone, narwhal-horns, and walrus-tusks. The commanders of these ships could as little resist the temptation of carrying home some specimens of the human inhabitants, in order to exhibit them on their arrival in Europe. After having ' killed a good many of them,' says the old record, ' they succeeded in capturing four alive, though not without running great risks.' The prisoners were so savage and unmanageable that the sailors were obliged to shoot one of them to reduce the others to order. On the voyage, however, they grew quite merry, and the captain trained them to jump about at a given sign from him when he nodded at them, and to go aloft with the sailors.

When these three ships had returned safely to Copenhagen in the same year, they attracted general attention, but of all the wares and curiosities they had carried home with them, nothing created such an excitement as some specimens of silver ore which the voyagers pretended to have discovered at one of the northmost fjords. The king, in the hope of acquiring a lucrative colony, levied a special Greenland tax throughout his dominions, and in the next year he equipped no less than five ships for an expedition, chiefly with the aim of mining silver ore. The stolen Greenlanders were appointed interpreters to the explorers. The accounts of this enterprise are not very detailed, but it has been reported that they reached the supposed silver mine, found it all right, shipped full cargo of ore, and bartered with the natives, of whom they stole five, whereas, in retaliation for other offences, one of the ships' crew who had been put on shore as a punishment for some crime, was torn to pieces by the Greenlanders. In October, the same year, the expedition returned, but, as it appears, resulting in utter disappointment. The purchases of Greenland articles had only been few, probably on account of the stores having been exhausted in the preceding year. No further mention is made of any silver mines, and it is supposed that it only proved to be the invention of a swindler, and that those who had been duped quietly put aside the mineral cargo after having ascertained it to be devoid of any metallic contents. The human specimens were exhibited, and their limbs measured and examined for the purpose of describing this new race. Later on, one of them died of home-sickness. Another made a desperate attempt at getting back to Greenland in his kayak, in which he perished. The third of the poor wretches died from being overworked, and compelled to go out fishing in winter as well as in summer. The last one tried to make his escape, but was overtaken and died of grief and vexation.

The result of these explorations had been particularly disappointing as regards the rediscovery of the ancient colonies. Desolate and barren rocks had been found instead of farms and green pastures, and the strange people of whom a few individuals had been brought home and been minutely examined, bore no resemblance at all to the reputed ancient settlers. It has taken centuries to discover the real cause of this disappointment, which undoubtedly must be ascribed to an overrating of what Erik the Red had considered an ' inhabitable country.' The want of success on the part of the explorers first led to the resumption of the old idea that the abandoned settlements had been situated to the east of Cape Farewell. Thither the king accordingly, in the following year, 1607, despatched an expedition, which, however, soon returned after several perilous and disastrous efforts to penetrate the belt of pack-ice encumbering the whole of the coast. With the failure of this expedition the government temporarily gave up all further attempts, whereas some private expeditions, English as well as Danish, visited Greenland in the same century, until the government again, in 1670 and 1671, sent out two ships, probably to the east coast, with what result is, however, unknown. These other voyages, in the mean time, gave rise to several commercial undertakings, fishing being tried in the new branch of the Atlantic discovered by John Davis. They were carried on by English, French, and Dutch vessels, and the whale fishery especially acquired a long-continued importance in Davis Straits after the whale had become scarce in the Spitzbergen seas. But only the Dutch seem to have carried on any traffic with the inhabitants of the Greenland coast in connection with the whale fishery. This commerce already flourished in the earliest part of the eighteenth century ; the whalers on sailing up and down the strait occasionally dropped in here and there, anchoring up in the bays, and awaiting the arrival of the natives, who used to bring out the products of their country for sale. Many cairns erected by them, and also many names of places and several traditions, indicate that the Dutch have thoroughly searched the coast from Cape Farewell up to 73° N. lat., but there are no signs left that any settlements or temporary fishing establishments have ever existed, or been attempted or intended by them, nor have their explorations in any way added to the general store of geographical knowledge.

Hans Egede and the Modern Settlements.—We have now come to the foundation of the present European stations in Greenland by the well-known missionary, Hans Egede. The motive that first prompted this extraordinary man, equally excelling in energy and in fervent devotion, to undertake this great task, originally sprang from the same source that gave rise to the first expeditions for the rediscovery of Greenland—viz., a belief that the posterity of the Norse settlers must still exist there. It was not before he had taken up his abode in Greenland, and seen the hopes of finding a people of his own race frustrated, that he embraced the idea of bestowing all his care and zeal on the present inhabitants. He then conceived the plan of procuring the necessary means of supporting a European establishment by help of the revenues of a trade with the natives. That the barter which used to be carried on by the whalers during their occasional summer visits was too insignificant in itself to defray the expenses of any commercial enterprise in Greenland was owing to carelessness on the part of the natives in not saving the produce of their catch, keeping stores, and accumulating property. If an establishment was founded where they could bring their wares for sale at all times of the year, it seemed probable that much would be prevented from going to waste, and might perhaps supply the necessary means for keeping up an establishment. We will omit the details of the series of difficulties, dangers, and hardships Egede had to endure before he was enabled to carry this plan into execution and prove its feasibility. It may suffice to remark that he at length succeeded in forming into a company certain merchants of Bergen, who were willing to fit out two ships for Greenland, and that the king, approving of the plan, appointed him missionary and governor of the intended colony.

On July 3, 1721, he landed with his wife and children on an island at the mouth of Godthaab-fjord, or Baal's river, where he reared his new home in the neighbourhood of a populous wintering place. The natives at first were extremely adverse to the idea of Europeans settling in their country, and it was only the prudent and conciliatory measures and gentle behaviour of Egede, that appeased them and yielded the new comers sufficient security as to their life and property. The traffic, however, continued to prove unprofitable. In the year 1726 the company at Bergen, discouraged by the loss of a ship, dissolved their partnership and abandoned the whole undertaking. The government was now obliged to succour the colonists by taking the sole charge of the trade, as well as supporting a mission. But it set to work in a most preposterous manner, and had recourse to a series of expensive measures, regardless of what had been ascertained about the resources of the colony. With a view of setting about matters methodically, a royal commissary was first sent out in order to make enquiries and ascertain how things could be best arranged. He finished his task in the same summer, and albeit his investigations may have been somewhat superficial, he, at all events, seems to have returned with a better impression of the country than his predecessors. In consequence of the picture he gave of its features, a commission was appointed, consisting of several persons of distinction, and, according to their proposals, a grand plan was drawn up for the formation of a regular colony.

In the same year, 1728, two armed vessels and two transports were fitted out and laden with whatever was required for building a fort of twelve guns in Greenland. A governor was appointed to head the expedition, attended by a captain, who was to be commander of the intended fort, besides a lieutenant, several subordinate officers, constables, gunners, and twenty-five soldiers. Eleven horses were added to the equipment, so that the governor and his attendants might make an attempt to ascertain whether the east coast of Greenland, which had proved to be inaccessible to navigation, could not be reached by going

across the country on horseback.   Five of the poor animals,
however, died on the voyage out, whilst the remainder
soon perished from hunger and hardships in Greenland.
At a later period, however, when the governor set out on the
intended excursion towards the interior of the country, he
may have experienced some manner of consolation for this
loss in the fact that the country which should have been
travelled over only exhibited one vast insurmountable
glacier.   Care had also been taken to supply the colony
with a population of a superior race to the natives.   Besides the soldiers, who were accompanied by their families,
ten male and as many female criminals were taken from
the houses of correction, married by the summary process
of casting lots, and despatched to Greenland.   The ships
reached Egede's place of abode in safety, and the work was
commenced by removing his houses and founding the new
establishment on the mainland where the present settlement, Godthaab, the 'capital' of South Greenland, is situated.   But the new houses were only half finished when
winter set in, to the great dismay of the new comers, who
had already suffered much during their removal.   After
this villanously unpromising batch of settlers had become
devoid of sufficient shelter, not only did disease break out
among them, but their discontent tended to open mutiny.
It is told that in winter the officers were obliged to shut
themselves up in the government house, mounting it with
guns and keeping guard during the night, lest they should
be attacked by their own people.   During this dreadful
winter, no less than forty Europeans were carried off by
sickness.

Notwithstanding the unfavourable news that must have
reached Denmark from the new colony in 1729, a new
project was formed, in addition to the above-mentioned
measures, in favour of peopling the country.   Ruins hav-

N.º 14. (1) Egede arriving at a hamlet.

N.º 14. (2) Egede threatening an angakok.

ing been discovered by Egede indicating the places where
the ancient Northmen had lived, the Danish government
resolved to send out six families from Iceland to Greenland for the purpose of settling down in these ancient
dwelling-places of their ancestors, and try whether they
could prosper there. In the year 1730 a sufficient quantity
of timber was sent out to erect houses for the Icelandic
settlers, but in 1731 the matter was cut short by the unexpected death of King Frederick IV. In this year a vessel
arrived conveying an order from his successor, Christian
VI., to the effect that the establishments for trade as well
as for missions were to be given up, and that the Europeans
should embark for Denmark, with the exception of Egede,
who was permitted to stay with as many of the crew as he
could prevail upon to remain with him. For those who
remained as settlers an allowance of provisions for one year
was granted, but without any prospect of further aid from
the government.

The thought of giving up the fruits of his labours, and
deserting his converts, whose language he had now for the
first time mastered, was the severest of all the trials that
had been inflicted upon him during his tedious stay in this
desolate country. He of course clung to the last hope
that had been pointed out to him, and having persuaded
eight or ten men to stay with him, he wrote a letter to
the king, in which he set forth his state of affairs, exercis-
ing all his eloquence in an appeal to his majesty's feelings,
and soliciting him not to abandon his poor subjects, who
tried to keep up the propagation of Christianity in this far-
away part of his dominions. This letter proved decisive
as to the fate of the colonisation. After having passed
one year of anxious expectation, he had the joyful satisfaction of receiving news from home, with an announcement
of the king's resolution to continue the trade on the go-

vernment account, and grant a certain sum annually for the support of the mission.

From that moment the European institutions in the country were provided for and ordered with discretion and thriftiness on a scale commensurate with its resources. During the lapse of a century the trade naturally extended by means of establishing throughout the whole coast small stations where the scanty and widely scattered population could exchange their home-products for European articles. Only two critical periods have since then occurred, threatening the whole undertaking with destruction, viz., a dreadful epidemic of small-pox in 1733–34, and an interruption of the intercourse with Denmark, caused by the war, in 1807–14. The trade was for some part of the former century made a private monopoly, but in order to keep up the commerce the government was finally obliged to take it up, and since 1774 it has continued to be a royal monopoly. Following the steps of the extending trade, the missionary institutions have gradually incorporated the whole population into Christian communities. The result of the European transactions thus carried on in Greenland for a century and a half, the present state and future prospects of the population, will be one of the chief subjects treated of in the present volume.

CHAPTER II.

CONFIGURATION AND GENERAL PHYSICAL FEATURES OF THE COUNTRY.

The Interior and the 'Inland Ice.'—In most geographical works or memoirs in which Greenland is mentioned or briefly described, it is generally spoken of as an extensive country, of which only the coast is inhabitable or accessible ; the interior presenting nothing but mountain heights, impassable on account of perpetual snow and ice. This description, however true it may be in the main, has given rise to misapprehension, by giving us the idea of a continuous strip or belt, accessible or iceless land, running from south to north along the shores of Davis Strait. On the contrary, the coast is known to be almost everywhere broken by deep indentations, and is, moreover, frequently girt by numerous islands throughout the whole of its extent. In fact, if we are to continue to consider the coast of Greenland as such a strip of land, it must be added that its breadth is not less than twenty to sixty miles, and that it includes numerous narrow and tortuous inlets of the sea. In the preceding historical sketch we have referred to a document illustrating the conditions of the ancient settlements. It is called the ' Speculum Regale,' and is said to have been written in Norway between the years 1154 and 1164, while some have attributed it to the next century. At all events, the author lived while the Greenland colony was still flourishing, and acquired his knowledge about it by carefully questioning travellers coming thence. Regarding its physical features, he says: 'Only a small part of the country is bare of ice, all the rest being covered with it, and people do not know whether it be large or not, because the mountain ridges as well as the valleys are hidden by the ice, so as to leave no thoroughfare anywhere. Nevertheless, in reality, some passages must be supposed to exist, either in the valleys between the mountains, or along the sea-shore, through which the (rein) deer can find their way, seeing that they could not migrate thither from other regions if no such openings where the surface is not covered with ice were to be found. People have often tried to go up the country and ascend the highest mountains in different places, in order to look out for ice-free and habitable tracts, but without discovering any such, excepting the parts now inhabited, which only extend a short way along the sea-shore.'

When now we recollect what we have stated about the first discovery of Greenland and the formation of the first settlements, the words of the old record strikingly agree with the present physical features of the country, and hint at no peculiar changes having taken place, especially as to the extent of perpetual snow and glaciers, during the subsequent six or seven centuries. But this statement also requires explanation, lest it should give rise to the same misconception as the recent accounts above alluded to. Of course, when the old document talks of 'inhabited places along the sea-shore,' it means the tracts in which the farms and hamlets of the settlers were situated, ruins of which are still to be seen. But now we must recollect that these places generally bordered the heads of long and narrow fjords or inlets running into the country, and that they lie hidden behind extensive mountainous islands and peninsulas. It is obvious that the ancient geographer has left this outer land wholly out of consideration, and, in speaking about the icy regions of the interior, only means what is situated still further in the direction of the fjords or beyond their terminations, whereas the land on the other sides of the settlement was by no means inaccessible, but crossed by many valleys, which afforded passages from one fjord to the other, as well as pasture for the farms.

The description given of the lands beyond the ends of the fjords only refers to those amongst the latter which were occupied by the ancient settlements, but the same features are met with throughout the whole coast, which is everywhere broken by indentations in the shape of fjords or sounds. Wherever these fjords have been followed to their terminations and an attempt has been made to penetrate the regions beyond, or to attain a view from the adjoining heights, the country has been found to exhibit the same continuous waste of ice. When visiting the southernmost portion of the mainland in the environs of Cape Farewell, near the latitude of Christiania, we meet with the very same hindrance as on the coast a thousand miles further north. On entering these southern fjords, we are first struck with the luxuriant vegetation, gradually increasing towards their termination. The charming scenery of the verdant valleys and slopes here displayed leads the traveller to suppose that a few miles still further inland the country will be covered with wood and change its arctic character. So far from this, wherever we follow a fjord to its source and try to proceed further in the same direction by land, we are suddenly arrested by a wall of ice rising abruptly from the ground, which in the immediate neighbourhood produces vegetation. But if we subsequently, in order to find some other passage, ascend a neighbouring hill, thinking that the ice wall probably belongs to some glacier of a limited extent, we see that it

forms the unbroken edge of an elevated icy plateau, sloping gently down towards the sea and occupying the whole
interior. As far as this plain can be overlooked from the
heights of the outer land, or has been travelled over (to a
distance of twenty miles from its nearest seaward border),
it only attains a height of little more than 2,000 feet, but
must be supposed to still rise very gradually towards the
wholly unknown interior, where no human foot as yet has
trodden. This elevation is much less than that of the outlying headlands which sever the inland ice from the open
sea, which to the north and the south frequently attain a
height of from 3,000 to 4,000 feet. This circumstance, combined with its uniformity and other reasons derived from
what is mentioned in the following pages, contradicts the
opinion that, like other glaciers or *mers de glace*, it rests
upon a high table-land. On the contrary, its probable
thickness and extent may rather be compared with an
inundation that has overspread the interior in course of
ages, only for some reason or other kept within a certain
limit towards the sea. The analogy to an inundation is
furthermore in accordance with occasional small insular
hills or rocks, called ' Nunataks ' by the natives. These,
however, seldom rise from the uniform horizontal surface,
representing the still emerging mountain-tops of the vanished
land, which on the whole, at least within the first 50 or 100
miles from its western border, seems to have been low in
comparison with the bold headlands which project as its
continuation seaward.

The Greenlanders entertain a sort of superstitious awe
regarding the icy interior of their country. These ' Nunataks ' are looked upon as the dwelling-places of people who
have fled from human society and acquired supernatural
senses, quickness, and longevity. Besides these, several monstrous and terrible beings have their haunts upon these

lonely hills and roam over the great glaciers. In summer, however, hunting parties often visit the margin of the ' inland ice,' and occasionally walk over it for short distances in pursuit of the reindeer, that during the warmest season usually retire to its vicinity. A few other wanderers have also tried a trip across the outer margin of the vast mysterious desert, the most remarkable of these excursions being that of the Swedish naturalists in 1870. When the wall of the ice has been ascended and its first part passed over, it becomes tolerably smooth and level, with the exception of the yawning fissures or ' crevasses ' which here and there unexpectedly traverse the road, and threaten, should a false step be made, a fatal fall of many hundred feet. Lakes are found here and there supplying shoal basins, and beautiful torrents which rush along their icy beds until they meet a fissure and turn into waterfalls disappearing in the bottomless abyss.

Area of Greenland.—The outlines of Greenland are very imperfectly ascertained ; its northern extremity is still quite unknown. Calculations, however, of the extent and *area partly of the inland, and partly of the whole complex,* may be made with some probability, if in both cases we are careful to avoid exaggeration, and rather agree to underrate the extent of the country yet to be discovered. If we suppose Greenland not to extend further to the north than where its outlines have as yet been traced, the circumference of the whole coast-line, including the interspersed branches of the sea, will extend to 3,400 miles, and its area amount to 512,000 square miles. If, furthermore, the whole circuit is supposed to be indented even somewhat deeper than that part of it which hitherto has been tolerably explored, estimating the fjords to run sixty miles from the outer islands towards the interior, the interior will make 320,000 square miles, an allowance of

192,000 square miles being made for the outer margin, or what we will call the 'outskirts,' with their sounds and fjords.   What we have here classified as 'inland,' is what by its size, continental character, and peculiar icy covering, distinguishes Greenland from other polar countries. A construction on the map, with a view to measure how far its central parts are from the coast, will show that a line may be drawn from south to north for upwards of 1,000 miles, with a distance in the middle part of 200, and towards the ends of 80 miles, from the nearest seashore. The Scandinavian peninsula, if calculated in the same manner, would leave an interior only half as large as that of Greenland, and a similar central line drawn up there could present distances only half as long as the corresponding distances in Greenland.   Iceland in the same manner would afford an interior measuring about $\frac{1}{14}$ of that of Greenland, with a central line of eighty miles at a distance of forty to sixty miles from the sea.   Among the coast lands projecting from the interior of Greenland, and uncovered by its ice, we find a peninsula presenting points nearly sixteen miles distant from the nearest shore.   On the whole of Spitzbergen we scarcely find any points further off the sea-shore than twenty or twenty-eight miles. The large islands north of the American continent may in these respects be ranged between Spitzbergen and Iceland.

Origin of the Floating Icebergs.—It is owing to the size and continental character of Greenland, as here explained, that it has become the only hitherto known home of real icebergs in the northern hemisphere.   Scanning our statements as to the icy mantle of its interior and the want of a regular drainage by the help of rivers, the reader might ask whether the accumulation of snow that has given rise to it by partially melting and again congealing into a solid mass, must be supposed still to continue in the central parts, and consequently to be likely to pile up the ice to an unlimited height. Nobody has as yet made direct or extended observations as to the physical conditions of the real interior, and of course we are not able to give a satisfactory solution of the problem, but we possess an important guide in the formation of icebergs. The fact that from certain points along the edge of the great inland glacier extraordinary masses of ice issue into the sea, and the question whether this discharge of water in a solid state may be likely to account for the drainage of the country, is what we shall here try briefly to explain.

A description of the monstrous fragments of ice which are called 'bergs' has so frequently been repeated in the accounts of arctic voyages, that we need only in a few words mention their size and general occurrence on the ocean. What in the Greenland sea is called an *ordinary large iceberg* rears its walls from the surface of the water either to a height of from 60 to 100 feet, with a somewhat horizontal surface, or in a more conical shape ending in pointed summits or ridges, in which it often rises 150, sometimes 200, and more rarely 300 feet, or even more, above the level of the sea. The circumference is from several hundred to some thousand yards. These dimensions only refer to the visible part of the floating block — viz., the top of it emerging from the sea. Considering that seven or eight times as much lies under the surface of the water, the whole bulk of an ordinary large berg must be calculated to have a thickness or height of several hundred, or even of a thousand feet, and its weight must be counted by millions of tons. In short, the visible portion of a large iceberg equals the largest buildings made by human hands, and its whole bulk is only to be compared with mountains. The icebergs, being in a manner themselves fragments, are liable to break asunder and produce more fragments. For this reason the same kind of ice that constitutes the ordinary large bergs occurs in pieces of every size inferior to that of the bergs here described. Every bursting asunder of glaciers or bergs by which fragments are discharged is called calving, and the fragments *calves* or *calved ice.* The latter expressions consequently also comprise icebergs, but are chiefly applied to masses too small to be called bergs. There is, however, no sharp distinction to be made between large and small icebergs and mere calves.

Floating icebergs are scattered over the Atlantic to an amazing extent. Numbers of them annually reach the shores of Newfoundland, and the fishing banks off this island are not unfrequently crowded with them. But stragglers occasionally travel as far south as the latitude of Spain, and one berg is said to have been met with on June 18, 1842, in 38° 40′ N. lat., measuring 100 feet in height and 170 feet in breadth. The whole mass of these strange productions, of a nature so widely differing from that of the regions over which they spread, have their sources in Greenland, are moreover *exclusively discharged from the inland ice* above described, and only emerging from a limited number of narrow branches protruding from it into the sea. The icebergs thus issuing from Greenland are mostly drawn southwards on both sides of this country, without spreading very far to the east and west of it over the rest of the arctic seas.

Glaciers in general have their origin in the snow on the mountain-tops which grows and slides down their sides, and are partly at least pushed on by the direct force of gravity. When they abut on the sea, and their icy walls are constantly washed and undermined by the waves, their projecting parts will of course be dismembered, and fragments will be thrown off and drifted away. This process is going on in numerous places along the arctic shores, but however considerable the fragments may be in many instances, we are still far from having accounted for the manner in which a large iceberg can be launched and set afloat. It is the margin of the inland ice dipping into the sea in certain places, and being broken asunder, which gives rise to this phenomenon.

On the coast which we here particularly treat of—viz., the Danish part of the west coast—these places lie hid at the heads of the fjords or behind islands, while on the same tract many stupendous glaciers present themselves from the ocean, and may give rise to the supposition that bergs are issuing from them. Bearing in mind that the fragment to be detached measures upwards of a thousand feet in thickness, as well as in breadth and length, the solid mass from which it has been severed must likewise be supposed to have at least the same thickness. If the fragment has to be loosened chiefly or more directly by the force of gravity, the main body must rest upon a ground sufficiently smooth and inclining. But in this case it would seem more likely to break asunder gradually, and we should have reason to believe that small pieces would almost continually be detached and rush down the sloping ground, whereas we can hardly imagine how so fragile a mass can be dismembered into parts of a mountain's magnitude. Moreover, granting this to be possible, there seems little probability that such blocks should come rushing down and reach the sea in an unbroken state. Finally, to be properly launched and set afloat they would require an extraordinary depth of water immediately outside.

All these difficulties will disappear when we regard the process which actually goes on in the interior of those inlets which, by reason of the bergs they produce, are termed *icefjords*. In reality the force of gravitation seems to have no *direct* influence at all in loosening the bergs from the firm ice, and even the movement of the glacier itself seems only in a small degree to be promoted by the inclination of the ground. The projecting and advancing branch or defluent of the inland ice that has taken its way down to an icefjord, and which might more specifically be called a glacier, continues sliding along the bottom of the sea until it reaches a certain depth where the buoyant action of the water begins to lift it and keeps its outermost part in suspension. In the sheltered waters of the said inlets the huge mass may still be pushed on for several miles without resting on the ground or losing its coherency. Being kept in suspension by the buoyant power of the water, it presents a nearly horizontal surface like the frozen sea. But from time to time external or accidental causes, such as, for instance, the tides in particular, will be apt to cause fissures to be formed, and the foremost part to be detached and go adrift. The results of this breaking asunder are the bergs. Consequently they are by no means formed by any 'launch' or 'fall,' but in a manner more in accordance with the breaking up of a frozen sea. The displacement of the water caused by the calving of the glacier is, however, violent enough to cause great disturbances.

Having thus considered the process by which the bergs originate, we have to account for the quantity of ice in this manner produced by an icefjord ; only thus can we form an idea whether it might in any way be likely to correspond to the water poured out by a river. The author has tried to estimate from direct observations the *quantities yearly drifting off from the mouths of large icefjords*, and has arrived at the conclusion that each of the most productive fjords yearly sends off at least 10 to 100, but rarely more than 150, and certainly not 250,000,000,000 of cubic feet. The vague appearance of this statement bears evidence of the rudeness of the estimates upon which it is founded. In fact we may say that we have had no real observations at all concerning this remarkable point of physical geography till of late, when, in the year 1875, the Norwegian geologist, Amund Helland, visited Greenland to investigate the action of the inland ice on the ice-fjords. Considering that the edge of the glacier, on account of its being continually wasted by giving off icebergs, in order to maintain its position, must at the same rate be pressed forward, this *movement of the glacier* or downslide of the inland ice gives a far more distinct and trustworthy indication of the ice production than the floating bergs issuing from the fjord. By measuring this movement, Helland. has gained the most extraordinary and interesting results. He has especially surveyed and explored two such branches of the inland ice, both of them belonging to those most productive of large icebergs. One of them he found to have a thickness of 920 feet and a breadth of 18,400 feet, and to advance at a rate of 47 feet a day during the summer season, when his observations were made. As far as the author has been informed, this velocity surpasses by twenty or thirty times that which has been observed in glaciers of the temperate zone. For the whole year these statements would correspond to a produce of 200,000,000,000 cubic feet of ice, while the other ice-fjord surveyed in the same way gave 79,000,000,000. But possibly the velocity is not the same during the other seasons. Now we must take into consideration that no glacier whatever is known to move down any mountain slope without being accompanied by a stream of water whose annual quantity always several times exceeds that of the ice, gliding over the same part of the river-bed occupied by both of them. In fact, no motion of ice on land can be considered possible

without such accompanying water, and as to the inland ice
of Greenland, we must suppose that the whole interior part
of it is permeated by channels and reservoirs of water, and
that its temperature is not influenced by the change of
seasons.   It has been proved by direct observations that
where this ice borders the sea, streams of fresh water issue
underneath the bottom of the ice, and rise to the surface of
the salt water in front of its edge.   If now we suppose that
a proportionate quantity of fluid water accompanies the
masses of ice discharged through an ice-fjord, we shall have
the facts necessary for calculating whether there may be
some probability that the *drainage of the mainland of
Greenland is effected through the ice-fjords.*

We have calculated the area of the interior at the low
rate of 320,000 square miles.   On the Danish part of the
west coast, up to 74° N. lat., twenty ice-fjords or outlets,
from which bergs issue, are spread over an extent of 1,000
miles.   We will suppose that at least 120,000 square miles
are contributing to supply these outlets with ice, so that in
accordance with their productiveness, each of the five principal ice-fjords has 16,000, each of the seven next in proportion to them 4,000, and each of the remainder 1,500
square miles for their tributary basins.   If now, for instance,
we assume a standard of 120,000,000,000 of cubic feet ice
for the production of a first-rate ice-fjord, it will be corresponding to a sheet of water from rain or snow $2\frac{1}{2}$ inches
thick, covering the 16,000 square miles.   But to this must
still be added the effect of water emitted in the shape of
sub-glacial streams.   Supposing these to give a multiple
of the ice—for instance, only a triple—the result, by adding
water and ice together, will be 10 inches.   By taking into
consideration that the calculations of the body of water
annually carried to sea by a certain well-known European
river have given the result that it corresponds to a sheet of

13 inches upon the surface of its basin, it will be found that our estimates, at all events, will lead to a result which lies within the limits of probability. It must be maintained that the third or least productive class of ice-fjords are of little significance, and yet we have been led to assume that more than a thousand square miles of the '*inland*' may be required to provide the supply for each of them. The most stupendous glaciers that issue from the mountain-tops on the *headlands* of Greenland, filling their sloping valleys or clefts down to the water's edge, only require the snow and rain falling upon a surface of 20 to 40 square miles. The most renowned glaciers of the Alps and their tributary basins may perhaps equal the latter in size, and even though we allowed them to be ten times as large, none of them could be compared with the lowest class of ice-streams that discharge icebergs into the Greenland seas.

While the calculations here proffered remain in any case very imperfect, we are still more at a loss to explain how the ice is actually transferred from the interior towards the outlets here pointed out. Several conjectures may be made, but a proper solution of this problem must be expected from future researches, and chiefly from exploring expeditions across the country, or, at least, to its central part, which the author considers to be by no means impracticable. Dr. R. Brown, in his memoir on the ' Physical Structure of Greenland,' has described some of the attempts to penetrate the interior, in one of which he shared. (See 'A Selection of Papers, etc., for the Arctic Expedition,' 1875.) Of late the Danish Government has voted funds for geological surveys of Greenland, and explorations of the inland ice.

General Configuration and Appearance of the outskirting Land.— Having explained what we understand by the interior or ' inland,' the following description will comprise only the coast region, more especially that part which forms the Danish trading districts. This portion of the west coast stretches from Cape Farewell to about 74° N. lat., and is, at 67° 40′, divided into North and South Greenland. Although its extensive and tortuous coast line has as yet only been very imperfectly surveyed, and the exact situation of its eastern border, viz. the margin of the inland ice, is still more hypothetical, we are nevertheless now enabled to give a rude calculation of its area. According to what has been already stated, it consists of projecting parts of the mainland, exhibiting more or less the shape of peninsulas and their off-lying islands. The total mass when surveyed and estimated on the map may be reckoned at about 20,000 square miles. The largest blocks of land consist of two peninsulas and one island (Disco), each of which measures from 1,800 to 2,000 square miles.

We have designated these coast regions as the margin of Greenland which has not been buried beneath the inland ice, but it would be a great mistake to imagine them free from other ice. On the contrary, they may be considered the very home of glaciers, several thousand square miles of their surface, at the least, being covered with perpetual snow and ice, rivalling any mountain-chain studded with glaciers in any other part of the globe. The coast is throughout very rocky and mountainous, which makes the first appearance of its summits, when sighted at sea at the distance of about 40 miles, seem to be that of snowy islands. On approaching them, they gradually expand into a continuous stretch of land. Near Cape Farewell almost the whole coast tract, which of old comprised the ancient eastern settlement, 140 miles in length, may be seen from a certain point at sea, presenting a most magnificent panorama, the mountains rising between 3 and 4,000 feet throughout its whole extent. The flat table lands are perfectly white, whereas the dark precipices and pointed summits are sprinkled over with snow and all the sloping clefts filled up with glaciers. On coming nearer the coast, the highlands seem gradually to retreat from view on account of the lower land becoming more and more visible, and during the latter part of summer the country in general, after having passed the outer islands, will seem perfectly free of snow. It nevertheless presents an exceedingly barren aspect, the only marks of vegetation observable being the brownish tint of some of the slopes and level spots, more rarely still passing over into green. On running further in and entering a fjord, vegetation becomes more prevalent, at the same time assuming fresher colours, and particularly at a distance of about eight miles from the entrance, the slopes appear literally covered with verdure up to a height of several hundred and even of thousand feet, chiefly because of the bushes and shrubs growing high enough to partly hide the huge boulders of the stony ground. At the same time numerous streams from the highland glaciers are seen to rush down the precipices, forming diminutive cataracts, while here and there the edge of a glacier presents itself to view, or may even be seen protruding down into the verdant regions. The average breadth of the outskirting land is thirty to forty miles, near Cape Farewell, but only eighty miles further north, in 61° N. lat., it is so narrow that the inland ice becomes visible from the open sea on both sides of the isolated headlands of Nunarsuit, probably identical with those to which John Davis gave the not inappropriate name of Cape Desolation. The dreary appearance of the surrounding country is increased by an ice-fjord sending a great amount of calved ice and small bergs out to the sea south of the promontory named.

The whole coast to the north presents a repetition of the features here described, the mountain tops only varying somewhat in elevation above the level of the sea, often surpassing 3,000 but rarely 4,000 feet, and the inland ice alternately retreating from and approaching the sea. Between 67° and 69° N. lat., there are scarcely any considerable mountain heights to be observed from the sea, although the country always appears hilly and uneven on this side ; here, in the middle part of Danish Greenland, the iceless coast tract also attains its widest extent. The fjords run for sixty or eighty miles into the country, and being ramified in the interior, their heads are separated from one another by isthmuses of low land with extensive lakes, navigable to the natives by means of their skin-boats, when engaged in the reindeer hunt. But these extensive hunting grounds have as yet been very little visited or explored by Europeans.

Between 68½° and 72½° N. lat. the configuration of the coast assumes a peculiar character, owing to the trap formation of the mountains here. The coast lines become less tortuous, and the sea forms wider and more spacious inlets, which deserve the name of bays rather than fjords. At the same time, the land appears less broken and divided, comprising as it does the island of Disco and the two largest peninsulas, remarkable both from the elevation of their peculiar table-lands, and their area. The latter border North-east bay or Umanak-fjord, in the interior of which all the most characteristic and magnificent features of arctic scenery seem to be centred. Icebergs of every description issue from its ramifications, spreading over the spacious inlet. Around these inlets the mountain heights of Greenland appear to culminate, rising about 7,000 feet above the level of the sea, and furrowed by valleys through which a series of glaciers like frozen brooks proceed towards the fjord, some of them dipping into the very sea. On the north side of the inner fjord a series of clefts rise in view, remarkable not only by their steepness but by the peculiar pinnacled shape of their tops. The precipices, rising abruptly from the sea to a height of from 5,000 to 6,000 feet, are especially beautiful, when, at the end of a winter night of two months' duration, their summits at mid-day begin to glow with a rosy hue, while the twilight in which the rest of the scenery is enveloped is rendered still darker by this contrast. Beyond the peninsula of Svartehuk, which forms the north side of Umanak bay, the mainland again opens out, forming a gulf studded with islands, some of which are pretty large and upwards of 3,000 feet high, while behind an ice-fjord of the first-class forms the head of the bay. This archipelago of islands and capes constitutes the northmost district called Upernivik.

CHAPTER III.

CLIMATE.

AN idea of the climate of Greenland will most easily be conveyed, by stating that in the southernmost part, situated between 60° and 61° N. lat., it very nearly resembles that of the northmost shores of Iceland and Norway, and that beyond these limits it exhibits a gradually decreasing temperature throughout the whole of its vast extent to the north. For this reason even the part which lies south of the polar circle, in the latitude of the Shetland Islands and Christiania, bears a thoroughly arctic character, and this peculiarity probably contributes to render the changes of weather still more irregular and incalculable than in other northern countries. In the following pages several striking examples of this changeableness will be given. But before we proceed to treat of the details of the climate it must be remarked that besides their stretching far from south to north, the regions in question have also a certain extent from east to west which must be taken in account. The distance between the outer islands and the interior inlets is certainly a short one to produce a considerable change in the climate; but notwithstanding, the difference arising from it is very remarkable. Everyone who has travelled in Greenland will have experienced how in summer the warmest and sunniest weather off the outer shores is almost every day suddenly succeeded by winds with icy fogs, which at any time will reduce the temperature to only three or four degrees above the freezing-point ; but on entering a fjord in such weather one generally encounters the brightest sunshine. The fog is whirled against, and encircles the headlands in the shape of dense clouds, but dissolves beyond them, and within the distance of a couple of miles there is a change like from winter to summer. In winter, on the contrary, when the interior inlets are frozen over and, so to speak, embodied in the *terra firma*, the thermometer on their shores will fall considerably lower than on the outer coast, where the activity of open water counteracts the severity of the frost so as to cause a difference of more than ten degrees. For these reasons it may be allowable to speak of the Greenland stations as having a *more or less seaward situation*, although in reality they are all near the sea-shore. On account of the chief settlements being mostly situated on the outer coast, we have very few observations from any fjord-station, and when, in the following remarks on the climate, nothing particular is mentioned about the conditions of locality, a seaward station is generally meant.

At the southernmost station, Julianehaab, the *mean annual temperature* seems as near as possible to be 33°, and at the northmost, Upernivik, 13°. But while the difference for the whole year is thus found to be 20°, the mean temperature of the three summer months is, for Upernivik 38°, for Julianehaab 48°, that of the three winter months respectively ÷7° and 20°, thus causing the difference of both places in summer to be only 10°, but in winter upwards of 27°. The winter at Julianehaab is not much colder than that of Norway and Sweden in the same latitude, while its mean temperature for the whole year is like that of Norway, 600 miles further north. In short, the winter of South Greenland can scarcely be termed a severe one, whereas its summer is wholly arctic. On account of Julianehaab having mostly a seaward situation, it might be questioned whether the same applies to the more inland parts. We have no observations from the interior of its neighbouring fjords in 60° to 61° N. lat., but in 64° N. lat. there is a Moravian missionary station upon an island called Umanak, in the interior of the Godthaab-fjord, where meteorological observations have been taken for several years. In almost the same latitude, but twenty-six miles nearer the open sea, is the station of Godthaab, where observations have been regularly made for a long series of years. From a comparison between these two places very interesting results have been arrived at, showing that the annual mean temperature is almost alike, but that the summer is decidedly warmer and the winter colder at Umanak than at Godthaab. In the course of the year the difference gradually decreases and increases, culminating in July, the mean temperature of which is 4° warmer at Umanak than at Godthaab, and in the same way the month of December has proved to be 6½° colder. However striking and instructive this fact may be, the general features of vegetation, even in the fjord-regions, prove that the summer in Greenland scarcely anywhere attains a heat surpassing that of an arctic climate.

After the mean temperature of the year and the seasons, the next question which must be treated of are the *extremes of heat and cold.* But before we proceed to speak of the highest and lowest degrees observed, it is of still greater interest to know what, in some particular place and at a certain season, may be considered a warm or a cold temperature by its inhabitants. For this purpose the registers of the same month and at the same station have been examined for a series of years, in order

to discover the utmost degree of warmth and cold for every
year separately, after which the means respectively of all the
lowest, the colds, and the highest heats recorded have been
computed. According to the results thus gained in South
Greenland, in summer the weather is spoken of as being
exceedingly warm when the thermometer rises to upwards
of 60°, whereas in winter the temperature must be a
couple of degrees below zero to make people feel particularly cold. In the most Northern settlement a temperature
of 52° in summer will be found an almost oppressive heat,
whilst in winter the thermometer must fall to something
like ÷ 28° before the cold is considered at all severe. As
regards the absolute highest and lowest temperatures ever
observed in Greenland, the author, after perusing numerous
registers and notes written down at different stations, has
arrived at the following conclusions. At the Moravian
station of Lichtenau (60° 31′ N. lat.) during a period of four
years, the thermometer was only once seen as high as 66°,
and only four times rose above 60°. At Upernivik (72°
48′ N. lat.) the highest temperature noted down has been 59°.
At Julianehaab (60° 44′ N. lat.) the author himself, once in
each of the two succeeding summers of 1853 and 1854, observed 68°, and even in Disco Bay (68° 48′ N. lat.) on June
28, 1850, he observed 64°. The 68° observed on the
occasion referred to is, however, the maximum of warmth
which the author with certainty knows to have been observed anywhere in Greenland. Of course a self-register-
ing thermometer put up at the interior of the southern
fjords would show instances of a higher rise, but how much
this might prove is not to be calculated ; however, there
are several reasons for believing that the difference between the inland and the more seaward stations will be
less conspicuous with regard to such single observations
than to the monthly mean temperatures. At all events, if

an observation of more than 70° is reported to have been made in Greenland, it cannot be accepted without some hesitation, especially as regards the question whether the effect of radiating heat has been sufficiently excluded, as it is generally a matter of difficulty to secure a perfectly shaded spot among the low hills whose rocky surface is heated by the sun. The most prominent agency tending to produce extraordinary warmth in Greenland is a peculiar warm land wind, the effect of which in bringing about sudden changes is remarkably little influenced by the difference of latitude. It not unfrequently causes a thaw to set in any time in January and February, and instances are known of the temperature rising to 42° in the depth of winter in the northmost settlements. In the same manner the absolute extremes of cold vary less according to latitude than might be inferred from the mean temperatures. At Julianehaab the thermometer fell to nearly ÷29° in 1863, at the southern Umanak (64° 28′ N. lat.) ÷42° have been observed, and the lowest temperature ever known in Greenland occurred at Upernivik, which is close to ÷47°; but, of course, the true extreme may at times have been greater. At Upernivik, in July, a day was once observed with a mean temperature below 32°, and a single observation in the same month has shown 27½°, whereas in South Greenland the temperature in July and August rarely goes down to 32°.

Among the *prevailing winds* in Greenland the *warm land wind* is the most remarkable. Its direction varies according to locality from true E.S.E. to true E.N.E., always proceeding though warm from the ice-covered interior, and generally following the direction of the fjord. It blows as frequently and violently in the north as in the south, but more especially at the fjord heads, while at the same time in certain localities it is scarcely perceptible. It often turns

into a sudden gale; the squalls in some fjords rushing down
between the high rocks, in certain spots often sweep the surface of the water with the force of a hurricane, raising
columns of fog, while the surrounding surface of the sea
remains smooth. But now and again the same wind blows a
gentle breeze, with a clear sky. Not unfrequently it sets in
accompanied by heavy rain, but generally when blowing for
several days it is very dry, sometimes causing the snow to
vanish without any water becoming visible. This wind in
consequence of its always blowing from the interior, and
having blown along a great part of its icy surface, must be
considered one of the most important agencies in counteracting the accumulation of snow in the central regions. As
regards other winds they follow the direction of the coast,
blowing from the south with snow and rain, and from the
north clearing the sky, or in summer frequently accompanied
by mist. Westerly winds blowing more or less on land generally appear as gentle breezes. Gales from this quarter are
very rare; in late autumn or in winter they may occur, but
are always of short duration. The general local land and sea
breeze are very common and regular in the Greenland fjords.
It is a mistake to believe that intense cold is always accompanied by calm weather. When the sea happens to be
frozen to a wide extent calms will mostly prevail during
the severest part of the winter, but in many places a
strong local wind from the east makes the cold almost
insupportable. The north wind sometimes also blows with
heavy squalls and a temperature of $\div 22°$.

The *mirage* is a very frequent appearance at all
seasons. Those cases are most common in which the
lower part of the land has disappeared, and the upper
part substituted, but in an inverted position. This makes
the low islands appear of an ellipsoid or globular shape, so
that they seem to float on the surface of the ocean. More

rarely the change is just the reverse, causing the upper part of the mountains to disappear, and substituting their lower parts, likewise inverted, which sometimes gives them the appearance of smoking volcanoes. The *halos* (parhelia, paraselenæ, and anthelia), and the *aurora borealis*, being too well known from other accounts to make any description needful here, we need only mention that the former phenomenon is equally common everywhere and at all seasons, but that the aurora increases in intensity and duration towards the south, where it is especially to be observed in autumn. The winter nights of the north, when lighted up at the same time by the aurora and a bright moonshine, are often very fine ; the shadows and outlines of the mountains, and the icebergs scattered over the frozen sea, may be discerned almost at the same distance as in broad daylight, the imposing impression of the scenery being augmented by the deep silence and rest reigning all around.

Finally we may add a few notes by way of examples, particularly illustrative of the striking *changeableness of the weather* in the same seasons of different years. On December 26, 1819, in 64° N. lat., a heavy rain was pouring down incessantly the whole day, with a calm and a steady thermometer from 54° to 57°, the mean of that month amounting to 26½° in the same year. On May 22, 1850, the author found a saxifrage blossoming very beautifully in 70° 30′ N. lat. On the last day of June and the first of July 1854, after a severe winter, he visited the headland of Nunarsuit, about six hundred miles further south, and traversed it on foot. The smaller inlets, as well as the lakes slightly above the level of the sea, were not only covered with ice, but the latter, as well as the adjoining country, was covered with snow to such a degree that the border between the ice and land was levelled and quite imperceptible. At Julianehaab in February 1855, the warm land wind set in with light breezes and a temperature of 32°, clearing the sky and lasting for about a fortnight, with beautiful weather, but was in March and April succeeded by heavy snowfalls, and on May 1 the gardens were still covered with a sheet of snow 5 feet thick. In the first week of June it snowed continuously for 36 hours, so as to make the roads between the houses almost impassable. Nevertheless the summer turned out unusually fine, and in all respects favourable to vegetation. In 1863 and 1864 the winters in regard to severity surpassed any of which the author has ever been able to acquire information from earlier accounts, and possibly we should have to go back a whole century to find their equals. In 64° N. lat. not a single drop of rain was noticed from September 27, 1862, to the 20th of May next, on which day the snow had obtained a height of 8 to 20 feet between the houses. At the southernmost settlement, during six days in March, the thermometer did not rise above $\div 17\frac{1}{2}$°. The succeeding winter was almost identical as regards the whole amount of cold, but the period of extreme cold both commenced and abated somewhat earlier. As regards the quantity of snow, a more recent winter has nevertheless surpassed those here mentioned.

CHAPTER IV.

THE GENERAL FEATURES OF THE SURFACE, THE WATERCOURSES, LAKES, AND SEA.

The Limits of perpetual snow, and of vegetation.— The contrast between the vegetation which is seen to spread more or less everywhere over the surface from the very sea-shore up the sloping mountain sides, and the snow-clad appearance of the mountain tops, induces us to question whether there is in Greenland a distinct *snow-line*, or a height beyond which the snow of one winter is unmelted before the setting in of the next. As regards the vegetable covering, it requires of course considerably more summer warmth than suffices to clear away the snow. For this reason we might also be led to ask the question whether an intervening space exists between the regions of vegetation and those of snow, where the ground is perfectly bare. But in trying to make out such a distinct snow-line we are often puzzled, inasmuch as we here meet with the strangest and apparently most contradictory features, such as almost *perpetual snow near the water's edge* in southern latitudes, while on the other hand in some localities much further north, the mountain sides will be found covered with *vegetation to an amazing height.*

Temporary glaciers or accumulations of snow partly

converted into solid ice and lasting for periods of a couple of years or more are frequently met with all over Greenland, covering smaller spaces close to the very sea-shore, but of course more frequently on the higher slopes and in clefts or ravines. As a curiosity it may be mentioned that such a temporary glacier has been forming for several years only a few hundred feet from the European houses of Godthaab in 64° 8′ N. lat. It was here seen to occupy a flat ground, only to some degree shaded by a low cliff. In some years the snow which is heaped up in this spot is melted by the end of July, but sometimes the warmth of the summer does not suffice to dissipate it. The ground thereabout always appears barren, and the rocks bleak and devoid of the ordinary covering of dark lichens. Not much more than a hundred paces from this spot the trader of the station has a small garden before his windows, where at any rate radishes and turnips are annually reared. Such accumulations of snow do not merely depend on its being heaped together by drift, but more especially on the action of running water which continues to percolate and overflow it during the winter. At the Umanak-fjord the author has seen two small ice-formations which originated from fountains, and are now apparently perpetual or real glaciers, though so close by the sea-shore. As the most striking contrast to these instances of perpetual snow in the lower regions must be mentioned the extraordinary height to which vegetation extends on the north side of a mountain chain bordering on the Umanak-fjord. The author ascended it from Karsok-point in about 71°40′ N. lat., on July 30, 1851, during a cold and unpleasant summer. A nearly uniform slope, only interrupted by a few terrace-shaped edges, leads from this point to a height of 5,000 feet in a distance of 5 miles. The foreland consisted of low rocky hills alternating with fresh green meadow-like glens, and exhibiting the usual shrubs, such as the willow, crowberry, and Andromeda. Crossing a plain scattered over with huge boulders, we arrive at a somewhat steeper slope or terrace, on the top of which, at a height of 1,000 feet, the clouds are often seen to lie, enveloping the upper part of the mountains. It generally happens that when the sky has become clear after rains in September, everything above this line appears scattered over with snow, while at the same time scarcely any snow has fallen on the lower land. Nevertheless the surface was found to continue almost unaltered up to a height of 2,000 feet, the ground, consisting of gravel and clay, was covered by a thick sod containing almost the same plants as the low land. Only here and there a small heap of snow was concealed in some of the sheltered ravines. But at a height of between 2,000 and 3,000 feet the vegetable covering seemed decidedly thinner, the grasses and Cyperaceæ which form the chief part of the sod disappear, and are succeeded by mosses. At a height of 3,000 feet the same mosses still entirely cover small boggy places adorned with blooming buttercups. But on arriving at 4,000 feet the vegetation ceases to form any continuous mass, the plants standing singly in the gravel while the flat hollows are totally barren. The arctic willow finally disappears here, and several heaps of snow lie scattered over the ground, their under sheet consisting of solid ice. Footprints of reindeer and very old antlers were found here. Lastly the increasing patches of snow at a height of 4,700 feet join to make a continuous sheet, leaving no ground visible. Close to the borders of the perpetual snowfield, among the numerous hillocks of ice and snow, at a height of more than 4,500 feet, the following plants were collected: Papaver nudicaulis, Potentilla Vahliana, Saxifraga tricuspidata, S. oppositifolia, S. cæspitosa, Alsine rubella, Silene acaulis,

Draba arctica, Festuca brevifolia, Carex nardina. Some scanty and stunted specimens of lichens, too defective to admit of their species being duly determined, were also found.

If we consider facts apparently so incompatible as plants in bloom at a height of 4,500 feet in 71° N. lat., and snow resisting the thawing action of a whole summer's heat in 64° N. lat., at less than 100 feet above the level of the sea, it will appear a rather difficult task to determine anything like a positive snow-line. In fact the formation of glaciers from snow, owing to its having lasted for several years and turned into solid ice, depends on many different local influences besides the height above the level of the sea. But still, on regarding the country as a whole, a certain degree of uniformity may be discovered in the appearance of the more considerable mountain ridges. It will be found that at a height of from 2,000 to 2,200 feet or more, flat surfaces of some extent, and more or less excavated surfaces, have in most cases given rise to fields of perpetual snow and ice. From these accumulations glaciers arise, and are moved onwards even to the edge of the water, but glaciers originating at a lower height than this are only exceptional. In the same way clear ground above 3,000 feet will be exceptional, and found to be caused by steepness, limited extent of a horizontal surface, and other accidental influences.

Lakes and Streams.—These are numerous everywhere. The lakes begin to freeze at the end of September, become wholly frozen during the course of October, and are not thawed up until the middle of June or July. The average thickness of their ice covering appears scarcely to exceed 3 feet in 61° N. lat., and 6 feet in 71° N. lat. At all the European stations drinking water is supplied by such lakes, or from rivulets issuing from them, during the whole winter. Such water-courses may continue in a diminished size throughout the whole winter, sheltered by the snow sheet, a deep and narrow hole being kept open, the sides of which are converted to solid ice.

In such a climate, the soil, if composed of earthy or porous matters, should be continually *frozen to a certain depth*, at least throughout the greater part of the coast. This occasionally also happens at the depth of one or two feet, but not everywhere, in the south at least. It is a certain fact that subterranean water reservoirs are kept open in many places during the whole year at smaller or greater depths. Springs are not unfrequent and of various temperatures. In Disco Island the author found rather remarkable watercourses proceeding from *springs* and running through caverns underneath the snow, paved with beautiful fresh green mosses, in which animal as well as vegetable life seems to live in the depth of winter. One spring in Disco showed a temperature of 54°. In another island, in about 68° 40′ N. lat., a group of springs are situated close to each other, one of them bursting forth as a jet from a fissure in the granite cliff, and keeping a temperature of 42°. But the most interesting springs are those in Unartok, an island about two miles in length, in 60° 29′ N. lat. At the foot of a rounded hill two basins are found, 12 to 20 feet in diameter, and scarcely 2 feet deep, from the sandy bottom of which hot water wells up. The temperature of the one is 104°, of the other 107½°.

The largest lakes seem to exist in the Nugsuak (or Noursoak) peninsula, about 71° N. lat., and in the tracts of the mainland between 64° and 67° N. lat., also containing the richest hunting grounds. The largest rivers communicate with the same lakes, some of them also receiving supplies from the inland ice, from the bottom of which water has also been observed to issue in winter. But none of them, as far as we know, appear in size to surpass what would correspond to the drainage of some 500 to 600 square miles.

The adjacent Sea.—It will be apparent from our description of the indented and intersected configuration of the coast line, as also of the inland ice, that the sea may be said to form the roads by which the interior to a certain limit is made accessible, and by which the inhabitants are enabled to keep up some intercourse with each other. At the same time it opens the channels through which an enormous annual surplus of ice produced in the interior is discharged, and prevented from burying the coast regions like the 'inland.' But its chief importance to man consists in making the land inhabitable by means of its abundance of animal life, which proves a striking contrast to the barrenness and inhospitable features of the land itself. A favourite topic in the accounts of arctic voyagers has been to describe the manner in which certain small organic beings fill wide areas of the arctic waters, and form the principal food upon which the subsistence of higher organised animals is more or less directly dependent. But near the shores of Greenland the sea offers frequent opportunity for observing an even more conspicuous display of its richness in animal and vegetable life. Its bottom is found to be overgrown with various kinds of seaweed, some attaining a height of from 10 to 16 feet, with leaves half a foot broad, and the rocks and stones more or less covered with zoophytes or shells. Among the swarms of different animals inhabiting the submarine thickets, some species of small shrimplike crustacea seem to be of peculiar importance in supplying food to the stationary and most common seals of the coast. An idea of the enormous multitude of these animals off the shores may be formed from the fact of their yielding the easiest means for getting all sorts of skeletons cleansed from the adherent softer parts, which is simply managed by sinking them for a few days in the sea. About the most lucrative fishing is carried on by angling in depths of up to 200 fathoms, and wherever a sample of mud is got by dredging, it will be found abounding in various specimens of sea animals. It need scarcely be added that the substances contained in several animals of lower orders, passing into those of a higher organisation which feed upon them, and finally in the shape of blubber from seals and whales, serve the Greenlanders for food as well as for fuel, thus supplying the means by which they are enabled to procure a subsistence even in the highest latitudes.

The difference between high and low water caused by the tides varies up to 12 feet, on account of which all the inlets are continually more or less in motion from the changing *currents* transferring a corresponding body of water into the fjords and back again twice a day. In some places where narrow entrances lead to extensive interior inlets, rapids are formed which can only be passed at the very moment that the tide changes. When icebergs happen to float into such sounds it is amazing to behold the manner in which these huge masses are hurled forth, crushing one another as they are moved about by the whirlpools. Besides the alternating tides, a regular current sets into Davis Strait, keeping close to the coast, but gradually decreasing in strength as it advances northward, and totally disappearing on spreading to the west, north of 64° N. lat.

The Greenland sea is *much less liable to be frozen over* than might be supposed from the severity of the climate and the masses of drift-ice of various kinds that are scat-

tered over it. The most sheltered interior inlets are of
course frozen over every winter even in the south, but on
the more seaward shores a firm sheet of ice requires such
an amount of cold that it is not till beyond 66° N. lat. that
sufficient ice is found for dog-sledging, and even at the
northernmost settlements the frozen sea at the usual fishing
or hunting grounds often breaks up in the midst of winter,
causing danger and damage to the inhabitants and their
property.

The Fjords in general are remarkable for their extraordinary depth, frequently exceeding 1,000 feet. The *ice-
fjords* especially require such a depth to carry off the
bergs. They are at the same time of peculiar importance
as regards the livelihood of the natives. The '*firth-seal*'
or *natsek* is the most common species all over Greenland,
with the advantage of being stationary or not regularly
migrating. It seems to prefer the ice-fjords, in the
remotest and most inaccessible parts of which these
seals are seen to herd in the greatest numbers, and
probably have their principal breeding-places. The author
once happened to witness a remarkable instance in proof
of this. In the ice-fjord of Jakobshavn the glacier is
said to expand much further over the inlet for some
periods of years than others before breaking asunder and
forming floating bergs. Consequently a part of the sea
which is generally only scattered over with bergs, will at
times be covered with the solid glacier, and in such a
case it may happen that some creek branching off the
main fjord is cut off from the sea by the glacier, thus
closing its outlet to the larger fjord. In May 1851, the
author, travelling by land, succeeded in reaching such
a creek. The small basin of course appeared to be
totally enclosed, partly by its surrounding shores and
partly by the enormous wall of the glacier which shut up

the only entrance to it from the sea side. When thus viewed in its immediate vicinity the glacier offered a strange appearance, being broken and piled up with enormous fragments by the friction between the moving ice and the shore, which was also perceptible by the roaring and rattling noise from the bursting and crumbling of the icy wall, and the occasional overturning of the pinnacles on its top. On perceiving the small basin thus effectually barred, it was a curious fact to find it inhabited by numerous seals which had crawled up and lay scattered over the surface of the bay-ice basking in the bright sunshine. One of them was shot, and proved to be a very big and fat specimen. The appearance of the isolated herd of seals here described, which at all events must be supposed to have lived in a state of seclusion for more than a year, sufficiently proves that the interior ice-fjords yield the necessary food for these animals to subsist. But other and weightier circumstances must concur to make these places their favourite haunts. In the first place, the calving motions of the glacier will cause the ice covering of the interior fjord to break up at intervals during the whole winter. The seals, requiring access to the open air for breathing, are evidently attracted by the numerous fissures and openings caused by these disturbances. Secondly, the bay-ice in front of the glacier is studded for several miles with bergs and broken ice of every dimension. In the ravines and clefts of this labyrinth heavy snowdrifts accumulate, beneath which the seals contrive to make caves, communicating with the water through a hole in the ice, and perfectly protected against the cold air from above. These haunts must of course be liable to occasional destruction, but nevertheless seem to offer convenient refuges for the breeding of the young seals towards the end of the cold season. It has been observed that the oldest and largest animals are caught in the ice-fjords, giving three or four times as much blubber as specimens of the same kind from the outer coast. If a severe winter happens to set in, and the seal hunt gradually comes to a stop on the outer coast, the ice-fjords are generally resorted to by the natives who live in their vicinity. But the seal hunt there is not without its hardships and dangers of various kinds. In order to form an idea of the bay-ice in front of the glaciers in the ice-fjords, it must be remembered that the ruggedness of its surface may properly be compared with that presented by a half-devastated town. The densely crowded bergs are in size like the largest and highest buildings. The interspaces between them are studded with hillocks of calved ice of every shape and description, and occasionally with high barriers of crushed bay-ice; a sheet of deep snow more or less covers the whole, and the ground on which the hunter stands is always liable to sudden 'bouleversements.' The calvings of the glacier as well as of the bergs already formed continue throughout the winter, causing the bay-ice to be partially broken, and more or less jammed up upon the shores for a distance of 10 to 20 miles from the edge of the glacier. It is not generally until the middle of June that the ice-fjords begin to be emptied of the bergs by sending them to sea ; this is continued at intervals and called 'the shooting out of the fjords.'

The *drifting ice* which, aided by the icebergs, more or less encumbers the passage along the coast in summer, consists of *pack-ice*, coming partly from the northern regions of Baffin's Bay, partly from the Spitzbergen sea. Only the latter kind of ice can be considered a real hindrance to vessels bound for the settlements. It immediately follows the track of the above-mentioned current which enters Davis Strait. It is pressed upon the coast by southerly winds, and again dispersed by those from the north. Its bulk is disproportionately small when compared with the length of the coast, which is sometimes totally locked up by it for the greater part of the summer. It usually reaches 62°, often 64°, but rarely 65° N. lat. This belt is often found to be quite impenetrable, though not broader than that ships sailing outside may be seen from the shore.

CHAPTER V.

PRODUCTS AND RESOURCES OF THE LAND.

Geology and Mineral Products.—The geological survey of the country is greatly facilitated by the bare, rugged, and intersected features of its surface. In whatever manner we may suppose these numerous and precipitous clefts to have originated, either by the bursting asunder of the earth's crust, or by its having been grooved out by the long continued passage of ancient glaciers, they present most excellent sections of the coast. In their walls the interior structure of the crust is most beautifully displayed, giving sections of one to three thousand feet in height, with a length of many miles. Although these cliffs are mostly inaccessible, the structure of the rocks may be inspected partly from a distance, because of the beds and dykes being more or less distinctly delineated in them, and partly from the stone-heaps forming the slopes at the base of the cliffs, containing fragments that have been successively detached, and consequently presenting a complete collection of specimens from the various parts which are visible in the cliffs.

About the three-fourths or more of the whole country consists of rocks which *may be called granitic and gneissose,* although they are always seen more or less stratified, intersected by veins and dykes, and containing various kinds of rock greatly differing from real granite, in some instances even passing into slates. The predominating rock is always obviously gneissose, with gradual transitions to the accompanying varieties, so that, at least at present, no distinct subdivisions of this formation have been determined.

At the termination of the Igaliko-fjord a peculiar compact *red sandstone* is found, which distinctly differs from the beds belonging to the granitic formation, and is proved to be of a later origin. It has been of very limited extent, only occupying the environs of the ancient Norse settlement in Igaliko, the houses of which have been built of this very sandstone. Another formation of a still later origin is the *trap* or *basalt*, with beds of sandstone and shale, including *coals and other vegetable remains.* It is distinguished not only by the peculiar features of the various masses constituting its mountains, but by its great extension, occupying the tract between 69° 15′ and 71° 20′ N. lat. As to their chief outlines these mountains present regular table lands, between 2,000 and 5,000 feet high, with walls more or less perpendicular or terrace-shaped, and separated from the sea by a narrow border of slopes or lower hills. On this projecting lower land, which forms the base of the mountains, granitic rocks in some instances appear ; above them the hills consist of sandstone, including coal and other vegetable remains, and finally the precipitous walls exhibit more or less regular horizontal layers of trap or basalt, the edges of which give rise to their terrace-shaped appearance. These trap-beds present the plainest indications of their igneous origin, or of having resulted from a melted mass bursting forth from the depths and spreading over the surface at intervals, so as to cause the streams to be filled up in a stiffened state. Although the sandstone only occupies a very limited area, its frequent appearance projecting from underneath the trap mountains suggests the idea that it forms an extensive part of the ground over which these mountains have been piled up during the igneous eruptions. Of the extensive deposits which must thus be supposed to lie hidden beneath the trap mountains, only the outer edges are consequently visible. Coal-beds appear in many places along the shore, and very interesting remains of plants have been discovered in the sandstone and strata of slate. It has been ascertained that the coal originally proceeded from a previous vegetation in the same places where the relics are now found. Trunks of tall trees, now converted into coal or fossil wood, are still standing upright with the remains of their roots inserted in the very soil that gave growth to them, but now totally included in the sandstone which is composed of the sand that of old, by some unknown action, must have covered the trees themselves. Perfect and complete impressions of leaves have been discovered in abundance in the surrounding rocks. Fruits, seeds, and even remains of insects are among these striking proofs of an ancient flora, which to all appearances must have required a climate like that of middle Europe at the present day. The coal-beds also afford a striking evidence of the igneous origin of the superincumbent trap, which on bursting out made its way through the said deposits. The coal is distinctly seen to have been altered in various degrees by the heat from the melted masses. In one instance a small trap vein crosses and spreads over a thin coal-bed for some extent. The coal in immediate contact with the vein was found to be totally deprived of its volatile bituminous ingredients, and changed into coke. In another place a coal-bed was found converted into anthracite, and lastly a most remarkable bed of graphite has been discovered, which leaves no doubt of its having originated in the same way, the heating and metamorphosing action having here reached a higher degree of intensity.

Besides the formations already mentioned, we must still add the *latest deposits of sand and clay* filling up valleys of a very limited extent, but not unfrequently met with throughout the coast, and forming the only flat spots the country presents near the level of the sea.

Of the *Greenland minerals* the following may here be worth mentioning, partly on account of their utility and partly as mere curiosities.

Beds of coal may, as already stated, be supposed to extend for many hundreds of square miles beneath the trap rocks. In the low cliffs, or the slopes along the shore, they appear of a thickness varying from that of mere strips to nearly 5 feet. They are of a much later formation and less valuable than coals from the true carboniferous formation, but very well adapted for domestic use. In some of them fossil resin (retinite) may be perceived in yellow amber-like grains. The worth of the coal as a contribution to the fuel supplies of Greenland is nevertheless somewhat doubtful. Owing to the scantiness of the population, they are able to supply the wants of their small households from different kinds of fuel to be found almost everywhere, and as the coal necessary for the few European residents in the country forms a convenient ballast for the ships, the demand for it in the country is too small to pay the expense of any regular mining. There are about eighteen places scattered along the shores of North Greenland, where coal crops out or appears immediately below the surface. Some of these coal-beds have now and then been worked in a very primitive manner, by merely removing the gravel or decayed rock covering the outer edges, more rarely by mining out of the steep cliffs as much as the overlying rock will allow of without tumbling in. The whole produce may be rated at 40 to 50 tons *per annum.*

Graphite is found in two varieties. Besides the kind above-mentioned as having originated from a coal-bed, another sort, of a more laminated or scaly structure, is often met with in the granitic rocks ; but the finest quality and the greatest abundance is found on an island close to Upernivik. Both have been the object of mining-speculation attempted by private companies, and several tons, especially of the former, have at different times been brought to the European market, but without a 'paying' price having been obtained for it.

Cryolite is the only mineral that has become an article of trade, and given rise to commercial enterprise connected with mining in Greenland. Its importance was not ascertained till the year 1856, when a chemical process was discovered, by means of which it may be converted into soda, and an alumina hitherto unequalled in regard to purity and fitness for the art of dyeing. It is found only in one single spot, called Ivigtut, and situated on the shores of the Arsutfjord in 61° 10′ N. lat. ; moreover, it has not in this place been found traversing the rocks for such an extent as to present the usual appearance of dykes, veins, or strata, but imbedded like a massive body in the granitic rock. The whole space occupied by it before it was worked may be estimated at 400 feet in length and upwards of 50 to 100 feet in breadth, the depth not having as yet been made out, but as far as we know, it at least amounts to 100 feet. Within these confines the cryolite formed the prevailing part of the rock, being almost quite pure for an horizontal extent of several hundred or, may be, a thousand square feet, but for the rest accompanied by other minerals in dykes, veins, nodules, or grains. A more remarkable collection of minerals than this will scarcely be found anywhere in a single spot. There are several metallic ores, such as of argentiferous lead, copper, zinc, and tin, crystals of quartz measuring a foot in thickness, magnificent crystals of tantalite, besides molybdenite, fluor-spar, zircon, and various others. Attempts have been made to work the metallic ores, but they were found too scantily spread to be worked with any promise of gain, so that as yet the cryolite is the only article of trade produced from the mine. This spot is the only locality in Greenland, and, with a single exception, on the whole globe, where cryolite has been found, and by a curious incident it has been placed so close to the seashore as to facilitate the shipping of it, a necessary condition for its being worked in Greenland. The same place happened to be chosen by the natives for a fishing-station in summer, and they had built up the foundation walls of their tents with blocks of this rare material. In 1857 a licence was given to a private company for working cryolite. The ground where it is found now presents a large open hollow, at the bottom of which, in the year 1871, cryolite was worked over a space of 32,000 square feet, and at a depth of about 40 feet beneath the high-water mark. The number of labourers employed in working it generally amount to a hundred in summer, and thirty in winter, besides the officers, viz. the superintendent and his assistant, the storekeeper, the engineer, the physician, the controller, and their families. On the hills about the mine were scattered about ten lodging-houses and sixteen storehouses, workshops, and suchlike buildings. In the first nine years 14,000 tons were exported in eighty ship-loads ; during the next nine years the total export amount was 70,000 tons, or on an average, twenty-six ship-loads per annum.

The Steatite or *pot-stone,* used by the natives for making lamps and other domestic ware, no doubt comprises several different minerals, all of which are soft enough to be cut with a common knife. It occurs in different varieties, from a coarse, gray, wholly opaque and somewhat slaty kind, to the more valuable, slightly translucent, greenish, black, white, and even marble-like sorts. This mineral is pretty common, but only in certain localities forms seams of a sufficient thickness and coherency. Even the ancient Norse settlers seem mostly to have had their cooking-pots made out of the same material. Now-a-days the manufacture of stone-lamps is greatly on the decline, and cooking-pots of the same material have almost become unknown. The green translucent steatite has, of late, been made use of for various fancy articles for Europeans. It could be made a very useful article of domestic industry, if the dust produced by cutting and filing the mineral did not prove injurious to the health.

Native iron has been found in different parts of Greenland attended by very remarkable circumstances. The first piece was found on the mainland in 69° 24′ N. lat., having a globular form and weighing 23 pounds, and afterwards three pieces more were discovered in different localities. The first three that were found were examined as to their texture and chemical composition and determined to be meteoric iron, and no doubt was raised against the verdict. But in 1870 and 1871 an accumulation of the same metal was found at Uivfak, on the southern side of Disco Island, extraordinary not only with regard to quantity, but on account of various indications of its having once been imbedded in the rocks, and consequently not of meteoric origin. A number of detached pieces lay scattered over an area of a few square yards between high and low-water mark. The largest of these blocks measured the enormous size of $6\frac{1}{2}$ feet in length by $5\frac{1}{2}$ in breadth, its weight being calculated at 46,200 pounds. The two pieces next in size were estimated to weigh 17,600 and 15,400 pounds respectively, and twelve minor ones trom 5 to 300 pounds each, besides fragments to the amount of 100 pounds. In close vicinity to this amassment of fragments, the rock, forming a ridge of basalt, contained just the very same kind of iron imbedded as laminæ and nodules. It has been proved that the latter constituted true native iron *in situ*, a discovery which seems to have totally subverted the theory of those iron masses having had their origin from meteorites. In 1871 a Swedish expedition visited Greenland, with the chief object of bringing them home to Europe. By dint of great skill they succeeded in shipping the largest block, and, finally, brought away the whole stock. But after having been brought to Sweden and lodged in its proper place, the huge specimen suddenly displayed a most alarming tendency to crack and become disjoined by fissures, finally threatening to crumble wholly away and fall into bits. After several experiments, a continuous humid state, brought about by irrigation, has, as far as we know, proved to be the only way of keeping the block entire, or in the same state as when it was in its old position on the shore between high and low-water mark.

Metallic ores have hitherto proved to be rather scanty in Greenland. In 1850 a licence was given to a company for exploring and working mines in the country. Six expeditions were sent out, and two ships lost, before 1855, from which period the explorations on the part of the company were continued by an English scientific traveller till the year 1860. Since that time the company seems to have abandoned its plans. Copper ore has been traced in several places, and in two of them mining was commenced. But both mines were exhausted within a few weeks on account of the ore occurring only disseminated as nodules or strips of a very limited extent, no real vein or stratum having as yet been discovered. The argentiferous lead and the tinstone at Ivigtut were attempted, but given up for the same reason. Traces of lead, tin, and zinc ore in other parts of Greenland are still more scanty than those of the copper ore. In 1849 or 1850 some very mysterious bits of native silver were found close to an inhabited house in 60° 43′ N. lat. They proved to be small laminæ of apparently genuine crystallised silver, but only occurring as loose fragments, in the ravines of the rock in front of the house, together with ancient beads and small pieces of wrought copper. These accompaniments suggested the idea that the fragments of silver, even if they were originally found somewhere in the country, must have been possessed by the inhabitants of the house before they were dropped into the fissures or imbedded in the sod that covered them. All efforts at trying to trace their origin further have been to no purpose.

Various other minerals have been found which are very interesting and valued as rare specimens for scientific collections. Among these may be enumerated sodalite and endiolyte, tourmaline, amazon-stone, precious garnets, allanite with zircon, fergusonite, anthophyllite, and several other varieties of hornblende, besides many zeolites.

Plants and Vegetable Matter.—In the preceding sections we have tried to show that the difference to be observed in the vegetation of the southern and northern tracts is much smaller than might be expected on account of the difference of latitude. For this reason the productions of the soil are only scanty and poor, but on the other hand much more widely spread. Indeed, if we mention that on passing the ordinary route between the islands from south to north, travellers find sufficient fuel for cooking their meals wherever they pitch their tents, and with few interspaces also in most years a good deal of berries nearly everywhere, and that the natives wherever they build their winter houses with the slightest degree of providential care are able to procure fuel for the whole winter,—these facts would seem to be at variance with the common conceptions of Greenland, as merely a home of perpetual snow and ice. On the other hand, we have alluded to the striking difference of fertility observed within short distances on advancing from west to east. If we imagine ourselves travelling from the sea onward towards the termination of one of the southern fjords, and compare the whole country with the tracts to be passed on this way, we will find that as regards the vegetable covering the first part, viz. the outmost islands and projecting capes, present almost the same appearance as the islands and promontories in the furthest north ; the next tract, comprising the mouth of the fjord, is like the most fertile and sheltered regions in the north, and finally, the remainder, or the environs of the interior fjord, present features peculiar to the south and not exceeding the latitude of 65°. In establishing such a classification, the author does not at all present it as having a scientific foundation ; there is a successive progress from the barren to the more luxuriant regions, and the only view of the supposed area of demarcation is to facilitate the following description of the chief features of the vegetable covering.

On the *lower outer islands*, as far as the ground consists of gravel or earthy matters, and moisture prevails, the prevailing plants are lichens, mosses, and sedges, while the dryer spots are partly overgrown by a matting of very low shrubs, especially consisting of the crowberry plant. The willow also certainly occurs, but is so low and creeping as to be scarcely recognisable, the wind and fog preventing any plant from rising more than a few inches above the ground. Where such loose or porous ground is not found, the rocks sometimes contain fissures in which a similar vegetation may take root, but the greater part of the hilly ground appears quite bare of vegetation, with the exception of black lichens with which the rocky surface is almost everywhere studded, and which gives the barren hills their peculiar dark gray hue.

The next division is chiefly characterised by the *willows and dwarf-birches* which here and there attain a tolerable size. South of 67° N. lat., the *juniper* may be added to these bushes, but it is always stunted, creeping along the ground or forming a flat cover to the top of stones or rocks. The dwarf-birch and willow occur almost everywhere, sometimes the one and sometimes the other prevail. They generally have their roots fixed in clefts, and likewise creep along the ground, reaching a length sometimes of six to eight feet; the stems, having a dia-meter of from one to three inches close to the root, are very much knotted and twisted. But in some spots they are found clustering together, and, in supporting each other, have reached a height of from two to three feet. Such *willow-copses* may even be found on projecting headlands at the foot of high cliffs, situated so as to give them shelter and allow them to catch heat from the sun, as is the case on the south side of Disco. They are still more luxuriantly developed in certain beautiful spots at a fjord in the interior of this island, where the copse rises to a height of from four to six feet, and the green slopes are adorned with beautiful flowers bordering the rivulets. The willow-copses are said to be found even in $72\frac{1}{2}$° N. lat., but they are always scanty to the north of 68°. The birch always appears more stunted. Throughout the whole coast, at least up to 72° N. lat., the berries also always ripen in the regions here treated of, though with some difference according to year and locality. Lastly, we have to mention the lovely flowering plants with which in July and August the green spots are frequently found to be embellished. The shores about 70° N. lat. are in this respect in no way inferior to those in 60° N. lat. The arctic species of *Rhododendron, Erica, Azalea, Saxifraga, Epilobium, Pedicularis, Campanula, Arnica, Ranunculus, Potentilla,* and several others offer a great variety of colours and forms, tending to diversify the common brownish green of the spots covered by vegetation.

The last division, or the *interior to the south* of 65° N. lat., may be characterised by the occurrence of the *alder* (*Alnus repens*), growing between 61° 10′ and 64° 50′ N. lat., and the *white birch* (*Betula alpestris*) which is only found south of 62° N. lat., accompanied, though only scantily, by the *rowan-tree* (*Sorbus*). Besides the bushes here named, those of the above-mentioned division are of course also met with, acquiring a considerably greater development. The juniper stems may attain a thickness of 5 to 6 inches, but in general they are not above 2 or 3 inches thick. The copses of white birch and alder occupy sheltered slopes and small enclosed valleys, at a distance of 20 to 30 miles from the outer islets. The loveliest spots of this description are found between 60° and 61° N. lat., but of course the total area only amounts to a trifling part of the whole coast region comprised within the same degrees of latitude. In the very centre of the southernmost peninsula of Greenland such a narrow valley is found, in which the growth of trees, if so they may be termed, favoured by sheltering walls rising to a height of 3,000 feet all around it, seems to have acquired the greatest luxuriance which the climate of Greenland admits of. This place is arrived at by entering the fjord of Tasermiut. Having passed half way up, the skin-boat has to be unloaded and hauled up a short but shallow and rapid brook to a small lake, on crossing which this ' Eden-like ' valley appears to the view about 4 miles further up the country. Close to the lake willows and juniper grow most plentifully, but still further up the birches become prevalent, and at the same time increase in size. Generally the largest stems lie prostrate, half-buried in mosses, with branches from 2 to 3 inches in thickness rising 8 or 10 feet above them. The biggest stems measured 8 inches in thickness. The *largest and tallest birch-tree* had attained a height of 14 feet, and was strong enough to support a man standing on one of its branches at a height of 5 feet from the ground. The growth of this specimen, the largest that the author has ever met with or heard of in Greenland, had been favoured by being enclosed between two immense boulders, which had contributed to shelter it. This was evident from the circumstance that the twigs protruding above these stones had died away. In the vicinity of this tree stands a remarkable ruin dating from the time of the ancient Norse settlers. Some huge irregularly-formed blocks of stone had been made use of in their original position as part of the walls, which are formed of stones piled up without the usual care shown by these people in selecting them and fitting them to each other. The walls are 10 feet high, and the entrance is covered with a flat stone. It is obvious that this enclosure was not intended for a habitation, but probably for a storehouse, whereas traces of the farm can, it is said, be found on the opposite side of the stream, which is very rich in salmon, and on the banks of which indications of a bridge are said to be discovered. A small glacier hangs over the edge of the cliff nearest to the river, and from underneath the ice a jet of water bursts

forth and falls foaming down the precipice into the valley.
A similarly charming spot is to be found at the head
of the Lichtenau-fjord, where the birch-copse surrounds a
small lake, the tallest bushes reaching a height of 12 feet.
A magnificent waterfall, one of the largest in Greenland,
falls almost directly into the lake. The northernmost of
the copses in question are found about 64½° N. lat., and are
composed of willows and alder, both kinds reaching a
height of from 5 to 8 feet.

Of *useful plants or vegetable produce* the *berries* first
claim our attention. There are three plants of which the
fruits might be used for food—the crowberry, the whortleberry, and the cowberry. Of these the *crowberry* (*Empetrum nigrum*) is the only one the fruit of which is used by
the natives. It is the plant most usually met with all
over Greenland. Except in the swampy and half-inundated
marshes, one can hardly cut out a sod anywhere without
finding it intermixed with parts of the crowberry-plant.
About 6 miles from the outer islands it almost every year
produces ripe berries, in some years very plentifully, and
further inland they are always to be found in abundance.
Formerly the natives regularly filled large sacks with them
for winter provisions, but this custom has almost fallen into
disuse. In warm summers berries begin to turn black in
the middle of July, but they are not edible before August.
At the end of this month the night-frosts prevent their
decay, and berries may be found throughout the winter by
scraping away the snow. They are perfectly fresh when
they come to light by the melting of the snow in May and
June. The abundance of these fruits in favourable years is
really surprising. Even in 69° N. lat. the creeping branches
may be seen so laden with fruit that they resemble bunches
of grapes and almost blacken the ground. As a dish crowberries are served up with morsels of blubber, and eaten by

the natives as dessert after meals. Immense quantities of them are consumed by the natives in August and September. When pressed, the proportion of juice is one third of their volume. By means of fermentation a passable sort of cider may be made from it, even without the addition of sugar. The bog whortleberry (*Vaccinium uliginosum*), is somewhat less plentiful, but almost as widely spread as the cranberry ; the fruit, however, requires a little more favourable circumstances for ripening. They are somewhat smaller, but perhaps sweeter than the European variety. Nevertheless the natives, strange to say, scarcely make any use of them, considering them to be unwholesome. The third kind, the red whortleberry or cowberry (*Vaccinium Vitis idæa*), is only found in certain localities and not eaten at all by the natives. Lastly, it may be added that the cloudberry (*Rubus Chamæmorus*), is pretty common in 64° N. lat., where it may be seen flowering prettily even on the outer shores, but the ripe fruit of this plant is so rare that the author has only once or twice met with it. The juniper bears fruit rather plentifully in the southern districts, but it is never made use of.

There are several *plants of which the flowers, buds, leaves, or roots are eaten*, generally, however, in a raw state. The *Quan* (*Archangelica officinalis*) is most liked. In the north it only exceptionally occurs in Disco, and even in 64° N. lat. it is only found some way up the fjords. The young stalks are eaten raw ; they are brittle and sweet, not unlike carrots in flavour. Occasionally the root is likewise eaten. This plant will grow to a height of 6 feet in favourable spots. The other edible plants used by the natives are Sedum rhodiola (the rose-root), Pedicularis hirsuta, Epilobium latifolium, and Polygonum. Two varieties of sorrel, and the scurvy-grass (Cochlearia), are very common on fertilised spots, especially house-ruins, but these plants are not at all used by the natives. The Icelandic moss (*Cetraria islandica*), is found everywhere, but in greatest abundance in the outlying southern islands.

Seaweeds may perhaps be considered the most important vegetable diet of the Eskimo, because they have in many cases saved people from death by starvation. The species most commonly eaten is *Alaria Pylaii*, closely allied to the edible ' Hen Ware,' or ' Bladderlocks' of Scotland; the *Suvdluitsok* (i.e., without hollowness), of the Greenlander, which has a soft stalk as thick as that of an asparagus, and headed by a broad leaf. Stalk and leaf are both eaten raw, only steeping them first in fresh water, and, if possible, adding some blubber. Besides being plentiful, this seaweed also appears to be of rapid growth. Another kind, *Chorda Filum*. the 'sea-laces' of the English fishermen ; the *Augpilagtok* (i.e. red) of the Eskimo, is considered more delicate but is less abundant. Both these kinds are also eaten when there is no lack of food, but there is a third sort, smaller in size and far more common, which is only resorted to in time of need.

The preceding description of the plants which are worthy of the name of bushes, if even not of trees, will have given a sufficient answer to the question whether Greenland is able to supply *wood* for its inhabitants. Trunks of trees fit to be used as timber are scarcely to be found in the country, and every bit of *wood for manufacture is furnished by drift-wood* or imported. But the bushes are very useful for *fuel*. The larger faggots from the southern fjords are only made use of by Europeans, but the twigs of the willow and dwarf-birch are gathered throughout the winter by the natives on most stations, excepting those situated in the extreme north and on the outermost islands. A stranger certainly would be at a loss to find anything like bushes on the snow-covered hills. But the native women generally find means to supply their most pressing wants from this source.

The drift-wood is carried up Davis Strait by the current round Cape Farewell and thrown up on the shores particularly where it passes through clusters of islands. It travels as far as the northernmost settlements, but of course greatly decreases in force towards the north. The length and straightness of the larger pieces of drift and timber show them to be coniferous trees, but other kinds also occur. Parts of the root and bark are often found adhering to them. In 1855 one piece was found 4 feet in length, with one end rudely formed into the shape of a human head. Although this drift-wood most probably comes from Siberia, various floating objects, obviously of American origin, are nevertheless also cast on the shores of Greenland, such as birch-bark from Indian canoes, with the sewing-thread still attached, and a certain kind of large bean a native of the West Indies. A kayak-paddle formed after the Labrador fashion was once picked up near Cape Farewell. The largest timber is of course found in the south. One piece 60 feet long came ashore in $60\frac{1}{2}°$ N. lat., and another which was found in 63° N. lat. yielded between two and three cords of wood. They are frequently 12 feet long, and a length of 30 feet is not rare. The annual gleanings upon the whole coast may be conjectured to be between 80 and 120 cords, of which scarcely more than the tenth part passes 68° N. lat.

The most common material for fuel is a sort of *turf or peat*, formed of those plants which here and there cover the rocky ground itself or the gravelly hollows between the bare rocks, which we have mentioned above. It is scarcely ever wanting, even in the outmost islands or in the remotest north, but the only objection to it is that it requires to be gathered and dried in summer-time for winter consumption, and this is just its greatest drawback in the opinion of the natives. The plants constituting this fuel are only partially converted into peat. The greater part of the turf is allied to the vegetation still growing over it. The obvious cause of the accumulation of the relics of former generations in a more unchanged state than would be the case in more temperate regions is the climate, which only allows them slowly to decay and crumble into mould. The dead leaves will even adhere to the still growing stalks for several years, and the thick tufts of plants which cover the ground may be said to grow not so much in earth as in a thick matting of dead plants still far from being converted into peat. The turf here described is the most common kind; it is not found so much in wet and swampy valleys as on the hill-sides wherever plants are able to root, and its thickness generally does not exceed 8 inches. But besides this common species there exist two other varieties. In the first place there are some of these boggy glens in which a formation of peat has taken place somewhat more akin to peat-bogs of temperate climates. This peat may even be 2 feet thick, but is not seen north of 64° N. lat. Another variety of turf is characteristic of the outermost islands, and derives its origin from the growth of plants, favoured by the accumulation of the ordure of birds that have had their resting and breeding-places there. Certain small hillocks, usually called 'gull-mounds,' on account of these birds often being seen resting or apparently watching on the top of them, consist of such turf, and are very common. A similar variety of turf covers several low islands at Disco Bay. On one of them this layer was measured and found to have a thickness of $2\frac{1}{2}$ feet, of which $1\frac{1}{2}$ feet must be supposed to be perpetually frozen. The

Greenland turf is in general very well fitted for culinary purposes. The Europeans use a good deal, but few of the natives cut turf for their own use.

Small *gardens* have been laid out at all the chief stations where Europeans have resided, and attempts have been made to raise some of the common *plants of the European kitchen gardens.* In the gardens of Godthaab, situated in 64° N. lat., and rather near to the open sea, turnips, radishes, lettuce, and chervil were almost the only plants that could be cultivated with any success, and, moreover, the turnip required a favourable summer to produce tolerable specimens. The leaves of green cabbage which are produced are not worth notice. But at two more inland stations at the fjord in the same latitude, about 30 miles north of Godthaab, the difference was striking. Here the turnips always came to perfection. The carrots prospered well, and attained the size of ordinary young carrots. The cabbage was unable to develop stalks of a tolerable thickness, but still it produced tolerably large leaves, fit for being stored up for winter provision. Attempts have also been made here to cultivate potatoes ; the tubers, however, became so small that they could at most be eaten only as a curiosity in Greenland, and would not have been able to compete with the earliest new potatoes in a European market. Green peas were forced, to produce seeds just recognisable.

In the southernmost district horticulture is practised at Julianehaab, 60° 48′ N. lat., at Nanortalik and at Frederiksdal, the latter being situated most nearly under the same latitude as Christiania. These stations have a rather seaward situation, and for luxuriance their gardens may be compared to those of the interior fjord-stations in 64° N. lat. At Frederiksdal good carrots were produced. At Nanortalik a forcing frame had been made, in which strawberries grew well and yielded fruits during several years, but then they died off, probably from the severity of one winter. At Julianehaab the turnips very often attained a weight of more than half a pound, and were fit for table in the middle of July. Radishes might be had at the end of June. Rhubarb plants grew pretty vigorously, and could be raised from seeds. Green cabbage produced fine leaves, but did not attain its proper taste and flavour. During several years a few potatoes have also been forced, so as to be kept up by propagation. Only in some years the plants produced flowers, and each of them generally yielded two or three tubers weighing from two to four ounces, while the remainder were only very diminutive, and the whole crop amounted to scarcely four-fold the potatoes sown, and would hardly have been judged eatable in Europe. Parsley would scarcely grow, and peas were only forced sufficiently to yield flowers. No experiments have as yet been made at fjord-stations in 60° to 61° N. lat., where horticulture might be expected to be brought to the highest perfection possible in Greenland. It has been said that the Moravian missionaries at Lichtenau once visiting the interior of the adjacent fjord for the purpose of fetching birch-wood, merely at haphazard sowed some seeds of spruce or fir-trees among the copse mentioned above. Several years later, when this experiment had nearly been forgotten, the Greenlanders brought a tree, the produce of these seeds, about 4 feet high. Though the truth of this statement has not been ascertained, it seems trustworthy, and suggests the idea that perhaps some of the hardiest species of fir could be transplanted to the sheltered tracts of the southernmost part of Greenland. In the north, at Jakobshavn, 69° 13′ N. lat., a garden almost yields the same as at Godthaab, but still further north, at Umanak and Upernivik, radishes will probably represent the highest pitch of horticultural art.

Finally it might be added that Greenland appears exceedingly well fitted for the *indoor cultivation* of European flowers, probably on account of daylight prevailing during a great part of the year. The only difficulty is that of protecting the plants against the frost in the severest part of the winter, which has been effected best by the help of cellars underneath the floor of the heated rooms. At Godthaab a hot-house 14 feet long and 6 feet high was built in the inspector's garden. The room derived its whole warmth from the sun, usually obtaining on fine days in summer a temperature of 82°. During the winter the building was totally buried under the snow, and not until the middle of May was there any opportunity of planting or sowing seed in it. In 1857 the author took different plants from Denmark, such as dwarf apple trees, currant, gooseberry, raspberry, and strawberry plants. They were planted in the hot-house, but partly taken into more or less heated rooms of the dwelling-house for winter. The result proved to be as follows. The strawberries could not withstand the winter cold of the hot-house, but could only be kept alive in pots in the house. The apple trees, raspberry and gooseberry bushes, were kept during winter in a room of the dwelling from which frost could not be excluded. They withered gradually and died off altogether within a few years. One apple tree, however, bore three apples the third summer. The currant bushes only were able to hybernate in the hot-house, where they were planted in the ground and grew up most luxuriantly. In the first two or three years they bore fruit, then completely ceased bearing until about ten years after, when they once more quite unexpectedly produced a good many berries.

Domestic Animals.—In the historical introduction we have stated that in ancient time many farms were to be found in Greenland, and herds of cattle were kept which even yielded produce for exportation to Europe. At present *the dog is the only domestic animal of any value*, and we may add that it is almost indispensable to the existence of the natives beyond a certain latitude. Nothing is more contrary to their usual mode of life than the custom of keeping animals which have to be foddered with plants, and in fact, of those who do not hold an appointment under the Europeans, only a single family has been known to have practised it. Consequently the breeding of cattle in Greenland is only to be regarded as a curiosity, but still its results, like those of the horticultural experiments, may throw some light upon the physical features of this arctic country.

Shortly after the foundation of the southernmost establishment, Julianehaab, some *horned cattle* were sent thither from Europe for the purpose of trying whether this part of the country, still so little explored, might be fit for the development of means of subsistence wholly different from the seal-catching of the Eskimo. In 1782 two calves were sent out to the missionary, and in 1784 two heifers and one bull, to be kept at the expense of the Royal Trade. About the same time the first merchant of this place having retired, settled as a pensioner at Igaliko, where he took up his abode amidst the ruins of the most renowned Norse village. Here his posterity still live, and amounted to thirty-seven persons in 1870, some of whom still continue to breed cattle, combining this employment with seal-catching and the usual occupations of the Greenlanders: this is the family above alluded to. They are quite independent of any European assistance, and may, for natives, be called wealthy people, but of course their farming has in some measure been influenced by the usual carelessness of their countrymen with regard to housekeeping, and for this reason more directly dependent on the irregularities of the climate than necessary. They turn their animals out to graze, and find their food as long as possible, but if there is any extraordinary deficiency of provender they slaughter them. Consequently the amount of stock greatly varies from year to year. Cattle-breeding at the expense of the Royal Trade was soon abandoned, but it was continued by several officials and the missionaries at their own cost. About the year 1855 there were in Greenland 30 to 40 head of horned cattle, about 100 goats, and 20 sheep.

As long as the ground is tolerably free from snow, the cattle themselves seek their supply of food, and there being generally less than 10 head in one place, pasturage is always abundant. The animals roam about at liberty over the surrounding hills, feeding on different grasses, shrubs, and leaves of bushes. At milking-time a boy assembles them, and thus they require but little care. The only difficulty arises from the long winter season, when they have to be stall-fed. Grass growing sufficiently thick and high to be mowed is very scarce, except in those spots which have received some sort of manure. In such places grass continues to supplant every other vegetation, and grows luxuriantly. Even the Norse ruins frequently appear covered or surrounded by tufts of grass. But the Europeans who keep cattle in Greenland only get their hay from fishing places and the abandoned huts of the present inhabitants. The rarity of these hay-fields will be apparent from a quarrel which arose between the merchant and the missionary at Julianehaab about the possession of the places for hay-making available to the station. The litigation was continued for several years, and ended in 1801 by a legal agreement, which divided between the two parties the chief part of the renowned eastern settlement of the Norse, this being the only source of the supply of fodder for the cows which had to furnish milk for their meals.

Of course sufficient fodder can only be obtained from such places by employing the cheap labour of the natives. The owners of the cattle scarcely know where their 'hay-fields' are situated. The whole business is carried on by the natives, a man being sent out with a skin-boat and some women rowers, who find out and bring home the grass in a few days. At Igaliko grass is found mixed with a kind of vetch with beautiful flowers. The ancient Norsemen cannot possibly have been confined to the use of such grass for their cattle, and certainly there must be an abundance of other plants suitable for animals. But how they managed to carry cattle in their ships on their voyages of discovery, and procure food for them in Greenland, nevertheless remains a mystery. Of late years the European residents have almost given up cattle-keeping and only retain goats, while in Igaliko it still prospers. In North Greenland not even goats can be kept on account of the dogs. Poultry have also been kept in some settlements, but not without much trouble and merely as a curiosity.

The dog-sledging of the Greenlanders is one of the most remarkable contrivances as regards cheapness and handiness. The sledge requires a couple of boards for runners, which are 6 feet long, and the cross-pieces which rest upon them and make the seat, and finally the necessary drift-wood for two upright poles offering the necessary hold, if the driver has occasion to follow on foot and steer the sledge from behind. The whole is kept together merely by sealskin thongs, which afford elasticity and prevent the sledge from being broken asunder by the rugged ground over which it has often to pass. Lastly, it must be remembered that it is drawn by dogs which feed upon the offal of the animals killed by their owners, and require scarcely any care. By these means of conveyance nearly as much as 16 miles may be done in an hour upon

N.º 10. Dog - sledges in front of winterhouses.

perfectly smooth ice, if every circumstance favours the speed. But on account of the numerous hindrances that are met with an average of only 4 or 5 miles can be calculated upon, and 500 pounds may be considered a suitable load for eight dogs. Both in summer and winter the dogs generally sleep in the open air; in the severest cold they may even be seen stretched at full length asleep on the icy ground. Sometimes, however, according to old custom, they are allowed to sleep in the passage or entrance to the house, especially those which have young whelps. They are very prolific, and occasionally whelp twice a year, giving birth to six or eight at a time. Considering that they have to live upon what their masters spare from their own provisions, it is evident that their life is a continual fluctuation between dreadful hunger and sudden satiety from devouring masses of flesh, intestines, and blood, and that this irregularity tends to render them wild and ferocious. As they run much easier when fasting, they are not fed until the day's journey is finished. Then when the entire carcase of a seal is thrown before them, they present a spectacle by no means pleasant; the seal, being torn into pieces within a few moments, speedily disappears. Of course they are also dangerous to man, especially to strangers. Children have occasionally been lacerated, but generally help is at hand, and the animals are as cowardly as ferocious. Only bending down as if to take up a stone will sometimes suffice to frighten them, but when they once become infuriated, and have got hold of their victim, they are veritable wolves. In times of famine, they are often killed to serve their owners for food, their flesh, moreover, being considered palatable. When the sea is frozen over and no open water to be found in the vicinity, the sledge is indispensable for the purpose of finding openings further off, and also for pursuing

seals which have crept upon the ice when the sun begins
to give warmth on fine days in April and May. A hunter
in roaming about at this season may even do nearly 80
miles a day. Sometimes, when in travelling along the
shore the ice is found to be broken in front of some
promontory, the driver has to go by land, and, not unfrequently, mountains have to be ascended and descended
which on account of their steepness and height look somewhat hazardous to a new-comer to the country. When the
sledge has to pass down such a dangerous slope the driver,
fastening all the dogs behind it, and, if necessary, binding
one of the feet of each animal, keeps hold of the poles and
tries to moderate the speed in rushing down. In some
cases, if the slope is more moderate, he goes backward in
front of the dogs, stopping them by means of his whip. At
last, when the steepest part has been passed, and the
remainder appears wholly covered with snow, he takes his
seat again and lets the dogs run at their own pace. The
sledge is then hurried down with railroad speed, unless
some of the dogs become entangled in the harness and drag
behind the sledge, until finally the whole will stick in the
deep snow at the foot of the hill. Much skill is also required in driving the sledge over broken ice. In crossing
broad fissures the dogs are first sent over, and then the
sledge pushed after by one brisk pull. But this supposes
that the runners are long enough to reach from one side to
the other, in default of which the driver must cut out a piece
of ice large enough to serve for a raft to float himself
and the sledge. But the situation is still more difficult if
one has to descend from a precipitous shore, and the nearest
ice is broken. A stick headed by a sort of chisel, and
called a 'tok,' is indispensable for dog-sledging.

During the last 10 to 20 years a remarkable contagious
disease has raged among the Greenland dogs, consisting of

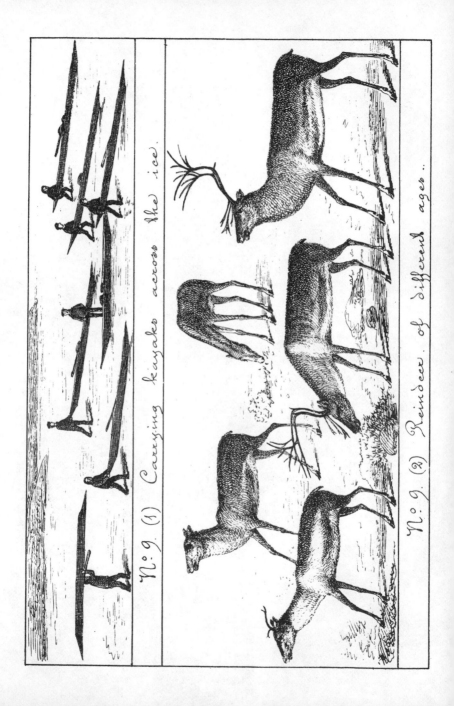

N.º 9 (1) Carrying kayaks across the ice.

N.º 9 (2) Reindeer of different ages.

a sort of madness somewhat akin to hydrophobia, which
is accompanied with a tendency to biting, but the disease
is not communicable by the bite itself. It generally causes
death within one or two days. The number of sledge-dogs
in Greenland is about 1,800 to 2,000, and of sledges about
320. The team used for a sledge varies from 4 to 12
according to the wealth of the owner. Although the
race has now and then been crossed with European dogs
the greater part have still most decidedly maintained the
appearance of the original Eskimo dog, or we may even
say, the arctic wolf, from which this dog is undoubtedly
descended. At the southern settlements the natives keep
some dogs of mixed races, only for the purpose of making
use of the furs for clothes.

Wild Land Animals.—Although the Greenlanders derive their chief sustenance from the sea, yet the chase by
land is by no means unimportant to them, not only in
supplying several necessaries, but more particularly by
affording, or properly speaking, having formerly afforded,
an opportunity for journeys and sports equally favourable
to their physical health and stimulating to their mental
powers, thus counteracting the dulness and inertness
arising from the usual life at the winter stations. The
travelling here alluded to was connected with the *reindeer
hunt*, which formerly occupied the greater part of the
population during two or three months in summer ; but for
a period of more than twenty years this custom has been
greatly on the decrease. The chief hunting grounds,
situated by the interior of the fjords, were the rendezvous
places for hunters from widely-spread wintering places. In
their skin-boats, escorted by kayaks, they carried their
families, tents, and all their necessaries. From the fjords
the boats occasionally were borne by land to the lakes, and
in this way the furthest accessible interior regions were

visited. The contrast between the desolate outer shores around most of the winter stations and the finest sheltered valleys of the interior, of the life in the huts to that in the tents, and lastly, the intercourse caused by the congregation of people from widely distant places, could not be without the greatest influence on people whose life otherwise, as regards the male sex, is a continuous struggle with hardships and dangers, and as far as women and children are concerned, is liable to produce dulness and torpidity from their being so much confined to indoor life.

According to what we have stated above, it is clear that there is not the least probability of valleys existing in the interior beyond the wall of inland ice which could afford pasturing grounds and safe refuges for the reindeer, and the possibility of any migration between the east and the west coast appears, at all events, highly problematical. The chase gradually increased, chiefly on account of the more common use of the rifle. It reached its culminating point in the period between 1845 and 1849, when the number of deer killed might be rated at 25,000 annually, the number of skins exported being about 16,000 per annum. But after 1850 the chase rapidly declined, and in 1868 to 1872 the annual export had dwindled to 6 skins, or, in other words, nothing, while the whole number of animals killed may scarcely be rated at more than 1,000 per annum during the latest period. On these longer excursions the hunters are generally accompanied by women, whose duty is to carry home as much of the venison as possible, which they effect by passing the strap from which the load hangs around their foreheads. Notwithstanding the great skill they have acquired in carrying burdens in this way, their assistance proved insufficient during the briskest period of the chase. We may suppose that during those years one half of the flesh was abandoned on the rocks, while a great many deer were killed only for the sake of the hide and the tongue. The somewhat sudden decline of the chase has tended to nourish the fancy of genial regions in the very interior of the Greenland continent, to which the reindeer herds might have migrated. But on taking into consideration the indiscriminate slaughter with the help of a weapon, formerly scarcely used, and still earlier wholly unknown in the country, it seems that here we have before us but an instance of a similar destruction of various kinds of game in almost every other part of the globe. Now since the animals have ceased to congregate in so great herds the pursuit of them never can become so ruinous, and it seems that during the last years the remaining stock has not been subject to any further decrease. Reindeer meat has of course ceased to be in daily use, but on the other hand it has as yet by no means become a rarity in Greenland.

The natives seldom eat it raw, except in a frozen state. On their marches, when they are unable to carry cooking utensils, they broil it, if possible, upon flat stones. But the frozen flesh is eaten as a dainty, and fresh meat will be given in exchange for that which has to some degree become tainted, and is for this reason preferred. But the most remarkable delicacy derived from the reindeer are the contents of the paunch, or the last food which the animal has swallowed. The author only once had the opportunity of witnessing the use of it, and must grant it to be an argument of great weight in favour of those who are inclined to rank the Eskimo, and especially their domestic life, as low as possible. At the same time one must remember that even amongst hunters of European race the same disgusting substance is said to be a favourite dish in the wilds of North America. The tallow is highly appreciated, and always eaten raw as a tit-bit. The antlers are almost indispensable for the manufacture of several weapons and kayak-implements. In the years following 1850 they were made an article of trade, and purchased at a price of about one penny per pound, and the quantity of them dispersed over the country proved to be so great that at one station more than 100,000 lbs. were brought for sale within a short period. Although hunting the reindeer was ordinarily a summer occupation, it also took place in winter, and in some localities reindeer were even shot close to the houses. Exceptionally the inhabitants of some places made the chase by land their chief source of sustenance, though not abandoning seal-hunting, to which they had recourse for the purpose of providing oil for their lamps.

Foxes are found in two varieties, *blue* and *white*, both of them being only an article of commerce, and not at all made use of by the natives themselves. There is a great difference in the value, the best blue skins having several times reached the price of 3*l.* in the European market. The foxes appear mostly confined to the mainland, though they live perhaps for the most part upon what they may find on the shore at low water. In summer they often visit the islands, and may be met with, having made their holes and bred their young in the immediate vicinity of abandoned winter-houses, apparently attracted thither by the garbage left by the inhabitants. The half-grown cubs may then be seen playing outside like whelps of tame dogs, and may be approached and taken by the hand. They are always easily tamed, and behave in this state just like dogs. The skins are only in season from November to March, the hair being shorter and of a dirty grayish-brown colour during the other months. Many of the foxes are caught in traps of a very primitive construction, formed of a flat stone so fixed as to fall down and crush or confine them when the bait has been touched. But most of

No. 4. A resting-place for reindeer-hunters on their march.

them are shot by hunters lying in wait when they come down to the shore in search of mussels or other food at low water. Of course this sort of sport is limited to those southern places where the sea off the shore is mostly open even during the first part of the winter. There the foxes are by far the most numerous, but even in the furthest north they are not wanting ; wherever seals have been caught in winter upon the ice, foot-prints of some fox that has been attracted by the drops of blood in the snow will generally be visible. But how these animals are able to find the food necessary for supporting life during eight months of the year at the northern fjords remains somewhat of a mystery. The sea being frozen over for hundreds of miles, the beach especially being covered by a crust of ice upwards of ten feet in thickness, and the birds having migrated to the south, the only other animals left to roam over the vast snow-covered tracts besides reindeer are hares, partridges, ravens, eagles, hawks, and owls. All these terrestrial animals are scarce, and seem to be unable to yield sufficient food for the foxes. Severe winters with much snow are favourable to fox-hunting, and such favourable years seem to have been often succeeded by periods in which the animals were unusually scarce. The number of foxes killed have been 1,500 yearly on an average from 1853 to 1872 ; the greatest number ever obtained seems to have been in 1874, when they amounted to 5,000. Of the whole stock about one half is caught between 60° and 61° N. lat.

The chase of the other, in a stricter sense, *terrestrial* animals is of little importance, only serving to procure food for the Europeans living in the country. *Ptarmigan* are pretty common, being in summer almost everywhere met with at heights of from 1,000 to 2,000 feet, while in winter flocks of them are sometimes seen close to the houses.

Very few are caught by snares, almost the whole of them being shot with fowling-pieces, and mostly by persons who are engaged and provided by the Europeans with the necessary implements for taking them. The whole annual production of ptarmigan may be rated at about 12,000 on an average, and that of the *white hares* at hardly one thousand. The *ravens* are assiduous guests in every settlement when the country is covered with deep snow, and when even berries, which otherwise seem to constitute part of their food, are difficult to be got. They then become almost tame, and follow people carrying seal-flesh or blubber in order to snatch the snow that may have imbibed some dropping blood or oil. Their flesh is eaten by few persons, and it is generally not considered worth while to shoot them.

The Polar Bear is almost an amphibious animal. Upwards of fifty of them are on an average shot yearly, of which more than one half are shot in the environs of the northernmost settlement, and of the remainder the greater part at the southernmost extremity of the country, where they arrive with the drift-ice around the Cape Farewell. Throughout the whole intervening tract bears are scarce, but still they may be found everywhere, and solitary stragglers may even be met with unexpectedly in summer in the interior of the fjords. Killing a bear has, in ancient as well as in modern times, been considered one of the most distinguishing feats of sportsmanship in Greenland. Erik the Red is said to have quarrelled with one of his best friends from envy on account of the latter having had the luck to capture a bear. About the year 1060 an Icelander named Audun came to Greenland and gave all his property in exchange for a living bear, which he brought as a present to King Svend in Denmark, who gave Audun in reward an honourable maintenance for life, and discharged his chamberlain on account of his having tried to extort money from Audun for being admitted to the king. In the north the bear is pursued upon the frozen sea by the aid of dogs. It often takes refuge on the top of an iceberg, where it is surrounded and held at bay by the dogs until it is shot, generally not without some of the latter being lost on the occasion. In the north the male bears at least seem to roam about in winter as far south as 68° N. lat., because wherever the carcass of a whale may be found, or a rich hunt of seals or white whales occurs in a certain place within these confines, there several bears are sure soon to make their appearance. In the south, where no dogs are to be had for assistance, the natives generally try to force the bear into the water, and often kill it with harpoons from the kayak. At the southernmost stations bears have often been shot close to the houses, being apparently attracted by the scent from human dwelling-places. Several years ago a bear had pushed the foremost part of its body into a house-passage at night, but getting into a difficulty on account of finding it too narrow, was killed by the inhabitants, who, after having been warned by their dogs, fired at it through the doorway and from the window. At another time a woman, staying alone with her child in a house, observed a bear outside. Thinking it might be likely to give her a call, she placed the burning lamp at the window, keeping some straw at hand. The bear soon came on, pushing its head through the intestine-formed curtain of the window, whereupon she threw the straw into the lamp, at the blaze of which the bear retreated. It then tried to scratch a hole through the wall from another side, but was killed by some passing travellers.

Sea-fowl.—In summer swarms of sea-fowl are scattered over the whole extent of the coast. It is well known that for the purpose of escaping their enemies, some of them,

especially the eider-ducks, breed in small and low outer
islands, while others inhabit precipitous rocks, the so-called
bird-cliffs.   The breeding-places of the *eider-ducks* are
limited to certain clusters of islets, which are regularly
visited by the natives in June and July in search of eggs
and down.   The eggs, even when containing little chickens,
are not at all offensive to their heroic taste.   The same
recklessness with which the natives now waste these eggs
has no doubt been shown by them in ancient times ; for
this reason it is rather surprising that a more constant decrease in the production of down does not appear to have
set in before the last twenty years, the average quantity
exported having diminished from 5,600 to 2,000 pounds
yearly during this period.   The only probable reason may
be found in a more general persecution of the bird itself
having of late been added to the devastations of the nests.

Compared with eider-ducks, the *sea-fowl which inhabit
the cliffs* are much less subject to have their nests and eggs
taken.   These precipitous walls rising abruptly from the sea
to a height of one or two thousand feet, or even more, with
all their protruding edges and their holes and fissures
crowded with birds, offer a curious sight on account of the
immense number of their feathered inhabitants, and the
enormous size of the beetling rocks when regarded from
a boat a few hundred feet distant from the shore.   The
appearance of such rocks is generally illusive to the eye by
appearing nearer and lower than they really are, for which
reason the size of the birds at the same time will appear
too small.   On seeing the innumerable white patches
with which the gloomy walls are dotted over, we are re-
minded of snow, while some single birds which happen
to be soaring in the air present the appearance of down or
feathers borne by the wind.   But on firing a gun, or on some
other sign being given, the white spots begin to move, in

a moment thousands of birds swarm over one's head, filling the air with their discordant cries, and the beholder then first receives a correct impression of the true size and height of the wall inhabited by them. Some of the bird-cliffs, and especially those of the furthest north, contain different species of sea-fowls ranged over one another, the auks occupying the lowest part, the kittiwakes being the chief inhabitants of the centre, and the gulls inhabiting the most inaccessible heights. The Greenlanders know nothing about those peculiar contrivances made use of in other countries in order to get at the nests ; they merely step from their skiff upon the rock and climb wherever they are able to find the least footing. Some cliffs are regularly visited by persons who have acquired extraordinary skill in this daring task, but of whom several have paid for their boldness by the loss of their lives.

Many years ago a company of travellers set out for the Nagsutouk-fjord (67½° N. lat.) ; the weather being fine and hot they had stripped off their jackets, when they happened to pass by a cliff inhabited by kittiwakes and other gulls. They all jumped ashore and climbed up the precipice to fetch some eggs, when suddenly they discovered that their boat had drifted off the shore. The half-naked people, left upon a resting-place a few feet wide, and hanging over the sea, were now surprised by cold and bad weather. The only means of keeping themselves warm was to lie down in a heap covering each other by turns. In this dreadful state they passed some days, seeking nourishment from shrubs after having consumed all the eggs. Finally some passing travellers rescued them, but not without having at first hesitated to approach them for fear that they might not be really human beings but ' Kivigtoks,' or some of the other weird unearthly beings which the Greenlander delights in peopling his desolate country with.

In winter all the sea-fowls migrate to the south, where open water may be found, and there, south of 66°N. lat., they afford profitable hunting to the natives, during a season when sometimes they have nothing else but fish for food ; the feathers furnish them with an article of trade, and the skins, with the feathers or down still adhering to them, form excellent clothing, being at the same time light and warm. Some of them, distinguished for their colour and softness, even yield a valuable fur for the European market in the shape of coverlets, or of articles for ladies' dress. By far the greater part of these birds consist of auks and eider-ducks, and although a great many of them are now shot, they are still chiefly taken from the kayaks by means of the bird-spear. Sea-fowl jackets are, on account of their lightness, much used by the kayakers. The whole amount of sea-fowls annually killed may be rated at 20,000 eider-ducks and other larger kinds, and more than 50,000 auks and other smaller kinds. The eggs yearly taken, chiefly those of eider-ducks, may be estimated at more than 300,000.

CHAPTER VI.

THE CAPTURE OF SEALS AND WHALES.

WHAT we have to treat of in this chapter surpasses in economical and commercial importance all the other means of gain and subsistence, and is to be considered the foundation of the whole peculiar mode of life of the Eskimo. The reason we have arranged these two different orders of mammalia together here is partly because they are caught in much the same manner, and partly because both their flesh and blubber supply the Greenlanders with their most nutritious food, and with the necessary means for heating and lighting their houses. But as regards their skins there is an important difference, the seals affording materials for clothes, boats, and tents, while the skin of the whales only yields a favourite nutriment. This edible skin is called Matak, and all the cetaceous animals are for this reason denominated Mataliks. It is almost always eaten raw, and consists of two sheets, the inner one very tough, while the outer, which is considered to represent the rudimental hair-covering, is more brittle. There are as many varieties of it as there exist species of cetaceans, from that of the small porpoise to the colossal whale.

The principle upon which the peculiar seal-hunting of the Eskimo is based is almost the same as that which has been resorted to in the ordinary European mode of killing whales ; viz. previously striking the animal with the harpoon, and keeping hold of, and wearying it by aid of a line attached to the harpoon, so as to facilitate the killing of it by means of the lance and spear. The use of the harpoons, lines, and lances is perfectly analogous among the European and the Eskimo hunting at sea. The chief difference in their proceedings appears to be the mode of retarding the animal while running off with the harpoon and lines. The Greenlander manages this by throwing out an inflated bladder attached to the other end of the line, but the European whaler still keeps this end of the line in the boat of the harpooner, only letting go so much of the line as is necessary to prevent the boat from being capsized and drawn down, while the terrified animal, being still in possession of its whole power, runs off with extraordinary quickness. The seal, or whale, having become sufficiently exhausted by dragging the boat, the mortal wounds are finally inflicted by help of the lance.

There is only one contrivance by which the harpoons and lances of the Eskimo essentially differ from those of the European whale-fishers ; viz. the peculiar manner in which the point of these weapons is fitted into the shaft, admitting of its being at the first pull sideways bent out of the shaft and only remaining attached by a line ; the point of the lance then remains attached to the shaft, the string forming a sort of hinge, whereas that of the large harpoons is wholly loosened from the shaft, and only remains attached to the line with its bladder. The sideways pull will of course occur as soon as the animal begins to sprawl after having been struck, and the flexibility of the weapon hinders the shaft from being broken asunder, and the harpoon point from being torn out again by the movements of the animal in its agony. The art of catching seals by the harpoon and bladder is still pursued in Greenland exactly in the same way as before Europeans had settled there, without the least change or improvement; and though some other means of capture have been added, viz. the rifle and the twine-made net, there is some reason to believe that the abolition of the ancient manner of hunting seals would prove fatal to the welfare, if not to the existence, of the present race of inhabitants. Still more indispensable to them is the kayak or skin-canoe, fitted out especially for this pursuit, but moreover almost as necessary in numerous other circumstances of daily life. It measures upwards of 18 feet in length and about 2 feet in breadth, and weighs about 55 pounds, so that the man on landing can take it in one hand and carry it along with him up the beach. It will carry a load of 200 pounds besides the man who sits in it. The paddle, or double-bladed oar, is fabricated most carefully, with the aim of adapting it especially to the purpose of enabling the kayaker to rise to the surface again if he happens to be overturned. To the kayak implements here mentioned must be added the kayak dress, viz. a waterproof jacket with mittens, which form one piece with the kayak, only leaving the face of the kayaker free. In a sheltered sea or in quiet weather, only a 'half-jacket' is generally used, which protects the man as far as to the arm-pits when he ships a sea.

In describing the different manœuvres by which the seals are captured, they may be divided into those resorted to while seated in the kayak, and those possible to the hunter if he has a footing on ice or land. Undoubtedly the kayak may be useful, or even indispensable, also in the latter case, and the application of the different weapons and implements may be mixed. The kayaker while roaming about in wait of seals may occasionally step out upon a piece of drifting ice, and shoot the game which he had at first intended to despatch by the harpoon and bladder ; *per contra,* if the hunter is standing on the beach or edge of the ice in water, the kayak will be required for the purpose of bringing or, in some cases, finally killing the seal he may have shot with his gun.   But generally there can hardly be any doubt whether the capture must be said to have been effected from the kayak or from the shore and the ice.

Kayak-hunting.—When the kayaker intends to strike a seal with his harpoon, he advances within a distance of about 25 feet from it, then throws the harpoon by means of a piece of wood adapted to support the harpoon while he takes aim with it, and called the 'thrower.'   At the same time he loosens the bladder and throws it off likewise. The animal struck dives, carrying away the coiled-up line with great speed ; if in this moment the line happens to become entangled with some part of the kayak, or if the bladder is not discharged quick enough, the kayaker in most cases will be capsized without any chance of saving his life by rising again.   But if the operation has been entirely successful, the bladder moving on the surface of the water indicates the track of the animal underneath it, and the hunter follows it with the large lance which he throws like the harpoon when the seal appears above the water, repeating the same several times, the lance always disengaging itself and floating on the surface.   Finally, when the convulsions of the animal are subsiding, he rows close up to it and stabs it with the small hand-spear or knife.   The right whale and other whales of similar size are caught from whale-boats or open boats, but the minor species of cetaceans or dolphins, especially the white whale and narwhal, are hunted exactly in the same manner as the seals. When the seal is only a small one the so-called bladder-arrow is used, being a small harpoon without any line, but with a small bladder fixed to its staff.   This arrow is likewise thrown, and generally remains in the body of the animal until it can be killed with the lance. The same missile is employed in the so-called ' halloo-hunt,' which is carried out by a number of kayakers for the purpose of forcing a shoal of seals into a narrow inlet or *cul de sac* and cutting off their retreat. In some cases seals are struck with the harpoon whilst resting on a floe of drift-ice, or the kayaker mounts the ice himself, stealing upon his prey and stabbing it with his lance.

The use of fire-arms has been introduced in various ways in connection with kayak-hunting ; generally the rifle is carried in the kayak, the occupant of which ascends an ice-floe and stands on the watch for seals chancing to pass by. Within the last twenty years it has occasionally been tried to shoot immediately from the kayak, and in some instances it has proved successful. But on account of the general incautiousness on the part of the natives, the carrying of guns in their kayaks has proved destructive to the lives and limbs of many hunters, and shooting from the kayak must, in particular, be considered one of the most hazardous manœuvres. The want of a suitable covering for keeping the gun dry generally causes it to be put into the kayak. On being brought forth again it so often happens to go off, that this occurrence in itself is thought very little of, but instances of hunters having their hand pierced by the ball are by no means rare, and mortal wounds are heard of almost every year. The gun may happen to go off in this way just as the hunter has landed, but if we picture to ourselves the same operation being performed at sea, where the kayaker has to creep or lift himself out of his narrow hole in order to get hold of his gun, and has to return to his seat before taking aim and firing, while at the same time he must be careful to prevent his frail skiff cap-

sizing without using the paddle, the danger of this proceeding will be sufficiently obvious.

Capturing from the Shore or from the Ice.—The different
modes of hunting described in this section have been greatly
influenced by the application of European implements.
The only modes of hunting on the ice which are still conducted after the original Eskimo fashion are the so-called
' slippery ice-hunting,' and the '*Maupok*,' and '*Itsuarpok*.'
The ice only rarely forms in such a manner as to make it
perfectly smooth and even. If the freezing in autumn
goes on at a temperature of from 9° to 5°, snow generally
accompanies it. If later on it happens to set in more
suddenly, at a temperature of more than 10° below zero,
the vapours from the water at the moment of congela-
tion cause the whole surface to be spread over with a
kind of rime like coarse needles or lamellæ, making it
quite uneven, as if covered with a thin sheet of frozen
snow. However, it may also happen to freeze over in calm
weather and with a moderate degree of cold, so as to make
the ice quite smooth and glassy, looking like the ocean in
a dead calm as far as the eye can reach. In such a case
the seals, being suddenly cut off from the air, are obliged
to form and keep open little holes in the new ice, to which
they may resort for the purpose of breathing. The opening itself is only an inch in diameter, and from the reiterated breathing its edges are gradually raised and the
surrounding ice kept thin, and acquiring the shape of an
inverted bowl, with sufficient room for the muzzle of the
animal. The respiration of the seal through such an aperture is slow, deep, and audible for a great distance, and
the experienced listener will be able to discern the direction from whence the sound proceeds. On attempting to
approach such a hole the least noise caused by the roughness of the surface will suffice to scare the animal away, but

if the surface is smooth as above described, the approach
may be accomplished speedily enough to take the animal
by surprise.   The hunter moreover guards the soles of his
boots by the help of shoes with the hairy side turned outward.   While standing on the watch with his harpoon, on
hearing the breathing of the seal he runs, guided by his ear as
well as his sight, reaches the hole and stabs his prey 'all in no
time.'   A hunter may capture from six to eight seals a day
in this way, but such smooth ice only rarely occurs ; upon
ordinary rough or snow-covered ice in winter, another mode
of hunting is resorted to, called ' Maupok,' signifying, he
sits or stands in wait.   It must be remembered that some
of the said breathing-holes continue to be kept open
throughout the whole winter, whatever thickness the ice may
attain.   But the seal being sure to perceive the least noise
from the surface of the ice, the only way to get at it from
the hole is to take up a position close by the same, either
standing or sitting, with the harpoon in readiness, and even
then the hunter has to use every precaution not to stir.

Such a state of perfect immobility has often to be
maintained for hours in the depth of winter, it may be
with a strong wind blowing and a temperature of ÷20°.
This hunting is much facilitated when a company of
hunters agree to watch all the holes for a certain extent,
so as to render escape more difficult to the game.   Another
mode of hunting, called ' Itsuarpok,' i.e., he pries or peeps
through a hole, is still more rarely practised and almost
abandoned now.   It is managed by two men in company,
who post themselves at two holes in the ice and have a long
pole headed by a harpoon-point.   One of the men lies
prostrate, and while he peeps through the first hole the
other keeps the harpoon dipping into the water in the
second hole.   The first man watches the approach of the
seal, and it is said that a certain art of alluring it was

formerly known. As soon as the right moment arrives he gives a sign to his companion, who instantly darts the weapon in the direction pointed out by the former.

On many occasions the rifle is used for shooting seals from the shore and from the edge of the ice. The most curious instance is that of the so-called ' *Savsat*,' which means animals secluded and confined to an opening in the ice. In winter the white whales and the narwhals seem to live in the vicinity of the ice bordering the coast, as they generally make their appearance whenever the ice happens to break up. If severe frost and calm weather at such time happens to set in simultaneously, so as to cause the sea to be frozen over suddenly and for a wide extent, the animals, which have meanwhile ventured too far towards the coast or up the inlets (perceiving the water to be closed up on all sides), for want of air are forced to resort to the nearest spot where no ice has as yet been formed, or at all events grown solid enough to withstand their united efforts. The hole having once been made and the course of the animals guided towards this only refuge, it is rapidly enlarged and kept open by the throng. As soon as the Greenlanders happen to discover a 'savsat,' the news will soon be reported to the neighbouring stations, and all the hunters who are possessed of sledge and dogs, at once set out for the spot and assemble around the border of the opening to join in the sport, which is mostly carried on with shooting weapons, but also by means of the kayak-tools, the latter chiefly for getting hold of the captured animals. This slaughtering is often continued for several days, giving sometimes upwards of one hundred animals in a day. Undoubtedly 'savsats' always occur somewhere off the coast every year, but only in some years they happen to be discovered and made use of.

One of the most lucrative ways of capturing seals is to

pursue those which have crept up on the top of the ice, and which are called *Utok*. In spring, when the weather grows milder, and chiefly in sunny days, the seals are very fond of getting out of the water to bask and frolic on the ice. The month of May is the proper season for utoks. The seals form oblique passages through the ice-crust, only large enough to allow their getting up and down. In all likelihood they make use of the breathing-holes from the water, enlarging them for this purpose by means of their warm breath, and by scratching them with their paws. Otherwise it would be difficult to conceive how animals of their size could manage to perforate ice of an average thickness of from 3 to 6 feet. At a distance of a few feet from this aperture they lie down ; sometimes they are seen to sleep, their heads reclining on the ice ; sometimes, turning round upon their backs, they try to scratch their big and clumsy bodies with their stumpy paws ere they stretch their limbs almost like human beings, suddenly lifting their heads and looking about cautiously, and then again lying down to enjoy the heat of the sun. Before the use of fire-arms had been introduced, the utoks were caught by help of the harpoon and line. The hunter lay down on the ice, pulled his sealskin jacket high enough to cover his face, and imitating the manners of a seal, crept towards his prey. But this mode has now been abandoned, whereas the use of the rifle has greatly promoted the utok-hunt, which at present has become one of the most lucrative sports in North Greenland. Nevertheless it is by no means an easy matter, or in any way to be compared with the usual seal-catch of European ships in the sea of Spitzbergen. In the first place it must be remembered that the seal, having a very acute sense of hearing, is always on guard and has its diving-hole, or 'atluk,' close at hand. On perceiving the least mischief astir it will instantly make escape. Secondly, it is necessary to hit the skull or the vertebræ of the neck, as no wound inflicted in any other spot will deprive the animal of the necessary power to roll its body down the hole and be lost. If a Greenlander sledging on the ice happens to see an utok and intends to slay it, he approaches it to a distance of some hundred yards, where he leaves his sledge, the dogs being trained not to stir from the spot until he has fired. He then produces his shooting-sail, a piece of white cotton stretched across a wooden frame, which stands upright upon a little sledge, serving him for a cover to hide behind while he tries to approach his prey. Keeping a steady eye upon the seal, and, if necessary, making a circuit in order to get at it from behind, he continues his approach on foot to a distance of about 200 yards, after which he lies down upon his stomach and creeps along, pushing his sail before him until he judges that he is within gunshot. He then takes aim, makes a sudden noise, on hearing which the seal lifts up its head, and at the same instant he fires. An ordinary utok-hunt yields four to six, and a very prosperous one upwards of twenty seals a day to a hunter.

Seal-hunting with nets is carried on in two different ways. One kind of net is small and only meant for catching one animal at a time by entangling it in its meshes when it happens to run its head through the same. These nets are chiefly set beneath the ice so as to cross the track of the seals along the shore, and are, on account of their cheapness, well adapted for common use by the inhabitants of the northern regions. Another sort of net is made upon a wholly different principle, viz. that of enclosing shoals of seals by cutting off their retreat. The nets used for this purpose are large and expensive, being made to bar certain sounds through which the seals have their track. Of these nets, two at least are necessary. The first one is lowered to the bottom, allowing the seals to pass over it, the second being spread a little further off to intercept their passage. When the whole shoal has passed over the first net, this is likewise lifted up and hauled tight, upon which the seals, being shut up within the two, are killed either with the gun or caught by running their heads into the meshes. This mode of capture has been practised in certain sounds between 63° and 66° N. lat., but ended in gradually sending away the seals from those inlets. It is in this respect, though on a smaller scale, analogous to the slaughter of the same animals by the European sealing-ships. In the period from 1838 to 1842 it produced 4,000 seals annually, excepting in 1839, when the whole coast was blocked up with drift-ice. Towards 1855 the yearly number was reduced to 1,000 seals and 100 white whales, and during the latest years to only a few hundred animals.

Whale-Fishing.—What more especially is termed whale-fishery, viz. the capture of the right whale or other whales of similar size, is at present only carried on in Greenland on a very small scale. The *right whale* was formerly chased by the natives from their open skin-boats, and struck by means of harpoons and bladders, but this practice has already been wholly abandoned many years. The present royal monopoly of the trade was from the beginning chiefly based on the whale-fishery being conducted from certain fixed stations in Greenland. It was soon found that an extraordinary profit might be gained by employing the natives for this purpose, partly because the skin and flesh of the whale, which the European sailors throw away, yield an ample supply of most excellent and palatable food for the Greenlanders, and partly on account of these people only being hired for the time during which the boats are in pursuit of whales, while they find themselves for the whole remainder of the year. This whale-fishery, carried on with native crews but with European boats and implements, was continued for many years from several stations, especially from two, and at times very successfully, but was found to be detrimental to the natives as regards their own business and self-reliance. In the course of years it declined, and only a remnant of it now exists at Holstenborg, where it is carried on from January to March, the sea being generally open in front of this settlement, while the interior inlets are all frozen over. During a long period it has averaged one 'fish' each season.

More peculiar to Greenland is the capture of the *Kepokak* or *Humpback*, one of the fin whales, which is almost as large as the right whale. The kepokak, on having been struck with the harpoon, runs with great velocity along the surface of the water, and is not so easily retarded by means of lines and boats as the right whale, which always 'sounds' or dives to the bottom, and sooner becomes exhausted. For this reason the kepokak is simply pursued by stealing upon it when it is found asleep, and stabbing it with the lance. Sometimes a harpoon is also entered with good effect after the strength of the animal has been reduced by the stroke of the lance. However, the kepokak hunt has likewise greatly decreased, and is at present chiefly confined to a single station, where European boats are kept to be lent to the natives for this purpose. But even yet a kepokak is at intervals caught by the natives also in other places, and by means of their own boats.

Number of Seals and Whales Killed.—The following calculations of the annual catch are based upon the exact returns of the export during the last twenty years; but into the calculation are also added those killed for the consumption of their skins and flesh in Greenland itself.

The Natsek or 'fjord-seal' (*Phoca fœtida*; *Pagomys*

fœtidus) is already mentioned as stationary throughout the coast. Only stray individuals of this species migrate to the main drift-ice of Baffin's Bay in July, and return to the coast when the first bay-ice is forming in September, or occasionally appearing whenever the weather has been stormy. But the chief stock, whose favourite haunts, as has been described, are the ice-fjords, does not seem to leave the coast at all. It is almost exclusively this seal that is captured as ' utok ' and by means of the ice-nets. It derives its scientific name from the nauseous smell peculiar to certain older individuals, especially those captured in the interior ice-fjords, which are also on an average perhaps twice as large as those generally occurring off the outer shores. When brought into a hut and cut up on its floor, such a seal emits a smell resembling something between that of assafœtida and onions, almost insupportable to strangers. This peculiarity is not noticeable in the younger specimens, or those of a smaller size, such as are more generally caught, and at all events the smell does not detract from the utility of the flesh over the whole of Greenland. Some experiments with seven seals of this kind gave a mean weight of 84 pounds for the whole animal, consisting of blubber 33, flesh including bones 28, head and paws 4, lights, liver and heart 6, entrails and blood 4, hide 4, fat scrapings from the same 3, leavings 2 pounds. The animals used for these experiments were perhaps somewhat below the middle size. The number of this species captured has been calculated at 51,000.

The Kassigiak or ' spotted seal' (Phoca vitulina ; Callo-cephalus vitulinus). This kind, which is widely spread and the most common seal of all on the northern shores of Europe, is, on the contrary, much less numerous in Greenland than the Natsek. It occurs here and there, however, throughout the coast, and seems to be as stationary as the former, with which it also corresponds in size. The skin is highly valued in Greenland for making clothes. The annual catch is doubtful; it may be guessed at 1,000, and at any rate scarcely amounts to 2,000.

The saddle-back seal (*Phoca groenlandica; Pagophilus groenlandicus*).—This species, which is well known as forming the chief object of chase to the European sealing ships in the Spitzbergen and Newfoundland seas, is a migratory animal, but must nevertheless be considered at home on the Greenland coast, on account of its haunting its shores and roaming over its sounds and fjords regularly during the greater part of the year. It is of inestimable importance on account of its skin, which yields the usual covering of the kayaks and open skin-boats. It appears regularly along the southern part of the coast in September, travelling in herds from south to north between the islands, and at times resorting to the fjords. They are then pretty fat, but their sheet of blubber is still increased during the course of winter. In October and November the catch is most plentiful; then it decreases in December, grows more scarce in January, and becomes almost extinct in February. The seals return as regularly off the southern coast in May, and on the more northern in June. They have then grown very lean, and lost more than half of their blubber. Having visited the fjords in numerous herds, they again disappear in July and return in September. Consequently this seal deserts the coast twice a year, and as regularly returns to it in due season, always first making its appearance in the southern, and somewhat later in the northern regions. It is also known that it wanders along the coast from the south to the north; but this is not the only reason of its appearance later in the north, inasmuch as the seals must be supposed to return in different latitudes, and consequently some of them must arrive at the northern regions without having touched at the southernmost. As to their whereabouts during their absence we are somewhat at a loss for perfect information.   There can be no doubt that in spring they retreat to. the icefields of the ocean for the purpose of producing their young.   It seems most unlikely that the seals from the west coast should have such breeding places to the east of Greenland in the Spitzbergen sea, which would require the whole stock of them to round the Cape Farewell at least twice a year.   But considering that just opposite to the west coast extensive masses of drift-ice from Baffin's Bay are moving southward throughout the greater part of the year, nothing seems more reasonable to believe than that the seals, having gone their usual beat along the west coast of Greenland, put to sea in various latitudes ; after which, on crossing Davis Strait, they almost everywhere will meet with parts of the drift-ice, which they will then follow on its course southward, and on returning they will make the coast of Greenland at some more southerly point, begin their usual migration, and so on.   But while the impending breeding-time may account for the departure of the seals towards the end of winter, the cause of their disappearance in summer remains more doubtful.

The 'saddle-backs,' according to their age or different stages of development, are divided into four or five different classes by the European sealers, as well as by the natives of Greenland.   In Greenland, however, in familiar language the only distinction made is between the full-grown animal whose skin has assumed the half-moon shaped dark marking on both sides of the body, and the half-grown ones, or 'blue-sides,' on whom these bands are as yet not sufficiently developed.   A full-grown saddleback of medium size was found to weigh 253 lbs.; the skin, with the blubber attached, amounting to 116 lbs., and the flesh to 100 lbs. The blubber, amounting to 80 lbs. in winter, is scarcely 24 lbs. when the seal returns in summer. The annual catch is calculated at 17,500 full-grown saddle-backs and 15,500 blue-sides.

The bladder-nose (*Cystophora cristata*), one of the largest seals, is well-known from the bladder on its forehead, which it is able to blow up at will. It is only occasionally found along the greater part of the coast, but visits the very limited tract between 60° and 61° N. lat. in great numbers, most probably coming from and returning to the east side of Greenland. The first time it visits us is from about May 20 till the end of June, during which it yields a very lucrative catch. It is very fierce, and when wounded not unfrequently attacks its pursuer, violently splashing and trying to bite him. This hunt, which is hazardous to a man in a frail kayak, has been greatly facilitated by the rifle, the hunters first hitting their prey from the ice-floes, and afterwards despatching it with their harpoon from the kayak. A bladder-nose yields about 120 lbs. of blubber and 200 lbs. of flesh. The annual catch is about 3,000 on an average.

The Ugsuk or 'thong-seal' (*Phoca barbata*), next to the walrus, the largest of the Greenland seals, measures 10 feet in length. It occurs only in few numbers, and chiefly at the northern and southern extremities of the coast, but is of the utmost importance, its big skin being the only one considered fit for making the hunting lines of the kayakers, whose life depends on the line running out easily without being liable to the slightest entanglement when pulled by the harpooned seal. The annual catch hardly amounts to 1,000.

The Walrus is only rarely met with along the coast, with the exception of the tract between 66° and 68° N. lat., where it occurs pretty numerously at times. The daring task of entering into contest with this animal from the

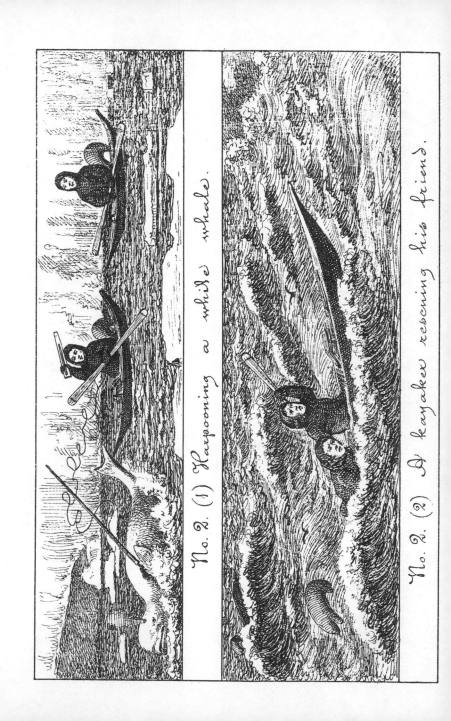

No. 2. (1) Harpooning a white whale.

No. 2. (2) A kayaker rescuing his friend.

kayak on the open sea forms a regular sport to the natives of Kangamiut in 66° N. lat. The number yearly killed has not been separately calculated on account of the skin being generally eaten along with the meat, and considered a very delicate dish ; but they can hardly exceed 200.

The white whale (Beluga catodon) has the habit of appearing on and travelling along the coast, chiefly in spring, as soon as the bay-ice breaks up, and in autumn before the new ice forms. It measures 12 to 16 feet in length, and yields about 400 lbs. of blubber, and an equal or greater amount of eatable parts. The number yearly killed may be estimated at more than 600.

The narwhal (Monodon monoceros) is much scarcer than the former, and almost only caught at the northmost settlements, especially in Umanak Bay. It follows immediately after the white whale, and is chased from the kayak in November, when the surface of the sea every moment threatens to be rapidly congealed in calm weather to the utmost danger of the hunters. The annual catch probably does not surpass 100.

The common porpoise (Phocæna communis) is now and then met with and occasionally caught by the seal hunters, but never in great numbers, the catch being of no importance at all.

The Common Whale or ' **Right Whale** ' *(Balæna mysticetus)* frequents the coast from 65° to 70° N. lat. in the months from December to March, and goes as near the land as the bay-ice will allow it, but, as has been already mentioned, it is now only hunted at one station, and during late years but one 'fish' has been got every year on an average.

The capture of the *'humpback' whale*, which is pursued in summer and autumn, depends greatly on the absence of drift-ice, and is often frustrated by the sinking of the killed animal before it can be towed to the shore. In the year 1844 not less than 13 were caught at one station, but in other years none have been got at all, and the annual mean catch can scarcely be rated at more than 2 'fish.'

If we wish to form an idea of the value which one of these largest animals of the whale-tribe is to the natives, we must first consider that the thick skin covering the whole colossal body yields one of their most favourite dishes, and is in fact a very wholesome aliment. Of course the flesh itself is coarse, but not much more so than tough beef, and to the natives it is undoubtedly as useful as beef. The kepokak-flesh can be preserved by salt and smoking, and in this state it may by European palates be taken for coarse smoked beef. A single right or humpback whale, in this way, after subtracting the blubber, gives probably much more than 20,000 pounds of what the Greenlanders consider delicate food, whereas it is thrown away by the whalers.

As regards other kinds of the larger cetaceous animals, such as the *tunulik* or '*big-finner*,' the *tikagulik* or '*little-fin-ner*,' and the *sperm-whale*, instances of their having been cap-tured by the natives are scarcely known but from traditional tales, but all kinds of whales, and especially the tunulik, now and then occur as floating carcasses of which the blub-ber and matak (skin) can still be made use of. As to the tunulik, it seems doubtful whether the carcasses that have been comprised under this name may not have belonged to different species, some of them, as is usually the case with the larger 'finners,' or 'rorquals,' having been of a size apparently surpassing that of the right whale, or we may say any other animal. A colossus of this kind has lately been found in the interior of a fjord about 67° N. lat. It is said to have measured between 70 and 80 feet in length, but was somewhat injured, the head being wholly crushed, and although the blubber was not very thick, nevertheless 50,000 pounds of it were brought for sale to the settlement of Holstenborg, where it gave an oil apparently of a finer and more fluid consistency than that from the tunulik and kepokak. The quantity thus brought for sale, besides what may have been lost or consumed and wasted, amounted to much more than what a right whale of medium size yields ; whereas the common big-finner, with regard to quantity as well as quality of the oil, is accounted almost worthless by the whalers. In connection with the carcasses may also be mentioned a remarkable coagulated oily substance which is occasionally found floating on the sea between 65° and 67° N. lat. It resembles a white soft fat or grease, occurring in lumps of different sizes, and after having been boiled and cleared it has proved saleable like the fin-whale oil. In the year 1854 not less than 24,000 pounds of it were purchased. The origin of this curious product has not as yet been ascertained.

Summary of the Seal and Whale Catch.—On running over what we have stated about the capture of seals and whales, we arrive at the conclusion that the animals killed amount to about 89,000 seals, 700 white whales and narwhals, 2 or 3 large whales, besides one or two carcasses of the same. In order to calculate the quantity of food these animals yield, we must remember that some of them in certain instances are eaten skin and all, excepting perhaps a part of the blubber, such as the fresh saddle-back that every hunter catches in spring, many bladder-noses and thong-seals, and greater part of the walruses. The seals thus eaten entirely may be estimated at 2,000, perhaps 3,000, and chiefly belong to the larger species. Then it must be remembered that a considerable quantity of the blubber is also eaten in addition to other edibles. Taking this into account, the food resulting will amount to 7 millions of pounds, not reckoning the refuse devoured by the dogs. If we moreover subtract 600,000 pounds for these animals, the rest will give about 2 pounds a day for individuals. Of the sealskins about 40,000 are exported and 49,000 made use of in Greenland. The whole production of blubber may be calculated at 2,050 tuns, of which 1,4˞0 tuns are exported, and 500 tuns are consumed in Greenland as lamp-oil in addition to 100 tuns which are comprised in the above-named food. Of the 90,000 seals and whales it may be supposed that 38,000 have been caught with harpoons and bladders, 38,000 by means of fire-arms, and 14,000 in nets.

CHAPTER VII.

THE FISHES AND FISHERIES OF GREENLAND.

THE capture of fish proper (apart from seals and whales which the reader need scarcely be told are only *fishes* in familiar parlance) has always been a subordinate trade to the Greenlanders whenever they have been in a prosperous condition, but the advantages derived from it have still been of importance to their households. In some of the most northern Eskimo territories fish seem to be very scarce. In the greater part of Danish Greenland, however, they are plentiful, and not only contribute essentially to the maintenance of the inhabitants, but may be considered of some value as supplying articles of export.

Sharks (*Somniosus microcephalus*) are found roaming about everywhere, and will soon appear wherever a large carcass is found or a plentiful capture of seals happens to take place. Those that are caught vary in length from six to sixteen feet, and the liver, forming as yet almost the only part retained for use, weighs between twenty and sixty pounds, in rare instances even several times more. This monstrous fish appears almost as indolent and torpid as it is voracious. Curious instances are related of the greediness and regardlessness of danger exhibited by them when crowding round the carcass of a whale, from which they are not to be scared away even by being severely wounded and mutilated, though there may be some exaggeration in the popular tales of sharks having been caught and deprived of their liver, thrown into the sea, and then instantly rising to the bait again. On taking their voracity into consideration, and the fact of their being attracted by carcasses, it is to be wondered at that instances have seldom, if ever, been reported of kayaks or skin-boats having been bitten by them. On the contrary, kayakers angling in deep water occasionally happen to hook a shark. The violent pull at the line soon indicates that such a fish has swallowed the bait, but by lowering the line at every subsequent brisk pull, and cautiously hauling it in again, the stupid animal is brought up close to the kayak merely by aid of a piece of common twine for a fishing-line; whereupon the fisher knows how to kill it instantaneously by severing the spinal cord with his knife. From this it will appear that the sharks may be caught in very different ways. Several modes of fishing them from open boats and by different sorts of hooks and lines have been attempted, but none of them have proved more effectual than the fishery through holes in the ice. This has been done not only with lines or chains, but also by drawing them to the hole merely by means of torchlight, and then taking them with sharp hand-hooks, two men being required to haul each of the larger fish up on the iec.

The catch being first successfully commenced in a certain spot, sharks will soon be attracted, and it may be contniued in the same place for a great part of the winter. The huge carcasses spreading over the ice then accumulate to several hundreds; at some stations, in favourable seasons, even thousands have covered the ice, attracting ravens, foxes, and especially dogs. But to the latter this frozen shark's flesh has proved obviously unwholesome when swallowed in large quantities, and forming their only food for any length of time. It renders them sluggish and

torpid, and subject to fits of giddiness ; on having pulled
the sledge a short distance their ears begin to droop, they
tumble from one side to the other, and finally fall into
convulsions, and cannot be compelled to stir from the
spot. The contagious disease already mentioned bears a
great similarity to this complaint, and as it commenced a
few years after the shark-fishery had gained its highest pitch,
there may be some reason for believing that this disease
might have originated from the same source. The bones
being merely cartilage, are considered good eating by the
natives, especially after having been kept for a certain time ;
a little of the flesh is cut into slices and dried, but by far
the greater part of the carcasses are thrown away. The
flesh has, however, proved to be very rich in oil, and there
seems no doubt that its unwholesome qualities merely ap-
pertain to it in a raw, and particularly in a frozen state.
A shark of middle size, weighing about 300 pounds, contains
about 100 pounds of pure flesh. The number annually
captured varies from ten to twenty thousand.

The Codfish of Davis Strait (Gadus morrhua) does not
spawn on the shores of Greenland. Spawners are only very
rarely caught, and during the winter the cod is wholly
absent. Sometimes in spring a great many quite young
ones arrive at the inlets between 60° and 61° N. lat., which
would seem to suggest that their breeding-places were not
far off, but they generally make their appearance after
June 20 on the fishing-grounds, which are situated between 64° and 68° N. lat., at a distance of sixteen miles
from the shore, and in July and August resort to the inlets
up to about 70° N. lat. With regard to number the occurrence of codfish on the Greenland shores is peculiarly
variable. Some years, or certain periods of few years, may
prove extremely favourable as regards the catch, whereas
others turn out a total failure. The number annually

caught by the natives may be estimated at somewhat about 200,000 fish on an average.

Salmon Trout (*Salmo carpio*) occur in the lakes and brooks, and at their outlets along the whole coast, but their capture will hardly ever attain any importance because it necessitates people who undertake it to stay in remote places during the best part of the summer time. A few are caught in nets to be exported, while the greater number are either harpooned or speared from the river sides, or from weirs built across the rivers.

The Natarnak or larger Halibut (*Hippoglossus vulgaris*) occurs on the banks as well as in different places outside the islands up to 70° N. lat., in depths of from thirty to fifty fathoms. Of late the capture of this fish has become an object of commercial speculation, and foreign ships, chiefly American, have been engaged in it, apparently with better success than that of the cod-fishery. A halibut of this species weighs from twenty to a hundred pounds, and its flesh is fat and much valued. Superior in taste as well as fatness is the smaller halibut or *Kaleralik* (*H. pinguis*), which is angled for in the ice-fjords at depths of about 200 fathoms. The '*red fish*' (*Sebastes norvegicus*), found only in certain, though pretty numerous grounds south of 68° N. lat., is hauled up from depths of 120 to 180 fathoms, and its flesh is likewise rich in oil, which occasionally, in times of want, is extracted by boiling, and used instead of blubber. The *Nepisak* (*Cyclopterus lumpus*), perhaps the fattest of the Greenland fishes, goes in-shore in April and May for the purpose of spawning, and forms at this season, during a couple of weeks, the chief food in certain places, the spawn being also collected, and considered a dainty.

The Angmagsat, or Capelins (*Mallotus villosus*) has from times of old yielded the most profitable fishery to the

Greenlanders, and may in a dried state, in winter time, frequently be said to have constituted the daily bread of the natives. They are shovelled on shore by means of small nets by women and children, and spread over the rocks to dry during four weeks of May and June, when they crowd to the shores of inlets south of 70° N. lat. to spawn. This fishery has now considerably decreased, but may still be considered to yield one million and a half of pounds weight or more of undried fish yearly.

Lastly, we have to mention certain kinds of fish which, although inferior in quality, are nevertheless of inestimable value to the improvident population on account of their being so widely spread, and generally to be had at a season when other provisions are most scanty. These are the *Ovak*, or smaller cod (*Gadus ovak*), the *frog-fish* or kanajok (*Cottus scorpius*), and the *Misarkornak*, or smallest cod (*Gadus agilis*). The two former are found together almost everywhere, though gradually decreasing in number towards the north, whilst on the other hand the latter seems to begin about the middle part of the coast, increasing so as to become abundant in the furthest north. If to the capture of these fishes we finally add the gathering of common *mussels*, which are generally to be found at low water where the shore is not totally closed up with ice, besides the above-mentioned seaweeds, we have enumerated the several means by which the final shortcomings of the yearly housekeeping of a Greenland family are made up for, and which almost every year, in some place or other, become the means of saving the people from direst want, and not unfrequently from death by starvation.

CHAPTER VIII.

HISTORICAL REMARKS ON THE GREENLANDERS.

The Eskimo.—According to what we have already stated, the population of Greenland, with the exception of a few European colonists or temporary residents, belongs to the Eskimo race, which comprise the scanty tribes that occupy all the arctic territories from East Greenland to the eastern corner of Siberia, extending for 3,200 miles from SE. to NW. Notwithstanding the wide distances which probably for more than a thousand years have divided the different branches of this race from each other, they exhibit the most striking uniformity in their language, habits, and mode of life. The earliest as well as some of the most recent explorers of Greenland and the other arctic regions have not unfrequently pictured this people in their original state as belonging to the lowest savages, devoid almost of anything deserving the name of religion or social institutions, and exhibiting the roughest, nay, even brutal habits. But a more careful contemplation of the mere facts mentioned in the accounts of almost every arctic voyager makes it appear that this conclusion is, at least, one-sided and partial. The Eskimo have settled down in those regions of the earth where no other nation is able to exist, and no other nation has ever surpassed them in surmounting the difficulties and hardships in procuring the immediate necessaries of life. A glance at the map of the northern hemisphere suffices to show that as regards the spread of man towards the pole, the Eskimo may be said to begin where all other human inhabitants end, and the whole series of arctic expeditions within the limits of Greenland and Behrings Strait afford numerous examples of the ability of these people to settle down and procure a comfortable livelihood by means of their simple implements, where modern explorers have only been able to sustain life for a couple of winters by means of an equipment corresponding to the present resources of the most civilised nations. This extraordinary capability of braving the severity of climate does not depend on their physical constitution, the polar climate itself having by no means proved unhealthy to Europeans. It must rather be ascribed to the application of peculiar contrivances, and a dexterity in certain arts acquired from the earliest childhood, in addition to a certain sagacity and knowledge of the nature and the resources of their country. These acquirements, however, necessitate the maintenance of a strict discipline within certain limits, as well as a careful observance of certain traditional rules, and consequently they are incompatible with a state of society in which the physical instinct prevails over the moral or intellectual, or, as it even has been termed, a state of savagedom and bestiality. Local exceptions may of course be found ; an unusual isolation of small bands, or the contact with the Europeans, having in some places suppressed development of the better elements amongst them. But if this unfavourable judgment refers to the race in its normal state, it rests upon insufficient inquiry, chiefly as regards their religious ideas and social institutions.

Influence of the Missionaries and First Settlers.—We have seen how Egede, after ten years' struggle with hardships, privations, and difficulties of many kinds, finally succeeded in establishing his settlement merely by founding it on the trifling but nevertheless sure profit that might be derived from the trade with the natives ; at the same time bringing about a more friendly intercourse between the latter and the Europeans, and putting an end to the acts of violence which had more or less characterised the earlier expeditions to Greenland. When the absurd plans of colonising the country, which we have mentioned, had been given up, and Egede had just got over the numerous troubles arising from them, another company of settlers arrived, who had formed the idea of joining him in his labours, but whose assistance proved a very doubtful boon to him. The Moravian Brethren had already, immediately after the foundation of their Society, been forming projects of founding missions in distant parts of the globe.

The reputation of having entered on a crusade against paganism seemed requisite to give their labours the apostolic appearance which was necessary for raising the new-founded sect in the opinion of the Christian world. No field could be more suited to them than Greenland. Its very name had a most deterring sound to the great public ear, calling to mind nothing but desolate icy regions, whose inhabitants were the rudest savages and pagans, while on the other hand, the missionaries might expect to have their existence secured by the protection of the Danish government and the vicinity of Egede's settlements. The first Moravian missionaries arrived in the year 1733, and took up their abode at a place half-a-mile from Egede's houses, which got the name of Ny, or New Herrnhut. In the Moravian accounts it is expressly set out how even in their external appearance they imitated the apostles, being but common craftsmen who were treated with disregard and scorn by their fellow travellers. It must also be allowed that in reality these Moravians displayed no small degree of zeal and self-denial. During several years they suffered privations, being miserably supplied, and in one year they did not even receive letters from their friends in Europe. It was not till the year 1738 that they succeeded in making their first convert. When we compare the social condition which was established by the united efforts of Egede and the Moravians with the sad picture of the earlier intercourse between the natives and the Europeans, no doubt can be raised as to their great merits, not only in behalf of Greenland, but in promoting the cause of civilisation in general. Yet, on the other hand, it must be remembered that they continued to be Europeans, without the least tendency to adopt aught of the Greenlandish mode of life, or to abandon the popular notion of the Eskimo belonging to that distinct order of beings called savages. Furthermore, their very struggle for existence in the country must have created a bond of union among the missionaries and the other European settlers, as belonging to a superior race entitled to rule the natives.

In discussing missionary work there seems generally to be too little attention paid to the difference that has prevailed between the propagation of Christianity by missionaries from a nation at a similar stage of culture to that of the people to whom they have conveyed their doctrines, and the conversion of what we are accustomed to call savages by emissaries from a nation in the stage of modern European civilisation. In the first place, the further dissipation and confirmation of the new faith is achieved by members of the nation itself to whom it has been transplanted; whereas, in the other case, the missionary is not only regarded as a teacher, but particularly as a member of a superior race, the most ordinary individuals of whom have a claim to be preferred to even the most distinguished ones of the race they are to enlighten. In other words, the propagator of the faith is acting more in the capacity of a 'white man' than in that of a teacher. This was particularly the case in Greenland, whose inhabitants, as regards their state of culture, were to be compared with people of the Age of Stone, to whom a needle was a precious article, who had never seen a tree, nor heard anything about agricultural or pastoral life, and on the whole had only from obscure traditions acquired a faint idea of the existence of other nations than their own. When such people saw ships suddenly arriving from the ocean, where they believed the world to have its termination, and people who possessed fire-arms, and hundreds of articles, the most trifling of which must have appeared wondrous to them, it seems natural that they should become filled with a sort of superstitious awe for the foreign race in general. The natives themselves, being greatly inclined to believe in supernatural influences, were of course induced to consider the owners of ships with all their contents as little short of conjurors. It is said that they used patches of clothes worn by the Europeans as amulets for their children, believing that they possessed a peculiar power, and likewise desired the Europeans to breathe upon their sick. It is not to be wondered at, that they believed the white men to be in league with the invisible powers, and to possess the same influence which they attributed to their own wise men, the 'angakoks.' Consequently, every European was to them somewhat of an angakok, and when, finally, to the other causes of mutual misunderstandings, we add those which arose from the language, the results in Greenland, more than in any other country, must have led to an implicit confidence in the teacher and obedience to him.

The Social State Modified by the Change of Religion.— The social organisation of the Greenlanders, like that of other more primitive nations, was founded upon the right of personal property within certain narrow limits, combined with a communism confined to a wider or narrower circle, and counterbalanced by certain obligations they were under individually to the community. The laws concerning the rights and obligations resulting from this social condition were maintained by public assemblies, which formed their courts of justice besides representing the public festivals. The laws and customs were, moreover, mostly closely connected with the religious opinions of the people, which were again acted upon by the angakoks, who had acquired their power and wisdom by applying to ' Tornarsuk,' who, on this account, must be considered to have been their supreme being. The disturbances caused in this system of social institutions and religious opinions will best be understood by mentioning them separately in the reverse order to that in which they have been alluded to here.

Tornarsuk, who, by the Greenlanders, was considered as the supreme being on whom they were dependent for any supernatural aid, and in whose abodes in the depth of the earth all those persons who had striven and suffered for the benefit of their fellow men should find a happy existence after death, was transformed into the Christian devil, and those spirits over whom he ruled, and whom he assigned to the angakoks as their guardian spirits, were presented as his subordinate demons. Consequently, their ideas concerning good and evil, recompense and punishment after death, were liable in some measure to be turned topsy-turvy. It might appear doubtful whether the strange definition of Tornarsuk which was transmitted to the Greenlanders, and by which, in a manner, the real existence of a false god and his whole suite of subordinate spirits was confirmed, could be brought into conformity with the Christian dogmas; in this place we only refer to it as the most striking illustration of the idea which the Europeans formed of the spiritual and social condition of the Greenlanders. One of the first reformatory steps was that of doing away with the angakoks. As a matter of course the high priests of paganism could not exist in friendly harmony with the propagators of the new faith. But here two peculiar circumstances have to be kept in view. In the first place, on account of the amalgamation of religious observances with the social customs and laws, totally subverting the authority of the angakoks was the same as abolishing the only institution that could be considered to represent appointed magistrates or lawgivers. Secondly, the class of angakoks comprised the most eminent persons, both as regards intellectual abilities, personal courage, and dexterity in pursuing the national trade. In so far that individuals can always be found who misuse their authority to promote their own selfish aims, the Eskimo, in this respect, exhibit nothing peculiarly distinguishing them from any other nation.

It seems to follow as a matter of course that the great veneration in which the angakoks were held could only be founded on real personal superiority, especially because no hereditary authority existed, and the respect acquired merely by physical strength and acts of violence was despised, and sooner or later punished as an offence. But evidence supplied by contemporaneous authors, proving that intelligence and personal respectability were no uncommon features amongst the angakok class, is not entirely wanting. As an instance of this kind we will quote the following words of the trader Dalager, in mentioning one of them, in his account, written about the year 1750 : ' The said angakok, inasmuch as he mostly lives quite close to the colony, visits me every day ; he likes to be informed about God and his divine works, which he never fails to

admire ; but there the matter rests, and in other respects
he maintains his own principles intact. On the whole, his
life is exemplary, and I must grant that I have acquired
my stock of experience of Greenland from conversing with
this eminent man.' If we take into consideration the importance of the angakok institution, it will be evident that
if its abolition was carried on in a reckless manner, every
authority within the limits of native society was liable
to be destroyed. That the angakoks were persecuted by
the Europeans and treated as the most wretched scum
of the people may be learned from numerous passages of
the early accounts. Missionaries and traders, Danes as
well as Germans, simultaneously joined in making them a
butt for scorn and derision to wanton youths, and the
task of course was greatly facilitated by the enormous
ascendency, as supposed conjurors, which the Europeans
had acquired in the opinion of the natives. But that satire
was not the only weapon resorted to, may be learned
from Crantz, the historian of the Moravians, who relates
how Egede, escorted by his European sailors, armed
with guns, tore the amulets by force from the child of an
angakok, and afterwards entered into a dispute with the
father, who ventured to assert that Tornarsuk was a benevolent spirit and no devil. The reverend brother Crantz
adds exultingly : ' This man wanted to revenge himself by
help of his wicked tongue (böses Maul), but got a blow on
his jaw, and when he tried to defend himself he was
obliged to put up with lots of the same kind.'

Next to annihilating the power and respectability of the
angakoks, the missionaries made the abolition of all
manner of public assemblies or national festivals one of
their chief aims. These meetings had to be considered
real courts of justice ; and a native judicial authority,
independent of the European control, was of course in-

admissible.   But in constituting the ordinary tribunals the
public assemblies at the same time were attended with
amusements, which must have tended in a high degree to
counteract the debilitating influences of an isolated life.
They consisted partly of recitals or singing and dancing
entertainments, partly of various matches and athletics
tending to exhibit strength and dexterity, such as wrest-
ling, boxing, sham-fighting, and other bodily exercises.
Dalager says about these assemblies : ' Finally, it must be
taken into consideration, that inasmuch as the climate
and the mode of life produce melancholy and heaviness,
no opportunity for counteracting which, by diverting their
thoughts, is to be found in Greenland, these plays and
dances, from which the inhabitants derive great mental
recreation, cannot deserve to be blamed so much.   Moreover, the same reasons have been adduced in justification
of balls and parties in our countries, where, however, they
seem less necessary because of the many other ways in
which the mind may be cheered without having recourse to
dancing-halls.   Perhaps in this instance the objection
will be made, that in Greenland also there are probably
various other sources of amusement suited to the coarse
taste of the inhabitants.   To this I answer, well and good,
but at the same time I beg leave to make the following
remark.   In our countries people dance merely out of vo-
luptuousness, but at the festivals yonder, faults are repri-
manded and considerable quarrels settled . . . the same
forum being the only one that preserves the Greenland
state.'

So far as checking in due time every tendency to
heathenish merry-making could go, none watched their
flock more carefully than the Moravians, of which the following instance related by Crantz is a striking proof.
Once, two young men were observed to have a beating

match, according to ancient custom, knocking one another
by turns on the shoulders to try who was the strongest
and hardiest. Such an occurrence happening in a remote
corner of the world would appear only to concern the two
antagonists who offered their fists and shoulders for the
performance. However, they were seized *flagrante delicto*,
a severe lecture was administered to them, and the case
reported to their supreme court in Herrnhut in Saxony,
having been ascertained to belong to those offences which
a renowned theologian has classified as being *next to
sin !*

Passing from the courts to the laws and customs of
the Greenlanders, the regard in which they were held by
the Europeans cannot be more clearly elucidated than by
the testimonies of Egede himself and of Crantz. The
former says : 'The heathenish Greenlanders have no ma-
gistrate, no laws, no order, nor any sort of discipline ; '
and the latter asserts, in mentioning what might be considered as corresponding to laws, ' such habits as gradually
have become a sort of law to the Greenlanders appear very
foolish to people who have other laws and customs. The
Greenlanders themselves are aware of the awkwardness
and unreasonableness of many of their customs, but feel
disinclined to alter them in any way for fear of ill repute ' !
From these statements it may be inferred that the Europeans only paid regard to the laws and customs of the
natives in so far as suited them.

The condition, both of the legislature and courts of the
Greenlanders, who on becoming baptised submitted themselves to the European rule, is most strikingly described
by Dalager : ' The intelligent and righteous natives,' writes
this shrewd trader, ' are now like people who have not
their wits about them, because to-day one missionary
treats a case in one manner, to-morrow another treats

it in the opposite way; and for this reason there are as many different customs as changes of missionaries take place, which puts the mind of the Greenlanders into such a state of confusion that they are liable to doubt the reality of the most self-evident truths.' But the missionaries were not the only legislators and judges. This will be apparent from the 'instructions of 1782' to the officials regulating the Royal Trade, especially the merchants, which served until late years as the Greenland code of laws. In this the following passage occurs; it represents the whole criminal law concerning the natives: 'If anything improper should be committed by the Greenlanders, such as theft or any other great misdemeanour, the merchant has to exhort them leniently to desist from such conduct. If this does not avail, or the crime should be very aggravating, they are to be punished conformably to circumstances and the nature of the crime.'

Amongst the chief influences acting upon the social state of the natives, we have lastly to adduce the trade and the immediate contact with the Europeans residing in the country. Setting apart the question whether a suitable choice of individuals was made in appointing the people who were sent to Greenland, let us consider the influence of the intercourse between the natives and them, merely in their capacity of Europeans. The liberty to accumulate property must be considered to have been kept within narrow limits, as custom made all that a person became possessed of beyond a certain stock of clothes and tools the common property of the whole family; what the family possessed more than customary would become the common property of the inhabitants of the same house, who again had to give a certain share to the inhabitants of the same hamlet; whilst finally such sort of game as was of an unusual size, especially a whale, became the common property of all who were able to be present at the division or sharing out of it.

This organisation of course was dependent on the single members being unable to transfer their catch or gains regularly to strangers living in their neighbourhood. If such an opportunity was offered, the seller would be liable to deprive his relations, housemates, or place-fellows of that contribution to the joint household which entitled him at other times in his turn to be succoured by them. This in a manner also applies to the labour performed by the single individuals in the service of the Europeans, while at the same time they at least in some measure continue to profit by the joint stock of their countrymen. But this unfavourable influence was especially enhanced by the disregard on the part of the Europeans respecting the right of allowing people to settle down in the same place, or to become housemates or members of a family.

The opportunity of borrowing in times of need rendered the practice of selling their catch even more detrimental to the independence and prosperity of those natives that lived in the neighbourhood of the foreigners, who in reality were considered the only persons entitled to bargain with the view of accumulating property. During a long period of years the sale of European provisions, especially bread, coffee, and sugar, was submitted to certain restrictions which were, however, gradually done away with. For this reason the impoverishment of the Greenlanders has been assigned to the import and sale of these provisions, and some people are in the habit of ascribing the whole national calamity to coffee in particular. The acquisition of these articles, however, seems to be an almost indispensable compensation for the deprivation of such recreation as the natives formerly used to derive from their national festivals, which were prohibited by the Europeans. The indemnification certainly seems poor enough, and we might be induced to question whether a state of culture which has been found incompatible with affording a right to buy coffee to the first men of the people, when they are able to pay for it, is entitled to be termed a progress towards civilisation from the original state of the Greenlanders.

We have now mentioned all the chief injurious influences arising from the intercourse between the Europeans and the natives. It must be admitted that their present condition does not agree with the idea of a process of civilisation having been carried on for a century and a half, nor with the picture given by various authors who have occasionally mentioned the Greenlanders in comparison with other nations in a low stage of culture. A complete understanding of their present state, therefore, above all seemed to require the evil influences to be treated of first, and for this reason we have endeavoured to trace them back to their very origin. But in thus regarding the weak points of the modern arctic civilisation separately without at the same time keeping in view the more successful part of the same, we should of course be in danger of suggesting a wrong idea of the whole. In the first place, it must be remarked that the social organisation and economical condition of the Greenlanders as a nation of hunters, has not proved quite irreconcilable with European trade and institutions. On the contrary, some experience has been obtained as to the possibility of accommodating the ancient social organisation to that of the Europeans and of improving the domestic life as well as the national trade by means of the advantages of European industry. Secondly, it must be remembered that the tendency towards suppressing the original institutions and the national life did not continue to prevail in the same degree, as above described, for any length of time.

When the Europeans gradually found their existence
in the country perfectly secured, and any conspiracy of
the peaceable and harmless natives against them prevented,
they became more and more unconcerned with regard to
what was considered heathenish superstitions and habits.
In the following pages we shall endeavour to show what
has still been retained of their ancient stage of culture,
and to explain how a sort of semi-civilised state has resulted from a combination of the ancient and the newer
elements. That the Europeans did not with the same zeal
continue to counteract even those customs which had been
considered the most dangerous ones may be learned from
a critical commentary on Crantz's renowned ' Historie von
Grönland,' which was written about the year 1770 by
the Danish missionary Glahn, and represents to us the condition of the Greenlanders about that time. In speaking of their festivals and entertainments being opposed by
Crantz, he says : 'I really do not find anything sinful
in it, if in the long winter nights a man entertains himself
and the other inmates of a house by beating his drum, nor
that the refrain of a song such as " Amna, Ejah, oh ! oh ! "
should be more blameable than the melody of a psalm ; nor
that a song of seal-hunting which must be likened to a
heroic poem for the encouragement of young people ; nor
singing a satirical song to his friend merely for fun, by which
in a fair manner he calls the attention of the friend to some
faults of his ; nor singing to children about the fights of
animals, should be in any way discreditable.'

In passing on to the true ' nith-songs,' used in the public
assemblies, the same author, although a missionary himself,
observes : ' So long as man continues to be man, and as
long as quarrels happen to arise between men, the Christian
religion, as well as good government, requires that strict
measures should not be resorted to so long as gentler ones

will at all avail. And what measures could be gentler than keeping men within the limits of propriety by help of shame ? Shame again can hardly be better maintained han by means of public disgrace ; nor could this possibly be done in any milder way than by the Greenlanders, who, by way of cutting capers and singing funny songs, tell their antagonist his faults, and who in blaming the vices of their enemy, praise the opposite virtues to all who are present.'

The Moravian missionaries have some claim to in-dulgence if their sway is more severe than that of the Danes. Originally, they even tried to make their whole community settle down at the mission-station close by their own houses, and Crantz calls the people who took up their abodes in these places 'sheep that were driven into their fold.' The Moravians had not the support which the connection with commercial establishments gave to the Danish missions. If their flock was not kept strictly separated from the surrounding Danish community, their presence in Greenland might at some time perhaps prove quite superfluous, and for this reason their proceedings may in some measure be excused, inasmuch as these have always until the present day more or less partaken of the character of a 'struggle for existence.' Crantz gives an interesting account of the organisation of their community in Greenland, describing how by means of the ecclesiastical ceremonies, and especially by withholding the right of ad-mittance to the Lord's Supper and of marriage, and by the awe in which they were held as Christian angakoks, they established an ingenious system of rank and of penal laws, and by the help of spies controlled the most private affairs of everybody.

The history of Ultramontane papacy and Jesuitism hardly exhibits proofs of a more refined interference with personal liberty than the control to which the Moravians submitted this people, to whom a certain independence was of vital importance for the development of vigour and prosperity. Glahn, in his critical review already quoted, gives a striking picture of the extreme haughtiness and spiritual pride which lay hidden beneath the brethren's paternal care in behalf of their hyperborean brothers and sisters. As a curiosity, we may here quote an example.

In olden times the native women used to adorn their chin, knees, cheeks, hands, and feet, with a sort of tattoo marks. Concerning this custom Crantz observes : 'that such as had been baptised by the Moravians had already long ago left off this vanity, which, foolish though it be, nevertheless tends to sinful enticement.' Glahn comments upon this passage as follows : 'We might with as much reason assert that they have cast off this habit in order to have a better chance of capturing a Danish husband, it being well known that the Greenland women are foolish enough to prefer the worst Dane to the best Greenlander ; or perhaps they may have done it only to imitate the European females. . . . But begging your pardon, author, why do you curl your hair, or powder and dress your peruke ? Why have your clothes folds and your shoes buckles ? Why do you have your face shaved ? . . . I think you would take it in bad part if anyone ventured to accuse you of wishing to captivate whenever you shaved your beards or bought a couple of nice buckles, or were to maintain that such things were nothing but vanity, which, though foolish, could only tend to sinful enticement. Dear author ! do request your brethren to have no concern whatever about the knees, cheeks, hands and feet of the Greenland ladies. Let them abide in these and other external things as they are. But let them strive to adorn their hearts with chastity and other female virtues. This, however, is not to be attained without a thorough-going instruction; it requires more than the observing of certain customs.' . . .

Secessions from the Christian Communities.—While it took more than a hundred years to found all the little trading stations and missions now established on the coast, and at the same time gradually to incorporate the natives into Christian communities, the transformation of the whole population into the present state of semicivilisation was accomplished almost as slowly. Now the question is very likely to arise whether it never happened that the natives made an attempt at trying to emancipate themselves from European rule, either by falling back into paganism, or by forming independent Christian communities? As to the former the author is not aware of any instances worth mentioning having occurred; but of the latter kind there have been at least two cases, both very characteristic, not only from a psychological point of view, but on account of their throwing light upon the stage of development of the natives.

In the summer of the year 1790 a woman named Maria Magdalena, living at the station of Sukkertoppen (65½° N. lat.), pretended to have had certain visions and revelations, and passed herself off as a prophetess. She directly made all the inhabitants of the place and its environs her adherents, and inspired them with an obedience sufficiently implicit to cause any person whom she might choose to point out to be killed on the spot. It is said that two women were actually put to death by her in this way. She had for her husband a man named Habakkuk, whom, on account of his extreme devotion, she called Jesus, and he became the real head of the sect that formed a settlement at the fjord of Kangerdlugsuatsiak. This native community had completely separated from the mission, and their excesses greatly alarmed the Europeans in the country. But the sway of Habakkuk was only of short duration. He and his adherents having lost the guidance to which they had been accustomed from the European control, speedily proved like persons who have lost their wits. They fell into a kind of frenzy, and were soon subdued again. Their excesses, however, are still remembered by the population, and of the respect once paid to Habakkuk slight traces are still retained by his descendants. A native of a place in the neighbourhood of his former residence has collected some of the traditions about him, of which we will here insert some fragments, quoting his own words :—

'Habakkuk and his wife Maria Magdalena had the misfortune to lose two children, which made them very sad. In spring, when his people started for reindeer-hunting, Habakkuk joined them, taking another woman along with him and leaving his wife at home. While staying alone Maria had a dream of what the reindeer-hunters were about, and when they had returned, and she had told them the dream, they were astonished to hear how exactly she had hit their very doings, and this turned their attention towards her. In the autumn Habakkuk once spoke to his wife about his having a second spouse, which made her very angry from jealousy. In the evening she said to him : " I shall take a European for my second husband when we remove." With these words she arose and went outside, while Habakkuk found himself unable to stir. When she came outside, naked as she was, she looked towards the east and perceived two persons standing on a hill, and recognised them to be Ole and his wife, who had died a long time before. On seeing two bright paths leading towards them she would directly go further, but the ghosts dissuaded her from doing so, saying, " Close thy openings (viz. eyes and mouth), they are all distorted, thou lookest dreadful," and they continued : " Maria Magdalena, during thy youth thy heart was fair, but now thou art so tied and fettered, wilt thou offer thy own person to those who are not thy brethren?" When they spoke thus Maria could not recollect anything, whereupon the ghost continued : " A little while ago thou saidst thou wouldest take a European for thy lover." On hearing this she remembered it, and she entered the house, whereupon Habakkuk again was able to move, and got up. One evening Mile and Barzillai were watching and relating tales. When later in the night they just went outside they observed two clouds of smoke above Umiusak-hill, one of them dark, the other bright, and they heard psalm-singing. Also by those inside the sound was perceived, whereupon Maria arose suddenly and seated herself on the pillow, grinding her teeth and trembling all over. From this time people really began to believe in them, but their story is rather difficult to narrate on account of their tricks and doings being so numerous. But during that first winter only three neighbouring places had Habakkuk for their prophet.

'In spring it is said two kayaks went to Maneetsok. One Simeon living in this place was just going to start in the morning when, looking over the ice-border (of the beach), he recognised those two visitors coming from Kangerdlugsuatsiak. Having climbed the edge of the ice they advanced, holding out their hands for him, but he could not understand why they did so, this not being at all the native custom. Both of them first shook hands with him, and then kissed him. Siméon could not conceive the meaning of it, but thought that perhaps they had done it on account of their having longed so greatly for him. When they had gone, he observed that already many people of the place had put belief in them, and from this time many people from the surrounding places repaired to

Nº 12. (1) Ancient dancing and singing.

Nº 12. (2) Singing of a Nith-song.

Habakkuk. When in autumn Habakkuk's second wife was with child, they said that it was by the Holy Ghost, and if it proved to be a boy, he ought to be called Christ. But she bore a daughter. Furthermore they said that none were allowed to be witches, and all those whom they considered witches they punished. They pelted the hands of a witch with stones and threw her into the sea. When so many men came to seize her, the poor wretch did not at all fear her murderers, but only gazed at the sky. Moreover, when they were going to kill her, she thrust her hand into her hood, drew out her snuff-box, and returned it again after having taken a pinch of snuff. And when they had seized her by the throat and were going to throw her into the sea, Habakkuk sent for them, informing them that in throwing her off they were to say nothing but, "thou pray'st for our sins." And thus they all shouted in casting her into the sea. Anangnia and Juitdle then just happened to be out kayaking; but when the body had drifted ashore, they also crushed the hands of the dead with stones, in order to have their share in her chastisement. In obedience to Habakkuk and his wife they also went to the graves, and holding one another by the hand, they formed a ring and moved round the graves; then they squeezed hands and kissed each other. Once Habakkuk held an examination, assembling them to know "how they were." He then cast lots among them to announce whom God favoured most. But the women he treated separately, beckoning to them from behind a curtain, and calling them to him to purify them from their sins. When his brother Juitdle, who was a stammerer, presented himself, asking how he was, Habakkuk answered: "Thou oughtst to be deprived of thy tongue," whereupon the poor man burst into tears. Once he set forth riddles to be guessed by them. "What does a gentle person resemble?" asked he.

"A large beast," replied one of them. "Yes, yes, yes," said Habakkuk. Once he was breathless and turned up his eyes. They all cried : "Woe is unto us, when he turns the whites outward, the world will be destroyed." It would sometimes happen that while they were assembled, all crying and sobbing, they would suddenly burst into a roar of laughter. It is also said that once in the first winter he called into the house : "To-day we have to be cheerful all the day, because Isaak's road to heaven has been opened," whereupon they continued to shout thus, and make merry the whole day. When anybody had caught a seal he gave a part of it to Habakkuk, and if a kayaker missed a seal he fell a-weeping for fear of being scolded by Habakkuk.

'Several men he named after the inhabitants of heaven, of which we can only remember one—Matias (Matthew). When he was coming home towing his seal, they shouted, "Jesus comes towing." At last in spring the missionary arrived, attended by Naparutak (the native teacher). Habakkuk would not go outside, but they entered his tent. Before they had said anything Habakkuk briskly put in, "The chief persons in heaven wish that men should love one another." Naparutak replied, "Certainly the chief persons in heaven have commanded men to love each other, but why hast thou altered the seventh commandment? Why hast thou not followed it ?" When Habakkuk gave no answer, Naparutak very cautiously accosted him, admonishing him in a gentle manner, and desiring him to leave off his habits. From this time their pranks began to cease, but still they would remain superiors, being unwilling to yield.'

So the tale still runs at Kangamiut of the first of the incidents above alluded to. The other is of a very recent date, having happened in the vicinity of the author's own place of residence. In the winter of 1853–4 the quiet life of the Moravian Brethren at Frederiksdal was disturbed in the most unexpected manner. This mission had been founded in the year 1824, and 222 natives belonging to it lived at the station itself. The 'sheep,' as Crantz says, were lodged in twenty-two folds, and supposed to be well trained and perfectly satisfied under the protection and gentle discipline of the Brethren. But now it happened that a young man named Mathæus, distinguished not only by his skill in seal-hunting, but also most remarkably by his school-learning, and intended by the missionaries for a teacher, suddenly became taciturn and reserved, and often sought solitude. Some time later the Brethren perceived that unusual assemblies were being held in the houses of the natives, who at the same time neglected to attend the daily prayers. They were then informed that this Mathæus had assumed the authority of a prophet, and had resolved to form a community of his countrymen, quite independent of the Europeans. He believed that he had had visions and conversed with the Saviour; he adopted the name of Gabriel, and soon gathered around him a crowd of adherents who put implicit confidence in his words and promised obedience to his commands.

The mutiny now rapidly expanded and soon left the missionaries with but few followers, the regular divine service and ecclesiastical discipline peculiar to the sect being entirely interrupted. Gabriel celebrated marriages and fulfilled other ecclesiastic duties, and sent off kayakers to other places for the purpose of enlisting votaries. Soon other individuals also spoke of having had revelations from heaven, and a sort of feverish frenzy seized the whole population. Some of them wounded their hands, asking others to suck them for the purpose of trying the sweetness of the Saviour's blood, others again were told to open their mouths, whereupon Gabriel breathed into it in order to impart to them the 'Spirit.' A grand project was planned, the whole band intending to depart in spring for the east coast, to go and convert the heathens and form a colony there. The missionaries now had only one way to act, viz. to hold their peace and go on with gentleness until the paroxysm had exhausted itself. Laying hands on the ringleader during the prevailing sensation would have been dangerous, and rendered the evil still worse. The extravagant excitement soon subsided and gave way to a sort of languor. The missionaries availed themselves of the opportunity in order to strengthen the trust of the few who remained faithful to them, and Gabriel was gradually abandoned by his partisans. The remainder of them removed to a place named Komiut, where they wholly devoted themselves to their reveries and frantic imaginations. Once Gabriel predicted that the world would come to an end in the ensuing night, and they threw all their implements out of their houses in order to be free from worldly riches at the setting in of the catastrophe. As, however, there was no sign of the world being destroyed, on the following day Gabriel, with some companions, climbed a wall, thinking they were going to ascend to heaven. They all wore their smartest dresses, and were washed and clean, and, as no ascension took place, Gabriel took off his boots and walked barefooted in the snow, supposing some adherent filth to have prevented the miracle. In the ensuing summer the rest of the sect seems also to have been dispersed. Even Gabriel gave in and suffered himself to be duly wedded by the missionaries.

Decay of the Greenlanders.—It must be granted that these examples give a very sad picture of the commonal spirit of the natives. They seem to suggest the idea that at present social order is only maintained by help of foreigners settled among them, their regard for ancient laws and cus-

toms being subverted, and the doctrines introduced by the
strangers proving to be so superficially rooted that they are
unable to replace their old institutions as guides for their social life. But, on the other hand, these incidents intimate the
existence of some feeling of independence and nationality,
however misled it may be, and as to the extravagances, it
must be remembered that the instances related are so few
that no trustworthy inference can be drawn from them as
to what would happen if the European sway suddenly
ceased throughout the whole coast. More serious are the
indications of physical decline, impoverishment, and the
development of a sickliness which have appeared of late
years. Already, in the ' Instructions ' of 1782 regulations are
given to the traders as regards assisting the Greenlanders
in emergencies, and when a famine had taken place in 1844,
these regulations were revised and renewed. From this
period the signs of the declining national prosperity grew
more general and evident.

In 1853–4 a very severe winter set in, accompanied by
the failure of the seal-fishery, and several individuals in
isolated places died from cold and starvation. But this
year of need was greatly surpassed by the disasters of the
winter of 1856–7, when about 150 people died from cold
and famine, and in the following summer an epidemic
carried off about 100 more. It must be remarked that
while a disregard of the old customs as to laying in
stores caused starvation, the deterioration of the houses
and clothing gave rise to a sickly constitution, especially
tending to chest complaints. Many difficulties, of course,
were met with here in trying to relieve the poor. The
distribution of food and other necessaries in time of need
was, moreover, entrusted to the storekeepers of the Royal
Board of Trade, of whom the greater part appointed at
the many small outposts were taken from European work-

men or persons of the labouring classes engaged for Greenland at low wages. The mere authority a man derived from his European extraction was considered necessary as well as sufficient for the task of a storekeeper and overseer of the poor. Now, on the other hand, every native considering himself indigent in comparison with a European, this way of relieving the poor tended to make the whole population dependent on these storekeepers for the chief necessaries of life during a certain season every year.

As this preposterous arrangement threatened the natives with certain ruin, a municipal institution was founded in 1857, tending to separate the administration of the fund for the relief of the poor from trade affairs, and to make the natives themselves participate in it. The Royal Board of Trade now pays to the fund of every district a certain tax on the wares purchased within its confines. The natives choose from among themselves representatives who hold regular meetings, and are moreover invested with the office of wardens or guardians of the community under them. The surplus of every year's income at the end of the winter, or of the usual time of need, is divided as honourable gifts among those heads of families who have abstained from having recourse to the fund to supply their wants. This institution has met with no peculiar hindrance as regards the possibility of adapting it to the faculties and susceptibilities of the natives, but in what degree it will be able to stop their retrogression cannot as yet be ascertained, it being still in its infancy.

Causes of this Decay.—The author cannot close this historical review without adding a few remarks tending to guard against misapprehension respecting the causes of the decay here mentioned. In reading this account, the reader will be liable to lay more stress on some of the causes enumerated than on others, so as to infer that the author had aimed at making certain persons, institutions, or doctrines peculiarly responsible for the mischief which he has tried to delineate. In various discussions on matters belonging to the history of culture, we even find the question treated, whether one nation may be considered more or less adapted for Christianity than another. This might appear to be rather a strange object of enquiry, inasmuch as every person, as well as every nation, who is able to conceive an idea of their Maker, seem to be equally able to adopt the main tenets of the Christian religion. But if judging merely from the outer appearance of the social state, this comparison has to be made, the laws and customs of the ancient Greenlanders might, even more than those of highly civilised societies, appear to conform to the social conditions of the earliest Christian communities.

Passing from the Christian religion itself to its first propagators in Greenland, the author is so far from accusing them of having the lion's share in the mischievous influences above mentioned, that on the contrary he thinks that they must be considered true benefactors to the natives, when we reflect on their intercourse with the Europeans previous to the foundation of the missions, and that as regards the subsequent period, the prospect would have been less discouraging if the greater part of the persons who have since been appointed to the service of the mission and the Trade, each within his duties, had shown the same earnestness and unselfishness as the earliest missionaries. But again, as regards these later officials, the blame cannot be laid upon them, in so far as they did their duty according to the instructions given them by their superiors. The qualities displayed by their first predecessors could not be claimed as official duties.

The next question is whether the Trade, in opposition to the Mission, has to be charged with a peculiar responsibility for the detrimental part of the European influences. We have already mentioned the coffee question. A theme still more popular is the low prices paid for the productions of the natives. In this respect, it may suffice here to remark, in the first place, that on account of many difficulties no regular trade could possibly be carried on with the natives of Greenland if their wares could not be had at very low prices, and secondly, that commercial speculation is so foreign to the ideas of the Greenlanders, that a mere change of prices, if even they became twice as favourable to them as they are now, would hardly have any perceptible influence on the economical state of the natives, which will be evident from what has to be explained in the following pages. Having thus in vain tried to charge the evil to any particular source, it has to be ascribed to the whole intercourse, or to those general causes which everywhere, more or less, have led nations and races to contend with one another. In Greenland only is the peculiarity met with, that the intruders merely consist of temporary residents in the country, and that should the natives die out it will become uninhabited.

CHAPTER IX.

THE INHABITANTS : THEIR MEANS OF SUBSISTENCE.

Nationality, Number, and Distribution.—Throughout our preceding pages we have drawn a sharp line of demarcation between Europeans and Greenlanders. The real contrast existing between both parties cannot be more strikingly denoted than by a phrase not unfrequently used by the Greenlanders themselves in speaking of their countrymen when they say, 'He is *only* a Greenlander,' but on attempting to define this distinction, we nevertheless meet with some doubtful points. In the first place, the distinction does not refer to a sharp difference of extraction. Without regard to the probable intermixture with European blood from the Norse settlers, a pretty numerous class of half-breeds has originated since the time of Egede, many Europeans belonging to the classes of labourers or sailors having married native women. These marriages seem to have been more prolific than those between the natives themselves, and to have had a decided influence on the increase of the population, although their number on an average has scarcely amounted to 4 per cent. of all the marriages, whereas the number of illegitimate children of mixed race seems to have been of less weight in the same respect, on account of earlier death from want of sufficient care. In the year 1820 the half-breeds were calculated at 14 per cent., and in 1855 at 30 per cent. of the inhabitants, but these numbers are very vague, and in the latest years it has not been possible to ascertain the relative numbers of these two classes on account of their blending almost imperceptibly into one another.

On first arriving in Greenland, one is surprised at seeing kayak men with light hair and perfectly European physiognomy and stature, while as to their language and habits they are as perfectly Eskimo. Others again, and indeed the greater part of the half-breeds, resemble South Europeans. Notwithstanding this intermixture, the Eskimo features are still by far the most prevalent, exhibited chiefly in a low stature, remarkably small hands and feet, and a brown complexion. The hair is coarse and raven-black, that of the male sex particularly is distinguished by its luxuriant growth, hanging down to the shoulders, and only sometimes cut off to a straight line across the forehead. The women, on the contrary, have their hair tied into an upright tuft, the size of which is a subject of pride, but this constant strain on the hair causes it to fall off early, especially at the sides, which greatly disfigures them. On the whole, handsome persons are more frequently met with among men than women, owing in some measure to the difference of their mode of life. While the business of the former is connected with daily exercise in the open air, the latter on growing old mostly take to indoor life. When once they are married, they care very little for their dress and appearance. The cramped position in which they sit on the ledge makes them bandy-legged, and causes them to waddle, while on the contrary the young women appear smart, and in some degree even graceful in their attitude and movements. Moreover, the plumpness of their faces gradually shrinks, leaving nothing but wrinkles, the little hair remaining is almost insufficient to be formed into a tuft, and these deficiencies, added to their filthiness and their crookbacked attitude, generally make the old women very ugly. The children are remarkable for their plump round faces, and taking the whole population on an average, their appearance seems to be at variance with what we have stated about the frequent occurrence of famines and a general disposition to sickliness. Their constitution exhibits a remarkable capability of regaining a good condition within a short time when they have happened to lose flesh by suffering from want and disease. Persons have been found who during the course of every year had their periods of fatness and leanness alternating as regularly as summer and winter.

If the marks of race or extraction offered insufficient means for determining whether the individual is to be considered as European or Greenlander, the education, on the contrary, will be so much more decisive as regards this question. In the following sections it will be explained how little the domestic life of the natives has changed since their becoming Christianised; the size of their habitations, their sustenance and mode of life, being almost the same as before the Europeans settled amongst them, and the language spoken by them has not suffered the least alteration. Between people brought up in the native houses, and those who have been educated in a European family, as sharp a difference will be perceptible as ever is possible between two classes of human beings, and this difference will scarcely disappear throughout the rest of their life, whereas an Eskimo child brought to Europe at an early age, and educated there, will as regards its abilities show but slight traces of its extraction. A peculiar intermediate position is maintained by the Europeans who are married to native women and have their children brought up as Greenlanders, while at the same time the household arrangements of the family are conducted wholly after the Greenland fashion. Some of them are quite unable to acquire any degree of perfection in speaking Greenlandish, and as generally neither wife nor child can be persuaded to pronounce a Danish word, their mutual conversation of course is kept within very narrow limits. Usually such a European tries to get a smaller room for himself and his wife, separated by a partition wall from the common room, in which their children and other housefellows are more at liberty to follow their own habits. In the census and statistical accounts, the rule has been maintained to count everybody a native who in any degree may be of mixed extraction; and in reality this mode of distinction will most nearly coincide with the division founded upon the education, because only very few half-breeds receive a European education, and scarcely an example is known of a European child having been brought up as a Greenlander.

In October of the year 1870, the number of natives in the Danish part of the west coast was 9,588, and of Europeans 237, the population being distributed among 176 winter-stations, viz. 1 with more than 300, 4 with 200 to 300, 19 with 100 to 200, 47 with 50 to 100, 47 with 26 to 50, and 58 with 25 or less inhabitants.

Means of Subsistence and Occupations.—We have already frequently alluded to seal-hunting as being the occupation on which the existence of the whole population more immediately depends, and we may add that the same more especially refers to that sort of seal-hunting which was carried on before the arrival of the European settlers, and which is still dependent on the ancient contrivances and the use of the same implements, without the least change in any respect. But as regards the livelihood of the single man or family, seal-hunting can no longer be said to constitute the only trade of the natives. First, it must be remembered that the European settlers have required the assistance of a certain number of persons who now gain their living by serving them ; and, secondly, many natives now maintain themselves by such kinds of fishing and hunting as formerly were only considered subordinate occupations occasionally resorted to by the seal-hunters. But no mechanical industry, handicraft, or commerce whatever has been developed, excepting in the service of Europeans by individuals appointed for such purposes. For this service young people have been trained up partly in Greenland, and partly by spending a couple of years in Denmark.

The author is of opinion that if we compare boys at the age of sixteen to eighteen years in Greenland, with the same class in Europe, as to their handiness and facility for learning various kinds of labour within a short time, the verdict will be in favour of the Greenland youth. This also appears in some measure probable when we consider how the latter from their earliest childhood have the opportunity in daily life of developing the faculty of helping themselves, the members of an Eskimo family being able to supply all the chief necessities of their common household by means of their own labour, and especially to surmount, by their own ingenuity, the various hindrances and embarrassments met with in travelling and roaming about in uninhabited tracts where no foreign assistance is to be expected. It can easily be imagined that by having shared in this life until the age of sixteen or eighteen years, a man will have obtained an advantage hardly to be acquired at a later period of life, viz. a capability of learning the rudiments of various manual arts within a short time, so as to acquire a further perfection by the aid of his own experience. Of course the natives are peculiarly fitted for being employed as sailors on board the coasting boats, but they have also, as carpenters, coopers, and smiths proved to be able to perform all the necessary work required by the trading establishments, their acquirements being of course limited when compared with artizans of the European race. Moreover, they generally combine with their chief profession a certain skill in various other manipulations, which makes them all the more useful in such isolated places.

The most necessary assistance may be had from them as bricklayers, glaziers, bakers, and brewers. As good bread and beer are generally made at the settlements as in the mother country, the art once taught having since been handed down by tradition. Native cooks are appointed at all the chief stations, and their performances in the culinary art have often been deservedly admired by strangers, while at the same time they make themselves useful to the European households by procuring fodder for the goats, and in various other ways act as expert and skilful servants. The author cannot omit adding one instance to illustrate this. Once he took such a boy with him to Denmark, where he stayed only one winter as apprentice in a printing-office, and acquired a skill in book-printing, lithography, and bookbinding, of which he has afterwards given proofs by managing, all by himself, without the least assistance, a small office in Greenland, the productions of which will be mentioned by and by. This young man is by no means a rare exception ; perhaps one out of ten may be found to be equally highly gifted. It cannot be denied that the half-breeds seem to surpass the original race as regards such perfectibility.

There is only one general deficiency tending to make the service of the Greenlander less useful to Europeans. It must be remembered that even the most skilful and respectable native continues to be considered as belonging to a nation, the best individuals of which, according to a deeply-rooted prejudice, are inferior to the worst of the foreigners. This creates a difficulty whenever it is desirable to place a native in a post that requires the exercise of any degree of authority. Of course, a clever, well-bred, and honest man acquires the esteem of his countrymen, but he still remains 'only' a Greenlander, and his authority is nothing in comparison with that of a European. When the mission founded by Egede began to extend its stations to the distant parts of the coast, the want of a sufficient number of teachers became evident. The natives lived dispersed in a hundred wintering places, so distant from one another that divine service and school instruction could not possibly be performed by the few missionaries in the country. At first the experiment was tried of sending orphan boys from Denmark to Greenland, where they were trained up by the missionaries so as to be enabled to undertake the duties of subordinate clergymen or schoolmasters to the newly-converted 'savages.' These settlers married native women, and it has been stated that they behaved well, and furthered civilisation, and it is a fact that they have given birth to a numerous offspring distinguished to this very day by comprising talented individuals. But besides these officials duly educated for the missionary service, in emergencies other Europeans who appeared fitted for the same task were occasionally employed. The missionary Saaby relates in his journal that about the year 1770, at a chief station at Disco Bay, the duties of the clergyman were committed to the charge of an old married Danish sailor, who once in his youthful days, by fighting when drunk, had lost an eye and broken his leg. That the instruction given by this man, he adds, did not prove successful, is what might be expected, and from this time the same missionary tried to avail himself of what assistance he could get from natives. This expedient was resorted to more and more as the mission extended its activity. The natives, invested with the authority of teachers or 'catechists,' underwent no preparation for this task, but were chosen merely on account of their having acquired more skill in reading than their countrymen in general, and being besides held in public esteem. The salary paid to them was so trifling that they must be considered to have accepted their positions merely as posts of honour. Most expert seal-hunters have sometimes been found among these clerical officials, clever old men who used to perform the duties of their office in the evening on returning from the seal-hunt, assembling in their own house the inhabitants of the place for prayers and teaching the children. In the year 1845 two seminaries were founded for the purpose of more systematically training young men for the service of the mission. The teachers issuing from these schools have been somewhat better paid, but still the greater part of them cannot be said to derive their chief means of subsistence from their salaries.

When the Trade was gradually extended by the addition of outposts, its administration was embarrassed in a similar way to the mission, the profit derived from these insignificant stations being too trifling to pay the appointment of a regular official. Of course, a Greenlander was considered too inferior to be trusted with the responsibility of a few barrels of biscuits, coffee, and suchlike luxuries; but in this case there was less want of individuals of the superior race. The sailors, labourers, and handicraftsmen engaged for Greenland not unfrequently proved to be well-qualified for managing the traffic of those small establishments. The native teacher, of course, was, in comparison with such a European merchant, but little more than a common Greenlander, sometimes carrying water and performing the coarsest servile work for them for a trifling pay. One circumstance, however, in many cases, tended to soften the apparent untowardness of this sway which thus followed from their position; the traders generally married native

women, and brought up their children as Greenlanders, and
frequently so as to become the most intelligent and skilful
members of society. Of late years, attempts have been
made to employ natives for these posts, and the experiment
has met with no great obstacle.

The ardour with which the whole nation devoted itself to
the practice of their hazardous and troublesome seal-hunting,
at the time when the first hunters were considered the aris-
tocracy of society, deserves our admiration ; but on glancing
over our account of the effect produced by the European intercourse, and perceiving how the seal-hunters are
now thrown into the shade, we are forced to wonder at the
assiduity with which the natives still continue to make use
of their kayaks. It has been alleged that they do so
merely from being coerced by hunger and want, but if need
is now required to compel them to activity, it must be immediately impending, and when famine is perceived to be
imminent, it will be too late to learn to manage the kayak.
The practice of this art has to be begun in boyhood, and
as a matter of delight and ambition rather than of necessity and compulsion. Still, notwithstanding all controversy,
public opinion is so generally favourable to the national
seal-hunt that if a boy is growing up in a place where circumstances tend to render him neglectful in this respect, he
only requires to be removed to another more favourable
spot, being then almost sure to become an ordinary kayaker
within a short time. The power of traditional custom, and
the peculiar attraction of a sporting and wandering life,
must afford a sufficient explanation of this fact.

Many strangers have practised kayaking as a sport,
some of them even acquiring remarkable skill in it within
a short time ; but if we fancy one of the same removed to a
place on the Greenland coast where no assistance was to
be had from natives, we doubt if it would be of any

essential use to him as regards obtaining his livelihood. The difference between practising an art as a diversion and as a means of subsistence is very great in this instance. The skill in manœuvring the kayak which is admirable in a foreigner, is as easy to a Greenlander as walking on *terra firma* is to us. If properly educated, he already learned the same before he was twelve years of age ; what to him is expertness in his art can hardly ever be attained by a stranger when grown up. A single one of the difficulties which the Greenlander meets with by hundreds in the course of a year, will suffice to impede his deriving any practical profit from the skill he may have acquired. Kayak-hunting becomes very troublesome in autumn and winter. Throughout half the coast no firm ice is formed sufficient to admit of any seal-hunt being carried on upon it, and where such ice occurs the use of the kayak is, nevertheless, in many instances indispensable as an additional expedient. It must be remembered that the sea is not covered with solid ice at once, and that its freezing over is very different from that of a lake. The rise and fall of the tide cause the first ice that is formed in autumn to be broken up along the shore so as to form a broad channel filled with fragments, which has to be crossed by leaping from one piece to the other in order to reach the solid ice. Moreover, even when the sea remains open throughout the winter, the beach becomes fringed with an ice border, which at low water may present a precipitous wall upwards of 10 feet high, and besides being slippery, the sea in front of it is often encumbered with pieces of drifting ice moved by the surf. Landing on such a coast is always dangerous, and, in a stiff breeze, often impossible. Surprising dexterity is also displayed by the kayak-hunters in passing over a sea partly open and partly frozen over, or filled with broken drift-ice, which requires the kayak to be carried by turns

upon the head in walking over the ice, and then launched
into the water again. What we have here mentioned only
refers to the use of the kayak as a means of conveyance,
but from this to catching a seal with harpoon and bladder
there is a wide difference. South of 67° N. lat., where the
sea in front of the outer coast places is always open, kayak-
hunting is carried on throughout the severest part of the
winter, seals having been caught in this way in a strong
breeze and at a temperature of ÷ 20°. In such cold the sea
is always covered with a thick haze, and the water in washing over covers the kayak as well as the clothes of the man
with a crust of ice. The sea is also filled with drifting
ice, and if it happens to grow calm, the kayaker may be
stopped and frozen in with his frail skiff without any hope
of getting assistance. When, on the contrary, a gale sets
in, he may be obliged to row against it for several hours
without being able to lift his hand in order to shelter his
frost-bitten face. If, finally, we add the short duration of
daylight in the depth of winter, and not unfrequently an
empty stomach and a bad condition of clothes and implements, hardly a more perilous and troublesome employment
may be found than seal-hunting. But to the Greenlander
such hardships are nothing but commonplace occurrences,
and even in his most impoverished and degraded state he
considers that either to boast or complain of them is beneath his dignity.

Formerly it must have been considered an ordinary
rule that a boy had a kayak of his own from his tenth
year at least, and in his nineteenth year on an average he
had caught his first seal with harpoon and bladder, but now
many youths are growing up without possessing a kayak,
and many kayakers never become seal-hunters, but only
take to fishing. One point of great importance to a kayaker is the power of rising again by help of his paddle when

he happens to be capsized. Men have been found who could perform this trick even without the paddle ; it has been said, by even keeping a stone in each hand ; but now the practice of it, even in the ordinary way, seems to be on the decline, and probably many lives are lost on account of this want of dexterity. Further, seal-hunters now differ much as regards their perfection. While the average number of seals annually caught by a hunter is fifty-six, those of the highest class used to get in the North about two hundred or more, and in the South about seventy ; the least skilful hunters in the North got about fifty, and in the South about thirty seals on an average per annum. Besides the grown-up men who may be classed as fishers, many boys, before having caught their first seal, contribute a considerable quota to the supply of the families to which they belong. It has been calculated that five such boys in one of the southernmost places had each on an average caught from his kayak about eight hundred fish and one hundred birds in a year.

The manufactures of the natives being confined to domestic industry, a man himself makes his boat and his kayak with all the appertaining implements : the women build up the house walls, cut up the seals, and prepare their skins, besides performing the usual female labours. A kind of waterproof sealskin clothing is the only manufactured article for sale to the Royal Trade.

In 1870 the total number of natives was 9,588. On being divided according to occupation or means of subsistence the different classes comprised the following number of individuals besides their families : 1,555 seal-hunting and 339 fishing kayakers, besides about 250 kayaking boys and 41 men, who are named as practising seal-catching only by help of nets. In the service of the Danish Mission were 53 appointed teachers, besides those teachers who are counted as seal-hunters or fishers. In the service of the Royal Trade were 12 appointed outpost traders, 15 head-men and boatswains, 14 carpenters and smiths, 19 coopers, 15 cooks, 54 sailors and labourers, besides 10 pensioners and 33 midwives; 5 officers were enumerated as natives, but at least 3 of them are rather to be considered Europeans.

In the same year the number of Europeans were 237, of whom 95 were engaged in the service of the Trade; 8 were Danish and 11 Moravian missionaries, and 38 lived at the Cryolite Mine, at Ivigtout.

CHAPTER X.

THE INHABITANTS : THEIR DOMESTIC LIFE AND HABITS.

Habitations and Means of Conveyance.—The Greenlanders have always built their winter houses out of earth and stones, knowing the snow-huts used by the Eskimo in other places only from tradition. The habitations of the Greenlanders are often referred to as proofs of their wretchedness and low stage of culture, and, of course, in many respects, an amelioration of them would be desirable ; but, notwithstanding their partial subterraneous character, they have their advantages, and are remarkably well adapted to the habits and mode of life of the nation. If the inmates happen to be industrious people and well off, according to native ideas, a stay in these houses need by no means be disgusting to a European. The author had the opportunity of observing this in availing himself, for a night or two at a time, of the hospitality of natives who lived in isolated places in Northern Greenland. No doubt the icy nocturnal wind blowing outside contributed to make him more indulgent to certain habits and scenes which, under ordinary circumstances, might have been calculated to shock him, but the impression of the whole was far from being that of disorder and offensiveness.

To give an idea of the suitable construction of these dwellings, in the first place the air-tightness of the walls and the roof has to be mentioned. On account of their

No. 11. Interior of a rich house.

being formed of stones alternating with sod, the walls are liable to subside, but then the roof, consisting of turf spread over driftwood, will follow them, and the whole being cemented by help of moisture and frost, will be perfectly impenetrable to wind. The windows, made out of seal-entrail, only admit a scanty portion of daylight, but during the greater part of the winter time the sun is absent, and when the days are lengthening day-time is mostly passed in the open air. The dwelling-room of the original houses had no chimney or fire-place at all, but the lamps served at once for lighting, heating, and cooking.

A small kitchen is sometimes found as a side-room close by the doorway. Ventilation is afforded chiefly by the long and narrow doorway which forms the entrance to the house. On first entering one has to descend, while at the other end a step upwards again leads into the room itself. To a stranger this passage is rather inconvenient, it being quite dark, and moreover the narrow space sometimes becomes the temporary refuge of snappish dogs. An astonishing adroitness is displayed by the native women who, though carrying a baby on their bent back, can run up this dark porch-tunnel at a tolerable speed, whereas a very tall clergyman who resided in Greenland some years ago was said to manage his visits by being shut up in his sleeping sack and dragged by a rope into the interior. By properly adapting the width and length of the house-passage the necessary ventilation is afforded, there having been formerly scarcely any door at all in the house, only occasionally a loose skin curtain being used to close the entrance ; a vent-hole was also made in the roof ; and the enormous difference of temperature outside and inside explains how so little as 100 cubic feet of space per inmate could then suffice. In the only room in the house a broad bench or ledge runs along the wall opposite to the windows, and is divided by help of low screens into separate stalls or recesses for the families.   The walls are hung with skins, and the floor paved with flat stones.   The chief cause of the repulsive appearance of these habitations when seen in summer is the rubbish of every description which lies scattered upon the surrounding ground.   The more indifferent the inmates are and the severer the winter has been, the shorter the distance to which they retire from their door for the purpose of getting rid of anything which, during the course of winter, has to be removed.

As long as the cold prevails the snow hides this accumulation of dirt, which is at once brought to light by the spring thaw.   In North Greenland all what, in the widest sense of the word, has been left or refused by men, is converted into dog-feed ; in the south, these winter-stations, when abandoned in summer, sometimes offer a still more disgusting appearance.   But it must be remembered that, according to ancient fashion, the inhabitants take to their tents before the snow melts away, remove to other places and enjoy at once more cleanliness and fresh air during summer.   On leaving the houses their roofs have to be taken down so as to let them be aired and washed by the rain before they are rebuilt in autumn.   In the south the winter-huts have to be protected against rain and thaw occasionally during the cold season ; in the north the frost generally prevails sufficiently to make this measure superfluous.   A tent well-fitted according to fashion, of course, has a far neater and more comfortable appearance than a winter house, being formed of a double skin covering stretched over the poles, one end of which rests upon a low semicircular wall and the other end upon the frame which forms the entrance.   A curtain made of seal-entrail, and transparent enough to give sufficient light to the in-

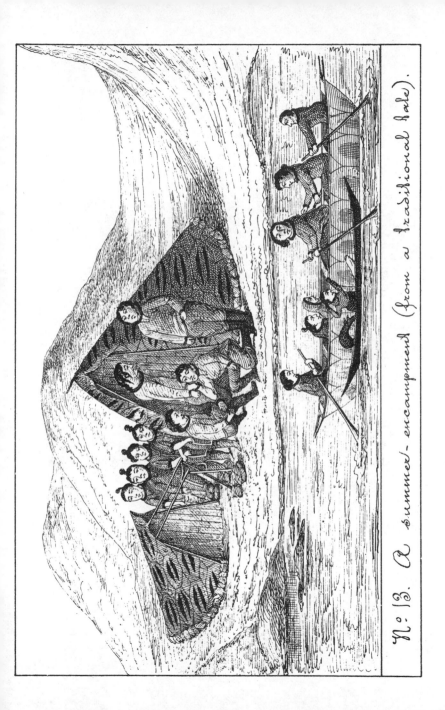

Nº 13. A summer-encampment (from a traditional tale).

terior, covers the opening, in front of which is an entry and a fire-place.

The women's boats or umiaks must be mentioned here on account of their being so closely connected with the tents, and with the removal of the family from one hunting or fishing station to another. They are 25 to 37 feet long, 5 feet broad, 2½ feet deep, and quite flat-bottomed. To a stranger who travels in them for the first time, it is curious to see how the skin-covering of the bottom and sides of the vessel becomes transparent from growing wet, and permits the motion of the water to be observed through it. They require to be managed with the greatest care, the stretched skin being liable to be cut by the first piece of ice it may happen to run against, or by the sharp edge of a single stone on being launched into the sea. But the perfect familiarity of the natives with this mode of travelling admits of their being used to cross fjords crowded with icebergs, when almost no thoroughfare can be discovered. As regards their usefulness in a heavy sea, they possibly might almost equal a whaleboat, as their flexibility in some measure prevents them from shipping seas. To this, however, they are only exposed in urgent cases, any exposure to the open sea being as far as possible avoided. The largest boats can carry 6,600 lbs., or 3 tons, the smaller only half the weight, and at present by far the greater number of umiaks belonging to the natives are of the smaller kind. As only the framework and the thwarts or rowing-benches are of wood, the rest consisting of a skin covering, a large boat may very well be transported by land, eight to ten men taking it keel upwards on their backs. For a boat covering, from twelve to twenty sealskins are required; in the south it needs to be renewed every year, while it will last for two years or even more in the north; but the worn-out covering still

serves for various purposes. The skins intended for kayaks
or for open boats are neither cleaned from fat nor expanded
like other skins, but are prepared merely by being put aside
to dry and shrink, and become saturated with oil till the
hair falls off.

Of course the Greenlanders' habitations have not escaped the influence of civilisation, but the advantages
acquired hardly counterbalance the deterioration caused at
the same time. The first-rate houses are now constructed
with a sloping roof including an attic or 'loft,' while the
living-room is wainscoted and furnished with a stove. The
roof is made of boards, and the window has panes of glass.
Undoubtedly some houses of this description are patterns
of cleanliness and order. The interior is fitted up with the
usual ledges, and only as a rare curiosity is a table or other
piece of furniture to be seen; the walls are adorned with
cheap prints and the shelves bear cups and other utensils.
But many of the houses thus constructed are a picture of
negligence and disorder, being even inferior to the better
ones of ancient form, and all of them have the inconvenience of being liable to become fissured on account
of the walls sinking while the room still rests upon the
framework of the wainscot. Another degree of improvement in the construction is to leave the flat roof unaltered,
but to furnish the interior with a wainscot, a boarded floor,
and a stove. These houses of course differ much from
each other. Whether on the whole a stove is to be considered an improvement to a Greenland household is somewhat doubtful, the stone lamp being indispensable, and
the stove generally being an insupportable addition to the
heat of the room.

Even in very isolated spots the author has met with a
few of these houses of which not only was the interior
nicely fitted up and swept perfectly clean, but even the

surrounding ground was cleared of rubbish ; but these rare instances are unable to compensate for the misery and wretchedness exhibited in a great many others. Above all, it is an irreparable detriment, when the tent is abandoned and the winter house has to be inhabited summer and winter. It is hardly to be doubted that even the best of the improved houses are unable to render the use of tents needless. But when the usual turf-huts continue to be inhabited in summer, they cannot but become pernicious breeding-places of disease and infection. The floor more or less covered with mud, combined with filth and rottenness of every description, being acted upon by moisture and heat, gives forth mephitic exhalations which render the air in such pestilential caverns poisonous to their inmates. It appears impossible that many generations will be able to maintain their existence in such pitiful abodes, surrounded with heaps of rubbish in every stage of foulness and putrefaction. At present scarcely half the inhabitants are provided with tolerably good tents, and many families are even totally devoid of worn-out boat coverings, which form one of the principal materials for the construction of the modern tents. The ominous expression of Crantz, when he called the natives 'sheep driven into folds,' has now become a sad reality in so far as the picture given here refers to the Moravian stations, Ny Herrnhut and Lichtenfels. On approaching these places, the visitor on being told that each of them contains about a hundred natives and two or three missionary families, will be at a loss to make out where the former have their abodes. The mission houses are pretty spacious, and, for Greenland, even stately in appearance. The stranger will probably be surprised on being informed that these buildings are only inhabited by the missionaries, because he discovers nothing like human dwellings anywhere else. Then his attention will be called to something resembling dunghills scattered over the low rocks, and partly overgrown with grass, and he will be surprised to learn that the native population of the place lives inside these dens. When some drift-timber has been collected in the course of the summer, on repairing the huts in autumn the roofs are furnished as abundantly as possible with spars and smaller pieces of wood, because in winter, when fuel becomes scarce, recourse is had to the ceiling, which is cut away as long as it can be done without fear of the roof falling in. But miscalculations are often made, and when frost ceases to bind together the earthy covering, it is liable to break asunder, for which reason roofs falling in used to be looked on as a sign of spring. The want of tents in these places has given rise to a peculiar invention, viz. that of building separate huts in spring of the same construction as the winter houses, but of smaller size. In 1855 there were 19 such summer residences at Lichtenfels, each of them from 8 to 10 feet long, and from 6 to 8 feet broad. Some of them had nothing but stones covered with moss for a ledge or couch ; in some of them the walls were hung with pictures, a melancholy sign of the last relic of the taste for improvement that is left in these poor people.

In the year 1870 the natives were distributed in 985 winter houses, of which 880 had less than 16 inmates each, the rest 16 or more, the highest number being 36 persons in one house. Of these houses there were, belonging to people employed in the service of the Trade and missions, 72 houses with sloping, and 90 with flat roofs, all furnished with stoves ; belonging to the natives free of service there were 30 houses with sloping, and 180 with flat roofs, but furnished with stoves, and 613 houses with flat roofs and no stoves. Between 1872 and 1875 the number of boats (umiaks) and sledges possessed by the natives were about as follows :—in the south, 203 boats ; in the north, 71 boats and 270 sledges, with the necessary complement of dogs.

Garments, Food, and other Articles of Use.—The most characteristic feature of the Eskimo dress is the similarity between that of the male and the female sexes. The narrow doorway alone would suffice to render any sort of petticoat or gown out of the question for the women; their trousers are very narrow, and reach only to the knees. The next peculiarity is the form of the jacket, which fits tight round the body without any opening excepting those for the face and the hands. The hood, or that part of the jacket which covers the head, is scarcely made use of by the women, on account of their hair being tied up in an erect tuft, which makes them cover their head by having a neckerchief tied closely around it ; but they have a jacket with a peculiar sort of hood called the ' amowt,' serving for the conveyance of children. Being of sufficient width for a child to be placed between it and the back, it affords an excellent means for keeping the infant warm and well protected. The unbecoming appearance of trousers as a part of female dress was originally in some degree diminished by the length of the jacket, and its further prolongation by flaps before and behind ; but civilisation has mostly discarded the flaps and curtailed the jacket, so as even to leave an open space between it and the trousers, offering the opportunity of at times displaying the whiteness of a chemise. The material, however, has been subjected to more alteration than the form of dress, it having become the fashion to furnish the jackets with a cotton covering, and coloured materials have now become the predominating feature of fashionable Greenland attire, especially that of the female sex. Men frequently use white cotton for their outer garments, in summer even for trousers. In the south there are scarcely any fur jackets to be seen with the hairy side outward, excepting the amowt, whereas in the north the winter-jacket of the men has been allowed, for obvious reasons, to keep its hairy appearance, as well as somewhat more of its length. The Eskimo foot-gear is so ingeniously made and so well adapted to the country that it has not only been subject to no alteration, but is invariably adopted by every European during his stay there.

The carelessness with which a great part of the population now look forward to the cold season as regards clothing is almost incredible. But most pernicious to the prosperity of a family is the want of the necessary kayak clothes, which hinders the provider from pursuing his business ; many seal-hunters are at times condemned to inactivity from this miserable cause. We have reason to admire the seal-hunter of the northern regions, who sleeps upon his sledge in the open air, without other equipment than his daily dress, while passing a night or two on his lonely hunting grounds. We may often have occasion to wonder how little is required by the natives to protect themselves from cold when travelling in rough weather, and even to make them perfectly comfortable. But how far they surpass the Europeans in hardiness and endurance is more clearly to be seen at the poorer stations when the winter is unusually severe even in the opinion of the natives. Persons may be seen dressed more like poor people in southern Europe than Eskimo. Children are seen in rags which scarcely hide their nakedness, their boots being frozen quite hard and stiff on account of not being taken off for several weeks.

A detailed calculation of the total amount of the edibles yearly produced in Greenland has given the result that each individual has for his daily consumption, on an average, 2 lbs. of flesh with blubber, and $1\frac{1}{2}$ lb. of fish, besides mussels, berries, seaweed, and other indigenous vegetables, to which may be added 2 oz. of imported food, viz. bread, barley, and peas. This allowance does not appear scanty, but when we consider the extraordinary inequality with which it is distributed throughout the year, it might appear in some measure remarkable that it can suffice. It will not be far from truth if it is affirmed that each family of five persons consumes 7,000 lbs. of these edibles in a year ; but we should be greatly mistaken in believing that every person usually has anything like the said daily allowance for his meals. In no other country in the world is there probably such a sudden change from superabundance to insufficiency during the course of the same year as in Greenland.

In Southern Greenland small storehouses are still found in a few places ; winter provisions stored up in summer are more commonly deposited in caves or holes well secured with stones, and often purposely rather far from the winter station itself, in order to render them more difficult of access, and thereby diminish the temptation of having recourse to them. Beside these provisions, consisting of dried fish and a little dried flesh, as well as skin bags filled with seal-oil, the seals saved from the catch in the principal hunting season are preserved in autumn by merely covering them with snow. The foresight thus displayed at the southernmost stations gradually decreases towards the north, and in the northernmost stations nothing at all is laid up from one season to the other, and nowhere in Greenland are the stores sufficient to secure a tolerable uniformity of diet. The contrast between the fatness and substantiality of the meals at different seasons is intensified by the possibility of refining them by the addition of European articles. An ample supply of seal-flesh always presupposes a corresponding acquisition of skins and blubber, and these goods are equal to cash. Then of

course the savoury repasts of fat seal-flesh are refined by
the addition of biscuits and a cup of coffee. Barley and
peas are sometimes boiled with the meat as a soup.   Then
perhaps recourse is had to more favoured kinds of fish for
variety, when the ordinary codfish, frog-fish, and mussels
are regarded with contempt. However, soon after the
tables are turned, seal-flesh becomes a dainty, sea-birds will
be highly appreciated, and a piece of blubber to some fish
is the only thing desired, and if coffee has been obtained,
the grounds are used a second time. So their ideas
of luxury gradually decrease, until frog-fish again make
their appearance on the table, and enjoy the same
esteem they did a year before about the same season.

Curious instances of excessive consumption, as well as
of living on short allowance, frequently occur here and
there. That the population of one station should consume
a dozen entire walrus every year during a week or two in
spring is not so much to be wondered at, because the hide
of these huge animals is known to be one of their most
favourite dainties for dessert. It appears all the more remarkable that people who were appointed to catch seals
with nets, and whose consumption could be pretty well
controlled, were calculated to have eaten as much as ten
pounds of flesh and blubber per head daily, during two or
three months, exclusive of a certain allowance of European provisions as pay for their services. Considering that
a whale must be supposed to give much more than 20,000,
perhaps nearer 50,000 pounds of edible material, it appears
strange that the inhabitants of Holstenborg are in some
winters favoured with one or two such animals, in others
with none at all, without any other difference being perceived in their condition, but that people kept a rather
better table in the one year than in the other.

In regard to the degree of scarcity required to cause

people to complain, a great difference prevails between
the south and the north. It is curious how little the
natives at one of the southern stations are able to subsist
upon without speaking of want. As a contrast, we will
quote what the native teacher at Upernivik, the northernmost station, where eighty natives live, writes in his diary
for 1868. At the end of September he says:—'For this
month the catch has not been good, having yielded only
ten seals and six white whales.' On October 15 he continues : 'The cold is more intense than it has been hitherto,
but the poor Greenlanders have only had scanty success in
hunting, as they say that there are no seals to be seen.
Sometimes they do not go out on account of bad weather,
and then they have nothing to eat.' On October 31 : 'For
the whole of this month the catch has been much better
than in September, the total amount for the month having
been eighty-two seals, two bears, two white whales, and one
narwhal.' Lastly, on November 12 he reports : 'During the
last few days, the weather having continued to be nasty,
with gales blowing, the Greenlanders have been unable to
go out hunting . . . The day before yesterday they began
to receive support from the public fund. . . . They get their
supply three times a week, viz. twice rye-meal, and once barley and peas, with the addition of a little blubber each time.'

As far as we are able to calculate from these statements, these eighty natives, children included, had, besides
more than the average quantity of European provisions, at
least two pounds of fat flesh per individual daily, during
the three weeks before they began to apply to the fund
for the relief of the poor, and suddenly passed to a diet
of perhaps half-a-pound of rye-meal or barley boiled in
water, with a small slice of blubber a day. The reader
no doubt will also find it strange that the report only
speaks of 'the Greenlanders' instead of 'the poor,' and

indeed this fact strikingly illustrates what in the following pages we have to proffer concerning the distinction
which in Greenland is made between natives and Europeans as regards the right of accumulating property.

The most curious feature of the fluctuation in the diet
and the value of eatables during the course of the year is that
it not only depends on the incalculable changes of weather
and of success in hunting, but also varies almost as regularly as the flux and reflux of the tide, and that no native
ever avails himself of this opportunity for speculation.
During the usual hunting season in autumn, carcasses of
seals, or as much as 100 pounds of meat, are sold for the
same price as three pounds of biscuit, although they are
known to be almost of inestimable value a few months
later, and there is not the least difficulty in preserving them.
In some places improvident hunters have even sold entire
seals to the European trader merely for the value of the
blubber and the skin, in order to avoid the trouble of
flaying them. Even fish dried and prepared for winter
provisions have usually been sold for one-sixteenth of the
value of bread, and, strange to say, it has been tried for
some years at one of the stations to catch and dry the
same sort of fish, and sell them regularly to the natives at
a rate four times higher than what they were paid for
them ; yet they were perfectly satisfied with the bargain.
But as a rule, when occasionally they buy from the Royal
Board of Trade the ordinary Greenland wares, especially
the blubber, they are always sold to them again at the
same rate at which they are purchased.

The peculiarity here described is easily explained if
we consider the ancient customs of the Eskimo. The trade
which they carried on amongst themselves was a very
limited one, and scarcely at all comprised articles of food.
Victuals were shared out after certain rules,—not indiscrimi-

nately, but still so as generally to protect anybody against suffering from starvation so long as the neighbours had a sufficient supply. The contact with the Europeans has altered this state of matters in several respects, but not in the main point. Speculation in victuals would be an undertaking so contrary to public opinion that no Greenlander has ever tried it. But, on the other hand, he will take no offence at seeing a European do so. The fixed low price of the blubber, being the chief article of trade, and at the same time serving for food as well as for fuel and lamp-oil, still more contributes to facilitate the subsistence of the poor and of those who live upon their wages.

The most popular articles purchased by the Greenlanders are coffee and tobacco. It is difficult to say whether they are to be considered as merely articles of luxury, or in some degree necessaries of life. As coffee is indispensable on any festive occasion, so is it valuable on the other hand on account of its enlivening and warming qualities to people who travel about in rough weather but scantily provided with the means for protecting themselves against damp and cold. A cup of coffee and a quid of tobacco perhaps in many cases serve as the last resources to raise the drooping spirits of the seal-hunter, and thereby become in some measure pillars of the Greenland commonwealth. When it can be afforded coffee is made pretty strong ; it is roasted darker than usual, and pulverised by being beaten in a skin bag, or at a pinch in a mitten or a boot. On longer kayak journeys, coffee, naturally, cannot be had, but still some kayakers have been known to manage it by eating the coffee and drinking cold water at the same time.

Tobacco is used in its three different forms. The first step towards civilisation is represented by snuff, the use of which has been adopted even by the heathens on the east coast, being one of the chief causes which induce them to undertake their annual expeditions to the trade station next to Cape Farewell. The natives prepare it themselves, and consider one sort of tobacco alone as fit for this purpose. It is dried, pulverised, and mixed up with a little limestone or cryolite. Next to snuff, chewing-tobacco is most in request as more convenient to the kayakers, while snuff is used by them as well as by the female sex. The want of these articles is considered to be nearly as bad as a food famine. A company of travellers being brought to this sad plight, and happening to miss another party whom they had expected to meet with, immediately examined the place where the latter had encamped in search of the stone which they knew must have been used for grinding the snuff. On finding it, it was handed round to the assembly to smell. It was also said that on a journey two kayakers, of whom only one had a quid of tobacco, made a bargain that when it had served its owner during the day it should be delivered to the other in the evening, and paid with a new hunting-line. Smoking tobacco is also common all over Greenland, but mostly in the north, especially at Umanak, where the women and even children have adopted it. But the pipes used there in winter must be very short, lest the tube should be obstructed by frost.

The importation of intoxicating liquor is limited to certain quantities granted for the use of the officials to be retailed to the labourers and to the natives for services rendered, and for use on solemn occasions. The quantity distributed in this way averages one gallon for each grown-up man per annum.

Their Trade and Property in general.—The trade-monopoly affords better than in other countries an opportunity of controlling the consumption of imported wares. Moreover, less difference of classes or of mode of life of course prevails here than in more civilised societies. Even the natives who live upon their wages differ but little from their countrymen as to their mode of life, inasmuch as their income only suffices to give them a share in the produce of the hunt by barter or by having hunters or fishers for their house-fellows. Subtracting from the annual import what may be supposed to be consumed by the European residents in the country and 200 natives, constituting the families of the Europeans who are married to native women, the remainder will show how much European produce each family consumes, supposing it to consist of five persons, and their value according to the latest fixed prices in Greenland.

Each family on an average has a yearly income of 8*l.*, which is spent as follows :—

	£	s.	d.
Fire-arms, gunpowder, and lead	0	6	8
Other weapons and tools for hunting and fishing .	0	3	1
House materials and stores	0	1	7
35 yards of various dry goods, chiefly cotton .	1	0	9
Other articles of dress	0	6	2
Domestic implements and tools	0	2	1
42 lbs. of coffee	2	2	2
188 ,, bread	1	9	10
58 ,, barley and peas	0	7	2
29 ,, sugar	0	16	8
Other imported victuals	0	7	0
12 lbs. of tobacco	0	15	2
Various articles	0	1	8
Total	£8	0	0

The income here calculated gives a sum of 15,016*l.* as the total incomes of 1,877 families, which is gained in the following way :—

For goods sold to the Royal Trade. . . .	£8,030
From the municipal fund	1,472
Fixed wages in the service of the Trade . . .	2,445
Fixed wages in the service of the Mission . . .	800
Occasional wages and pay for labour and articles used by the Europeans	2,269
	£15,016

If we will now find out the whole yearly consumption or expenditure of an Eskimo family in Danish Greenland on an average, we must add what the natives use of their own productions, being according to what has been stated above per family : 26 sealskins, 480 pounds of blubber, 6,400 pounds of flesh and fish, besides various other skins and articles of food and other things of little value. If we estimate the flesh and fish at one-quarter of the value of blubber, all these products will amount to 6*l*., and the whole consumption to 14*l*. If the price is taken at one-half, the products of a Greenland family will amount to 9*l*. 10*s*., and the whole consumption to 17*l*. 10*s*. When compared with the consumption of those who merely live upon their wages, the first supposition seems to be nearer the truth, and consequently the total expenditure or consumption of a family may be estimated at about 15*l*.

It must be granted that the first of the accounts here given, however trifling it may appear, indicates a decided tendency to prodigality, especially on account of bread baked in Europe or biscuits, being a mere article of luxury to the Greenlanders. Experience has sufficiently proved that whenever the income of the natives surpasses the usual rate, almost the whole surplus is spent on coffee, sugar, and especially on bread. From this fact it may be guessed what would be the case if the assortment of articles of luxury was increased, and how little real progress in prosperity would result to the natives merely by their obtaining a higher price for their goods.

To the account here given of the annual income and expenditure, an estimate of the actual estate of a Greenlandish family will form a necessary supplement. For this reason the author has procured inventories of the possessions of about ten persons with their households. The following three will serve as examples which will suffice for all the other native inhabitants of the coast.

The first family is that 'of one of the richest native Greenlanders. He owns a small but good house, with a sloping roof of boards, in which he lives with his wife, his son sixteen years old, and three younger children, a married brother, a sister, and the widow of a deceased brother with five children, comprising fifteen persons, or in a stricter sense three families. The interior of the house contains about 200 square feet. Moreover he possesses a boat for the same number of persons, and a small tent constructed very much according to the model of the ancient tents, one stove, one large copper kettle, some iron pots, twelve different stoneware vessels and four skins for ledge-covers. He himself possesses one kayak with all the clothing and tools appertaining, the bladder and line being in duplicate, one rifle (besides one inherited from his brother), one chest of tools containing axe, saw, files, and plane ; of clothes he has one reindeer-skin jacket and another of birdskin, with two stuff-coverings, and three to four suits of the other articles of dress. The son has his kayak, and he as well as the other children and their mother are well supplied with clothes. The brother and his wife are also well provided with clothes ; he owns a kayak and a rifle, but no house utensils of his own. The widow and her children are also well dressed. The whole party moreover possesses a hut for a temporary refuge at an isolated hunting station ; this, although valueless in itself, is nevertheless a very rare possession to a native.

The second man whose possessions we are about to describe, was not considered poor. He owned a miserable house which contained eighteen other inmates, and a stove, but he had neither boat nor tent. He had one kayak furnished with clothes and tools, comprising one supernumerary hunting line ; one chest of tools (formerly he had owned a watch and a fiddle), and about two complete suits of clothes. Of his eighteen house-fellows, three were kayak-owners and one had a rifle. They were all worse off in the item of clothes. As common property they had three lamps and a small fishing-line, but scarcely any other house utensils worth mentioning, these articles having to be borrowed from others.

Our third example is a poor man who owned a perfectly worthless house and a bad kayak with a good fishing-line. Of other kayak-implements he used to acquire some in autumn, but again he sold them during the course of the winter. Of clothes he had scarcely one complete suit at all, and these were in a miserable condition. His wife also only owned one suit of clothes, but of a better quality. They had an iron pot, a lamp, and an old harpoon which he used as a knife, but no other utensils or tools whatever.

The examples here given are taken from the middle part of the coast. In North Greenland a sledge and dogs must be added to the property of well-to-do people. It is a very rare exception when a man possesses a European boat, and the author has met with but one native who had a canvas tent to be used for shorter excursions. But as regards money, until recently scarcely a native could be found who had saved as much as 5*l.* from his own gains, independent of European sources. A larger sum has sometimes been acquired by one of them by inheritance, or from other accidental causes, but in such cases an arrangement has generally been made by which the capital became submitted to European guardianship in order to protect it from being wasted. What we have here stated concerning property and estate, more especially refers to those who are in an independent position; as regards the natives who live upon their wages, their position under European control enables them to ameliorate their domestic life a little, but their property on the whole only a very little surpasses that of their countrymen, and with few exceptions they are prone to contract debts as soon as they are able to obtain credit. They always inhabit the best houses, some of them have sledges and nets for seal-catching, but very few own a kayak and scarcely any at all an umiak. In the years 1867–8 a savings bank was opened for the use of the natives and the Europeans of the subordinate class whose families were Greenlanders. In 1873 the following deposits were lodged in it: contributions to the support of illegitimate children 200*l.*, sums gained by inheritance or on other accidental occasions, 199*l.* 10*s.*, savings belonging to people living upon fixed wages, but chiefly the Europeans amongst them, 791*l.*, savings belonging to the rest of the population, 121*l.*

What we have here stated will be sufficient to prove that the efforts made to civilise the inhabitants have been hitherto attended with little success as regards promoting a desire to accumulate property. It may be asserted that the foreigners settled in the country are the only class able, or in some measure privileged, to lay up stores or possess money beyond a very limited amount, on account of their being exempt from the obligation of sharing with their neighbours in times of emergency. In Greenland, whenever want or famine is spoken of as impending in some hamlet, people only calculate how much there has been taken in hunting or fishing there, but there is never any question as to whom the provisions may belong.

Any native who may try to secure the prosperity of his family by saving and accumulating property, will sooner or later be obliged to help his more careless kindred or neighbours. The limits of what he is considered entitled to keep for his private use are evidently even narrower now than in former times. If he tries to surpass them by saving money and provisions, his life will become a continual struggle against solicitations for coffee and biscuits from his house-fellows, and for blubber and dried fish from his neighbours. If he keeps supernumerary utensils and implements he will be obliged to lend them to others, and to lend is the same as to lose. The result of his efforts will first be the title of niggard, and it is very curious to see the readiness with which the European residents who are well lodged amidst their storehouses, join in accusing such men of being avaricious. In his embarrassment three ways are open to him. The first is to make his house smaller and thereby narrow the circle of his house-fellows. The second is to remove to another place in order to get rid of troublesome neighbours, and the last one is to apply for the European's protection, especially by entering their service. All of these expedients are now and then tried, but, as we have seen, the seal-hunters have troubles enough merely from their own daily occupation, and the result of this additional inconvenience is that, sooner or later, they become disheartened, throw up the game, abandon themselves to indifference and resignation, and very often the greatest seal-hunters and most industrious men end their lives in want and misery.

CHAPTER XI.

KNOWLEDGE AND ENLIGHTENMENT.

Language and Traditions.—From their ancient stage of culture the natives still retain two treasures unaltered, viz. their language and their traditional tales. There are three important obstacles which have contributed to secure a remnant of independence and national feeling to the natives by keeping them separate from the foreigners, viz. their habitations, their language, and their traditions. The houses have already been described. The language we may assert has not suffered the least alteration, being the ancient Eskimo idiom spoken with a few variations of dialect from Greenland to Labrador and the north-eastern corner of Siberia. It differs from the whole group of European languages, not merely in the sound of the words, but more especially in the construction. Its most remarkable feature is that a sentence of a European language is expressed in Greenlandish by a single word constructed out of certain elements, each of which answers in some degree to one of our words, and moreover the order in which they are arranged is almost the opposite of that in which they are placed in the corresponding sentence in our own languages. Of course strangers who have not passed their childhood in Greenland will seldom acquire any real familiarity with the language, although several missionaries have spoken it with tolerable fluency and correctness. On the other hand, the Greenlanders are very disinclined to learn Danish. Hardly 1 per cent. of them is able to speak a few words, and probably not 2 per cent. understand it in the least. As it is always very difficult for foreigners to understand Greenlandish perfectly, the traditional tales narrated in this language will be still more unintelligible to them. It must be remembered that to people like the original Eskimo, their traditions represent their literature, history, religion, and poetry. Tales which are handed down unaltered, some for hundreds, others for thousands of years, only by means of verbal narration, of course require to be popular. Above all, they must be perfectly intelligible without explanation, and for this reason adapted to the mode of life of the inhabitants and the physical features of the country ; but for the same reason they appear trifling and childish to people who have grown up in countries more favoured by nature and civilisation.

Another circumstance makes them at the same time unintelligible and mysterious to the European listener, viz. the ancient religious ideas which are thoroughly interwoven in these narratives. The folklore is the source from which the successive generations have continued to learn the opinions of their ancestors concerning the supernatural world, and by which the ancient faith has been preserved. But on the other hand, the tales are far from being didactic, or on the whole appealing rather to the intelligence than to the imagination. The narrators insensibly imbue their auditors with doctrines which they mention or hint at as being well known to them beforehand, and which consequently are learned in the same way as people learn to speak their mother-tongue. For this reason the stranger meets with the same difficulty here as in trying to make himself familiar with the language. The traditional tales in some measure form the definite boundary which separates the natives from the foreigners. We may imagine a European settler acquiring a perfect familiarity with the language, marrying a native woman, taking up his abode in a true native hut, and even pursuing the seal-hunt as well as he can, in short turn in almost all respects a Greenlander. Even in this case he will scarcely acquire any taste for the stories which will still form one of the chief entertainments of his house-fellows. They will remain to him childish, nonsensical, and obscure, if not quite unintelligible. As to the tales and traditions themselves, and the ancient religion, the author must refer the reader to the book which he has published on these subjects. Here we have only to consider the folklore in general as far as it may be necessary for the purpose of understanding the opinions and the intellectual development of the modern Christianised Greenlanders.

Ancient Superstitions. — What we define as ancient superstition still maintained by the Greenlanders in reality constitutes a system of belief, by which their ancient religion has been so altered as to make a reconciliation possible between it and the Christian doctrine. The ancient faith involved a very distinct conception of the soul as in some way independent of the body. The whole visible world was ruled by supernatural powers denominated ' owners,' and the soul might probably be considered as such an owner or ruler of the body. There existed an under-world and an upper-world to which the souls of the deceased departed, the under-world being preferable as it afforded happy abodes to all who had striven and suffered much in the present life, whereas cold and hunger were encountered in the upper-world. Men were able to obtain supernatural assistance from the invisible

powers by the help of prayers and amulets, but this assistance was always more or less directly derived from the
priests or angakoks who had acquired their wisdom and
power from the supreme invisible ruler Tornarsuk, who
gave them some of the subordinate rulers for 'tornaks,' or
guardian spirits.   Consequently some idea of godhead has
been connected with Tornarsuk, and there existed a whole
system of doctrines concerning the supernatural assistance
to be obtained from him through the subordinate powers.
But besides this aid, which was considered good and lawful,
there existed another supernatural influence which was
wholly opposed to that derived from Tornarsuk.   The art of
invoking this power corresponds to what we understand by
witchcraft, being the worst form of evil, or representing
selfishness in the narrowest sense.   It was always practised
in secret, and with the object of injuring others only for
the gratification of the practisers.

    We have already stated that the first missionaries, after
having deprived Tornarsuk of his rank as the supreme
being, installed him as the Christian devil. This position he
still greatly occupies in the imagination of the Greenlanders, he being now only awful and terrible.   He is at times
said to have been seen here and there, the lower part of his
body always quivering, and he always disappears suddenly,
sinking into the earth.   Another supernatural being of high
reputation, the Arnarkuagsak, an old woman who resided
in the depths of the ocean, ruling over all the inhabitants of
the sea, was made the grandmother of the devil.   She is
still called 'the mother of him below there,' and believed to
have some power over the seals and whales, but she is not
considered an evil being.   The natives avoided the collision
which would arise between the upper-world of the pagans
and the Christian heaven, by placing the latter still higher,
or beyond the solid blue vault which was supposed to expand

over the former. Traditions exist of apertures having been
observed forming in the vault, through which psalm-singing
was heard, and, according to others, travels have been
undertaken by souls who were temporarily delivered from
the body, and wandered through the ancient to the Christian
heaven.

But a greater embarrassment was met with in trying
to reconcile the idea of the Christian hell with that of
the ancient happy abodes of the deceased. The traditions describe how the souls of the last angakoks who were
unwilling to become converted were perceived after death
to sink roaring into the depths of the earth. As to the
ideas of good and evil, a revolution in the ideas of the
natives could not be avoided. The moral evil of the
heathens, of course, was all that was contrary to laws and
customs, as regulated by the angakoks, and for this reason
derived from Tornarsuk, while the height of evil was witchcraft, or applying to an occult power in opposition to
Tornarsuk and the whole order of society maintained by
the angakoks. Invoking the supernatural powers under
the rule of Tornarsuk was chiefly comprised in what they
called 'serranek,' which may be most closely translated by
'prayers,' and in some measure also included the acquisition of amulets. Witchcraft being the opposite to serranck
was signified by 'kusuinek,' and the perfected practice
of it by 'iliseenek.' But now the Christian teachers confounded both kinds of invocations, comprising them under
the common denomination of 'serranek,' paralleling the
witches with the angakoks, and considering both together
as devil-worshippers.

On the other hand, Egede being in want of an adequate
expression for the notion of 'sin,' formed a new word,
hardly pronounceable by Greenlanders, out of the corresponding Danish denomination. The result of these trans-

formations in connection with the imperfect conversation by means of the Greenlandish language, could only be that the natives conceived the idea of virtue and sin as what was pleasing or displeasing to Europeans, as according or disaccording with their customs and laws. To this very day the members of the Moravian communities are divided into the 'obedient' and 'disobedient,' viz. with respect to the missionaries. The ideas of 'kusuinek' and 'serranek,' however, being too incompatible, the natives have made a compromise by still considering the former to be the essence of evil, while the second is only to be abstained from on account of its being unbecoming or indecorous in baptised people.

Supernatural Beings.—According to the ancient faith the whole universe was filled with the supernatural rulers we have already referred to, each of whom had his separate dominion. The existence of this spiritual world was confirmed by Tornarsuk being made the devil, and the others his servant demons. Consequently, to this very day the natives maintain the existence of all the supernatural beings who inhabit the vast interior country, or roam about on the sea or in the air, and who make themselves visible only under peculiar circumstances or to certain people. The particulars of this subject must be sought for in the Traditional Tales, and the account of the ancient religion which the author has given as an introduction to them. A few remarks may suffice here. The spiritual world is always more or less dreaded, and visions from it are considered to be dangerous, and require peculiar measures to be taken lest they become injurious; but on the other hand the invisible powers are able to render assistance to man in various cases. As a rule it is maintained that baptism, which must be performed, or at least confirmed, by a European, at once protects man against any hurtful

influence from the spiritual world, and in some degree makes
other measures superfluous. Most especially people are
inclined to lay aside their fears as far as the invisible rulers
required abstinence to be observed or inflicted other con-
straint. But on the other hand, as regards the favourable
influences from the same world, its aid is not refused if
offered spontaneously, and in many cases complete reliance
is placed in it. Probably exculpation is sought for on the plea
of the aid being rendered by the subordinate demons, and
not by the devil himself. Some of the supernatural beings
derive their origin from still existing beings, men as well as
animals. The dead are believed to reappear as ghosts,
making themselves known by certain signs, the gentlest
one being that of whistling. Nobody has greater power to
appease them than the Moravian missionaries; not even
the least whistle is perceptible from those who have
been duly buried in their church-yard. Everybody who has
stayed in Greenland will have heard people speaking of
'kivigtoks,' viz. persons who for some reason or other,
especially on account of being ill-treated or offended, have
fled from the society of man and taken up their abodes in
the interior country, from whence they will for ever threaten
their offenders. They are now supposed to enter into
alliance with Tornarsuk, and, as some say, they will live till
the day of judgment. Another sort of spectres most frequently mentioned in the tales, the 'anghiaks,' or ghosts
of children who were born in secret and killed, although
formerly considered some of the most terrible, are now but
little regarded. The kayakers who perish at sea have
totally ceased to be revived, and return as 'anghiniartoks,'
the mere sight of baptised people being sufficient to scare
them away. In the southernmost places they are seen now
and then, owing to the vicinity of the heathenish Eastlanders.

Of the numerous classes of supernatural beings who are not akin to mankind, the 'ingnersuaks' are the most popularly known. They live beneath the surface of the earth, having their abodes in the cliffs along the sea-shore. They are divided into two classes, the upper or the benevolent, and the lower or malignant ingnersuaks. The former accompany the kayaker, assisting and guarding him, but are invisible to himself, and only to be seen by others at a certain distance. The latter, on the contrary, persecute the kayakers, and draw them down to their abodes, where they keep them in painful captivity. Even the most enlightened native entertains not the least doubt about the existence of these spirits, at once the guardians and the enemies of the kayakers. Proofs of their having rendered them assistance are found in cases of escape from imminent danger, and the wounds discovered on the captured animals bearing evidence of having been inflicted by other weapons than those of the hunter himself. On the other hand kayakers who did not return have been supposed to stay with the malevolent ingnersuaks. Various beings, partly resembling mankind, partly beasts, people the vast interior of the country. The most renowned 'inlanders' are the 'tuneks,' who have their dwellings also in regions frequently visited by man, the entrances to their habitations being covered with sod and shrubs. They are twice, or even several times, as large as men, and very conversant with sorcery. But the 'Inuarudligaks,' of whom many stories are also told, are a sort of dwarf people who have taught the Europeans the art of manufacturing fire-arms, being possessed of a 'pointing weapon' by which men and animals may be killed merely by aiming at them. They are also highly esteemed on account of their cleanli-ness, their habitations being as handsome as those of the Europeans.

As supernatural means of summoning help and averting evil influences from the spiritual world, amulets are still frequently made use of, and some 'serratit' or magic spells must also still be known, both, however, being kept secret. A curious instance of a complicated superstitious ceremony was observed in South Greenland some years ago. A kayak which was put upon land and secured as usual was perceived to move apparently by itself. The owner of the kayak on being informed of this applied to a certain man amongst his comrades, asking him to fire two blank shots with his gun into the kayak, one towards the stern, another towards the prow, each time pronouncing certain words. On making enquiry as to the meaning of this proceeding it was found out that the owner had believed the motion of the kayak to have been caused by a witch who, in an invisible state, had crept into it for the purpose of bewitching it. The man whom he had selected to fire at her was a 'piarkusiak,' *i.e.*, a man born by a mother whose preceding children had died at an early age, for which reason he was considered peculiarly proof against all kinds of deadly influences, especially witchcraft. The words pronounced were, of course, a magic spell.

An extraordinarily effective amulet for the purpose of restoring health to a child and conferring longevity on it is supplied by its navel-string, which, for this reason, is sometimes carefully preserved. European articles, strange to say, such as coffee-berries and pieces of newspapers, are also used for amulets, probably owing to the original and still existing belief in the virtue attaching to anything that has been in peculiar contact with the civilised strangers. But it appears remarkable that scarcely anything that refers to the Christian religion is used as an amulet, or with other superstitious aims. The only examples of this kind which the author has become acquainted with, are, perhaps, the habit of making the sign of the cross to calm delirious people during their state of delirium, and to scare them away 'when they reappear as ghosts after death,' and the custom of using leaves out of psalm-books for gun-wadding in shooting at certain dangerous spectres. The mysterious formalities which the Moravians attach to the participation in the Lord's Supper, specially in admitting no spectators to it, have given rise to the belief that anybody who witnesses it without permission will be struck blind.

If the first Europeans believed they had convinced the natives that their angakoks were impostors, they were greatly mistaken, because even at present no Greenlander doubts that they once possessed the powers for which they are so greatly admired in the traditions, only allowing that they derived their powers from their alliance with the devil.

Greenlanders' Names.—One remarkable feature of ancient superstition is connected with naming the children. According to pristine custom, directly after birth the child was named after another person, generally a deceased relative. This act seems to have been performed by pronouncing a certain spell, and much importance was attached to it. It was supposed to secure rest to the dead, and to create a sort of peculiar relationship between him and his namesake. But if the latter had died only a short time before, or under peculiarly grievous circumstances, the name was not allowed to be pronounced without necessity, and chiefly for this reason everybody generally had at least two names, one of which was given afterwards and only intended for common use. Now the missionaries in baptising the first converts declined to give them Greenlandish names. The natives on their part were also much pleased at acquiring European names, though the ancient custom of adopting the names of the deceased was too deeply rooted to be abandoned. For this reason they have continued to the present day to name the children directly after birth, and in this way the national names of their ancestors have been handed down to the present inhabitants. They call this name 'atekok,' or 'remnant of name,' and everybody has one of this kind, but it is never used, and the habit of giving it has been kept so secret that it has almost escaped the observation of the missionaries.

Meanwhile the natives, from a tendency to ape the foreigners, took such a fancy to adopting European names, that the missionaries were at a loss how to put a stop to the multiplicity of names which the parents wanted to confer upon their child at its baptism. It was not without much difficulty and resistance on the part of the natives that the number was limited to six. Moreover, the European names are so incompatible with the Greenland tongue that the natives are much disinclined to pronounce them. It has happened that parents, on applying to the missionary to have their child baptised, could only notify the name to be given to it by circumstantial description of the person after whom it was to be named, and could not be induced to pronounce it themselves. In some cases the Christian name is wholly altered, such as Alfred to Faffaree, or Leopoldus to Pustusee, but a Greenlandish nickname is very often adopted for daily use. Moreover, according to ancient custom, the name is altered in case of its being the same as that of a recently deceased relative or friend.

To these remarks on the habits referring to personal names we may finally add that the Greenlanders are very reluctant to pronounce their own names. On being asked they generally give a sign to some other person who may be present, desiring him to take the task of answering, but when this one also happens to be more than

usually bashful, the result may be the following scene :—
The man to whom the question is directed only answers
by a push to his neighbour, who then reluctantly whispers
something to him, whereupon the first one plainly replies,
' **Jakugôᴋ**,' i.e. '*he says* (that my name is) Jacob.'

Traditional Tales.—From what we have here stated about
the remains of the ancient religion which still exist, it will be
evident that the traditions exercised a wider dominion and
are more deeply rooted than what generally we understand
by superstition in other countries, where Christianity is not
imported and maintained by strangers who only take up a
temporary residence amongst the people whom they have
undertaken to civilise, without blending or amalgamating
with them in the least degree. One of the difficulties met
with by the author in persuading the natives to communicate their traditions to him was their fear of being sus-
pected of maintaining heathenish ideas, and, on looking
back to our preceding account, it will be evident that they
have sufficient reason to guard themselves against being
misapprehended and treated in a reckless manner as regards
their national peculiarities. It appears by no means improbable that on perceiving that the superstition of the
Greenlanders is nourished and supported by their traditional tales, some European might attempt to prevent their
repetition by accusing of paganism those who participated in
this amusement. When such a proposal could be made
with a view to help the material prosperity of the Greenlanders as that of prohibiting their purchasing coffee, the
thought of promoting their mental welfare by dissuading
from telling their old stories seems not to be so very improbable. But we may also as surely assert that such effort
will be futile ; that the traditions, perhaps, may become
corrupted and rendered more stupid, but that they never
will vanish as long as the habitations, the mode of life,

and the social conditions of the natives arc the same as now. It must be remembered that to the natives they are *almost their only poetry.* It is obvious that daily life at a Greenland winter station offers only scanty variation and subjects of conversation to its inhabitants, and that it has lost a great part of its means of excitement by the cessation of their ancient national festivals. The long time which has to be passed in their winter huts, whose narrowness renders occupations as well as amusements difficult, has to be filled up.

The Greenlanders, on account of their free sporting life, are not stupefied by their pauperism in the same degree as the lower classes of more civilised countries. Their imagination retains a certain degree of vivacity, and requires a nourishment which their present intercourse with foreigners is unable to afford. It is, therefore, not to be wondered at that they cling eagerly to their old stories, which, being narrated in their houses, are withdrawn from European criticism, and will be as necessary to their mental requirements as food is for their physical nutriment. The tales, of course, reflect the taste and ideas peculiar to the people who have preserved them through the lapse of ages, showing what they consider merry and great, or, on the other hand, sad and detestable, in nature and human life. As regards nature, they mostly give us a picture of the difficulties and hardships with which man has to struggle, and, on the other hand, almost the only object required to make people merry is success in hunting, an ample supply of seals, or, to use a Greenlandish phrase, ' bringing home seals in such a quantity as if they had crept on shore of their own accord.' This being the case, the Greenlander is heedless of the severity of the season, of the snow, and barrenness of the soil around his abode, and does not at all long to bask in the sunshine of the more genial regions which he may visit occasionally in his summer travels.

But the greater the difficulties to be vanquished by the hero the more attractive, of course, grows the story. The narrators have a peculiar inclination to begin with picturing a child in a state of extreme weakness and destitution, and then make it pass through different stages of development, until it becomes 'saperfêrutoĸ,' *i.e.* having nothing impossible to oneself. Or their hero makes his appearance as a suitor who by his marriage acquires several brothers-in-law, all clever industrious hunters, while he prolongs his honeymoon, squandering his days in utter idleness, feasting upon their game without caring for their reproaches. But then a severe winter sets in, seals become scarcer, and at last famine threatens them. When all the brothers-in-law have given up their hunting and resolved upon staying at home, when the last bit of blubber is about to be consumed, then the time has come for the hero to show himself in all his glory. Then he digs out his kayak deeply buried under the snow, or he ascends the highest mountain tops for the purpose of looking out for openings in the ice where seals may be found, and from this moment he alone provides abundantly for the whole household. Pursuing the seal-hunt of course is the first duty of a man as long as his strength and state of health will allow it ; but indulgence is shown if an aged provider leaves his duties to his grown-up son and rests on his laurels, or, as sometimes the narrators say, ' to have a luxurious life for his only aim.'

However, old age offers him an opportunity of acquiring the highest pitch of admiration by braving its infirmities ; this is what has secured immortal fame to a certain Nivnitak, who was father and grandfather to a number of vigorous men. When the usual calamities of a severe winter had caused all the active youths to throw up the game and lie prostrate on their couches prepared for death by starvation, the old man ascended the highest mountain top, from which he perceived openings in the ice many miles out to sea visible from the haze resting over them. Thither he repaired, and in the evening he returned to the house in profuse perspiration, pushing a seal before him through the entrance. In this way he saved the lives of all the inmates, and so he continued for several days until he was weary of this monotonous life, and one morning made his escape by running right out to sea. There far out he had observed the track of a sledge, and now he followed it and arrived at the fabulous country of Akilinek ; and that the adventures he had gone in search of were not only those of sport he proved by falling in love with and taking two young wives there. After having performed great deeds and outdone the heroes of Akilinek, he became wearied also of this life, and began to long for his home. But now he had the greatest difficulty in getting rid of the ties in which he so thoughtlessly entered, on account of his being carefully watched by his house-fellows. Making his escape from them was his masterpiece as regards dexterity and quickness, and for this purpose he had ordered his wives to make a very narrow dress for him. So he returned to his old country, crossing the frozen sea again, and there he lived till he had seen his grandchildren's grandchildren.

The ideas of the supernatural world displayed in the tales by means of their allegoric sense also tend to enliven the pictures sketched in them. We need only refer to the benevolent 'ingnersuaks' as revealing the confidence in a superior guardianship which strengthens the kayakers in encountering the dangers figuratively embodied in the malevolent ingnersuaks. Both of them live in the cliffs which he has to pass every day, but when he ventures

further out to sea of course the risk increases, and it is not
to be wondered that there he meets with the ' kayariaks,'
that is to say, men in kayaks of extraordinary size, who by
help of charms can raise sudden storms, or with the monstrous gulls who have carried off many kayakers, taking
them as food for their young.   How strikingly does the
belief in kivigtoks paint the regret for having offended or
ill-treated relatives, and the painful thoughts which will
torment the offenders as long as they live !   In the amulets
and spells inherited from their ancestors we find expressed
remembrances of their carefulness and love, encourag-
ing the owner to encounter dangers by following their
example.

The traditional tales are adapted to attract the attention of every age and sex.   The boy listens open-mouthed
to the praises of exploits which also are to become the aim
of his life.   The task which lies before him was once the
only way to honour and prosperity for a man.   Now
although it is still as necessary as ever for the welfare of
society, its praise only sounds in the narrow habitations ;
there it still tends to strengthen his courage and instigate
his ambition.   But the female sex is by no means excluded
from the story-teller's tale.   The wife is the only one who
takes care to economise in the time when need is impending ; in many cases lives have been saved by means of the
small portions of blubber and dried fish which she had
laid by and did not share out until want had reached its
extreme limits.   But especially is there celebrated the bene-
volence and mercy of the old widow, who takes care of
the poor orphan child that has been rejected and ill-treated
by the rough and haughty men of the place, and she is
amply rewarded by her foster-son soon growing a clever
provider for her.   Finally, when the entertainment passes
to its most favoured subject of mirth, the old bachelors, then

none are more ready, or, indeed, more entitled, to burst into laughter than the female sex, and numerous are the oddities and ridiculous tricks which are imputed to the poor fellows who resolve or were obliged to live in 'single blessedness.'

On passing from the folk-lore preserved merely by verbal tradition to the printed literature of Greenland, we must mention that a few old manuscripts have been found in the possession of the natives containing stories of European origin, which they had preserved in this way by copying them, such as 'Pok : or a Greenlander's Journey to Denmark,' 'Sibylle,' 'Oberon,' and 'Holger the Dane.' The existence of these documents proves that European tales may have some attraction for the natives, but not so much that they have been able to remember them without writing them down. The details of these stories in their Greenland versions of course frequently appear very curious.

The Literature of the Greenlanders.—The literature of the Greenlanders printed in the Eskimo language amounts to about as much as might make fifty ordinary volumes. Most of it has been printed in Denmark, but, as already mentioned, a small printing-office was established at Godthaab in Greenland in 1862, from whence about 280 sheets have issued, besides many lithographic prints. As regards its contents the Greenlandish literature includes the following books, of which, however, many are very small or mere pamphlets.

The Bible, in four or five larger parts and some smaller sections as separate parts.

Three or four volumes, and several smaller books, containing psalms.

About twenty books concerning religious objects.

About ten books serving for manuals in spelling, arithmetic, geography, history, &c.

About sixteen books, with stories or other contents chiefly entertaining.

About six grammars and dictionaries in the Eskimo language for Europeans.

A Journal : **Atuagagdliutit, nalinginarmik tusaruminá-sassumik univkât,** i.e. 'something for reading, accounts of all sorts of entertaining subjects,' published in Greenland since 1861. Up to 1874 it comprised 194 sheets in quarto, and about 200 leaves with illustrations.

Official reports concerning the municipal institutions, 1862 to 1872, in Danish and Greenlandish, comprising about twenty-six sheets, besides many lithographic plates containing accounts and statistical returns.

Church and Public Instruction.—For *missionary affairs*, comprising church-matters as well as public instruction, the natives are divided into the Danish and the Moravian communities ; the former numbered 7,703, and the latter 1,945 souls in the year 1860. We have already mentioned the native catechists or schoolmasters, and the extreme difficulty of affording regular school instruction to a poor people so widely dispersed. Under such circumstances the fact is rather surprising that the ability to read and write may be said to be as common here as in any civilised country. We can confidently assert that the greater part of the inhabitants are able to read tolerably well out of every book in their own language, and that every child learns to read at least the chief passages of their usual school-books. The art of reading is not only familiar in every house, but reading also forms a favourite occupation. As to the objects of this reading we refer to the list before given of the Eskimo literature. Of course the religious part of it is still the most popular, or until of late, we may say, the only one commonly used. The New Testament especially, and a psalm-book, are found in every house. As regards skill in writing

it must be said to be at least more than half as common as
in reading. Carrying on correspondence by letters has
become pretty frequent between the natives of the different
stations, and whenever something has to be communicated
to or by a Greenlander in any station, there is scarcely
ever any doubt as to the possibility of settling the affair
by letter. Moreover, the natives seem to be peculiarly
talented as to acquiring a good hand in writing. The
Eskimo language has always been written with the common
Roman letters, with addition of the letter к, signifying a
very guttural **k**, and of accents which are of great importance. As regards orthography a great irregularity has
prevailed, until of late a very ingenious and simple system
has been invented by Mr. S. Kleinschmiedt, who has published a grammar and a dictionary of the language.

Religious instruction is mostly imparted through the
Holy Scriptures themselves, but class-books are also used,
especially with regard to the chief Christian doctrines.

We have already stated that the obstacles to public instruction, caused by the scantiness of the population and
its dispersion, have only been overcome with help of the
native teachers. Formerly only very few of them received
any particular preparation for this task. Now all the more
populous places are furnished with schoolmasters, who
have been trained at the two seminaries, which in 1875
were reduced to one, established at Godthaab. At these
two schools it has been the custom for from ten to sixteen
young natives from different parts of the country to study
for some years, and to receive instruction in the following
studies. Exegesis ; explanation of the leading Christian
doctrines ; Bible history ; geography of the Holy Land ;
passages of the Bible learnt by heart ; exercises in writing
on different subjects, mostly religious ; mental exercises by
reading and explaining books of no religious tendency ;

elements of history, mostly relating to the origin and the propagation of Christianity ; elements of geography, chiefly with regard to physical geography ; an introduction to natural history, with a special description of the mammalia ; the elements of arithmetic ; caligraphy ; organ-playing and singing, together with catechistical and homiletical practice. The Danish language has also been among the branchés of education taught, but with little success. It has been a rule that during their stay at the seminaries the pupils should continue to practise kayaking, and for this purpose they were ordered to have their kayaks in a proper state, and certain days were devoted to going out in kayaks during the lecture ' term,' while they had the whole summer at their own disposal for this as well as other national occupations.

Scarcely any country exists where children are so ready to receive school instruction as Greenland ; it is almost considered more a diversion than a duty. Attending divine service is not less popular, and is scrupulously observed by the population. Most likely this inclination is favoured by the holidays now offering the only opportunity for festive assemblies, and by the natives on these occasions feeling themselves equal to the Europeans. But it is a mistake to believe that they would prefer to have a clergyman of their own nation officiating. On the contrary, at Godthaab, where the Danish and the Moravian stations are situated close to each other, it has happened that when the native ' vicar ' had to preach in the Danish church, the members of the community repaired to the Moravians only for the purpose of hearing a European officiating. No displeasure at all is taken at the imperfect pronunciation of the Eskimo language, to which the usage of more than a hundred years has perfectly accustomed them.

We must add that the natives seem to be more than

usually gifted with a taste as well as a talent for music. No chief station is in want of a musician whenever people wish to have a dance ; playing the fiddle is a very common accomplishment all over Greenland, and in some places a sort of cithern is also used. Of course the musicians have always learned merely by ear, without any regular instruction. A few of them have even made their fiddles themselves. They have also nice voices, but except singing psalms at divine service, singing is generally only practised by women in attending children and in rowing. There exist a number of melodies for these purposes which are very characteristic, and evidently to a great degree the fruit of native composition. Whether any of them are of unmixed native origin, representing a relic of the ancient art of singing, is doubtful, but not improbable ; a few of these which are heard at the southernmost stations sound very agreeably. In the winter houses here and there, especially in isolated places, the old monotonous songs, perhaps also accompanied with the drum, are said still to be used, but rarely when Europeans are present.

CHAPTER XII.

CUSTOMS AND LAWS; STATISTICS.

Courtship and Marriage.—When on the introduction of Christianity marriage was made a religious ceremony, it could not but become a subject of European interference. The peculiar mode in which the ancient suitors used to practise their courtship, viz. by resorting more or less to force, gave the missionaries immediate occasion to take the management of the whole affair into their own hands, although the apparent ravishing of the bride had, no doubt, in the main been nothing but a ceremony. The missionary Saaby, in his Journal from the years 1770 to 1778, gives us an account of the task thus forced on the missionaries which is so characteristic that the way in which matrimonial connections have since been effected cannot be better explained than by quoting his words.

'These violent wooings,' he says, in his peculiar sincere and simple style, 'of course we could not allow to be continued by the baptised Greenlanders; for this reason they trust the matter to the priest, and the proceedings then are as follow. The suitor comes to the priest, saying, " I should like to have a wife." " Whom?" He names her. " Hast thou spoken with her?" Sometimes they will say, "Yes, she is not unwilling, but thou knowest womankind." More frequently they will answer, " No." " Why not?" " It is difficult; girls are prudish, thou must speak to her." In this case the priest summons the girl. She comes, and after some casual questions he begins the proposal in the following way. " I think it is time now to have thee married." " I won't marry ! " " What a pity ; I had a suitor for thee." " Whom ? " The priest names him. " He is good for nothing, I won't have him." Then the priest enumerates his good qualities. " He is a young clever provider, throws his harpoon with dexterity and power, and above all he loves thee." She listens to his praise with attention and, as her manner indicates, with pleasure, but still she answers, " I won't marry ; I won't have him." " Well, I will not force thee, I shall soon find a wife for such a clever fellow." The priest then keeps silence, as if he considered her " No " as a decisive answer. At last she whispers with a sigh, and with tears in her eyes, " Just as thou wilt have it, priest." " No, as thou wilt ; I will not persuade thee." Then follows with a deep groan a " Yes," and the matter is settled.'

No doubt the programme here given has been the general form for these negotiations, but it will be evident that the power which was thus put in the hands of the missionaries could not fail to be made use of sometimes for other ends than merely arranging the matter to the satisfaction of the parties concerned. Saaby himself in the same diary mentions an instance of this kind, when merely for the purpose of maintaining the authority of his position in the opinion of the natives, he entered a house and by force compelled a father to give up his daughter, whom the missionary wanted to marry to a young man who had fallen in love with her. In the same way the Europeans interfered with affairs within the circle of the family itself. In former times the husband had the right of divorcing his wife, or inflicting slight personal chastisement. These rights were abolished and at the same time other circumstances rendered domestic discipline more difficult to the head of the family. According to Eskimo custom, scarcely any compulsory measures are resorted to in educating children : but it is the common opinion of the present Greenlanders that children were much more obedient in ancient times. When we remember these unfavourable influences, we not only wonder that the good behaviour of children who have passed the tenth or twelfth year, but that the ancient custom of a friendly way of conversing and of abstaining from high words and quarrelling is still generally maintained.

Family Festivals and Customs.—Few people pay so little attention to family festivals as the Greenlanders. As regards marriage, a tendency now exists to avoid having recourse to the aid of the missionary in settling the preliminaries, but in every case the man who resolves to give up his bachelor state will generally meet with hindrances which tend to deprive the nuptials of their solemnity. The object of his affections will still be liable to show the shamefacedness which renders it difficult for him to get a decisive answer, although such an agreement is necessary before he applies to the missionary to perform the ceremony, and moreover, he is not free from bashfulness himself. At the chief stations, where a missionary resides, there is more time to arrange the matter, but at stations where he only makes a short stay when on his travels, the embarrassment of the bridegroom is often so great that he puts off his communication till the very moment when the minister is getting into his boat again to depart. A curious instance of another but similar kind happened at such a place a few years ago. The communication to the minister having been made by the relations of the bridal pair, the community had assembled, and were all waiting for the fulfilment of the solemnity

with the exception of the bridegroom himself who was still
wanting. The following conversation then ensued between the minister and the assembly. ' Where is the
man whom I am to marry to this woman ? ' No answer.
' Have none of you seen him ? ' No answer. On running
his eyes over the assembly his suspicion was raised by
observing a man sitting with downcast eyes, and the evident
appearance of being in an uncomfortable position. ' Is not
that the very man, he who sits there ? ' No answer. ' Thou
there, hadst thou to be wedded to this woman ? ' The
answer was an affirmative nod. ' Thou hast perhaps
changed thy mind ? ' He nodded assent, and the ceremony
was at an end.

While in this way nuptial festivals are almost unknown
in Greenland, on the other hand conviviality on various
occasions connected with the children of a family is not
uncommon, such as when a boy has brought home his first
game, and, above all, when he has caught his first seal.
The christening of a child is also, if possible, generally
followed by a coffee-party, and in some cases the parents
imitate the Europeans in celebrating its birthday.

In cases of death some of the ancient customs of
mourning are still more or less observed, such as abstaining
from labour and neglecting their dress. Using the tools
and clothes of the deceased is also avoided, but if in certain
cases the inheritance has to be equally divided according
to Danish law, a blow of the auctioneer's hammer suffices
to break the spell. Funerals are performed in a very neg-
ligent and indifferent manner. The ancient mode of
burying under stone-heaps, built carefully on the top of low
hills, was abandoned as a relic of paganism. But on the
other hand the rocky soil, especially in winter, scarcely
admits of a proper interment according to European custom.
For this reason the burial-places often now display a very

sad appearance, the covering of sod and stones being
insufficient to conceal the corpses which have been either
laid down in rude coffins or sewed up in skins.

On account of the sort of community or partnership
with regard to certain property which arose from numbers
of families living together at the wintering stations, it was
a law of great importance that nobody could settle down
in such a place without consent of its inhabitants, This
law was of course completely disregarded by the Europeans,
but is still as far as possible maintained by those natives
whose dwelling-places have not as yet been made trade
stations. At the chief trading stations and missions the
ancient custom of distributing flesh and blubber gained in
the seal-hunt has been modified so as to refer only to
certain circles of the inhabitants, whereas in other places
it is still retained less altered. The intercourse between
the most distant parts of the coast which formerly arose
from the travelling life in summer has almost ceased.
Journeys are now mostly made only within the limits of
the district belonging to each chief station, and many
natives may be met with who have seen nothing of that
part of their country which lies more than 40, or even than
20, miles from their birth-place. This isolation, of course,
is in many respects detrimental to their prosperity and
intelligence.

Since the abolition of the ancient national festivi-
ties, the church festivals have become the only occasions
of public assemblies, and perhaps for this reason they
are also highly favoured and appreciated. Above all,
Christmas is celebrated by everybody, in so far that
they appear in their best attire and have a little
extra to feast upon. Early on Christmas morning young
people, headed by the catechist, go round and sing a psalm
before each house. At Easter, in some places, the custom

of the kiss of peace has been introduced, and whenever they have attended the Lord's Supper they have the privilege of shaking hands also with every European living at the place. The Greenlanders have no national mode of salutation either in meeting or in parting. The old Eskimo habit of rubbing noses is universally employed in petting children, and it is not quite out of use among grown-up people ; but generally when a guest arrives or enters a house not the least sign is made either by him or the hosts. On leaving a place they now sometimes say ' **inûvdluaritse,**' *i.e.* live well ; and to a European guest who leaves a house ' **aporniaкinatit,**' *i.e.* don't hurt thy head (viz. against the ceiling of the doorway), the latter probably being the most national of these phrases.

At the chief stations dancing in the European fashion is a very favourite amusement. Nothing else is required but permission to clear the workshop, the only preparation necessary for an ordinary ball. If a glass of corn brandy to the male, and a cup of coffee to the female members of the party be added it becomes a luxurious one. The presence of sailors from a ship tends to render it still more attractive. We have already mentioned that remains of the ancient singing entertainments still exist in remote places, and are resorted to in the long winter evenings. It is said that even nith-songs still may be connected with them.

When a Greenlander offers anything for sale he always leaves it to the buyer to settle the price of it. This habit arises either from his deeply rooted disinclination for commercial speculation, or his antipathy to binding himself by contract. For the same reason it was a long time before it became customary to enter into the European's service. Now, on the contrary, the position acquired by such appointment is considered superior to that of the free seal-hunter, and almost causes a man to pass to the opposite extreme, viz. that of having no will of his own.

Without intending to pronounce any judgment on the morality of the natives as regards their private life, it may be asserted that any sort of licentiousness or indecency that might give rise to public offence is rare amongst themselves. But as regards their intercourse with strangers their behaviour is just the reverse. The scantiness of this intercourse in comparison to the number and dispersion of the natives prevents its having any generally obnoxious influence, but in certain places peculiarly favoured by the presence of an unusual number of foreigners—the scandal caused by them is surprising even to people who are well aware of the present state of the natives in general. That the female sex yield to the vanity excited by attracting the attention of members of the superior race is less to be wondered at than the complete want of self-respect and jealousy displayed by their countrymen and relatives on these occasions. As regards other vices or crimes it may suffice to say that making free with the property of others cannot be said to be common in Greenland.

Laws.—In reference to what we have already said concerning the ancient laws and customs, we may add that the following standing rules are still maintained, though modified in some degree by the contact with the Europeans.

As regards inheritance in cases of death the boat and tent, with the duties of a provider, pass to the eldest son, or to the nearest relation, if there is no grown-up son, and this relation adopts the children of the deceased as foster-children. Although widows with children are still more or less provided for by their housemates or kindred, they set up separate households, perhaps more frequently than in ancient time. Nevertheless the number of poor relatives who lay claim to the assistance of a provider seems to be greater now than formerly.

Lost property is generally considered to belong to the finder. With regard to wrecks of course this principle has not been maintained, but goods from such wrecks, or stranded goods in general, taken by the natives before the authorities could take possession of them, have mostly been recovered from the holders by a low payment. The right to drift-wood is made good by the finder carrying it above high-water mark and putting stones upon it. If a seal, after having been harpooned, makes its escape with the harpoon in it, it becomes the property of the finder, if the bladder has become detached, but the weapon still belongs to the proper owner.

All animals which on account of their size or from other circumstances are rare in the place where, or at the season when, they happen to be captured, are especially considered common property, generally only the head and the tail being reserved by the hunter for himself. As regards animals of the largest size, viz. the largest kinds of whales, which were formerly considered common property, certain restrictions have now been made when they have been captured by help of the boats and implements belonging to the Royal Board of Trade. Drift-whales, although taken possession of by the officials of the Trade, are nevertheless considered the property of the natives who take part in flensing them, inasmuch as full pay is usually given to them for the blubber and the whalebone. If a man happens to lose or injure tools or weapons which he has borrowed from another, he is not generally considered bound to make compensation for the loss or damage which he has caused to the owner.

Municipal Councils.—The municipal institutions we have already alluded to. They were commenced in 1857

for the southern, and in 1863 were extended to the northern
district, and adapted to both of them by regulations issued
by the Ministry of Home Affairs on February 1, 1872, of
which the chief points are as follows. A tax of 20 per cent.
on the amount paid annually by the Trade for produce purchased without the confines of each chief station is paid to
' The Greenlanders' Fund,' or the municipal fund. The
council of each chief station consists of the missionary as
president, some other officials of the trade and mission, and
a certain number of representatives elected by the natives
at the rate of about one to 120 of them. Only clever
kayakers are eligible, or men who have been so, and have
abandoned seal-hunting merely from bodily infirmity. The
natives cannot appeal to the council except through their
representative or guardian (**parsissoκ**). The council holds
two meetings every year, and the discussions are held in
the Eskimo language. Two kinds of aid are supplied by
the fund, assistance to people whose poverty is evidently
caused by their own idleness and negligence, and assistance
to a more deserving class. The relief to the poor has to be
given chiefly in the shape of the necessary tools and clothes
for enabling them to help themselves. In spring the
accounts are made up, showing the balance from the last
year, of which the greater part has to be distributed
among the providers who have received no aid at all from
the fund. The guardians have to divide them into three
classes according to their ability, and their shares are pro-
portioned accordingly. It is also the duty of the council
to investigate crimes and punish the offenders, to settle litigations and divide inheritances. The council imposes fines
for smaller offences, while more serious cases or crimes are
reported to the inspector. In cases of high misdemeanour
corporal punishment may be applied. In 1874 the municipal fund amounted to 7,271*l.*, and according to the returns

of the two years 1873 and 1874, the annual share from the Trade had been 1,721*l.* on an average, while the annual expenses had been—relief of the poor 279*l.*, other support 225*l.*, administration and printing-office 263*l.*, savings divided amongst the 'providers' 758*l.* During the first ten or twelve years the following causes were submitted to trial. One single cause of having in passion occasioned the death of a person, and another of openly threatening; four or six instances of grosser theft or cheating, and as many of concealment of birth and crimes relating to matrimony; every year a few petty thefts, and instances of making use of the tools of others without permission, or suchlike disorders, and several trifling litigations.

Census and Population.—Egede estimated the number of natives to have been 30,000 on his arrival in the country. This seems to have been an exaggeration, although very likely the coast was more densely peopled in ancient time than now. The statements of the number having been 5,122 in the year 1789 and 6,282 in 1820 are also somewhat doubtful, but for the latest forty years the census has been more trustworthy, and especially since 1850 they may be considered very accurate. The number of natives in Danish Greenland was 7,356 in 1834, 8,501 in 1845, 9,648 in 1855, 9,588 in 1870, while during the same time the number of Europeans has varied from 196 to 237.

The proportion of females to males has been on an average as 1,118 to 1,000, while in Iceland it is 1,102, and in Denmark and the Faroe Islands there are 1,018 females to 1,000 males. The same comparison made for different ages shows a remarkable variation, proving that greater mortality is prevalent among the male sex in the prime of life, inasmuch as females are to males in an age below 15 years as 961 to 1,000, between 15 and 60 years as 1,199 to 1,000, and above 60 years as 1,920 to 1,000.

In the year 1860 out of 1,000 persons there were, under 15 years of age 419, between 15 and 60 years 551, over 60 years 20, of unknown age 10. This proves a remarkable predominance of the infantile age, the number of children under 15 years being for Denmark 337, for the Faroe Islands 324, for Iceland 344, per 1,000.

In the disastrous year 1857, the number of births was 233, of deaths 566, while during the subsequent three years the average number was 330 births and 279 deaths.

The increase of the population during a long period after 1820 gave rise to the opinion that its state on the whole was prosperous and promising. We have tried to show that the increase proved to be only temporary, and, as regards the conclusions drawn from it, illusory. An examination of the causes of death enumerated in the annual registers tends to corroborate this suggestion. A calculation founded upon a number of 4,770 deaths, which occurred between the years 1782 and 1853 in South Greenland, has given the result that 13·4 per cent. of them were caused by infantile diseases, and 25·9 per cent. by complaints of chest, whereas in the years after 1860 the same causes seem to be represented by 19·3 and 35·0 per cent. The deadly influences indicated by these numbers seem to refer to defective habitations, clothes, and disorderly mode of life, and are likely to gain ground as long as no improvement of these conditions may be perceived. But on the other hand, severe cold and short allowance seem to produce no *immediately* obnoxious effects as far as can be inferred from the number of deaths and the general state of health during the course of the year. In South Greenland the variation from prosperity to want, according to the seasons, is most regular. A calculation of the monthly average of deaths, which has been made up from the church registers of the southernmost stations for 26 years, gives the following results :—

Supply of food and mode of life	Per cents. of the number of deaths for the whole year
WINTER. Seals decreasing, fish are had recourse to instead of flesh—Occasional want of food—Staying in the winter huts—Diarrhœa being the chief sickness.	December, 7·5 January, 6·1 February, 5·6 March, 6·1
SPRING. Want of food rarely occurring—Partly favourable catch of seals and fatter kinds of fish—Removing from houses to tents.	April, 4·6 May, 5·4
SUMMER. Seal hunt increasing—Want of food never occurring—Travelling and dwelling in tents.	June, 7·1 July, 7·6 August, 11·8
AUTUMN. The chief seal-hunting season—Frequent intemperance in fat animal food and berries—Removing from tents to houses—The prevailing complaints being inflammation of the chest, with stitch, influenza, and obstructions.	September, 11·7 October, 13·3 November, 13·2

The average annual number of men who perish in kayak has been 23, or about 8 per cent. of the deaths.

CHAPTER XIII.

SKETCHES OF GREENLAND LIFE BY NATIVES.—A SE-
LECTION OF ARTICLES FROM THE 'GREENLAND
JOURNAL,' WRITTEN BY NATIVE GREENLANDERS ;
TRANSLATED FROM THE ESKIMO LANGUAGE.

(1) **A Perilous Adventure of the Inhabitants of Southern
Upernivik (about 72° N. lat.) on January 3, 1873.**

[It must be remembered that what in this report is
meant by 'day' is only a few hours' twilight.]

On the morning of this day all the hunters set out
upon the new ice for the purpose of shooting. Just as they
had posted themselves at the border of the open water a
breeze sprang up that soon turned into a heavy gale, for
which reason Hans, Jens, and Mathias, and the three sons
of the Europeans repaired to their homes. But the following people—Benjamin, Martin, Thomas Ole, the teacher
Peter Ville, Mathæus, Carl, Zacharias, Frederik, Jörgen,
Peter, and Jacob remained. A little later, Martin, on
going homeward, was stopped by a fissure in the ice on
account of which he returned and warned the others.
They then all set out together and came to the fissure,
which they found had enlarged, and none of them having
a kayak they were at a loss how to cross it. They turned
back speedily and made for the point of Kingitok (Island),
but before approaching it they perceived that the ice had

loosened from the shore and moved, being drifted towards the open sea. On account of the darkness setting in rapidly they lighted a fire with the shafts of their toks (sticks headed by a chisel), nourishing the flame with blubber from their catch, and fired their guns to make themselves heard. At last people on shore, being on the look-out, perceived the perilous state of their countrymen. Those who are mentioned as having returned had made the land in another place, and did not come home before nightfall. They would fain have succoured them in their kayaks, but the new ice rendered it quite impossible. Keeping a continued look-out, they at length towards morning lost sight of the fire and believed that all of them had perished. The day came, then night set in a second time, when the wind veered to the seaside, making the ice drift towards the coast again. The men upon the ice then tried to reach the point of Ingnerit on the mainland, but they found the ice broken. After frightful exertions they at length approached the shore, but before they could gain a footing on it, the east wind set in afresh. When they were again drifting towards the open sea they made for their homeplace (situated upon an island), crawling upon their knees across some parts of the fragile ice. Benjamin then fell through, but the others assisted him, lifting him up on the ice again. A long time they took him with them, although he desired them to leave him, but at last, when he was quite unable to walk, and the ice proved to be too bad, they abandoned him to his fate. Later on, Peter, Mathæus, and Frederik also fell through, and one of them lost his rifle. They continued to move on for that night, and day broke again; they had now approached their land, but the ice being now quite impassable, they remained stationary and only waited for death. But daylight having set in, the people on shore

were surprised to see those whom they had already for a
long time believed to be dead still abiding on the ice.
Later on, the guardian Hans, and Mathias and three other
young people, set out in an open skin-boat, and following
a fissure they reached them at the utmost risk of their
own lives, and at length brought them to the shore.
Some of them suffered from frost, but the others were
soon after able to go out hunting again ; but all of them
felt aches in their arms and legs, and chiefly in their knees,
which had swollen from crawling along the ice.   Frederik,
however, was the only one confined to his couch from frost-
bitten feet.

(2) A Married Couple passing the Hunting Season lonely up the Country.

[This occurrence took place in the environs of Holstenborg (67° N. lat.) about the year 1866, and was written
down by the man in 1869.   Their whole equipment consisted of their clothes, a gun and ammunition.   The
manner in which he describes their changes from want
to abundance, from fears to composure, his dear companion being always his first care, is not without feeling
and picturesqueness.]

When first I began to go out hunting the reindeer and
they were still plentiful, I used to be very fond of that
sport, and only wished they had so continued.   Once
when the boat-parties set out for the fjord, a desire possessed me to follow them, although I was well aware that
the reindeer had now become scarcer.   Longing for the
sport, however, I only watched a chance of conveyance,
but in vain, till at length every one of the boat-owners had
left Kerrortusok (his dwelling-place), after which I started
by land on July 10, with Maria for my only companion.

At the beginning of our march we perceived that the snow
had not wholly disappeared on our way, and we crossed
the Kakarsunguit hills to avoid the largest snow-heaps.
On reaching the end of Kingartarsuit, we found the snow
as soft as foam, and taking hold of each other's hands, we
descended a rather steep declivity to gain the Kangerdluarsuk fjord.

At length we arrived at the head of the fjord wet to
the skin with fog and drizzling rain.   The brook being
swollen with muddy water we thought it impassable except
at low tide, for which reason we lighted a fire to warm
ourselves and waited for the tide running out.   Before it
was quite low, we crossed it and fitted our resting-place on
the other side.   The next day being fine we started and I
set out for the reindeer, but without getting sight of any.
At nightfall we again went up country, passed the brook at
the end of the Isortuarsuk-lake, and later on the following
day we tried to sleep but found it impossible on account
of the mosquitoes.   The top of the mountain we had to
ascend was enveloped in clouds, and it began to rain.   We
went to look for a place of shelter, because the rain was
pouring down faster and faster, but the only cave that I
knew of to be fit for sleeping in was still four miles off, the
day was wearing (of course no darkness existed during the
nights), and we had had no sleep for a couple of nights.
We persevered, however, being so much in want of rest,
and at length reached our goal, the cave.   We found it
perfectly dry inside, and there we had a good sleep.   We
awoke in the hopes of more favourable weather, but the
rain was still coming down in torrents and continued the
same the whole day.   On the third day I left Maria in
order to look for reindeer in the neighbourhood, but I
never got sight of a living thing.   The rain and mist did
not cease, and we were quite destitute of provisions.

At length the heavy rain lessened and ended in a drizzling mist, and with the aim of shooting some birds for a meal, I again took Maria with me, knowing that geese used to be found at the end of the Isortuarsuk-lake. Towards evening, to our great delight, we procured three geese, and our place of retreat was pretty comfortable, situated below a beetling rock, lined with fine grass, and sheltered by a hill like a low wall. So the rain passed by on the outside and we had no need to build up walls. Right in front of us was the small lake, and we could see the raindrops falling without getting wet ourselves, but we could not walk about, and only had the geese that resorted to the lake for our food. When two weeks had passed by in this way and fine weather set in, the geese totally disappeared, and my poor companion feared she would suffer from starvation. I wholly complied with her desire of repairing to the people of Sarfanguak, but on reaching the river we had to pass over, we found its waters had risen and overflown its banks, offering no possibility of fording, for which reason I again returned to the north with her. When I was most distressed on account of her suffering for want of food, I spoke to her, saying: 'A father will strive as hard as he can to prevent his children dying from hunger, and yet he may not be able to hinder it, but I know that God has created me and will not permit me to die from starvation, and he is capable of prohibiting it.' We now climbed the south side of the Igangnak-hill, and at noon I got a couple of ptarmigans which we broiled and ate. Having wandered the whole day without catching sight of the reindeer, at nightfall I again shot two ptarmigans, which we also made a meal of. After our night's rest, on the next day, I shot a reindeer. On July 28 we at length fell in with them.

When we had chosen a new resting-place on the land-

ward side of Pisigsarfik, the weather again changed, and
the next day set in with snow and cold, the small watercourses were frozen up and ceased to flow. If I had got
no reindeer we should have suffered much from cold. But
on the following day, when the weather had somewhat
improved, on taking a walk, I shot three reindeer, and now
how vain all our fears of starvation had been ! Still when
I was out hunting and had been obliged to leave Maria
all by herself, on my way home, I used to be haunted with
fears that some wild beast might have torn her to pieces,
and often when I approached our place of retreat and
beheld her standing outside, it was indeed a joy and relief
to me. Sometimes, however, she accompanied me in my
ramble. We had now commenced to dry the flesh and
had abundance of food, and it once happened that after a
rainy day the sky cleared off again.

While I was busy cooking and having a hard job with
blowing the fire and making it burn without any other fuel
than wet shrubs, and Maria employed in soling boots, she
suddenly broke the silence by crying, 'A large reindeer !'
But being annoyed with the smoke, and my poor eyes
smarting and watering, I was unable to see anything at
all. I rubbed them, but after a while I gave it up, thinking
on account of her laughter that she must have been fooling
me, when, all of a sudden, I perceived the deer bounding
off, accompanied by a young calf. Having observed that
it fled towards the south, I went in search of it the following day and got both of them in one shot. When I
had made our neighbourhood quite devoid of deer, we
deposited all our dried flesh in a hiding-place beneath
some stones, and travelled north till we got sight of the
upper part of the Isortok-fjord, and the encampment (boat-
place) there. I quite believe that in our wanderings we
had passed over sixty miles, though in a straight line the

distance may have been shorter. Surely having travelled a
great part of the summer and been absent as long as the
boat-parties without having encountered any danger is very
pleasant. When we had finished preparing my ten reindeer, the flesh of which had to be carried on our backs, we
began our homeward march, but we had too much to be
taken at once, and had to go back for one load. Having
first brought away the dried flesh, which was easy enough
to carry, we had to turn back and fetch the second lot,
consisting of moist and rather heavy meat.

Thus we passed the whole day in hard work and were
quite knocked up and exhausted at night. But after
going on in this way from early morning till close upon
sunset we met with no dangers. Of course when first we
set out on our journey we suffered some hardships; at the
time that we had not a morsel of food and no other people
were living in the neighbourhood whom we could reach in
a day and get something to eat from; when unable to
turn back, as our only way lay across a river which had
been rendered impassable—then to be sure Maria was in
great distress. But now on our home-passage, when we
got sight of the river again, the stones could be seen above
the water and we had no concern about our food. We
crossed the river, and our path now lay before us without
any danger, and requesting her to fit up a resting-place, I
left her a while. It was my intention to hunt a large deer
for the purpose of adding to our stock of tallow, and I
succeeded in getting one which proved to be very fat. I
laid down the whole of it, covering it well up with stones
in a place on the road we had to pass.

The next day we continued to move onward, having
now to proceed in a straight line towards our home. We
at first passed by my deposited store, and when we arrived
at the ancient summer-stations at the north side of the

Isortuarsuk-lake, we made halt to provide a resting-place, and turned back to fetch my reindeer. I never in all my life beheld such swarms of mosquitoes as in this same place. At night when it had grown calm they were almost stifling, finding their way into our nostrils and eyes, although we closed up our couch as tight as possible. We scarcely had any sleep the whole of that night, but tried by means of smoke to keep them from entering through the openings of the roof which we had formed of reindeer-skins.

The whole night we kept up a smoking-fire, and we perceived a dropping noise as of something falling from our roof which proved to be only mosquitoes. Indeed, had we happened to have had a baby with us, I think it would have been stifled by them. The tallow which we had spread over our bed was covered with dead mosquitoes, as if it had been sprinkled with coffee. I have travelled far about in the country, but never in my life saw a place with so many mosquitoes. When we started from this station and approached our home-country, we rejoiced at seeing how its high mountains gradually lost their bluish hues. We arrived at the summer stations of Kangerdluarsuk, where we intended to stay a few days in order to lessen our burdens by drying the flesh more properly, while in the meantime I pursued my hunt, as it was my intention to lay down a store of meat in this place, but I never caught a glimpse of game. I knew that deer used to be found on the top of Isunguak, and at length I observed the footprints of a single reindeer at a gallop, but they were of no recent date. We only stopped for two days in this place, the weather being remarkably fine, and I was beginning to long to see people. When the middle of August had passed we went back to fetch our remaining stores, each of us having still two loads to bring home, taking one of them at a time and then returning to fetch the other.

We started early in the morning, and at noon reached a cave below a large fragment of rock, which the boat-parties to Kangerdlugsuak use for their sleeping-place. In this place we rested and had a meal. I climbed the rock and was eating my share at the top, when I heard a roaring noise like that of running water, and as nothing was to be seen, I supposed it to be some underground watercourse and did not mind it. But fancy! the sound proceeded from some bears that lay behind a rock a little above us, and it was their growling I had heard. Having finished our meal we continued our march, fearing no harm and resting whenever we felt tired.

When we set out to fetch our second load, I left my gun and my game-bag, and had nothing at all to carry in my hands. On approaching our things, I observed some white patches behind a large stone, but not thinking them to be of any consequence we continued our walk towards them. Maria, who did not feel very well, was foremost, and crossing a small watercourse we looked round to make out what they were, when one of them began to move. (It was a bear). All of a sudden we now perceived the danger that had overtaken us, and if they should happen to advance towards us I had nothing at all at hand to scare them with and was at a loss to think of some means of defence. Giving me a look, Maria said, 'Why hast thou left thy gun?' In default of a better answer, I only replied, 'If we are to become their prey, they will probably come towards us.' But we pursued our march in a seaward direction, having just got a glimpse of them within shooting range, and if they had lifted their heads they would certainly have seen us. They lay down rolled up like dogs, two of them only being visible; the third was almost hidden behind them. Being unable to flee we only proceeded towards our goal, and having fetched our loads we travelled homewards, observing them still lying in the same attitude. On the whole of our walk every now and then I looked round; and when at length I came nearer my gun, that poor little object appeared to me like a whole company of men coming (to our relief). I let my dear companion go foremost, but we moved on rather slowly because of Maria having a pain in her chest and being wearied from overwork.

When we had arranged our couch the weather grew quite calm, with a thick fog so as to allow nothing to be discerned. On lying down to rest, for fear of what might happen, I placed my gun pointing out through the small aperture and kept my bag open in order to be able to get hold of the balls quickly, and I also had two knives ready. Sleep, however, was very difficult to be had, but at length Maria did fall asleep, and at daybreak I also began to conquer my fears, and closing my eyes, I had a little of rest. When Maria awoke we went outside and hurried to make ready for our departure, and started while the weather cleared a little, our only desire being that we could have carried the whole of our burden at once, so as to leave nothing to turn back for. When we moved onward we perceived the roar of the bears to the north of us gradually withdrawing, and sounding from that side which was wholly enveloped in mist. There was nothing more to apprehend. We were satisfied on perceiving that the bears seemed to remain on the north side of the Kangerdluarsuk-fjord, as we had to pass along its southern side, and we chose our sleeping-place at the trout-fishing station. When I first saw them there was good reason for being afraid on account of my not even having a stick to protect my poor little wife with. It really seems such a stupid thing to get frightened at beasts, which perhaps would take to their heels if they had perceived us. Animals bear reverence to men and are afraid of them. However, some of them we know are dangerous, and in summer, bears are said to be ferocious. If I had been alone, I should have been less frightened, but my little companion, being a woman, and I having come off quite empty-handed, we had some reason for being afraid.

While we spent a great part of the summer far up the country, no human voice, and not even a gunshot, was ever heard, and we would not have liked to meet with anything frightful. Every evening before going to sleep we read from some little books which we had carried along with us, and when I had roamed about all day leaving my dear companion unguarded, and going home got sight of our little abode, I was greatly concerned as to how I should find her on my return. When I then saw her busy cooking, I praised our protector in heaven. It was a strange fact that though we had met with no harm during the whole summer, when we again approached our fellow-men I was taken with fear lest we should fall in with the objects of my suspicion. Having left the salmon-fishing place at Kangerdluarsuk, we strived to reach our home the same day by taking as much as we were able to carry and securing the rest by covering it well with stones.

When it was growing dusk I got sight of our own sea and I fired my gun, thinking that there might be persons near who would answer the signal ; but when we approached the houses and were most anxious to see some people, we at length arrived without finding anybody. When we had slept and awoke, we were really annoyed on account of the absence of our people, and the more so as we had not even had the smell of coffee for so great a part of the summer. Later in the day I ascended the hills, and on looking round I suddenly descried a sail, the boat itself being still hidden. At the pitch of my

voice I thundered out, ' A boat ! ' Maria, peeping through
the window, first gazed at me and then drew back. Fancy !
she was seized with fear, thinking that I had suddenly
gone mad. . . . Having all this time longed to see
other people, we at length again enjoyed the society of
man, having supplied our stores with eatables highly
esteemed even by the Europeans. It will now be apparent that people who like to have (furs for) warm winter
garments need not be idle, even if they are possessed of
no boats and have to go ever so far off in search of them.
Food and clothes do not come of their own accord to folks
who always stay at home. The man who is eager in his
business and no idler will benefit himself by his labours.
If we were to speak like that to certain people, perhaps
they would reply, 'It is too tiresome, we prefer to look
for some other sport.' Well, but when now other animals
happen to get scarce, and their number are diminishing
year by year, we must strive to gather stores whenever
there is anything to be had, and when we to the best of
our ability endeavour to put by something (for the evil day),
then let others who dislike labour famish !

(3) **Tidings from Kagsimiut (situated in about 60° 48′ N. lat.)
in the year 1862—Kayakers frozen up in new ice—
Seal-hunters drifted out to sea on the pack-ice.**

[The writer of the following narrative is the father of
two men who perished on the drift-ice whilst they had
gone kayaking with several others ; he watched in vain for
their return. The pack-ice, generally called the 'great-
ice,' means the drift-ice from Spitzbergen which doubles
Cape Farewell.]

*Concerning Thomas, a teacher who was frozen to death,
and the marvellous rescue of his companion, a kayaking boy.*

——In February of last winter our northern neighbours went out kayaking, but were soon caught in a snowstorm. They resolved on turning back, but the wind suddenly turning west they found it impossible to pull their kayaks through the crust of ice and snow quickly forming around them, and finally their progress was totally arrested. Thomas had his kayak-jacket on, but the boy had only a half-jacket (viz., a skin-covering only reaching from the kayak up to the armpits). Later in the night Thomas was frozen to death, and the kayaking boy kept watch over his lifeless companion ; not ere the moon had appeared did he leave him. He laboured hard to move on his kayak, but finding the new ice setting all his efforts at nought, he rose out of his kayak and went crawling along the surface of the new ice, dragging his kayak after him, and when at length he arrived at the edge of the open water outside the shore, he again slipped into his kayak and safely reached the land.

About the kayakers from Kagsimiut who were drifted out to sea.——On April 14 last, the great-ice having arrived off the coast, and the hooded seals also, the weather being cloudy, with only a slight breath of air, the kayakers all put to sea. At noon snow began to fall ; two kayakers returned, and I expected that my sons would soon follow, but, alas, in vain. In the afternoon Markus came home, bringing with him a large seal and accompanied by three other kayakers. On approaching the shore they asked whether the others had arrived, and were surprised to learn that some were still wanting. When the seal was killed, they said, they had caught a glimpse of their companions through the snowy air and given them the usual shout. thinking that they would come to secure their share (viz. of the seal, according to custom), but none of them appearing they made for the shore, whilst a heavy squall came up

from the south, but all of a sudden it fell a calm and
changed to a slight breeze from the north.

This perhaps (we thought) might have caused them to
lose their way, but on account of their being so many
together we did not trouble ourselves much as to how long
they would gain the shore ; they were seven men from this
place and two from our neighbouring station upon Nunarsuit. However, towards night we really grew anxious,
some kept watch, and those who lay down found no rest.
At daybreak, at length, the snowstorm abated, and it blew
a tolerable breeze from the north. But when we ascended
a hill to have a look-out, the wind freshened and soon blew
a regular gale. About two o'clock four kayaks arrived.
On seeing that my sons were not among them I still was
in hopes that they might have landed on one of the
islands, and directly engaged some kayakers to go in
search of them, carrying clothes and provisions along for
them. But when those whom we had seen approaching
touched the shore, they informed us that they had left my
sons and one man more ascending a monstrous floe of
drift-ice out to sea beyond the outer islands. When they
had come on shore they gave the following report :—

At the time they were caught in the snowstorm and
heavy squall from the south, they no doubt had taken the
right course towards the land by keeping the wind on their
right hand, but wondering at their own folly, they went on
to relate how when the calm set in and the wind afterwards
changed, they first had a dispute but then followed the
advice of their oldest companions ; who, however, being
mistaken continued to keep the wind on the right hand
(and taking them straight to sea), until at night they met
with the ice which they ascended, and lying down there
tried to sleep but failed. At dawn the sea had gone
down a little ; they resolved upon leaving the ice, but could

see no land on account of the haze. However, when the sun had risen a little higher in the sky, the summits of Cape Nunarsuit became visible to them. During the night it had blown a gale from the north, and the sea continually washed over the ice upon which they had stopped. One of the company being only provided with a half-jacket, they had to take him in tow, but he soon ceased to row, saying his arms were too weak, and he told them to leave him behind, feeling so wretched he said it were better he died, and so they left him. And when they came to the open water between the pack-ice and shore, my eldest son, who began to give up the hope of saving his life, ascended a piece of ice in order to observe the wind, and his brother joined him, besides the man from Nunarsuit, who told them not to despair, saying they would be well taken care of, and that all were continually watched and taken care of by the Almighty.

(4.) A Perilous Walk of some Men from Igaliko on the fjord-ice in the year 1863.

[Igaliko is supposed to be the ancient Brattelid. The writer lived at the trading-post of Narsak in about 60° 56′ N. lat., 20 miles from Igaliko, at the mouth of the fjord which the wanderers had to pass.]

One morning in January, when the days began to lengthen, we arose and perceived the sky to look dull and overcast, although no snow had as yet appeared and the east wind blew with less force than usual. On the same morning Pavia and Amos at Igaliko went out before dawn, and finding the sky serene and the weather in no way threatening, they made themselves ready and set off on foot, intending to cross the ice to Narsak in order to do

some trading. When they had gone a good distance to the
westward and daylight began to break, they saw that the
clouds were gathering fast and looked very threatening,
but considering it impossible to get back in time they pursued their way to the westward. In the afternoon a gale
from the east sprang up, and the ice along the shore, where
they had to go, was covered with 'deep snow. It so happened that Jakob (a man from Narsak) was out kayaking
(along the edge of the ice), and just discovered them when
it began to snow. He informed them well about the road
they must take, and left them in order to go home. But
in striving to gain the spot where they had to go on shore,
the two men were suddenly overtaken by a tempestuous
snowstorm from the east.

In proceeding towards the shore they could see nothing
but what was close before their feet, and were thus incapable of avoiding the dangers of the road, and only
took care to try the ice in front of them by help of
their staff. But as it was utterly impossible to discover
every dangerous spot, Pavia fell through the ice, but his
companion succeeded in hauling him up again ; and now
they proved to be men of great prudence, inasmuch as
he who fell in continued to proceed in front of his companion who had kept dry. If both had got wet probably
neither of them would have been saved. Continuing their
journey without being able to see aught on account of the
snow, the first of them again fell in, and when he did it the
sixth time his head only remained above the surface, and
being seized by the current below his companion had well
nigh lost hold of him in pulling him out. Being thus
drenched with water and almost benumbed with cold,
Amos brought him to the shore, and there they made a
resting-place in the deep snow ; but Pavia, who had six
times fallen into the water, almost went off in a swoon on

approaching land. By a lucky chance there was no great frost that day, and the man was exceedingly hardy. When at length they had got on land his companion dug a hole in the snow, and here they spent a pitiful night, one of them wrapping the other up in the foxskins which they carried along with them and trying to keep him warm. The next morning they set out to the westward along the edge of the ice, hoping to meet some kayaks, as Jakob had seen them the day before. Again they made themselves a couch among the stones in front of the open water, and here Jakob, who had gone out in search of them, at length perceived their voices, and having found them repaired to Narsak, from whence he fetched two kayaks and clothes to them, and thus they were rescued.

(5) **Kayakers cast ashore in a Snowstorm.**

[The following account is part of a report written by a native of the interior of the Godthaab-fjord ($64\frac{1}{2}°$ N. lat.), who went out fishing in his kayak with some companions on February 21, 1866. Having left the shore in fine weather they were suddenly overtaken by a furious snow-storm, and he with his brother and one man more were thrown upon an icy shore by the breakers. He then continues as follows.]

On finding that my brother was still breathing, I got him out of his kayak and made him go to the old ruin ; the other one I saw running straight thither and I was satisfied, thinking that since he was so quick he must feel well. We also tried to proceed. At first my brother could walk by himself, but he soon tumbled, and I did my best to get him along, partly by carrying him on my back, partly by leading him. Our steps were greatly impeded by the tiresome snow. When we arrived, our companion had fetched some straw (such as is wont to grow on ruined house-walls), with which he rubbed himself and stuffed his clothes, and therefore I thought he was out of danger. I now took care of them as well as I could, scratching a hole in the snow that filled the ruined entrance, and spreading straw on the bottom, and tried to cover them with the same, as we had nothing else, every stitch of our clothes being wet, only my boots were as yet tolerably dry ; but the terrible snowstorm still continued and more soaked us with moisture.

While I was still busy at pulling out straw I perceived that Christian got worse and would soon be frozen to death. On account of the miserable state of his garments, the very skin of his knees being visible, he could not of course withstand the cold. But my brother still survived a while, and I was in hopes that he would recover ; if he only had got some dry clothes he might still have pulled through. Towards low-water time his state grew worse, and he could not move his one arm on account of his side having been hurt. When I perceived his hopeless state I began to admonish him on account of his misery, saying, that when he was dead and his mental eyes were opened, it would be dreadful if also yonder he found himself in a desolate place. He then answered that he had no fears whatever, although he could see no rescue, because yonder Jesus Christ was our only Saviour and Redeemer. And when he thus spoke I grew more hopeful and my mind was at rest, for I feared that because of his thoughtlessness his end would have been a sad one. I now exhorted him to put his trust in God and a blissful life hereafter. When he could not hear any more I gazed upon him and saw how his spirit vanished. On beholding him thus I was seized with anxiety and tribulation, but while I was watching him in his dying state he turned around and smiled at me, and then drew his last breath.

(6) An account from Kangamiut in the Winter of 1865–6— Walrus-hunters in distress upon an Islet.

[Kangamiut is a small trading post in about 65° 49′ N. lat. The narrative shows the difficulties of kayak-hunting in the depth of winter, and especially that of landing and again setting off from the shore in unsheltered places that have been resorted to on account of sudden gales, the men having only their ordinary kayak clothes to protect themselves against the cold during such a stay.]

The first disaster happened to us on October 2, when Frederik, a very clever youth, disappeared in fair weather and was never seen any more. A long time after, a kayaker found something floating on the surface which he considered to be the lungs of a man. Later, on December 12, all the kayaks put off to sea in a light breeze from the east and the finest weather, but out to sea the air looked thick with snow. In the afternoon a sudden gale from the north-west burst forth, with a snow-drift so dense as to cause nothing at all to be discernible. The children who played in the open air knew not whither to go, and could only be found by their crying. When all the people had entered the houses none of the kayakers had as yet returned. I was greatly concerned about those who didn't understand the art of righting themselves again in case of being capsized, but when the heavy snow subsided a little the young kayakers all came in sight from the shore. They had not been far off when the squall came on, and had just succeeded in taking the right way. In the course of the evening the seal-hunters successively returned, three of them with catch; some of them had failed in finding the harbour at once, and had first landed somewhere in the vicinity. Seth Egede had come behind our

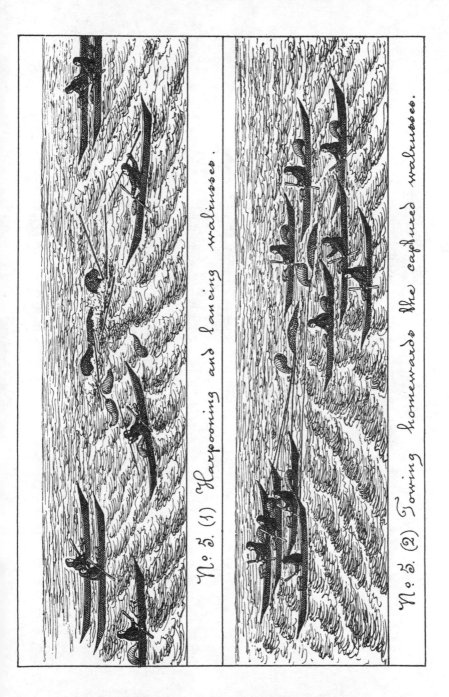

No. 5. (1) Harpooning and lancing walrusses.

No. 5. (2) Towing homewards the captured walrusses.

island, and on coasting along it he met with one Gaios, our only fiddler, who, now on the point of being frozen to death and incapable of going any further, had sought refuge in the cave of an iceberg. On account of the poor man being only a bad hand at kayaking, his rescuer found it rather difficult to bring him home. When all the rest had returned Adam was still missing ; not till the next day did he appear, and was then accompanied by our eastern neighbours, to whose place he had been driven in the squall. On being washed over by the heavy seas his one hand had twice lost its hold of his paddle, and he was nearly drowned. He then threw away his mittens, being only a hindrance to him, but having no mittens he could not go back against the wind. Later on, at the eastern station, Esaias perished in his kayak ; his place-fellows believed him to have been crushed by the calving of an iceberg, and they never found him. On the day that he was lost the weather was as fine and calm as could be.

Some time later, a southern gale having crowded our shore with drift-ice, a dead body was seen to protrude from the edge of the ice ; they tried to fetch it out, but did not succeed on account of the pack-ice moving too rapidly. Afterwards, when the large drift-ice had neared the shore, walrus made their appearance, but on account of the heavy ice the hunters were unable to pursue them properly until February 23. Simeon caught the first walrus, and Isaak got another one, being with young. On the 25th the six kayakers put to sea, and one of them having killed a walrus with young they tried to land it on account of a strong breeze blowing from the east and the weather looking very bad. But they were driven to a small islet, where they could not get into their kayaks again on account of the heavy surf, while at the same time the night set in with heavy rain and a strong gale from the south. The petty island being quite flat, and no snow being seen sufficient to build a wall for shelter, they seated themselves on their haunches closely huddled together.   But the sea and the surf rose higher and the water almost touched them, so that they were obliged to retreat from the shore, and now they got a place rather worse than the first one.   Here they awaited daybreak, while it continued to blow a tempest, and the sea dashing against the shore never ceased to cover them with spray, so as to wet them to the skin.   And now the sea was nearly reaching them and almost carried off their kayaks. Notwithstanding the dreadful darkness and storm, they were obliged to seek another refuge, and they scratched a hollow in a little snow, and tried to make a sheltered resting-place by heaping up the snow about them, but the wind immediately dispersed it.

However, during the darkness of the night they had scarcely felt any anxiety, but at dawn when the wind had changed to the north-west, and intense cold had set in, they felt that life could not last in such a place, nor was it possible on account of the surf to start from the shore in their kayaks.   For fear of being frozen to death they searched the whole circuit of the islet, and having found a small prominent cliff they went to fetch their kayaks.   But one of them, by name of Seth, in trying to let his kayak slide down a slope, had the misfortune to break its prow and bent so as to make its point turn backward ; however, without the skin-covering being injured.   The others remarked that to people in a less wretched condition it must have been funny to look at. The first who ventured the plunge into the sea was Mads. Having tightened his kayak clothes well, he allowed himself to be pushed off the rock and reached the sea safely. But when Isaak was ready to start, the one who pushed him happened to make an awkward pull at his kayak so as to hurl him keel upwards into the sea ; however, he soon managed to right himself. Now James got into his kayak, and Adam was to have shoved him off, when at the same time a heavy sea came dashing over them both. Adam still kept hold by the stem of the kayak with one hand and with the other grasped the edge of a small fissure. When the next sea came sweeping on, it tore the kayak from out his grasp, but Jens stopped it and hauled him up the rocks. The sea now washed over them a third time, but without doing them any harm. But Adam, who had so nearly es- caped being drawn down, had now taken fright and did not venture a second try. Mads and Isaak, who could not be hauled on shore again, left them, and coming home they said that on turning their backs upon them and leaving them behind, they fell a-weeping for pity to think of their poor companions.

When now they were gone, those who were left upon the islet felt themselves utterly forlorn in great misery. Their clothes becoming stiff with frost, they tried to pull out some straw and sod from beneath the snow and stuffed it inside of their clothes, and then they built up a wall for shelter, and here Jens, Adam, and James crouched down, but Seth walked about, knowing he would only be the worse for a rest. When now again he care fully examined the shores of the island, he discovered a furrow ending in a precipice. If a kayak was sloping along it, it would tumble over the precipice upside down into the sea, but at high-water time it was not unfeasible. He then repaired to his comrades, but when he came up to them and they turned towards him they offered a pitiful sight he afterwards said. He asked them to come and look at the place, and being obliged to take their kayaks with them they tried to carry them on their heads, but tumbled on account of their weakness, and were obliged to drag them along the ground. When they came to their place of embarkation they found it fearful to behold. The fissure was just wide enough to allow a kayak to run down without being overturned on either side, but still it looked an appalling sight. Meanwhile they talked with each other, considering that if they stayed there the night over they were not likely to remain alive till next morning, and whether they died upon the island or in the sea mattered little. Seth took the lead, rushed down the furrow and safely reached the sea, but on account of his jacket not having been fitted tightly enough, the kayak on being washed over by the waves shipped a good deal of water. Then came Adam and James, likewise getting safely off the shore, and Jens was the last on account of his not knowing the art of righting himself in case of being capsized. When they had thus safely put to sea and rowed off they talked together of their mutual joy, and began to feel warmer in their kayaks, and came safely home in thick snowy weather.

(7) A Walrus-hunt at Kangamiut, in 1869.

Later on, when the drift-ice had been cleared away, the walrus-hunters again got three large walrus. The shore was bordered by a strip of firm ice as far out as Karajugtut. Thither the kayakers repaired, and following its edge they soon saw a great many walrus, and captured three of them, but the weather appeared threatening and a heavy swell had set in, when watching their return we saw them coming forth from behind the point of Umanak and safely reach the shore. On the same day it happened that some others had set out merely on a seal-hunt, not in pursuit of walrus, and on seeing two large seals they

threw their harpoons at them but missed their aim, and
the seals diving down, a lot of walrus made their appearance swimming in front of them, and one of the ferocious
ones was amongst them. On pursuing the seal, and
before they had overtaken it, the walrus emerged ; it had
been startled at the sight of them and was now coming on.
One of the kayakers just pulled towards it, but when it
turned and faced him he silently kept out of its way, but
another kayaker, Hans, tried to go behind it and waited
for it to emerge, when all of a sudden he found himself
right on top of it. At first Hans wanted to go back, but
when he found himself on the point of being capsized he
persevered and succeeded in forestalling it, the creature
thumping his elbow with its muzzle, and he striking it
with his oar, while the walrus aiming at the man only
struck the kayak behind him, not with its tusks but with
its muzzle only, though at the risk of capsizing it. The
kayaker took himself off quickly, while the walrus pursued
him for some time, but soon turned away in another direction. Giving up the seals they had chased they made for
the south, always expecting that the wicked beast would
turn up afresh. Later on the drift-ice again blocked up
the shore, and as there was no more open water they could
only make use of their guns.

(8) **News from Narsak in the Winter of 1863-4.**

[Narsak is a small trading-post 12 miles south of the
chief trading station, Godthaab, in about 64° N. lat.]

From the beginning of December directly a heavy
frost-smoke set in. While the haze continued with few
interruptions the sun at length began to rise higher, and
the wind blowing very violently continually cleared off the
new ice. We endeavoured to continue our hunting, but

when the weather was too unfavourable we did not go out kayaking. Thus it happened that on January 31, with a gale from the east and a thick frost-smoke, we did not go to sea. Towards ten o'clock, when all were repairing to rest, someone who had been outside entered the house saying that Ungaralak had arrived. When he came in his eyes were nearly glued together, and both his cheeks dreadfully frost-bitten. He came hither after having tried to go from Kangek to Nuk, but was stopped on his journey by ice; having started at ten in the morning he arrived here at the same hour in the night (viz. he had rowed the whole day with the wind in his face). The next day he repaired to his home in good case. Afterwards we had news from the people about Nuk stating that they were all doing well. On some days when the weather was tolerable we went out kayaking.

Once on a beautiful morning, February 16, we set out for Ekaluk Bay, but we had just arrived at our hunting ground when the sky became overcast and a storm appeared to be gathering, so we turned back and had hardly arrived before a heavy gale from the east came rushing down upon us. At the same time we just got a glimpse through the snow of another kayak coming in, and of people looking out for kayaks. When we had landed, those who came down had a fearful tale to tell us. On the morning, the same day when the weather had been so fine, a couple of men had set out from Kangek to pay us a visit. On the way they fell in with some birds, and having been separated, each setting off in pursuit of his prey, one of them suddenly observed that his companion was capsized. He rowed towards him, but was too late, and only found his kayak—the man having already sunk. These people belonged to the Moravians. Afterwards the severe frost was suddenly interrupted by wind from the south during two days. On the morning of the third day the weather became beautiful, but none of us could start in our kayaks on account of our shore being wholly blocked up with pieces of ice. Early in the forenoon a gale from the south suddenly sprang up. If a suitable place had been found for putting to sea some of us would certainly have perished, there being no possibility of landing speedily on account of the drift-ice and the high shore-ice. As good luck would have it none had set off to sea. On the same day one of the kayakers from Nuk perished. The storm continued four days, whereupon we had fine weather and roamed about as usual.

(9) A Bear-hunt at Narsak, in 1865.

[The place is the same Narsak as that mentioned in the preceding narrative, where bears are very rare. A party of seal-hunters having put to sea observed a very strange animal swimming. The narrator thus continues.]

While we pursued it on its track towards Sordlagtorsuak Island, it turned landward, whereupon we gave it a sign by calling out a halloo for bears. Once at our shout it turned to us, but on seeing us it turned back and instantly let its voice be heard. To people who are not accustomed to it, its frightful roaring and hissing is most extraordinary. At the same time it sounded just as if one more was approaching, but it only proved to be the echo from a small island in front of Sordlagtorsuak. When gradually it came near to the shore without having yet been wounded, we spoke to each other of setting about it, and having backed our kayaks astern we took out our guns, but on cocking mine I observed that the percussion-cap had dropped into the oakum. Whilst I was getting hold of another, Adam fired, and when I was aiming Andreas also fired, and then I likewise gave it a shot. It was really amusing to observe the animal, which I never thought would move so quickly.

While the others were reloading I put my gun aside and pursued it, thinking my lance would now be better, but fearing to come too near I kept a proper distance and threw my lance, but managed it awkwardly, hitting the beast on the nape of its neck. On being hit it stooped down without turning aside in the least, and the lance directly fell off. The second time I missed. When they had loaded anew Andreas gave one shot more, after which it appeared quite stiff and I supposed it to be dead, when suddenly it turned its head towards us and began to wheel round. Adam then gave it the last shot. Again it appeared stiff, but I still expected it would revive, and therefore gave it the finishing stroke with my lance, when it was done for and quite immovable.

We had heard people say that the bears had a knack of feigning death, but having got its head so severely wounded it really was dead, and just as we had killed it a kayaker appeared from the north side who even before we fired had heard its loud roar, so awfully does it resound. The place to which we intended to tow our game was close by; we hauled it ashore and began to cut it up. To people who have never seen such a beast its fatness is really surprising; unto the very feet nothing but grease is to be seen. On dragging it up the beach I measured it, and was just able to span its body completely. On being opened, its inward parts glistened as white as those of a full-grown fat reindeer. When we had finished the flensing, four kayakers appeared from the east side, namely Otto, Kunarat, Apuluse and his son. They were likewise lost in wonder, although Apuluse had once before caught a rather large bear, but almost devoid of fat.

(10) **Rescuing a Man who had fallen through the new ice.**

[The narrator, living at Ketertarsuatsiak, in about 63°
N. lat., tells how he went out with a friend on the ice in
January 1869, and continues.]

When I was walking behind my companion, all of a
sudden he fell through, at the same• time losing his gun,
which went to the bottom. On the point of sinking he
stopped himself by stretching his arms and hands as far
out on both sides as possible, and resting them on the ice.
On seeing him in this state I hurried towards him, but he
warned me lest I too should fall through the ice. On due
reflection I found no expedient but to take my bird-spear,
and grasping it at its point I told him to get hold of the
other with his teeth, thinking that if he tried to catch hold
of it with his hands he would fall backwards and be carried
away by the current which had caused the ice to be
so fragile in this place. Taking my advice, he kept it
firmly between his teeth, I slowly began to draw him up,
and when he had been lifted a little he suddenly tried to
rise by pressing his hands against the surface of the ice
notwithstanding its being very unsafe, and lastly, when I
could reach his head, I grasped it and dragged him up.
When he had arisen he said, 'If I had been alone I
should not have succeeded in getting up.' The cold being
very severe I feared he would be frozen, but without touching his dress, he only took my neckcloth and the skin seat
of my kayak to put them on his loins ; whereupon he
hastened to reach home.

(11) **A Greenlander's Advice to his fellow-hunters.**

[The author of this article is a young man living at Sardlok, at the Godthaab-fjord, being himself one of the ablest

kayakers and belonging to one of the most industrious and
intelligent families, whose prosperous state in a great
measure was owing to their having carefully avoided the
immediate vicinity of a trader's shop, as well as having
improvident and indigent people living in their dwelling-
place. As a curious fact it may be added that the same
man, one of the handsomest youths to be met with in
Greenland, had much difficulty in getting a wife from the
Godthaab, merely on account of the girls there preferring
to live at a European station, and moreover, disregarding a
common seal-hunter.]

Concerning the age of boyhood.—When a young lad first
gets possessed of a kayak, whether he has any parents or
not, when the kayak has been furnished with a skin covering
and he tries it the first time, if he has a father the latter
should repeat the following words to him, 'When thou art
obedient thou shalt have this for thine own kayak.' If he
be an orphan another man amongst his house-fellows shall
say the same, and he must not be treated with disregard,
inasmuch as this is written in the commandments of the
Lord, that is the fourth commandment. It is likewise
necessary that the boy should practise kayaking according to his ability. When a youth has acquired a kayak
in the aforesaid manner, he shall keep in mind the received
injunctions, because a disobedient youth is sure to grow
more corrupt continually. These latter years have turned
out worse and worse for the Greenlanders. We have tried
to find out the cause of their misfortune, and wish to have
the following inserted in the Journal. May our counsel to
you not be in vain, young kayakers! One of the providers
has endeavoured to write the present lines concerning the
Greenlanders beginning to suffer from want and cold in a
pitiful manner.

Some of the most hurtful things to the seal-hunter.—The

bad success of a hunter is chiefly owing to disorderly
habits, such as neglecting to look after the kayak-tools,
and not cleansing his gun for a long time ; furthermore his
laziness in hunting and working ; also not keeping the
women of his household in proper discipline, and being
disinclined to keep his children under control, and to teach
them all that might be necessary for them to learn ; also
being disobliging towards their fellow-hunters ; also being
too much addicted to coffee ; also being prone to over-eat
himself when he happens to have abundance of food,
although provisions that can be preserved may become
very useful when stored up. Probably he consoles himself
in a wrong way by misconstruing the words of the
Scripture, ' Take therefore no thought for the morrow, for
the morrow shall take care for the things of itself. Sufficient
unto the day is the evil thereof.' It is also objectionable
when providers who are house-fellows do not assist or
love one another ; and it is also untoward to be too poor
in clothes, inasmuch as being insufficiently clad makes
one susceptible to the cold, which is a great impediment to
hunting ; it is also hurtful to go shopping too much ; it
is also blameable to contract debts. When, notwithstanding
one's old debts, one tries to borrow still more, the debts
continually increase. Our country is not like what it was
formerly, as game is decreasing, and want growing more
and more common every year. The Greenlanders have
great need of acquiring an approximate idea of their home
affairs.

Concerning the trading-stations.—The wintering-places
which have a trader are worse off than those which have
none, on account of being more impoverishing ; as the
hunters are apt to become prodigal if they sell their skins
on the spot, inasmuch as being stripped and brought to
need is the first step to indigence. Some years ago, when

the inhabitants of Sardlok had a merchant, they were brought into great want.

Several things tending to the bodily welfare of the providers and the Greenlanders in general.—A provider has to see that a proper use is made of his game, as his profit depends on the way it is employed. It is also his duty to assist those who are most in need according to his means, such as the orphans nearest related to him, and to show charity to the neediest people. A provider must not be blamed for acting thus, and the Invisible One will reward him. Furthermore, the owners of boats ought in summer, while the weather is favourable, consider what is likely to be useful for the winter, setting their women to work properly, taking care of everything that belongs to a kayak, viz. the skin covering and the kayak-clothes. A provider who is generous in sharing out his game is not to be blamed ; however, those who are able to make a return will be more useful to him. To be poor in kayak-clothes is the greatest drawback to a hunter.

The most populous wintering stations are the worst, for the following reasons :—When a man has caught a seal and divides it to the people, males as well as females, it won't suffice for them all and will only go to waste. . . In the same way, when people wintering in the same place are too numerous they are apt to rely too much on each other; thus they do not care to store up all manner of provisions, thinking they will be able to get a supply from their place-fellows. It is also hurtful to providers when relatives settle down in a wintering-place where there will be only two or three providers ; in case one of them should happen to meet with an accident or die, the only remaining one will be too solitary. But when more than three, say five or six, providers live together in a wintering place, that will suffice. When the number of place-fellows is about equal to that of the inha-

bitants of Sardlok it will almost be best, and in this case
they ought to adopt a plan similar to what we used to do
at Sardlok, viz. every other time that a man catches a seal
he regales the others, and alternately he omits to do so.
But in times of need all the place-fellows get their share of
the catch.

(12) On the Inhabitants of Southernmost Greenland.

[The author of the present article was appointed as
teacher at the trading-station of Nanortalik, in 60° 8′ N.
lat. Pamiagdluk is situated in 59° 58 ′N. lat. He begins his
account by praising the Southlanders as surpassing their
countrymen further north in kayak-hunting, whereupon he
continues in the following way.]

Some of them are praiseworthy on account of their
dexterity in managing their kayaks, especially the inhabitants of Pamiagdluk. Above all, I have heard two men
in that place highly commended for their indefatigability
and skill, namely Christian and Nathanael, both being young
men ; the latter I have seen myself and have admired his
rare dexterity, his nice dress, and the neat appearance and
excellent construction of his kayak. There are some
tales of his childhood relating his extraordinary intrepidity
and expertness. When a mere child he owned a kayak,
and he once saw a dovekie diving off the shore. He instantly brought his kayak down, seated himself in it, and
when the bird had come up and dived a second time, he
pulled straight towards the spot and watched it from above,
spearing it at the very moment it rose to the surface, and
brought it to the shore. Probably he has repeated the
same trick many times. I only mention it here as an
example. Being like that in his childhood, he finally grew
up a thorough seal-hunter and kayaker. Once he happened
to see a small seal swimming before him. He rowed towards .

it and harpooned it, whereupon he grasped the hunting-line and hauled in his game, and finding it rather heavy when he had brought it close to his kayak and examined it, he discovered that he had got two at once. Now they say that he has spitting of blood, but still he is uncommonly clever. The seal-hunters there in the south are renowned not only for their skill but also for their prosperous circumstances. Most of them have both more money and better houses than those who have appointments in the Trade's service. The last year, certainly, some of the Southerners suffered from want, but others experienced no want at all, especially those living at Pamiagdluk and Nunatsiak, who caught seals and were well off during the winter. Those from the south do not care much for money if it is offered them in payment. They have no use for money; some of them do not care about it at all, while others gather money and have commenced to acquire a tolerably large amount. But they are very desirous of European provisions. A whole large seal without skin and blubber is sold by them for one loaf of fresh bread or six biscuits; some of them also give it away without getting anything at all in return. At Pamiagdluk, when there is an uninterrupted catch of seals, many pieces are left to spoil without being used, the entrails are not esteemed and the scrapings thrown away. Perhaps even entire carcasses are spoiled, and when they fall short of fuel they burn a great deal of blubber in cooking. But it is not every year that they enjoy such abundance; sometimes they are subject to want, though this only rarely happens. In summer they lay in stores of angmagsat, dried flesh, and skin-bags filled with blubber. But the inhabitants of Sermilik suffered much from want during the last winter, having consumed all their provisions and blubber, and not even a codfish being caught. When the most provident of them had succoured the others who were on the point of dying from hunger with their scanty stores, they were finally saved and began to get seals and fish. Two men arrived here some time ago for the purpose of bargaining, and started again on the fifth day, there being much new ice as well as firm winter-ice. When they found it impossible to proceed further they tried to go back, and fell in with a strip of new ice which they had to cross on foot. One of them, who was rather old, managed to get out of his kayak, but fell into the water alongside of it. The poor man in his decrepit state was almost benumbed with cold and much exhausted. They reached the shore, however, where the old man went into a cave beneath the ice-border and seated himself in his kayak, and the other remained close to him in order to keep him warm. But on finding himself unable to rise out of his kayak he besought his companion to leave him. At length the other went, but turned back again and stayed with him, and did not leave him till there was no hope of recovering. Then he left him a second time, and having encountered great danger, he arrived here.

(13) On the Greenlanders making their Houses smaller by separating.

[Kakortok is the principal south station, Julianehaab situated in 60° 43′ N. lat.]

When I was a child I never visited other inhabited places, but always stayed at Kakortok, and I grew up quite unaware of the conditions of people in other places. Therefore I had for a long time no idea of my country-men's poverty But having now arrived at manhood, and having travelled round to other inhabited places, I have observed the following facts. The Greenlanders have com-menced to live more separately, reducing their houses proportionately, and that, I think, is one of the causes of their decline, on account of which I have written this, wishing that they may reflect well on again congregating together and mutually loving and assisting each other. When I was yet a child at Kakortok there were very large houses with three windows, and the inmates all loved and assisted each other in procuring the chief necessities of life. Sometimes when kayaks had become leaky, three might be seen to be brought into the house at the same time to be sewed and dried. And when a kayak had to be covered with skin, they used to do it in the house, and all the inmates assisted one another without applying to the Europeans ; they had a storehouse and engaged one of the oldest women to take care of their stores. They possessed beautiful tents for removing to in spring, taking to the outer islands or to the fishing places. When, during my boyhood, I saw my countrymen thus well off, I believed that people dwelling in other places were in similar prosperity. This was also the case when the ship arrived. All the people from the environs repaired to Kakortok, where they pitched their nice tents all around the harbour for the purpose of looking at the ship.

The decline of the Greenlanders is the result of their having given up their former mode of living together in big houses, and this is the cause of their shortcoming, although some, on the other hand, believe this to be the cause of their separating, that when they commenced to make use of European dainties and articles of clothing, the housemates did not like joint possession and mutual assistance as regards these things, which only yield an enjoyment of short duration. When then, for some of them, this enjoyment had come to an end and they had to witness others leading a luxurious life, they would grow angry and take offence, and this is perhaps the reason why they separate. But this we disapprove of, because such people do not take into consideration what follows after rejoicing and what follows after need.

(14) The Famine in Tasermiut in the year 1862.

[The Tasermiut-fjord is situated between 60° and 60½° N. lat. Iluilek is the same as Nanortalik. This article is written by the same author as that of No. 12. He gives a description of the fjord and its various resources, and then continues.]

In the year 1862 it happened that some people wintered here, having amongst them two seal-hunters, and consisting of 14 souls in all, including an infant, who were brought to distress from want, and died one after another, three of them only being rescued. Two, however, cannot be said to have died from hunger, one being carried off by sickness and another drowned. Those who were saved were a widow and her little son, and a young girl. The latter, however, when removed to Iluilek and properly nourished there, died soon from the effects of previous hunger. It began with one of the providers, called Stefanus Lazarus or Leepa, falling sick. His state rapidly grew worse; finally he was unable to stir, and afterwards he died. It is said that the other, Josef Simon or Jukasik, had paid a visit to the inhabitants of Igdlokasik, and that the cause of his disease had been eating too much there. He had travelled to this place on foot, although it was at a good distance and situated upon an island. These people did not succour them in their need, and it was a long time before the tidings came to Iluilek, from whence some people directly endeavoured to reach them and bring them provisions. Afterwards they again exerted themselves to the utmost in order to carry provisions to them, but being overtaken by bad weather and a gale they did not succeed, and in the meantime the sufferers perished. When the time of need set in, Jukasik, from feeling very solitary, yielded to despair, his spirits continued to droop, and finally he did not rise from his couch. The insufficiency of his clothing contributed to enfeeble his body, and he died from hunger. But notwithstanding the miserable condition of their clothes, they used them for food as well as the skin hangings of the walls and various kinds of rubbish. A woman amongst them, named Else Christiane, made herself very useful to the others, being the only one who provided for them when they all lay exhausted with hunger. For a long time she supported the others by procuring them sea-weed. Finally she fell through the ice while engaged in this task and perished. Now the few persons who remained alive could not endure to be housed with the naked corpses which were passing into putrefaction, and although in a state of the utmost feebleness they removed and made them a miserable tent out of skin-rags, on the top of the doorway, which was almost as bad as being in the open air on account of its narrowness even for three persons. When they had taken refuge in this wretched shelter and began to give up all hope of rescue, and were in a state of utter despondence, the people from Iluilek came to them in an umiak just in the very nick of time. What must their feelings then have been ; how they must have been overcome with gratitude and delight ! All their dead were buried at once in the interior of the house ; they covered up the putrefied and bad-smelling corpses and left the place. Probably the disaster that happened to these people was owing to their insufficient dress, though their want of stores also contributed to it. Indeed if they had not, from lack of clothing, been unable to get warm, they would not have been enfeebled to such a degree, in which state, and not having sufficient food, they became very susceptible to the cold and disinclined to go out.

Note.—The above articles are written by eleven different natives. The author of No. 3 had received a half-European education, and the author of No. 1 likewise forms an exception, as he had been specially instructed and prepared for the office of a missionary, to which he was appointed in 1874. Of the others, two have been educated at the seminary in Greenland, but the remainder have received no school-instruction beyond what is received by the Greenlanders in general. The same Journal contains a great many more pages written by similar authors, all of them in the same style. These remarks may perhaps contribute to make the articles here given serve as a supplement to the chapter on 'Knowledge and Enlightenment.'

CHAPTER XIV.

THE GREENLANDERS SKETCHED BY THEMSELVES.

SCATTERED through this volume are various plates show-ing Greenland ways of life. These lithographs are the exact copies of partially coloured drawings executed by natives entirely after their own ideas, and without any information or guidance whatever in the arts of drawing and painting. The greater part are the work of a man named Aron, living in Kangek (64° N. lat.) He was only a common seal-hunter, who falling sick was prevented from going in kayak. On account of his being confined to his bed for several years, the author of the present book by way of pastime and occupation furnished him with paper, pencil, and colours, and asked him to draw sketches of native life and of old traditions after his own ideas and choice of subjects. During the course of some years he not only delivered pictures, but also engraved many of them on wood, which have been published in other works by the author of this volume. The poor sufferer performed this task lying on the 'ledge' in the crowded room of his narrow hut, but seemed to derive much satisfaction from it, and took a great liking to this occupation. On sending his last pictures (Nos. 4, 8, 15, and 16, in January 1869) he complained of his increasing illness preventing him from doing any more, and ends thus: ĸasuvdlunga agdlagkáka kipiváka, kingorna ĸanoĸ isanerpugut ; i.e. 'from exhaustion I must cut short my letter, in the future how will our fate be like?' and shortly after he died. Nos. 5, 12, and 13 are by a native of Kangamiut, an expert seal-hunter and a clever and intelligent man, who was appointed trader in the place where he lived, and for this reason abandoned seal-hunting. He has written down a great many legendary tales and several articles for the Journal, and also drawn numbers of pictures, some of which are rather characteristic and not without a glimpse of genius, but very rude, especially as regards perspective. Nos. 6 (1), 6 (2), and 9 (1), are from a native of Arsut, who once of his own accord sent some of his attempts at the art of drawing to the author. Nos. 7 (1) and 7 (2), painted by persons unknown to him, have been added chiefly in order to give an idea of the most primitive attempts at the same art. All the remaining ones are by the above-mentioned Aron.

No. 1 represents the *ordinary Eskimoseal-hunting* with harpoon and bladder. The nearest man, in a white cotton jacket and a kayak half-jacket, kayak-sleeves and mittens, has captured a seal which he is towing home. A small bladder is attached to it to assist in keeping it afloat. The designer perhaps has made the kayak a little too short, although its position requires it to be contracted. The second figure is a man in a regular kayak-jacket, commencing his pursuit of a seal. Having approached it to a certain distance, he keeps his paddle with one hand and with the other he is in the act of throwing his large harpoon, (**ernangnak**, properly signifying the shaft, **tukaᴋ** the point of it) placed upon the thrower, viz. the piece of wood which he grasps. The coiled-up line is ready to run out as soon as he throws, and then he instantly has to throw out the bladder (**avataᴋ**) placed behind him and fastened to the other end of the line. The third man represented has finished this first part of the catch. The

bladder is seen floating on the surface, dragged by the seal
which has dived and tried to run off with the harpoon-point
sticking in its body.   Now the moment it emerges he is
ready with his lance (**anguvigaᴋ**), which is thrown in the
same manner as the harpoon.   The point of the lance has
no barbs, for which reason it falls out again after having
pierced the animal, and the hunter catching hold of it
repeats the throw, until, if necessary, he advances close to
his game and finally despatches it with the small hand-
spear (**kapût**) or knife.

No. 2 (1) may serve as a supplement to the former.
The white whales are caught exactly in the same way as the
seals.   The man here has struck the animal (**nâligpâ,** ' he
strikes or has struck it with the large harpoon '), still holding
the thrower and having as yet not thrown out the bladder.

No. 2 (2) is an illustration to one of the recent tales.
Maningak already as a boy distinguished himself as a
daring kayaker.   His father who lived upon one of the
outer islands, on seeing how the boy ventured out upon the
open sea, merely for fear that this locality should become
fatal to him, removed to a place up the Godthaab-fjord,
and when the son nevertheless succeeded in extending his
excursions beyond the outer islands, he removed still
further up the sheltered inlets.   Here Maningak got a first-
rate hunter as a companion, but when the wind blew very
hard he dissuaded him from going out, because he had
noticed that he was not able to follow him.   When nevertheless his companion, disregarding his advice, had once
ventured out in a gale of wind, Maningak, keeping an eye
upon him, saw him suddenly swamped by a heavy sea,
after which he first caught sight of the kayak and then of
the man swimming after it.   Maningak brought him to
the nearest shore in the manner here pictured, and seized
the opportunity of duly scolding and mocking him.   Man-

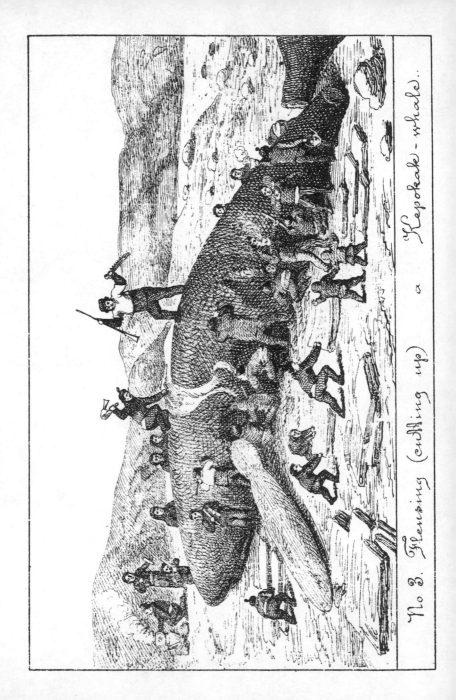

No. 3. Flensing (cutting up) a "Keporkak-whale."

ingak was a heathen, but his two sons when grown up were baptised and received the names of Esaias and Lars.

No. 3. People 'flensing' a Kepokak or humpback-whale. Having towed it as close to the shore as possible when the tide was in, they are now busy cutting it up at low tide, and obtaining the blubber as well as the flesh. Here there are only a few people seen to participate in this lucrative sport. It is probably a drift-whale, found in some out-of-the-way place, and the news has not as yet spread far enough to attract more people. This is confirmed by the fact that no proper tools are seen to be employed, but only such implements as are at hand by chance. The woman on the top evidently does her best with the usual axe of the natives, consisting of a broad chisel inserted in a handle of wood, apparently in the same way as the stone chisels from the prehistoric age have been fitted for use. The man in front of her, who has likewise ascended the slippery surface of the colossal animal, seems to be looking for the most suitable spot to apply the weapon which he holds in his right hand, and which seems to be a 'tok' or stick also headed with a chisel, while with the left hand he holds a saw, which at all events will come in handy for cutting across the bones. The men standing on the ground seem to make use of their kayak-knives. A pretty large quantity of blubber has already been cut out to be brought to the nearest trading-station for sale, and with this prospect of soon being able to acquire a new supply of various articles of luxury they have thought it needless any longer to save their store of coffee. One of the women is busy with her kettle, sharing its contents out in the only three cups they possess, while another in the background has taken upon herself the more serious task of preparing a substantial meal out of the kepokak-beef.

No. 4. The scene here pictured transports us to *the hunting grounds for reindeer far up the country.* The hunters have left their chief encampment near the shore, being only accompanied by a few women and a boy, and are of course unable to carry anything along with them except their guns and ammunition. For want of shelter they used to build up low walls of stones or sod to protect them against the wind whilst sleeping. In the present case, in favour of the designer we will suppose the ground inside the enclosures to be a little deeper than outside, so as sufficiently to account for the total disappearance of the nether part of their occupants. It would seem that they have duly deserved to enjoy all the comfort which their improvised encampment is likely to yield them. The two women descending the hills with heavy loads on their back, and the foremost one busy stretching skins for drying, shows that the day's hunt has been successful. The persons to the left have their hands full of the kitchen-work of the party, consisting in broiling slices of reindeer flesh upon a flat stone, gathering fuel for this purpose, and serving up the cooked food upon another flat stone. As to drink, each of the travellers has to provide for himself out of the watercourses in which the country everywhere abounds.

No. 5, *The walrus-hunt,* is a rare sport in Greenland, chiefly practised at Kangamiut, in 65° 40′ N. lat. The proceedings hardly require any further explanation, being much the same as the ordinary seal-hunt represented in No. 1. The only difference is that the extraordinary size and ferocity of these animals makes the contest with them too hazardous to be entered on by a single kayaker. To make up for this, we see that the company before us has seized the opportunity of taking two at once. The lances, however, must have pierced the huge bodies many times

N° 6. (1) Harpooning an Herbivorenk (Dolphin).

N°.6. (2) Greenlanders dressed after ancient fashion.

(3). A full dressed kayaker and another in half-jacket. —

(4). A girl in head-fringed jacket and another in cow-rying a child in "Amout".

before the kayakers could proceed with fastening the two bladders to them in order to keep them floating on the surface whilst towing them home. As for the rest we refer to Nos. 6 and 7 of the above articles, the author of which is identical with the artist who has designed the illustration. *No.* 6 (1). The title given this sketch by the designer was, ' **ârdluarssuk nâlerкâra sarpigârкasitdlardlunilo ernînak tauva avatârpunga ;** ' i.e. ' I harpooned an ardluarsuk, and when it suddenly stretched its tail up high (dived), I threw out the bladder.' An ardluarsuk is a rare sort of whale, only known from the description of the natives, for which reason there exists some doubt as to the determination of the species. (It is probably a grampus.) At all events, it is one of the larger kinds of whale animals, so large indeed that we must not wonder at the hunter evincing a little pride in his powers, and especially exulting at having thrown out the bladder at the right moment. Had it remained fastened to the kayak a moment later, he would certainly have been capsized and unable to rise to the surface again.

No. 6 (2). ' **kâlâtdlit sujugdlît ilait ;** ' i.e., 'some of the ancient Greenlanders.' The designer has tried to sketch these dresses from tradition. It appears that he has made the jackets both of the man and the woman too short.

No. 6 (3). *Greenlanders making ready to start in their kayaks,* one of them in full dress, the other in a half-jacket only. As regards this garment we must refer the reader to the description we have already given of kayak-hunting in general. The rows of white spots in the full-jackets are the bone fittings of the straps, to raise its lower border at pleasure, and of a lace to tighten it around the face.

No. 6 (4). *A girl in festive garb,* wearing a white jacket fringed with red embroidery. *Another girl with a child in 'amowt.'* Both of these jackets have retained the flaps of the original female jackets, which have now been totally

abandoned as regards the ordinary jacket, or 'anorak.'
The bead-jacket has a covering of white cotton ; white
boots being worn on the same occasions as this jacket, the
whole attire is very becoming to young women. The
amowt is merely made of skin, if possible of reindeer-skin,
and probably differs but little from the ancient fashions.

No. 7. The original bears the following title : **'pula-
jartorput inukatitik taᴋussarângamikik erᴋarfigissarpait ; '**
i.e. 'They are going into a fjord (to hunt reindeer), on
meeting with their fellow-men, (literally) they fire a salute.'
It is not without reason that this travelling party rejoices
and gives vent to these merriments, because now they have
overcome the hardships of the winter, which, especially towards the end, may have brought with it many days of
slender fare and other privations. They now not only are in
expectation of an abundance of game, and all the delights
of the hunting grounds in the interior of the country, but
for the first time they meet with other members of the
human race, viz. with people from other wintering stations,
from which they have been cut off for more than half a
year. No wonder therefore that they fire a salute.

Especially the women and children may rejoice, for
during the winter they have been even more confined to
the dull life at the winter huts than the men, and the artist
has taken particular pains to let us know that the party
includes women and children, partly by means of the most
striking emblem of the former, viz. the hair-tuft, partly by
the diminutive proportions of the latter. The edge on both
sides of the middle of the boats has been heightened by
means of boards in order to give room to the luggage,
which comprises all the household furniture of the family,
and forms comfortable seats for the older women and the
children, while the young women act as sailors. But now
they have put in the oars, profiting by the fresh breeze,

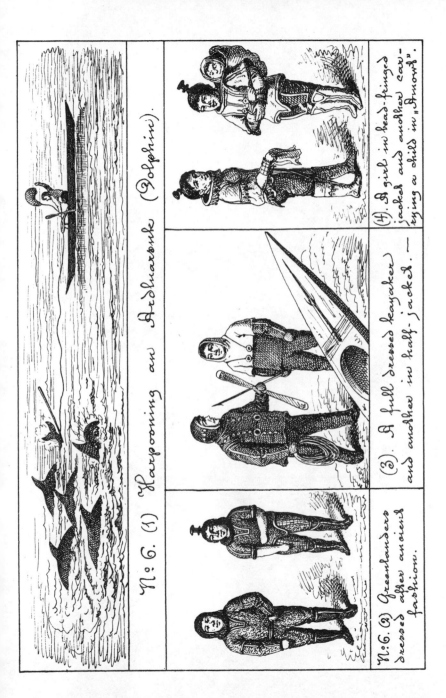

No 6. (1) Harpooning an Ardluarsuk (Dolphin).

No 6. (2) Greenlanders dressed after ancient fashion.

(3). A full dressed kayaker and another in half-jacket. —

(4). A girl in bead-fringed jacket and another sewing a child's "Amowt".

No. 8. Reindeer-hunters in their encampment.

which being favourable to them proves to be the sea-breeze which in summer commonly prevails during the warmest part of the day in all the fjords. In this instance it is almost blowing a little too hard, as is evident not only from the waves but also from the kayakers, who seem to be ready to cling to the side of the boat, as is their habit, in order to prevent its shipping a sea.

No. 7 (2). An empty umiak rowed by women sets out to fetch fuel or some other load.

No. 8. Here a hunting party has reached its nearest goal, the chief encampment at the head of a fjord. Two tents are pitched, but the two boats set up in an inverted position, sloping so as to form a roof over a room accessible from one side, also afford excellent shelter to some of the travellers. The iron pot over a fire also indicates that seals have been caught during the last few days, and to those who are anxious to know the national mode in Greenland of eating meat, it is fortunate that a man has seated himself in the foreground, just as if for the purpose of explaining it. The meat being served up in pieces larger than a mouthful, and no forks being made use of, the operation is performed by taking one end of a piece between the teeth, and cutting off the bit as close as possible without hurting the nose.

No. 9 (1). Kayakers being stopped in their course by new ice having formed, now make for their home by carrying their kayaks across the ice.

No. 9 (2). Reindeer of different ages and sexes, for which the Greenlanders have peculiar names.

No. 10 gives a representation of a hamlet or wintering station in the north, where dog-sledging is carried on upon the ice in front of the houses. The sledges with dogs attached have been sketched from memory or description, because the designer lived where no dog-sledges existed.

No. 11. The interior of a house belonging to people in prosperous circumstances. It is not one of the first-class houses, however, as may be judged from the ceiling indicating a flat roof covered with sod. It is rather small, and seems to be inhabited by two families related to each other. The younger man is probably absent pursuing his seal-hunt, while his father, seated on the main ledge, entertains another who occupies the side ledge, and seems to be a guest. The main ledge appears to be designed a little too narrow.

No. 12. These illustrations, made for certain traditional tales, represent the ancient manner of dancing and singing. In both of the groups here represented there is one chief performer, who accompanies his song with the drum, gesticulating and dancing at the same time. In the first one the song seems merely intended to amuse, without any satirical aim (**katissutáinaᴋ kimiaᴋángitsoᴋ**) and the party surrounding him are probably moving in a slow dance and singing a refrain. But the other delivers a regular satirical song or 'nith-song' (**pisek**) on his adversary (**iverpâ**, ' he sings on him') named Ajakutak, the man to the left, whom he reproaches for neglecting the kayak-hunt, saying:

> O ! behold this Ajakutak, he will not do like me,
> Not in the hard east wind of the Amerdlok-fjord
> Abreast of his hunting-bladder he will watch the seal.

At that time Ajakutak could make no answer, but anxious to revenge himself he made enquiry about the life and behaviour of his adversary, and having been informed that he was addicted to licentiousness, at the next meeting he gave a song upbraiding him with all his bad habits, and ending, ' To be sure Ajakutak will not be like thee.'

We have mentioned that remains of the old manner of singing is occasionally to be found among the Greenlanders, especially in the remote places. It is designated by the name of tivanek, which means at once the dancing and the singing part of the performance (**tivavoκ**, 'he dances,' **tivaneκ**, 'dancing.') It is very characteristic that the natives, on seeing the European manner of dancing, considered it to be a kind of entertainment perfectly differing from tivanek, and called it **kitingneκ** (**κitigpoκ**), which signifies wild and indecent merrymaking! A native more than usually gifted and educated, who was appointed an outpost trader, has given us a description of the tivanek which he witnessed at Sanerut (61° N. lat.) in the year 1869, and he explains his opinion on the subject in the following way: 'Many who read what I have mentioned here will probably consider it indecorous and preposterous, but the ancient dance and song are neither blameable nor wrong. In other places where Europeans live, the natives use kitingnek, or dancing to European tunes which are wholly strange to them. If kitingnek be not hurtful, tivanek cannot be so. But if kitingnek be wrong, tivanek will be wrong too. What some people may perhaps consider wrong is that they chose Christmas time for their tivanek, but there is nothing sinful in that. Whether they dance after the ancient or the modern fashion they commit no sin; it can only be called immoral when at Christmas or on other holidays people indulge in drunkenness and debauchery. At Sanerut the dancers could not be drunk, for they had neither beer nor brandy, and young people did not at all run about outside during the dancing, but in other places I have observed that during the kitingnek they sought an opportunity for licentiousness.'

No. 13 is an illustration of one of the modern tales in which the renowned Habakkuk, who afterwards passed himself off as a prophet, is mentioned as a youth. But here it may give an idea of a summer encampment in general, due allowance being made to the disregard of the rules of perspective, as well as to the peculiarity that the umiak is rowed by men instead of women. The passage of this tale which refers to this scene is as follows:—It is said that amongst those who stayed at Kasigisak to wait for the new seals were the parents of Habakkuk. They say that he was then a youth, and happened to row northward in pursuit of a small seal which he had just caught and placed on the top of his kayak, when he met with a foreign umiak rowed solely by men. He approached and followed them, but from timidity he was unable to address them until their old crone named Ajugaussak broke silence, saying, 'We are nearly dying of hunger, give us a bit of flesh from thy seal. We lived in Sokak, where our house-fellows have perished of famine, for which reason we have travelled this long way without once taking our boat on shore. Our provisions have consisted of half-boiled boat-skins.' On hearing this, Habakkuk advanced towards them, replying, 'Well, take the skin and the blubber and liver of my seal.' The boat's crew then seized the seal, but from exhaustion were unable to lift it until Habakkuk raised it from below.

No. 14. These drawings, like the former, represent a wintering-station in general, although referring to a certain tale. The upper one shows the winter-houses from outside; to the left the umiaks are seen resting on boat-pillars as usual in winter. In the other we see the interior of one of the huts. The following words were written underneath the original pictures:—

(1) palase **Egede kalâtdlinut tikerârniartoκ sákulersord-lutik sôrssúkaluarât; palasivdle unersuissâta kalâtdlip oκar-figai: κavdlunât angákûnerssuat ilaussok; tauva nuánârtors-sûvdlutik ilasiarât;** i.e., When the priest Egede came to visit the Greenlanders they took up arms, but the priest's native guide said to them, 'The great angakok of the Europeans

No. 15. Tents in a sudden gale of wind.

is with them,' at which they grew highly delighted and
received them with friendliness.

(2) **Egedip angákok tikerssûpâ, kitorne náparsimassoᴋ
angákuartormago**; i.e., Egede threatens the angakok for
having conjured over his sick child.

No. 15. On pitching the tents much care is generally
taken to secure them by means of stones, and to turn
the entrance to the opposite side from which the heaviest
gales of wind may be expected, but the present drawing
shows that a squall may nevertheless sometimes carry the
tents away, especially when on a journey they have only
been intended for a short stay.

No. 16 forms a supplement to No. 3.—A sufficient
cargo of blubber having been procured, the next step is to
bring it to the trading station and exchange it for European articles. The scene represents the front of a storehouse where the blubber brought for sale is received and
weighed. The eyes of the spectators are fixed upon a man
who stands somewhat elevated above the crowd, and is
noting down in his book how much blubber eaᴄh of the
sellers has delivered. His occupation and dress indicate
that he is either the agent of the place or his clerk,
and the artist has evidently endeavoured to suggest the
idea that he belongs to the Caucasian race by giving him
a tall and slender form. Whether the same may be the
case with the man at his side remains somewhat doubtful,
although he is of similar stature, and his bearing hints at
a distinguished and important position, because we have
seen that several natives serve in the capacity of craftsmen,
boatswains, or foremen to the other labourers, and as such
they also often render most valuable assistance to their
superiors, and are favoured with their particular confidence.

CHAPTER XV.

THE TRADE, EUROPEAN PUBLIC INSTITUTIONS, AND
EUROPEAN LIFE IN GREENLAND.

Royal Trade Monopoly.—The present *Royal Trade Monopoly* was founded in the year 1774, and the regulations which refer to its privileges are embodied in a Royal Statute, dated March 18, 1776, entitled, 'A Renewed Statute and Prohibition against Illicit Trade in Greenland.' What we have stated in the preceding sections will sufficiently illustrate how the traffic between a European country and Greenland is rendered difficult by the peculiar habits and mode of life of the natives, on account of their laying in no stores of merchandise at all and their great dispersion. In order to purchase and collect the products from the 176 inhabited places scattered over a coast 1,000 miles in length about sixty trading stations have to be maintained, at which the blubber is received in portions of from 50 to 100 lbs. at a time; it is then packed in casks, and that from the out-posts is forwarded to the chief stations, where it is manu-factured into oil, requiring an ample stock of casks and much cooperage. The value of these products in the European market does not on an average amount to 800*l.* annually for each of these establishments.

When moreover the difficulties of the Greenland navi-gation are taken into consideration, this trade, as regards its profits, may more properly be compared with whale-fishery and seal-catching carried on from ships by a European crew, who in this way gain their cargo themselves, than with ordinary commercial speculation founded upon supplying cargoes to the ships by means of purchase. The ships of the Royal Trade are kept at sea on each voyage quite as long as the whalers, and much longer than the sealing-ships, while the smaller number of the crews in the former ships is in some degree counterbalanced by the expenses connected with keeping permanent establishments in Greenland. From these statements it is evident that the traffic can only be made profitable by means of extraordinarily favourable prices in Greenland, and by being made a monopoly. The whole profit is derived from the low prices of the products in Greenland, which during the course of years several times have been fixed for longer periods, and each time raised. According to a calculation founded upon an average of the sales during the last few years, about 22 per cent. of the value in the European market are paid for the products in Greenland, out of which payment five-sixths are given to the sellers, and one-sixth to the Greenlanders' public fund. The prices to be paid for the European articles imported into Greenland are fixed every year, a certain rate of profit being added to the prime cost.

Articles for hunting and fishing are sold at prime cost, several other necessaries, such as bread, are sold at prices which scarcely pay for the purchase and carriage, and on an average the sum added to the cost price does not amount to 20 per cent., while at the same time people in Greenland are allowed to order goods from private agents, freightage to be paid at the rate of 2½*d*. per 10 lbs., or 1*s*. 6*d*. per cubic foot. This system has been maintained chiefly in order to make sustenance as cheap as possible to people who have to live upon fixed wages. It is evident that if the profit necessary to support the business had to be gained equally from the imported and exported goods, the livelihood of all the persons in the service of the Trade and the mission would require their salaries to be twice as high as they are now, while at the same time the control necessary for maintaining the rights of the monopoly would become almost impossible.

The whole coast tract is divided into the southern and the northern portion, and each of them again into districts, each of which is attached to a chief station or settlement. Each of the two portions has its superintendent or 'inspector,' while each of the chief stations is managed by an agent, called the *Colonibestyrer* or 'administrator,' who again has his subordinate outpost-traders or agents at the smaller stations situated in the same district. The chief stations generally are called 'colonies,' and in accounts by foreign travellers of their visits to Greenland, an agent of a trading-post there even frequently has received the title of 'governor.' The agents are aided by clerks, some of whom are called 'assistants,' others 'volunteers,' and who also sometimes superintend an outpost. The inspectors are the superiors of all persons belonging to the Royal Trade, and moreover are authorised to act as local magistrates in general, when doubtful questions occur which have to be settled by the government. The salary of an inspector is 328*l.*, besides a residence. According to the budget for the year 1876-7, the number of agents was 11, with an average salary of 250*l.*, and clerks 18, with an average salary of 106*l.*, besides residence, fuel, and attendance. The entire number of persons belonging to the subordinate classes, viz. outpost-traders, boatswains, craftsmen, sailors, or labourers, was at that date calculated at 182, including apprentices, and their wages averaged 25*l.* each, besides a percentage on the pur-

No. 16. People selling Blubber at the European Station.

chase-money which is granted to the outpost-traders. Of these salaries none exceeded 67*l.*, and some did not amount to 12*l.*

Danish Mission.—The Danish mission in Greenland is a government institution, subject to the Minister for Public Worship, by whom the missionaries are appointed and paid. They have their peculiar instructions, and are subject to no control or superintendence in the country itself. According to the budget approved for the year 1870, there were to be eight missionaries, whose combined salaries amounted to 1,207*l.*, besides two new-comers, who were to stay one or two years at the seminaries before being allowed to act as missionaries. But of late years several posts occasionally have been vacant for want of candidates. The salaries of the catechists were calculated at 666*l.*, expenses relative to buildings 866*l.*, and the total expenditure of the mission 3,898*l.* for one year. Since the year 1872 steps have been taken to promote several reforms in missionary affairs, chiefly conducing to the appointment of native missionaries. At present the Danish missionaries usually stay about ten years in the country.

The Moravians.—The Moravians have four chief stations, besides two auxiliary ones, or outposts, and usually number twelve European teachers, of whom about eight are called missionaries, while the rest only officiate as assistants, at the same time preparing themselves for the position of a missionary. When their pupilage has come to an end they return to Germany in order to be ordained missionaries and marry. Afterwards they usually revisit their native country when their children have arrived at an age to be placed in the Moravian educational establishments, whereas the missionaries themselves go back and generally remain in Greenland until their old age. The Moravian mission is maintained by charitable contributions, while the

Danish government only contributes to it by granting a slight diminution in the freight to be paid by them for their goods. But it must be remembered that the natives contribute indirectly to their support by furnishing each station with ten or twelve serving women, who constitute the crew of their boats, and are chiefly supported by their own labour and by gifts from their countrymen.

It appears somewhat strange to see a number of European missionary teachers, amounting to one for every 160 natives, employed in places in which, with the exception of the southernmost, for the last half century scarcely any heathens have existed, and where the inhabitants are so closely connected with their countrymen constituting the Danish communities, that their remaining under the control of European missionaries, as regards their church affairs, would be almost certain, if even the Moravian stations were given up, which might well be done as they have now completed the task of converting the natives to Christianity. On taking into consideration the field which other parts of the world offer to missionary undertakings, it appears evident that the Moravians are bestowing more care on Greenland than on any other country. The reason is what they call the 'historical importance' of their Greenland stations, their work being supported by charitable contributions which again depend on their reputation, or their credit derived from a favourable public opinion. The interest which the European public take in their work is to a great extent maintained by the number and the dispersion of their missionary stations over the world, and by the obstacles and hardships which are supposed to be encountered by their missionaries in these places. An atlas has been published showing the surface of the globe in its relation to the Moravian establishments, and the United Brethren endeavour to maintain the interest bestowed upon them by eulogising both in writings and in speeches the deeds of their missionaries to the present day. For a century and a half the name of Greenland has rendered marvellous service in increasing the reputation of the sect. When we remember that European travellers are still able to discover proofs of martyrdom in the settlements of the Society in Greenland, it is not to be wondered that to the great public in Germany Greenland is now just in the same state as at the time of Crantz. The auditors accustomed to attend the church-festivals in Herrnhut, when lectures are given on the history of the Greenland mission, would never be able to comprehend the reasons given above that prove these settlements to be now superfluous. Abandoning them, therefore, would be the same as subverting one of the pillars by which the credit and the prosperity of the Moravian missionary work is supported. For this reason the missionaries not only watch their flocks in Greenland, lest individuals should pass to the Danish communities, but in order to maintain the present number of their own stations they try to keep them as detached from one another as possible, preventing marriages being made between individuals belonging to different stations, and when a family removes to the confines of another station they continue to be noted in the census as still properly belonging to the former community.

Medical Attendance.—Medical attendance is very scarce in Greenland. There being only three medical men appointed for a coastline of more than 1,000 miles, sending for them in cases of sickness is generally out of the question. However, they have to make regular official journeys, visiting every trading station of their districts at least once a year. There are also small infirmaries established in the places in which the physicians reside, in order that they may pursue a particular course of treatment with certain patients.

Medicines are sent out to all the trading stations, and distributed to the inhabitants. Midwives are appointed in many places, some of whom have spent a year in Denmark in being trained for this position. Of course medicine, as well as every sort of medical aid, are given gratis to the inhabitants. But it must be granted that their public sanitary institutions are very imperfect. The great distances are not only hindrances to regular medical attendance, but the mode of life and the domestic circumstances of the natives in most cases render proper treatment difficult, if not impossible, even where the doctor resides. Moreover, he is at a loss how to induce his patients to follow his directions. In former days a great many rules of diet and living had to be observed, partly referring to the ordinary routine of human life, partly as given by the angakoks for peculiar cases. All these observances were conscientiously maintained as religious duties, but for this reason were wholly abandoned at the introduction of Christianity. Of course this disregard of old customs could not but cause some derangement. If none of them were hurtful, and half of them had sanitary importance, it was of no consequence to the state of health whether the other half were foolish or not, and when the rules given by a European physician are not followed, the ancient observances, although nourishing superstitions, have nevertheless been more advantageous as regards hygiene. The total medical expenditure has averaged of late 944*l.* per annum, out of which 505*l.* was spent on the salaries of the physicians.

Mode of Transport; the Posts.—In order to transport goods and products between the chief stations and the outposts, four small vessels which have crossed the Atlantic, and about sixteen transport boats, are stationed in Greenland. Letters are forwarded between the stations by kayaks, and in the north, in winter, by dog-sledges, the post going

regularly two or three times a year to the inspectors, besides
expresses sent on many occasions. In this way communication is also afforded two or three times a year by kayaks
between North and South Greenland. To Upernivik, however, no kayak-posts are sent, letters being conveyed fur·
ther by a sledge-post sent once every winter from Umanak,
and by the ships in summer. Between the extreme
points Julianehaab and Umanak, express posts may be sent
in summer for any distance required. The whole route,
under favourable circumstances, would take about five
weeks, and the expense amount to about 16*l.* No postage
at all is paid for private letters sent by mails of the Royal
Trade. The kayakers generally are rather proud of being
trusted with the conveyance of letters. To avoid mischief
by accidents, two kayakers are generally employed at the
same time. Post-kayakers may be recognised at a great
distance by their rowing closely abreast of each other,
neither deviating from their course nor throwing their
javelin, as the kayakers have the habit of doing merely as
a pastime. When these kayakers are perceived, it is directly announced by shouting '**paortut**,' and the people
shout louder than usual when the postmen, raising their
paddles, indicate that they bring tidings of a ship having
arrived from abroad.

European Settlements. — The European buildings in
Greenland are mostly constructed of wood, the roofs also
being made of boards. In some instances, however, the
walls are constructed of stones, and for some roofs European slates have been employed. For these walls stones
are collected in the environs and used in their natural
state, their interspaces being filled with clay, and the outside with a little mortar. Some of these walls are well made
and extraordinarily air-tight and durable, but when intended
for dwellings, the inner sides have to be furnished with a

covering of some non-conductor of heat. For this purpose, between the wall and the wainscot a space is left which is filled up with turf and moss ; if then a stone should accidentally protrude so as nearly to come in contact with the wainscot, it will be indicated by a spot on the wall of the room being covered with ice. Particular attention has to be paid in the choice of a proper site for dwellings, when the substratum consists of gravel and stones percolated by springs. In certain winters when snow happens to be scarce, the outlets of such water being closed up everywhere, it rises to the surface and flows out where it is unable to form a crust of ice, which will be the case when a building covers the spot and protects it against the cold air.

A curious instance of this kind happened a few years ago. A new school-house having been erected, nicely built with stone walls in a perfectly dry place, presenting no indication of watercourses, when this building had been used for some weeks in winter, a well suddenly burst out underneath the floor, so rich that not only was there no possibility of keeping school in it, but it became the common fountain from which all the inhabitants fetched their drinking water, especially towards spring, when the usual fountain was frozen up, and people would have been obliged to melt ice if they had not been able to get their supply from the school-house. The original and still most common, as well as in all likelihood the most convenient manner of building European houses, is that of constructing them like log-houses, of hewn and squared pieces of timber, which render it possible to have perfectly warm and sheltered rooms by means of walls not more than 9 inches in thickness. Several of them have lasted for more than a hundred years, and have only been replaced by new ones on account of the exigencies of time as to size and comfort having made themselves felt even in Greenland. The rooms of these houses being furnished as in the home-country, especially in depth of winter they make their occupants wholly forget the remoteness of the country in which they live. But on arriving at the settlements in summer, their outer appearance almost makes an opposite impression on the new-comer, reminding one of the temporary refuges of people who have been compelled to stay for some years on the shores of a land which can never become their true home. Besides the dwelling-houses, there are three or four other buildings, consisting of storehouses, workshops, the oil manufactory, and finally a church. A flag-staff forms an indispensable adornment of the diminutive colony, the arrival and departure of officials and other distinguished travellers, and the holidays, being always announced by hoisting the flag. The first-named occurrences also used formerly everywhere to be made known to the population by firing a salute from the guns before the flag-staff; but some serious accidents having been occasioned by the carelessness of the gunners, it has now been partly abandoned. Undoubtedly in most places care has been taken to make the appearance of this collection of buildings as neat as possible, a red colour being mixed up with the tar that serves for preserving the roofs, and the white colour of the window-frames enlivening the dark tarred walls of the log-houses, and in a more pleasing country they might look rather pretty. But what especially contributes to their dull appearance here seems to be the absence not only of trees or bushes, but in most places also of verdure. Beside the huge stone masses, the houses appear still smaller than they really are, while at the same time the bleak and barren colour of the rocks generally predominates in the scene.

The garden plants which we have mentioned cannot

be discovered before bending over the beds in which they grow, and in order to get the sight of verdure and flowers one has generally to pass over the nearest hills. In this respect, however, there is some difference between the north and the south. In the northern places the traveller on landing is received by flocks of howling dogs, which roam about among the houses, frequently fighting murderously. The native habitations there generally consist of nothing but simple earth-huts with flat roofs. In the south, vegetation around the houses is not quite so scanty, goats are seen instead of dogs, and the houses belonging to the natives in the service of the Europeans are almost always furnished with sloping roofs of boards which give the settlement a more village-like appearance. Notwithstanding the shelter and warmth afforded by the timber walls, the effects of the winter cold in North Greenland are felt in a manner which is unknown in the home-country. The windows must always be furnished with sashes, otherwise, in heated rooms, the ice-covering of the panes will not only acquire a thickness so as to allow very little daylight to penetrate, but the ice will fill the window-sill and overflow it like a glacier. The heads of nails and other metallic parts protruding from out the walls of a heated room are covered with ice, and when in spring the timber walls have been acted upon by the sun in the daytime, cracks are repeatedly heard from them at night as loud as pistol-shots. Victuals that are liable to get damaged by frost can scarcely be preserved anywhere but in the bedrooms; cellars are found in most houses, and can be free of frost in the south, whereas in the north the cold penetrates the ground so as to reach the cellars towards spring. Cupboards placed next to the walls of a heated room are likewise penetrated by the frost, on account of their being, in some measure, separate rooms.

On the other hand, the preservation of meat and fish is greatly facilitated by the cold, and generally venison hanging on the shady side of a house will not become tainted during seven or eight months of the year. It is only liable to get too dry, which, however, may be prevented by keeping it covered with snow for some time. Of course ice-cellars might be easily constructed in such a climate. To heat a room for the winter, on an average, about two tons of coal and half a cord of wood will be sufficient. A whole household does not require more than five tons of coal and one and a half cords of wood. In the north only, during the greater part of July and August, heating the rooms may be dispensed with.

Mode of Living of the Europeans in Greenland.—Each of the settlements is usually supplied with a stock of the most necessary provisions sufficient to last a year in advance, in case the ship should be prevented coming by some accident. We have already mentioned that beer is brewed and bread baked for the common supply of all the people who are engaged in the service of the Trade and the mission. The European kitchen is supplied with several of the most necessary ingredients, and even with some dainties from the products of the country itself. Most Europeans, after a short stay in Greenland, overcome the prejudices with regard to the use of seal-flesh as a contribution to their table, and not only find the soup prepared from it unexceptionable, but the meat also, when just sufficiently boiled, yields a nourishing and palatable dish. A great many of them even come to the conclusion that a little blubber remaining with the flesh answers the same purpose as a similar portion of the fat intermixed in the beef of oxen ; that the nausea raised by the mention of the former is caused by the idea of train-oil lamps, and that people who only know ox-tallow from very old tallow-candles would very likely become prejudiced as to the flesh of the animal that has yielded its fat to the manufacture of them. But there is no accounting for tastes, and besides, some people might urge a certain mawkish sweetness peculiar to seal-flesh, making it distasteful to many, and aver that the example of the Greenlanders themselves tends to weaken the argument about the old tallow. The author cannot wholly deny the former assertion, and though reluctantly, he must confess the truth of the latter, inasmuch as a common tallow dip is not only relished by the children as a delicious tit-bit, but also, according to trustworthy witnesses, is a highly appreciated article at a coffee-party, being considered to yield a fair substitute for cream when the coffee is stirred with it !

Of course there is also not the slightest reason to consider the habit of eating seals and whales as indispensable to a stay in Greenland, especially as the country yields several other viands as well as fish, sufficient to supply, not only the most necessary wants of a European palate, but even to afford some variety to allure the taste. Leaving the Greenlanders to feast upon their seal-flesh and blubber, let us return to what has been stated in the preceding pages concerning the other productions of their country, at the same time adding a few remarks in regard to their utility to settlers. The time has passed when reindeer-tongues were consumed as a cheap substitute for pork, and quantities of them were salted for winter use, or in some cases even sent home for sale. But still, at most stations excepting Julianehaab, reindeer beef, which is quite equal to ordinary venison, is no rarity, and at the latter place excellent indigenous beef of oxen now and then makes up for the want of it. In several places the annual consumption in a household of reindeer-flesh still amounts to a couple of hundred pounds, and it hardly anywhere costs more

than 1⅔d. per pound. Formerly it was still cheaper.
Ptarmigan yield a more usual contribution to the European
table, and are more generally to be had than reindeer venison, especially because the natives care nothing for them.
Most of the households consume at least 500 ptarmigan
in a year, at a cost of from 1d. to 1⅔d. apiece. Hares,
which cost from 3⅓d. to 6⅔d. each, are consumed at
about the annual rate of 20 per household. When the
game here mentioned happens to be scarce, recourse may
in most cases be had to seafowl, and what we have said
about them in a former chapter vouches for their being able
to make up for other deficiencies in the kitchen. Eider-
ducks which yield more than two pounds of flesh are bought
for 1⅔d. apiece. Other kinds of ducks considered more delicate may be had by way of change, to say nothing of the
scantier geese, which have sometimes also been caught alive
and fattened in order to render them more equal to tame
geese. The breeding of poultry, on account of being both
troublesome and expensive, is only practised by few people,
for which reason the eggs of seafowl are made use of in
great numbers. Those of the eider-ducks are the most
common, and the only ones that are gathered for winter-
stores. Towards the egg-season the Greenlanders used to
apply to Danish families for a 'tub,' offering to fill it for
them on their intended trip to the egg-islands. This talk
of a tub is a phrase implying that a little money in
advance to defray the expenses of the equipment for the
journey is also greatly desired, and in fact absolutely necessary, if one wishes to secure a sufficient supply of the said
indispensable article for the larder. The eggs, being almost
twice as large as hen's eggs, are sold at about 3d. for ten
In the south they are laid down in lime and protected
from the frost, in which state they may be preserved quite
fresh till the next egg-season, and even longer. In the

north, on the contrary, they are preserved merely by frost, but then they will only last for a few days when first they have been thawed up. Other eggs considered more of a treat, and eaten during the egg-season, are the delicious but small eggs of the tern or sea-swallow, the white of which is bluish and translucent when boiled.

Passing from meat to fish, we need only add a few remarks to what has been stated about them in the section on the products in general. It is only in rare instances that any sort of fish is sold at more than a halfpenny per pound, and generally the price is much lower. The large halibut, in quality and taste perfectly equalling those which in European markets cost more than a shilling per pound, are in Greenland sold at about eightpence for one fish weighing from twenty to fifty pounds. But the smaller halibut, or kaleralik, which is chiefly caught in the ice-fjords of the north, are highly preferred. At Jakobshavn and Umanak it yields an excellent dish in winter, and is occasionally sent from thence in a frozen state to the neighbouring stations. This fish is extraordinarily fat, and when dried is considered a dainty to be eaten without any further preparation. For this purpose a certain number of fish are gathered in the course of winter, and towards spring, when the fresh, mild weather sets in, they are cut into narrow strips and hung to dry in the cockloft. A similar article is also known in Iceland and Norway. Of the more palatable kinds of fish, salmon-trout are the most generally distributed ; they occur in the far north, but are more abundant in the south. Real, or 'scaly salmon,' may be had in a few places, but are very scarce. As a mere exception herrings occur, and are annually caught in one single locality in about 62° 15′ N. lat. Crabs of an extraordinary size are caught in several places in spring, and may, as a dish, be considered perfectly equal to lobsters.

These are the resources of Greenland for supplying a European kitchen with fresh meat and fish. They are so distributed over the different parts of the coast, and the different seasons, that people who really show that provident care, for the want of which we blame the natives, need have no concern about these important necessaries. As regards vegetables we have nothing to add to the account which we have given of what the Greenland soil yields by itself, and especially when submitted to cultivation. A real want to many is that of potatoes, because those which are sent out to the country generally do not reach their consumers much before everybody in the home-country has begun to use the new crop. In this respect, however, the cold climate proves favourable, at any rate, for preserving the old potatoes in the same state in which they have been received. Although the author is sorry to state a fact so discreditable to the horticulture of Godthaab, he must mention that it was proved by experience there, that as soon as the potatoes arrived with the ship, the easiest method to prevent their sprouting was to tumble them into a bed in the garden, after first digging a hole, placing a tub in it, and covering them with straw. By using ice in a proper way they have been kept quite fresh till the February of next year, and with sufficient care they might be kept even much longer.

Many settlers in Greenland have wholly adopted the native dress, that is, speaking of the male sex of course, and in some instances it is quite indispensable ; for instance, when travelling in winter in the north, and as regards the foot-gear and the very convenient clothing for children. A double fur-jacket, dog-skin inside and seal-skin on the outside, made in the Greenland fashion, is the most practical outer garment for a man in sledge-travelling, being at the same time almost impenetrable to cold and easy to move about in. The European functionaries sometimes ameliorate the equipment by an additional pair of trousers enveloping this jacket almost to the arm-pits, and likewise by an extra pair of boots the legs of which again cover the trousers to the knees. Notwithstanding their huge appearance, even these latter additions to the usual attire by no means constrain the free movements of the travellers. For protecting the face from being frost-bitten by the wind no satisfactory improvement of the dress has as yet been invented. Anything directly covering the face is of no use, as the breath would soon convert it to an ice crust continually enlarging; the only practical way of affording shelter is by making the border of the jacket around the face project as far as possible. The boots of the Greenlanders are especially useful on account of the softness of the soles, which make them peculiarly adapted for walking over the rocky surface of the hills. On account of the roughness caused by the dry lichens covering the rocks, they yield a sure footing on the numerous slopes that have to be passed over, and neither male nor female settlers in the country think of using any foot-gear but the boots made by the native women. Lastly, we must mention the sleeping sack, the inside of which is lined with bearskin, the outside being made of waterproof sealskin. It is considered an indispensable article of equipment for European travellers, and is constructed so as wholly to envelop its owner.

The Greenlanders and the Danes.—We now have enumerated the articles of use which Greenland offers to strangers who take up their abode on its shores; the chief contribution to their support it, however, yields through the aid which may be derived from its inhabitants. We have already shown that from a commercial point of view Greenland without Eskimo inhabitants would, with the exception of one single spot, be a worthless possession.

But, in addition to this, the Greenlanders are almost in every respect indispensable to the European residents and travellers as regards their immediate daily wants. The stranger who arrives there the first time can hardly put his foot ashore without having already had an opportunity of appreciating the assistance rendered him by a native. The coast being so insufficiently known and surveyed, even the most experienced masters of Greenland ships are generally very desirous of having some guidance in making the land. Kayakers who roam about the outer islands usually get the first sight of a sail, and are then very eager to gain the vessel if possible. On approaching the land, accordingly, a sharp look-out is kept, and nothing is more welcome than to discover something like a bird moving on amongst the waves. This soon turns out to be the paddle of a man who seems to sit on the very water.

On coming close to the ship a rope is lowered to him, and a moment later he is hauled on board, sitting in his skin-covered skiff or kayak. It frequently happens that a master of a ship, on account of the weather and the difficulty of recognising the inlet, hesitates to steer for the harbour, and that a piece of advice given by such a pilot on putting his foot on deck is acted upon and may shorten the voyage by several days. In such a case none has more reason to praise the daring kayaker for his assistance than the passenger who, wearied with the adversities and tediousness of a passage around the Cape Farewell, now sees the ship moving gently up a narrow sound sheltered by the rocky islands that separate him from a boisterous sea which has proved a source of discomfort to him for several weeks. But on the whole, the service of the Greenlanders is most especially valuable when travelling. In the south an umiak is the most usual means of conveyance; this being the native mode of travelling, one need have no concern about the boat and the navigation, with which none but the natives are familiar. Five rowing girls and one man for steering constitute the appropriate crew of a boat, while at the same time a kayaker is engaged to follow it, not only for the purpose of supporting the boat in a heavy sea, but also to be employed as a messenger to be sent to the nearest station for information, or to bring out necessaries if the boat should happen to be blocked up anywhere by ice, and sometimes it is the task of the kayaker to look out for a clear course in such places where the sea is densely crowded with drift-ice. The wants of this crew are easily satisfied. The boat being brought on shore and turned keel upwards serves for a tent. The women have a little luggage wrapped up in a skin, the men often carrying none at all of their own. The women are also always provided with sewing implements, and when the boat has been injured by a rent they are ready with their needle and sinew-thread, and soon put it in repair. The wages paid to the crew are very different, but a sum of 7s. or 8s. a day for the whole party, victuals included, may generally be considered a maximum. As regards judging of the weather and of the ice, the steerer and kayaker are generally perfectly to be relied upon. They will hardly ever omit to make use of what they really consider a favourable opportunity for proceeding on the voyage.

When they are doubtful of success it will never be advisable to go ashore where landing is difficult. But if when before crossing an open fjord or passing a steep coast a direct question is put to a Greenlander as to whether he thinks that the weather will hold out until a fair shore may be reached, instead of assenting he will generally answer, 'If the weather continues so there is no difficulty,' which is a phrase meaning, 'I expect so, but

should our passage nevertheless turn out badly, I will not
be responsible for it.' When the voyage happens to be
protracted, the crew cares but very little for the insufficiency of provisions, although on the other hand good fare,
especially with a cup of coffee twice a day, is highly appreciated, and they also have a great liking for visiting inhabited places where they may have an opportunity of
making a favourable barter with their biscuits for loads
of fresh fish and blubber, or whatever eatable they can
get hold of. On halting, the women are on the alert to
pitch the tent and make a fire for cooking, being as
clever and useful servants on shore as they are indefati-
gable rowers, and they always set about their work with
readiness and merriment, often even indulging in more
fun the more difficulties.

The only thing that will make them dejected is getting
wet to the skin with snow and rain, so as to make it impossible for them to arrange a dry couch by means of their
poor garments. An ordinary day's journey with an umiak
may be rated at between 30 and 40 miles. In urgent
cases even 60 miles can be made without halting for more
than a few hours. In the north, journeys are mostly performed by sledges in winter, and in summer European
boats with men as rowers are made use of.

We have mentioned that the Moravians at each of
their stations used to have a regular staff of ten to twelve
servants, besides occasional helpers. The other settlers in
Greenland cannot generally boast of an attendance so
ample, but, indeed, they would be badly off without the
assistance of native domestics. At first, of course, only
European labourers and servants could be had. As regards the Royal Trade, the important business of a cook,
with the meaner work belonging to it, was the first situation entrusted to the natives. The Eskimo cooks have

now everywhere supplanted their Danish colleagues, of whom only a few specimens still existed in the furthest north some years ago : this speaks sufficiently for the superiority of the former. The fact is so much easier to comprehend, when we remember that their work requires handiness as well as the aptness at learning all sorts of manual work, and helping themselves, which we have mentioned as being peculiar to the Greenlanders. In winter, early in the morning the cook, on removing the shutters from the windows, is heard to clear away the snow by scratching them with his nails, and with the same naked hands he immediately afterwards stirs up the very fire in his kitchen if in any way possible, because no Greenlander thinks of using tools where his hands will suffice, and in every case they prefer the simplest means for supplying their wants. In the depth of winter, when the mean temperature of the kitchen sinks below zero, a European lady is only too glad to have such hands as are proof against fire and frost for her assistance. Besides the cook, a female servant is indispensable for doing the work of a chambermaid, and in particular to take charge of the foot-gear ; and where there are children another one must be employed as a nursery maid, a duty for which the Greenland girls are exceedingly well fitted.

It must be granted that the service to be had from the natives in their present state is only of inferior quality as regards the management of stores and commanding or directing other people. But complaints are even frequently heard of their being unfit for such common servant's work as we have just mentioned, as well as of not rendering the necessary assistance to travellers, by guiding them and giving them information about their country. We will briefly consider some of the most common assertions of this kind, which are partly maintained by people residing in

Greenland, and may partly be here and there met with in the accounts of arctic travellers.   In the first place the Eskimo race has often been accused of mendacity, and of being even peculiarly inventive in lies and fictions.   There is one occasion, it must be admitted, on which a Greenlander rarely tells the truth, and this is when he has to apologise for his being unwilling to undertake a task or make a contract proposed to him.   Anybody who has travelled in Greenland knows the phrase 'kameĸángilanga,' i.e. 'I have no boots,' by asserting which a man always makes his first attempt to escape being engaged for a journey which he dislikes to undertake.   If then a pair of boots are offered him into the bargain, he will most likely try to back his refusal by referring to the critical state of his trousers, and so on.   But from the very fact that this excuse is so frequently made, and may almost be considered as a conventional phrase, we ought to conclude that it does not bear the character of a lie in the strict sense of the word.

For instance, how many lies are spoken in civilised society, if such excuses as saying that a man is 'not at home,' when a person wishes to call upon him, or that he 'is not well,' when he is asked to a party, had to be verbally understood?   In fact the talk of the boots is merely a phrase of this kind.   The Greenlander knows very well that in declining the proposal he will directly be called to account for the reason, and partly from timidity, partly from civility, he avoids making the real cause of his disinclination known, in case it might look as if he mistrusted the questioner as to the manner in which he would be treated during the journey, for how long a time he would be taken from his home, or such like.   For this reason he prefers to make use of excuses of a more vague character, which neither can be contested nor taken offence at by

anybody. As regards the accusation brought against the
Greenlanders or Eskimo in general of more obvious or
intentional lies and fictions, the author believes that the ill
repute into which they have fallen has originated principally from misapprehension, and also from prejudice,
founded on experience derived from other nations in a
similar stage of development to the Eskimo.

The author had a singular opportunity of putting the
Greenlanders to proof as regards the question whether they
are prone to invent stories, not only for fun, but also from
more selfish motives. For the purpose of gathering the
traditions still existing among the Eskimo, he directed an
appeal to people all over Greenland, desiring them to write
down all sorts of tales actually existing and forming a part
of the general entertainments in the native houses, and he
added to his summons a promise of reward in cash to the
natives who could procure contributions to the intended
collection. The result was a store of 500 tales, from fifty
native storytellers, which were carefully scrutinised with
regard to the questions whether it contained anything invented or composed merely by a single person, or after the
summons had issued, but with the exception of perhaps
three or four dubious instances, not even the slightest
attempt was noticed either at making fun or money in
that way. The stories sometimes contained recitations,
and were written down in a manner obviously intended
to fill up as many pages of a manuscript as possible, but
there was hardly any sign of a tendency to lengthen them
out by inserting passages invented by the writer himself.

This fact apparently proves that any speculation of
this kind agrees but little with the character of the
Greenlanders. The accusation of untruthfulness which is
not unfrequently brought against the Eskimo in books of
travels is undoubtedly to a great degree founded upon

misapprehensions, the origin of which is not difficult to explain. What is considered a lie or fiction, ascribed to a certain person, is more properly a rumour originating among the population in a similar manner to traditional tales, viz., without anyone being able to trace it to its first author or inventor. Credulity and superstition concur to create the most curious gossip in some stations, which is soon spread from thence to the neighbouring places. But the stories originating in this way grow all the more curious when they are intermixed with rumours from abroad, or with the conjectures which the natives make about unusual visitors to their country, such as ships and exploring expeditions, whose intentions and interests in visiting Greenland are a complete mystery to them.

A traditional remembrance of the acts of violence committed in ancient times upon their ancestors is still apparent from a remarkable fear of kidnapping which has sometimes been observed when such vessels were in port. This fear gives birth to rumours that some such incidents have really occurred; even cannibalism has sometimes been spoken of. The war tidings from abroad also suggest ideas which render such stories still more fabulous. The author is of opinion that the information given by Eskimo which has been brought forward in proof of their mendacity, generally belongs to this class of rumours. Misunderstandings arising from insufficient knowledge of the language have contributed to make the questioners believe that what a man speaks of as a rumour, or even a tradition of former times, which he has heard and in most cases has been credulous enough to rely upon himself, is a lie deliberately invented by him.

The next vice of which the Greenlanders are commonly accused is the habit of breaking their agreements. The European housewives in Greenland frequently lament the recklessness with which servant girls quit their service; they stay away without giving notice, or all of a sudden they say, 'soraerpunga,' i.e. 'I have finished,' and retire at once. Travellers who have engaged guides on making excursions, likewise complain of their having been deserted by them before they had reached their goal, and declare them to be not only untrustworthy, but destitute of perseverance, and even of courage. In most of these cases it is scarcely probable that any contract can have been broken, because it is very unlikely that any Greenlander would have given a real promise. When he has undertaken an ordinary duty, the obligations of which are well understood by him, such as an appointment in the service of the Trade, the conveyance of letters, or steering a boat for a certain route, &c., he will prove to be as conscientious, persevering, and trustworthy as any man of another race. But in taking upon himself other charges he is very cautious. The natives are very sensitive as regards their treatment ; they fear nothing more than passionate imperious words and a hot-tempered leader. When on excursions of exploration and discovery, of course they are unable to conceive the plan or real aim of the undertaking, but we know from experience that some European new-comers proceed in a reckless and presumptuous manner, displaying their ignorance of the country, and at the same time disregarding the advices of the native guides as long as no immediate obstacle or danger is perceptible ; but nevertheless afterwards claiming their assistance when they get into some dilemma. Moreover, it must be remembered that to the foreign explorer the excursion is a task which may bring him renown, while to the native guide it is a domestic drudgery for a daily pay, requiring him to leave his family and his private business for an uncertain time during the most profitable season. Supposing that the natives perfectly

understand the aim as well as the terms of their engagement, and that they believe the leaders of the expedition
to be worthy of their confidence, they will undoubtedly
display as much perseverance, courage, and skill as travellers' guides in any other country., This also has actually
been proved by examples from the arctic expeditions, and,
as regards Greenland, it must be remembered that almost
every rare and curious mineral there, every interesting relic
or ruin, in short almost every remarkable or useful thing,
has been discovered and pointed out to the foreigners by
natives, and that a great many details entered in the maps
we possess of the country are founded upon sketches drawn
by them.

Lastly, we have to mention the most grievous, but probably the most unjust charge that has been brought
against the Eskimo, viz. that of thieving. This assertion
is almost a traditional one, dating from the first discoverers, in whose accounts the Eskimo are unanimously
represented as being very thievish, pilfering whatever they
could lay hold of on board a ship. In order to judge
this accusation in a proper way, we must remind the
reader that personal property beyond a certain amount was
actually unknown to the original Eskimo, inasmuch as such
property always became the joint possession of the community to which he belonged. When, moreover, we consider
that everything, especially metallic articles, were of enormous value to the inhabitants, it is evident that their
behaviour when suddenly brought into contact with
strangers cannot be judged according to ordinary rules.
The ancient accounts also expressly assert that when the
strangers had once settled in the country, and the natives
became better acquainted with them, they wholly left off
pilfering. At all events it can now be confidently asserted
that at present few countries exist where property is so little

exposed to danger from theft as in Greenland. Pilfering European victuals which are all delicacies in Greenland, not unfrequently occurs, and liquors especially have to be well guarded; but taking the temptation here offered duly into account, the crimes committed in this way are, in most cases, to be ascribed as much to the carelessness of the sufferers as to the offenders themselves. Taking into consideration all that we have now stated concerning the Greenlanders in their relation to foreigners visiting or residing in their country, of course it must be admitted that on engaging them for any service, due attention must be paid to several peculiarities of their character, and that the information given by them must be made use of with a similar caution, but that on the whole they are as useful, willing, obliging, and unpretending natives as a traveller or settler can ever hope to meet with in any half-civilised country.

European Life in Greenland.—The rediscoverer of Greenland, John Davis, named the first point he saw of it Cape Desolation, and until the present day its name has been more or less connected with the idea of exile and banishment, of hardships and privations. It has been the common opinion that people who repaired thither for a long stay must be induced either by devotion or unselfishness, or compelled to it by want and despair,—the first class of course being chiefly represented by missionaries, the other more especially by people engaged at low wages as labourers in Greenland. Before taking these assertions more closely into consideration, we must remark that a great difference prevails between what a residence in this far-off country offers to female and to male settlers. To the former it must be admitted that Greenland is still more devoid of attraction than to the latter, and that although many of them have spent happy years there, on the whole they are entitled to consider Greenland a desolate and melancholy country. For this reason the following remarks in favour of it particularly refer to settlers of the male sex.

It cannot be denied that the early history of the settlements can boast of men who displayed great activity and self-devotion in their desire to benefit the Greenlanders as well as their own country; but such martyrdom has long ceased to exist in Greenland. Nevertheless, the idea of self-sacrifice still clings to it, and is occasionally maintained by the tales of travellers who seek in this way to flatter not only the missionaries, but also European residents in other positions. Thanks to the efforts of Crantz, the Moravians rank highest amongst those men who are still believed to lead a life full of privation and self-denial in favour of the poor Greenlanders. Consequently they may serve as an illustration of this feature of Greenland life, and if a closer examination should deprive them of a portion of their reputation for self-sacrifice, the other settlers in Greenland will have to share the same fate. The Moravians in Greenland indeed up to the present day have always been honourable and pious men, leading an exemplary life, conscientiously discharging the duties prescribed to them by their superiors, and not unfrequently they are possessed of such good breeding and learning as to be highly appreciated in Greenland.

But it must be remembered that they are now merely officials, who on entering upon an engagement for Greenland have secured for themselves a maintenance for the rest of their life, and often rise by aid of their missionary career from the humblest positions to a considerable degree of respectability in their mother-country. They are protected against the severity of the climate by houses which more than any other dwelling in Greenland are constructed so as to afford comfort and convenience, and they are bountifully supplied with provisions of every description by their European friends. As each household consists of two or three families, and their social arrangements are very conducive to comfort, they are in this respect generally better provided for than Danish settlers in general, and pay extraordinary attention to their domestic affairs. They are so far from having any heathens to convert, that on the contrary the natives who constitute their communities have already for generations been trained up in implicit obedience to their teachers, and with more reason might be called their slaves or servants than their persecutors as supporters of paganism. The fraternal organisation of their own Society is in little accordance with the position which they have granted to the natives on incorporating them in their communities, inasmuch as they even surpass any other class of the European race in degrading them to a set of subordinate beings. In short, their duty as the propagators of the Christian faith amongst their 'brethren' in Greenland is an obsolete institution, and the renown which they still derive from it is merely founded on ancient tradition and modern misapprehension.

The reader will probably already have received the impression that want and despair, as little as devotion and self-sacrifice, have been necessary to draw settlers to Greenland. Of course people take up their abode there, like other emigrants, owing to their having some reason for discontent with their condition and prospects in their native land ; and we will willingly grant that on an average perhaps these motives may have been weightier with those who have preferred Greenland to other colonies, but in other respects there has been no difference. There are few Danes who have spent a portion of their life in

Greenland without carrying away a pleasant remembrance of their stay. Many labourers and sailors who had very low wages to subsist upon, after the expiry of the three years for which they are generally engaged, have frequently resolved to prolong their stay in the country, many even marrying and remaining there for life. Some of the same people having become tired of Greenland go home, but afterwards so long for it that they return thither as soon as possible. It must also be admitted that circumstances bordering on want and despair have brought many people to Greenland, and that some of these have been sent back again for bad conduct, but it must be said to the honour of the country that many of them who in their native land would perhaps have been ruined by a dissolute life, have turned out clever and industrious people in Greenland, and become the fathers of respectable Greenlanders.

Experience seems to prove that Greenland is a healthy country. Nowhere do children thrive better than there. When they are able to leave the 'amowt' of the nursery-maid, which at once protects the infants against the severity of the climate and affords a most excellent means for their conveyance, they play with the native children and run about in the open air summer and winter The preceding chapters of this book will have shown that the country affords ample opportunity for different kinds of sport, thus greatly contributing to the preservation of health there. Hunting and fishing may be pursued at any time of the year, while the beautiful and magnificent scenery of nature makes rambles over the hills and travelling attractive. Excursions in summer are very pleasant, especially in the south, where a few hours' travelling up the inlets is sufficient to change the scenery. The view of the open sea is excluded, the inlet assuming the appearance of a lake situated in a mountainous country, and the slopes of the hills are clad with a verdure contrasting strikingly with the dreary appearance of the rocks surrounding the settlement. The tent is pitched on the bank of a brook, murmuring softly amid dwarf bushes and flowers, and the crew amuse themselves in fishing and gathering kvans or berries.

In winter, on the other hand, the north offers more variety by means of dog-sledging. In the environs of Disco Bay the long winter nights already begin with the month of November, on account of the few hours' daylight being generally darkened by a cloudy sky, with tempestuous and unpleasant weather. The sea still continues open off the outer shores, and a tremendous surf breaks upon the projecting rocks of Disco Island, where the settlement of Godhavn is situated. As southern gales with snow alternate with icy winds from the north, the temperature is gradually lowered. In the interior inlets the sea is then frozen and the sledging season sets in, but Disco Bay is not covered with ice before Christmas. Then all of a sudden the most striking change takes place. Instead of a pitch-dark and boisterous sea as far as can be seen, a white plain presents itself to the view, the uniformity of which is only broken by icebergs scattered here and there which have accidentally been frozen up in it. Then the temperature generally sinks lower than 10° below zero, and a strange repose and deathlike silence reign everywhere until the time when the sun again begins to lighten the mountain tops at noon, and a few days after appears above the horizon.

In the course of a couple of months afterwards, there is a change from almost continuous night to continuous day. From the middle of January, communication by sledge is generally opened between the stations, and as it lasts till late in April, an opportunity is afforded of paying visits to neighbouring stations and making excursions to the ice-fjords and remotest inlets, which in summer are often difficult of access. Such trips are especially pleasant when they can be made in the month of May by crossing the lakes and sheltered inlets, which continue to be covered with solid ice. At that season the sun never sets and the air at noon is quite summerlike; the snow melts and the fresh berries peep from beneath it, but at night the crust of snow is again hardened by the frost. In South Greenland no communication exists between the chief stations from October to April; the settlers have to confine their winter-excursions to the immediate environs of their houses. Snow-shoes are almost indispensable to everybody who wishes to take the necessary daily exercise. The snow-shoes used in Greenland are similar to those of the Lapps, the only difference being that the under side is covered with sealskin with the hair inclined to the heel, which, as it makes them more slippery, adds to the speed of the wearers and prevents them from gliding backwards. This sport is sometimes pursued also by ladies, and is pleasant as well as healthy. But the natives very rarely possess any kind of snow-shoes excepting staves, which are used by young people who sometimes display extraordinary adroitness in running down the slopes in this way.

An anecdote is often related in Greenland of an old Moravian missionary, who having retired and taken up his abode in Saxony, was asked how he liked living there. Whereupon he answered, that he found it rather dull. In Greenland, he said, there was always some variety and some news astir, but in Saxony one day ended like the other. Very likely other feelings also had contributed to raise Greenland above Saxony in the opinion of the old man, but at any rate it is proved by experience that nobody need be in want of occupation and entertainment in Greenland, and living there is not much more dull than in some very isolated places in the mother-country. The chief want is the absence of news from abroad for nine months in the year, the mails only arriving by the ships which are successively despatched from the end of March to the end of June. The anxiety with which ships are watched for in spring can hardly be conceived by people who have never experienced a similar isolation. For many years the English whalers brought the first news to Greenland, and they still sometimes render this service to the northern settlements. Letters have been regularly conveyed by them, or occasionally they have delivered some newspapers; but sometimes the first news is nothing but what kayakers who have visited a vessel out at sea have picked up by conversing, as best they could, with the crew, and for want of better information, of course they are eagerly questioned. This may serve to explain how the curious rumours which we have just mentioned can originate and spread along the Greenland shores. At some of the chief stations only one or two European families are to be found, viz. those of the agent and his assistant; in others there may be found four or five, as at Godthaab, and under extraordinarily favourable circumstances their number there can even be augmented to six, besides the Moravians, who live only half an hour's walk from them.

Statistics of the Trade.—In order to facilitate *the Trade*, bills of credit—paper money, indeed—have been introduced as a currency, only accepted as a payment at the trading-stations in Greenland. During the twenty years from 1853 to 1872, the average *annual exports*, besides the cryolite, consisted of 1,185 tuns of oil, 35,439 sealskins, 1,436 fox-skins, 41 bearskins, 811 waterproof jackets, 1,003 waterproof trousers, 3,533 pounds of raw eiderdown, 6,900 pounds of feathers, 2,300 pounds of whalebone, 22,500 pounds of dried codfish, 550 pounds of narwhal-teeth, 87 pounds of walrus-tusks, 1,817 reindeer skins. What is here called oil means the oil ready for sale which has been made of the oil and blubber sent home from Greenland by boiling and clearing it in Copenhagen. The raw eiderdown is likewise cleaned before selling, and in this way loses about two-thirds of its weight. During the period from 1870 to 1874, the mean annual value of the products received from Greenland was 45,600*l.*, that of the cargoes sent thither 23,844*l.*, and the mean expenditure on the ships and navigation 8,897*l.*

During the period from January 1, 1853, to March 31, 1874, or 21¼ years (the yearly accounts being made up on March 31 instead of December 31 after the year 1867) the net revenues of the Greenland Trade amounted to 140,985*l.*, or about 6,600*l.* on an average yearly. This sum, which does not comprise the royalty paid by the Company which works and exports the cryolite, has been calculated by subtracting every expense whatever concerning Greenland and its inhabitants, but not interest on the capital which the government has sunk in the trade, and which has been fixed at 64,426*l.*, the Trade at the same time having been its own insurer. The revenues from the cryolite-tax for the same period were 58,924*l.* It has always been a prevalent opinion, maintained by the government as well as by men to whom it has applied for advice concerning the affairs of Greenland, that the profit gained from the settlements must be considered a balance merely intended to be laid out for their benefit. The whole amount of net revenues from the present Trade during the period from 1790 to 1875, the interest of the capital as well as the income from the cryolite being subtracted, has been estimated at about 160,000*l.*

CHAPTER XVI.

TOPOGRAPHY OF THE TRADING STATIONS AND THEIR APPERTAINING DISTRICTS.

It has already been remarked that the coast is divided into districts, each of which has its chief trading-post with its outposts. North Greenland comprises 7 and South Greenland 5 such districts. Where not otherwise stated the census of October 1870 has been followed in this section.

Julianehaab.—This district comprises the coast from Cape Farewell to the northern point of Nunarsuit. We have already mentioned it as being the most pleasant part of Greenland as regards vegetation, and in all likelihood including the localities famous as being the ancient eastern settlements of the Norse. The inland ice, however, is nearer to the outer shores here than in North Greenland, the distance being between 30 and 60 miles near Cape Farewell, and between 16 and 20 miles in the environs of Nunarsuit. The coast regions thus left uncovered may perhaps be calculated at 1,800 square miles, of which, however, by far the greater part consist of barren mountains, partially covered with ordinary glaciers or highland ice and snow, many of their summits being almost inaccessible. In about ten different places branches of the inland ice project into the sea, some of them throwing off considerable quantities of calved ice, in one fjord, moreover, the northern

Sermilik or Ikersuak, to such an amount that it may be ranged amongst the ice-fjords.

Trade.—The district contains the following trading-stations : Julianehaab, Narsak, Kagsimiut, Sardlok, South-Pröven, Sagdlit, Nanortalik, and Pamiagdluk. Of late it has yielded about 300 tuns of oil and 4,000 sealskins yearly, while at the same time it furnished about one-third of the foxskins exported from Greenland.

Census.—The number of inhabitants in 1870, was 2,570, who were distributed in the following places :—

North of 60° 35'. — Julianehaab 223, Nunarsuit 32, Sakamiut 32, Kagsimiut 105, Karmat 28, Avatarmiut 33, Narsak 25, Niakornarsuk 19, Narsarak 23, Kusanga 9, Sigsardlugtok 14, Igdlumiut 5, Kingatsiak 16, Niakornak 13, Tugdlerunat 14, Ukevisokak 3, Igaliko 37, Kangermiutsiait 74, Kepokarmiut 17, Ikerasarsuk 65.

Between 60° 35' *and* 60° 10'.—Upernivik 20, Ikerasarsuk (Sardlok) 100, Karusuk 8, South-Pröven 90, David's Sound 17, Isua 33, Sagdlit 65, Igdlorpait 76, Anartusok 44, Igpik 25, Kernertok 13, Kerortut 6, Kanajormiut 36, Sermilik 19, Lichtenau 205, Kekertarsuak 19, Karsuk 42, Arnat 13, Nunatsiak 94, Akuliarusek 24.

South of 60° 10'.—Sigsarigsok 62, Iluilek (Nanortalik) 201, Tuapait 30, Ikerasarsuk 14, Tunugdlek 16, Ikigait 5, Pamiagdluk 139, Igdlorsuatsiait 50, Kungmiut 73, Anordluitsok 21, Nuk 26, Augpilagtok 23, Frederiksdal 172, Igdlukasik 48.

Of this population 1,056 natives belonged to the Moravian communities in the year 1872.

Julianehaab (60° 43' N. lat.), situated on the outer side of the peninsula which separates the supposed Erik's and Einar's fjords or the Tunugdliarfik and Igaliko. The route from thence to Igaliko may be made on foot, but will most likely prove extraordinarily troublesome and perhaps even take a couple of days, although it does not appear more than 25 miles. The centre of this peninsula is occupied by the craggy mountain ridge called Redekam, the height of which has been estimated at between 4,000 and 5,000 feet. The houses are built up on both banks of a small river somewhat hidden in a valley, so as not to become visible when approached from the sea until the last moment. On one side are situated the houses of the natives, the oil manufactory, and further up the dwelling of the missionary and the church. A bridge leads to the other side, where are situated the houses of the Trade officials, the physician, and also of several natives, together with storehouses.

The little village corresponds to its southern situation, inasmuch that none of the other stations can boast of so nearly resembling what we are accustomed to see in a more temperate climate. This impression is owing to the narrowness of the plot enclosed by green slopes, and the gardens in front of the houses looking a little less forlorn than other gardens in Greenland. Moreover, besides goats, cows used to graze on the surrounding hills. The nearest heights are marked by beacons ; one of them, named Sakarsuatsiak, on the east side of the harbour, rises 500 feet above the sea, and offers a beautiful view from its summit on the inland side, the foreground displaying the environs of Agpatsivik, celebrated in the traditions regarding the last Norse settlers, beyond which the Redekam and other lofty mountains rear their snowy summits. Close to the houses, a little higher, the very indistinct remains of a little building, dating from the time of the ancient Norse, may be observed.

The present settlement was founded in 1775. A small schooner is stationed in the harbour. To the European residents Julianehaab, with all its amenities, has the inconvenience of being almost the most isolated of the Greenland settlements, although the nearest to Europe. On account of the drift-ice from the east coast a ship has been known but once to have run into the harbour directly from the sea. Generally it must touch at some more northern post, and wait sometimes a couple of weeks, and sometimes even two or three months, before it is able to make its way southward between the ice and the land. In September the pack-ice usually disperses and opens a passage in front of the settlement, allowing the ships to go to sea.

Igaliko has been mentioned partly on account of its historical significance, partly in treating of the breeding of cattle, it being the only place where native farmers are to be found. The road thither along the north side of the Igaliko-fjord presents no landing place for a long distance, on account of the extraordinary steepness of its shore. On almost the first spot where one is able to get a footing, a narrow and secluded valley appears, intersected by a deep river-bed, named Sisardlugtok (not the above-named dwelling-place). Here several ruins, in a tolerable state of preservation, and traces of a bridge are to be seen ; they are supposed to have been the ancient 'dalar' (i.e. valley), a farm belonging to the bishop's see, Garde, now Kagsiarsuk, on the opposite side of the inlet. A footpath can be traced from one of the houses to the others, the origin of which appears very mysterious, as it might almost seem impossible that the impressions in the sod could have been preserved during centuries, while at the same time there is not the least probability that they have been formed by Eskimo wanderers.

Narsak, being 24 miles north of Julianehaab, and more distant from the open sea than the latter place, causes the vegetation thereabouts to be much richer. Some years ago an old Danish cooper managed the Trade here, and availed himself of the opportunity for farming ;

he generally had three cows, three calves, one bull, and twelve sheep. But the natives of the neighbouring places, who subsist for the most part by fishing in the sheltered inlets, are very poor.   Here begins the supposed Erik's-fjord, in the interior of which the richest farms of the ancient settlers seem to have been situated. Ten miles from Narsak, at Ipiutak, the first of the chief ruins is found, a dwelling with some outhouses, surrounded by a willow copse eight feet high. About eight settlements have been traced along the north side of the fjord from thence to its termination. The most remarkable of these ruins are those of another Kagsiarsuk, where also the remains of a church are found, and the sites of several farms can be traced. From thence the best route lies across the penin-sula to the ruins situated at the next inlet, the ice-fjord of Sermilik.   This road is said to be about eight miles long, and for the most part to lead through copses. Even the walls are overgrown with bushes, and alternately succeeded by charming valleys and lakes. Ruins have been traced on this route about one mile from the shore. A narrow eastern branch of Korok fjord adjoins the inland ice, and is said to be sometimes difficult of access on account of calved ice ; to this locality the sagas seem to allude in speaking of some people of Erik's-fjord as living near the 'glaciers.'

Kagsimiut, 44 miles west of Julianehaab, is situated upon an island near the open sea at the mouth of the Ikersuak sound, through which the Sermilik-fjord sends out its icebergs.   Still further seaward, upon *Nunarsuit*, some people live, renowned as skilled kayakers ; they have a very unsheltered sea for their hunting ground. Here the author saw a boy twelve years old who caught seals with harpoon and bladder to perfection, and had a rifle of his own. A narrow sound leads into an inlet on Nunarsuit remarkable for an extraordinarily strong current, and for the numerous seals with which the entrance is crowded at a certain season. The kayakers, therefore, repair to the sound at spring-tide and lie in wait for the seals, which try to swim against the current, but are unable to master it, and on their return are attacked by the kayakers. The catch is sometimes very abundant, but rather dangerous on account of the violent agitation of the water. The interior sounds being frozen up from November till June, the way further north into the confines of Frederikshaab has to be made by rounding Nunarsuit, which is a hazardous route for small boats on account of the heavy swell from the ocean. But in summer an agreeable passage may be made inside, the boat being carried across the isthmus of Itivdliatsiak.

Sardlok, more properly Ikersak, is the northernmost place for the real bladder-nose seal hunt in spring.

Lichtenau, a Moravian missionary station, is situated 3 miles from the trading post of South-Pröven, a footpath leading thither along the shore, which is, however, rather dangerous in winter. The missionaries have a spacious two-storied dwelling, the upper part containing accommodation for three families, the ground-floor being used for schoolroom, kitchen, and storerooms; but the church forms a separate building. The settlement stands a little within the entrance of the fjord named after it, at the foot of a mountain chain, the slopes of which are rather abundantly covered with verdure. We have already mentioned the beautiful spot at the head of the fjord where the missionaries get wood from the birch copse. But the rest of the mainland surrounding this fjord, and the next also, the southern Sermilik, present but very little low land. Amongst the islands in front of this tract the Sermersok is distinguished by its height and ice-crowned summit.

The others contain several inhabited places, amongst which the following two :—

Igdlorpait is an auxiliary station to Lichtenau, established a few years ago not far from the small island of Unartok, the remarkable hot springs of which we already have described. It has been asserted that a Norse ruin formerly was to be seen near the hot-water basins. The author did not see any other remains than those of an Eskimo tentwall, but some traces perhaps may have existed near the sea, which seems to encroach gradually on the beach of loose gravel and boulders.

Sagdlit, an outpost which has been established upon one of the islets bordering the ocean in front of Sermersok. Hardly any dwelling-place in Greenland offers an appearance more desolate and dreary than this, being on one side exposed to the open sea, which during the autumn tempests almost washes over the island, covering the very houses with its foam ; while on the other side the eye rests on the bare cliffs and ice-covered summits and clefts of Sermersok. In summer the islands are generally surrounded by drifting ice, and the prevailing fogs and salt-water spray combine to check vegetation. The only attraction of the place is the seals, which are extraordinarily abundant, especially the bladder-nose, at the season of the arrival of which the population from the surrounding places pitch their tents there.

Nanortalik (also called Iluilek) situated upon an island at the mouth of the Tasermiut-fjord, is an outpost, but furnished with buildings more like those of the chief stations, having generally been managed by an assistant who had the superintendence of the neighbouring outposts.

Frederiksdal, a Moravian missionary station almost exactly in 60° N. lat., was established in the year 1824 for the especial purpose of attracting to their community the heathen Eastlanders who occasionally visit the west coast. The missionaries inhabit a spacious and comfortable house, which has been built close to the church and school-house, so as to afford a passage from one building into the other. From thence there is an easy walk of less than two hours along the sea-shore to the southernmost point of the mainland of Greenland, whereas Cape Farewell is part of an island and situated about 28 miles further to the south-east.

Pamiagdluk is the southernmost trading station, situated upon an island in about 59° 57′ N. lat. at the mouth of the Ilua-fjord. The amount of products annually purchased there rivals that collected at one of the chief stations further north. To the west, pretty far out to sea, is situated a group of small islands, the Kitsigsut, where the bladder-nose hunt is carried on by the inhabitants of this southernmost tract.

Some Remarks on the East Coast.—To the east of Cape Farewell, or Kangersuak, which is situated about 18 miles from Pamiagdluk, no dwelling-place is found occupied by natives belonging to the Christian communities or comprised in the census of the population of the Danish trading districts. It is well known, however, that the southernmost part of the east coast has been explored by Captain Graah, who, at least up to 65° N. lat., took possession of it in the name of the King of Denmark, and gave it the name of the Coast of King Frederick VI. Natives from these regions every year visit Pamiagdluk for the purpose of trading. Between 1848 and 1854 two or three umiaks yearly brought on an average for sale 1,000 lbs. of blubber, six bearskins, twelve foxskins, and 200 sealskins, which they chiefly bartered for tobacco and ironware, but not for coffee at all. During the last few years they also had acquired a couple of guns and ammunition. Later on the author has gained more special information concerning the east coast from an assistant, Mr. U. Rosing, who officiated at the southernmost places for several years, and knowing the language to perfection availed himself of the opportunity offered of conversing with the Eastlanders, not only to collect all we possess of their traditions, but also various notices concerning their present state and the coast tract inhabited by them. The following brief abstract of this account, which bears date of the year 1861, may appropriately be inserted here :—The island of Cape Farewell itself contains two inlets, in which house-ruins and spots covered with a rich vegetation are found. Upon the same island, or in its vicinity, the first dwelling-place of the Eastlanders was discovered. The island of Aluk is situated where the coast of the mainland turns to the northward : here natives from the west coast sometimes meet and barter with their heathen countrymen. From thence it took seventeen days' journey by kayak to reach the northernmost inhabited place called Angmagsalik.

From this remote station only once, in 1860, an umiak arrived at Pamiagdluk, but the stay of the travellers was so short that only scanty information could be acquired about it. The boat-owner, named Samik, seemed to be a smart, intelligent fellow. He had lost his toes and the tips of most of his fingers; from the appearance of the stumps the mutilation had been caused by some act of violence. He was an expert kayaker, nevertheless, threw his javelin with his left hand, and was just able to grasp the paddle with his stumpy fingers. Angmagsalik was said to be very populous ; some years earlier, thirteen umiaks had gone from thence to the north, but only three of them having returned, the others were supposed to have been wrecked, the coast further north being very steep and dangerous. The next hamlet was Umivik, four days' journey to the south, containing ten houses, and then

Igdlutuarsuk, with thirteen houses. The latter was situated on a fjord, from the interior of which a great many icebergs issue. From thence to Cape Farewell fifteen inhabited places were met with, most of them only containing one or two houses. The whole number of inhabited houses on the coast tract in question was fifty-three, besides those of Angmagsalik. According to these statements, Rosing estimated the whole number of inhabitants, the latter place included, at between 800 and 1,000. They chase the bears by aid of their dogs, and sometimes stab them in their dens in the snow. Dog-sledging is practised everywhere almost exactly in the same way as in the northern part of the west coast. The ancient modes of catching seals which we have mentioned as almost entirely abandoned on the west coast are also still made use of there, and at Angmagsalik some harpoons were still made of bone for want of iron. The kayakers are not very experienced in the art of righting themselves, or rising to the surface with the help of their paddle on being capsized, but they frequently practise swimming as a means of rescue in that case. Nobody knew anything of ruins of buildings constructed by former inhabitants of the country of a race different from their own. The strong current which runs along the coast often carries the drift out of sight in a single day. Several tales are told of wrecked ships having been seen in the ice, and formerly dead whales not unfrequently drifted ashore, offering an opportunity of getting fishing-lines from whale-bone. According to the statements here given we have reason to suppose that Angmagsalik is situated not far beyond the northmost point reached by Graah on his exploring expedition. In the year 1871 a party of Eastlanders, probably from Umivik, having visited Pamiagdluk, on returning were obliged to set up winter quarters on the east coast before they could reach their home. In spring they made once more for Pamiagdluk, but on arriving there they fell sick, and in a few days eleven of them died, only leaving two grown-up women and four children.

Ancient Geography of Julianehaab District.—As a supplement to what we have often stated concerning the situation of the ancient Norse settlements, we will here glance over a topographical description of Greenland supposed to date from the fourteenth century. It is generally called 'The description by Ivar Baardson,' and has been written down from the verbal narration of this man, who officiated as a manager at the bishop's see of Garde for many years, and whom we have mentioned as having been sent to explore the western settlement when it had been attacked by the 'Skrellings.' This account begins by describing the route from Iceland to Greenland; it continues by stating that the easternmost dwelling-place in Greenland is Skagefjord and that the next one is Herjulf's Næs. We have shown that the latter probably is Ikigait near Frederiksdal, whereas we are not aware of any ruins having as yet been discovered corresponding to the former, which, however, is no proof that no such ruins exist. Further eastward several localities are then mentioned, which were occasionally visited by the settlers, but none of them were inhabited, the easternmost being Korsö, beyond which 'nothing was to be seen but ice and snow by land as well as at sea.' From Herjulf's Næs westward the first fjord was Ketil's-fjord; his description of it agrees with Tasermiut, at the end of which the remains of a church have been traced. Then the account continues: 'Item, next to Ketil's-fjord is Rafn's-fjord, and far into it is the sister-monastery Ordinis S. Benedicti; this monastery owns the whole to its termination, and towards the outside to the Vaage church, which is consecrated to St. Olaf. The Vaage church possessed the whole country outside the fjord. In the fjord are situated many islands, which are the joint property of the monastery and the cathedral church. Upon these islands there is much warm water, which in winter is so hot, that nobody can approach it, but in summer is moderately hot, so as to allow of bathing in it, and many people recover their health there after sickness.

'Item, the next one is Einar's-fjord, between which and Rafn's-fjord there is a large farm belonging to the king, and called Foss, i.e. waterfall; and there stands a costly church consecrated to St. Nicholas, which the king has to enfeoff: and in the vicinity is an extensive fishing-lake filled with fish, and when much rain has fallen and the water again subsides and decreases, innumerable fishes are left upon the dry land.'

If we now survey our present maps we find that between Tasermiut and Igaliko or Einar's-fjord there is a wide bay, one chief branch of which is the Lichtenau-fjord, while its outer part includes many islands. This fjord terminates in two small branches, the Amituarsuk, with its beautiful waterfall, and the Sioralik, where the remains of a church and cemetery have been found. From Amituarsuk is a route by land to the supposed remains of the bishop's residence at the Igaliko-fjord. Around the outer bay ruins have been found in eight or ten places, while the hot springs exist upon one of the islands in the centre of it. It will be apparent that these facts agree in a remarkable manner with the fragment of the description above quoted. From this it passes on to mention Einar's-fjord, after which two smaller fjords are enumerated, which we may recognise on both sides of Julianehaab, after which follows the Erik's-fjord, corresponding to the Tunugdliarfik of the maps. Then many islands are mentioned as well as several smaller fjords, of which two are called 'ice-fjords.' One of them bears the name

of 'Utiblik's-fjord,' in which the common Eskimo local
name Itivdlek, also written Itiblik, is most distinctly recognisable, and as far as we know, the only trace of such
Eskimo appellations in the sagas.

In passing to the north the population is mentioned as
growing scantier and scantier until the uninhabited tract
begins which occupies the space between the eastern and
western settlements, the latter being supposed to begin in
64° N. lat. This will suffice to give an idea of the researches by which it has been possible to recognise the
localities of the sagas in the present Danish Greenland.
By means of these investigations every spot where ruins
have been found has been identified in the ancient
records, and but few localities mentioned in them remain
unrecognisable from the absence of ruins or traces. The
discordance between the description given by Ivar Baardson
of the physical features of the country and the appearance they present at present may arise from the author of
the written record having confounded Greenland with
Vinland, as he had visited none of these countries himself.
The western settlement will be mentioned in the following
pages. For further details we must refer to ancient documents themselves, and especially to the remarkable explanation by Rafn contained in his 'Ancient Geography
of the Arctic Countries of America.'

Frederikshaab.—To this settlement belongs the next
coast-line up to 62° 30′ N. lat. At both of its extremities
the inland ice projects almost to the open sea, while
throughout the remainder of the district the average breadth
of the coast region is 34 miles. It is indicated by seven
fjords, besides many smaller inlets, two of them being regular ice-fjords. In its southern part mountain heights of
from 3,000 to 4,000 feet occur, with enormous precipices
towards the open sea.

Trade.—During the last few years about 68 tuns of oil and 1,000 sealskins annually have been exported from thence, the trading stations being Frederikshaab, Avigait, Narsalik, Kangarsuk, Arsuit, and Sanerut.

Census.—In October 1870 the number of inhabitants was 821, distributed in the following places from south to north : Sanerut 42, Isua 29, Ivigtut 52 (of whom 38 were Europeans), Arsut 77, Tigsaluk 41, Kangarsuk 57, Neria 38, Narsalik 51, Iluilarsuk 21, Kekertak 27, Kvan Island 73, Frederikshaab 129, Storö 78, Kuanek 18, Avigait 88.

Sanerut has been tried as a trading-post, but with little profit, on account of the scantiness of its population and its remote situation. The houses stand on the southern side of a rather large island which presents a very high and precipitous headland to the open sea. A narrow and very shallow channel, Kepisako, separates it from the mainland, which is here almost wholly covered with inland ice.

Ivigtut has already been sufficiently mentioned in giving the details of the cryolite mine. At the entrance to it from the sea, at the foot of the lofty mountain Kunak, is situated the trading-post *Arsut*, which, however, now will be abandoned. Several Norse ruins are found on the environs of these places, especially in the Ivigtut-fjord. The most difficult route for umiak travelling in South Greenland lies between Arsut and Frederikshaab, on account of the steepness of the shore, the unsheltered capes projecting far into the sea, violent gusts of wind rushing down from the highlands, or blowing with tremendous force through the narrow channels between the precipices, to which must be added the difficulties of the passage over two ice-fjords. North of this unsheltered tract an enormous quantity of calved ice, including numerous icebergs of medium size, issues from the Narsalik-fjord, but further northward the mainland becomes lower, and the coast offers sheltered passages behind numerous islands. Upon one of them, called Igausak, ruins are found of Norse origin. On a small plain the foundation walls of tolerably large buildings can be traced, but they have become somewhat indistinct from being overgrown by luxuriant tufts of grass. The isolated situation of the place and the want of pasturing grounds thereabouts, denote that it has probably been a fishing station.

Frederikshaab (62° N. lat.) is situated on a point of the mainland consisting of low hills projecting far out to sea, but the harbour is well sheltered and surrounded by numerous islands. The settlement contains one larger dwelling-house, with accommodation both for the officials of the Trade and the missionary, a church, and seven or eight other buildings, besides fourteen houses belonging to the natives. The nearest environs consist of low rocks alternating with swampy plains, presenting rather a barren appearance, owing to their exposure to the fogs and icy sea-winds prevailing here during the best of the summer time.

Avigait is the nearest place to the so-called 'ice-blink,' a low sandy beach stretching about eight miles in front of the inland ice, which here is separated from the open sea by almost nothing but a strip of low alluvial land intersected by watercourses issuing from the glacier. Only a few low rocky hills are scattered over the plain, and some islands just of the same appearance yield very insufficient shelter to travellers who have to pass this tract in an umiak. Several Eskimo ruins are found upon the islets, and tales are told of the extraordinary bravery and expertness displayed by the seal-hunters who have inhabited these desolate regions.

Godthaab.—This district comprises the next tract from the middle of the ice-blink to about 64° 50′, or 150 miles in

a straight line. In its southern half the distance of the
inland ice from the outer shores varies greatly, but is generally not considerable, whereas in its northern part the
breadth of the coast region, free from ice, is from fifty to
seventy miles. The coast is indented by six or seven larger
and many smaller fjords. The most remarkable amongst
them is the Godthaab-fjord, which runs in a north-eastern
direction for seventy miles, and near its termination sends off
a branch to the south-east, twenty-five miles long, through
which icebergs of smaller dimensions are discharged ; its
centre is wide and includes three rather large islands, while
its mouth in one place is only two miles broad, which
causes a strong current to run in front of the settlement,
especially at spring tide. To the north of this inlet the
land is remarkably low, while on the opposite side the
mainland, as well as the islands encompassed by it, rise
3,000 or 4,000 feet above the level of the sea. Further
southward the highest tops of the mainland seem to be
nearer 2,000 feet. The greater part of the coast is sheltered by clusters of low islands.

The *Trade* carried on by means of the stations of Godthaab, Narsak, Kornok, Kangek, Fiskernæs, and Atangmik
has of late years yielded about 74 tuns of oil and 1,000
sealskins, on an average, per annum. Godthaab is the
southernmost station for eiderdown, and formerly also for
reindeer skins. Codfish were also formerly caught and prepared for exportation, but this trade has now been almost
abandoned.

Census.—In October 1870 the number of inhabitants
was 999, distributed in the following places, passing from
south to north : Kangarsuk 12, Lichtenfels 143, Fiskernæs
90, Tornait 42, Karajat 14, Narsak 76, Kangek 102, New
Herrnhut 110, Godthaab 149, Kigutilik 15, Karusuk 6,
Sardlok 35, Umanak 68, Atangmik 51. As regards eccle-

siastical matters the population is divided between the
Danish and the two Moravian communities. The latter,
viz. Ny (or, New) Herrnhut and Lichtenfels, numbered 773
souls in the year 1855, 711 in 1860, and 538 in 1872. This
striking decrease is not owing to any accidental cause, but
merely to a prevailing mortality arising from the miserable
condition of the natives belonging to these communities,
as regards their habitations, clothing, and whole mode of
life. The disposition to sickliness is most likely enhanced
by marriages being exclusively contracted between members of the same community, and consequently it is rather
probable that they will become nearly extinct within the
next 50 or 100 years.

Godthaab (64° 8′ N. lat.) and *Ny Herrnhut* are situated on a point of the mainland at the mouth of the fjord,
only half a mile from each other. Besides the usual Trade
officials, one or two Danish missionaries, who manage the
seminary, and two or three Moravian missionaries, the
Royal Inspector or Governor of South Greenland and the
physician for the northern part of it, reside in this place.
In addition to the seminary, Godthaab has a church of
rather imposing appearance for Greenland, but too large for
the community, and built of brick, a material very little
adapted to the country. The houses of the natives, almost
all with sloping roofs of boards, look very pretty, but at
Ny Herrnhut they offer a sad appearance. The latter station
has a two-storied building, containing accommodation for
the missionaries, schoolroom, and church, or ' meeting-hall '
as it is called. The peninsula, at the extremity of which the
settlement is situated, is rather barren and low, but several
considerable heights within a distance of eight miles give
sufficient variety to the views from the surrounding hills,
such as, close to the harbour, the ' Little ' and the ' Great
Malena,' the latter rising 2,400 feet, and a little further off

the Hjortetak or Kingigtorsuak, and the Saddle or Sermit-
siak. Both of the latter rear their summits more than 3,000
feet; their northern slopes are covered with glaciers extremely worthy of a closer examination, and will amply
repay the trouble of a short excursion, especially a visit
to a narrow chasm of the Kingigtorsuak, only si:- miles
from Godthaab. In order to come to the nearest copse of
willow and alders, one has to travel ten or twelve miles.
The harbour is about two miles distant by sea from the
settlement, in front of which it is not always safe for vessels
to ride at anchor, on account of the rapid current, drifting
ice, and sometimes a heavy swell.

Kornok and *Umanak* are situated upon islands about
thirty miles further up the fjord, the latter being an auxiliary
station to Ny Herrnhut, and occupied by one missionary,
for whom a nice, comfortable dwelling was erected in
the year 1862. These settlements possess all the amenities which nature affords in the interior fjord regions, more
warmth and a clearer sky in summer, while the sheltered
sea branching off in various directions offers convenient
communication with the surrounding shores. We have
already given a detailed account of the attempts at horticulture here. Of course the most luxuriant copses and other
products of the vegetable kingdom, which used to be
found in the part of Greenland lying under this latitude, are
at no great distance. Ptarmigan and reindeer are also
more numerous here. No wonder that when a boat arrives
from these places at Godthaab it is generally expected to
bring a supply of these different articles, which, strange to
say, cost between two and four times as much in the former
place as in the latter.

Kangek, situated eight miles from Godthaab, upon an
island of the outer entrance to the fjord, presents the most
striking contrast to the places just mentioned. Besides the

uniformly barren hills of the low islands, nothing but the ocean is displayed to the view, the sea washing over the shores near the houses, and breaking upon the numerous rocks and shallows in front of the islands. The narrow plot upon which the dwellings are crowded is evidence of its having been a favourite wintering place for many generations, the soil having been undermined by the sea, and displaying an unusual accumulation of relics from ancient houses, and from the animals which have served the former inhabitants for food. This statement is confirmed by the traditional tales, in which Kangek is frequently mentioned and spoken of as a favourite goal for travellers. But it requires its inhabitants to be amongst the most hardy and expert kayakers, their usual hunting 'grounds' being quite unsheltered and even far out at sea.

A few miles to the north of this place are the remains of Egede's first colony, now called Igdluernerit. The foundation walls are still preserved of a house fifty feet long and twenty feet wide, about four feet high, and built of big stones with turf interposed. In the centre of it some brickwork is observable, probably the foundation of the chimney; coals lie scattered around the ruin, in the vicinity of which three or four smaller buildings can be traced. A continuous cluster of innumerable islands and rocks extends hence northwards for forty miles, affording favourable opportunity of collecting eiderdown and driftwood. The mainland thus bordered presents some of the most extensive tracts of low land in Greenland, where formerly a productive reindeer hunt was carried on. In the autumn of 1791, a party of travellers coming in an umiak from the north, and being stopped by drift ice, tried to cross this peninsula on foot, but four of them died from cold and exhaustion; only three of the wanderers, in a pitiful state, reached an inhabited place on the Godthaab-fjord.

Fiskernæs (63° 3′ N. lat.) was formerly a chief station, and in the years 1845 to 1849 furnished a considerable amount of oil and skins, especially from the seal-fishery, carried on by means of nets in narrow sounds. After the decay of this industry, codfish, which here are more abundant than anywhere else along the coast, were made an article of trade, but the continual decrease and impoverishment of the population belonging to the Lichtenfels community at last made it necessary to retrench the expenses connected with the establishment by making it merely an outpost. The little settlement, however, has a pretty appearance, being situated some miles up a narrow fjord between low rounded hills. About 8 miles further up the fjord the country abounds in copses of willow and alder. In one of the valleys an isolated Norse ruin is found, about 40 feet long, the interior having formerly been divided into one large and two smaller rooms, and the remains of a smaller building can be traced in the vicinity. The walls are low and overgrown with willows. A tolerably level plain extends from this spot to a lake, covered with a beautiful vegetation of shrubs alternating with groups of bushes, and pleasingly diversified with numerous angelicas and light-green ferns.

Lichtenfels is situated upon the same island as the last station, but further towards the sea and more exposed to its fogs, for which reason its environs are more barren. The missionaries inhabit a house similar to that of Ny Herrnhut. We have already mentioned the dwellings of the natives. The community has decreased to nearly half the number of persons which it comprised thirty years ago ; without doubt they have sunk lowest of all the inhabitants of Greenland as to their state of prosperity.

Ancient Geography of the Districts.—We have mentioned that north of the regions which are supposed to

have comprised the most populous or chief part of the
Eastern Settlement, some ruins are found scattered in the
environs of Arsut and upon the island of Igausak. Sixty
miles further north remains are said to exist in a fjord
called Agdlumersat ; then comes the ruin at Fiskernæs just
mentioned, but from thence the author is not aware of any
having been discovered for a distance of 90 miles, until
we arrive at the regions which have been conjectured to
be identical with what has been called the Western Settlement properly speaking, and of which we will now try
to give a sketch. The Norse ruins discovered in the
Godthaab and the Amaraglik-fjords are all situated at so
great a distance from the open sea and on such sheltered
inlets, that in choosing the localities for their abodes, the
settlers seem to have been guided by the special desire
of having in their neighbourhood a sea more constantly
frozen over in winter, and thereby offering an opportunity
for a seal-hunt, which must have been especially practised
by them.

The tract thus formerly inhabited occupies an area
extending 64 miles from N.W. to S.E., the numerous
branches of the fjords which intersect it included. Between twenty and thirty spots spread over this tract,
remains of dwellings or farms have been discovered,
situated in the valleys or lower and level parts of the
mountainous country. Intercourse between the dwelling-
places was afforded partly by sea, and partly by valleys or
narrow passes crossing the mountain chains. This tract
is about 25 miles distant from the outer shores, while on
the inward side it is bordered by the vast glacier of the
interior. In the remotest north-eastern corner of the
Godthaab-fjord, called Ujararsuit, stands the ruin of a
small church, the walls of which in the year 1829 measured 8 feet high, and contained an entrance $2\frac{1}{2}$ feet

wide. The remains of several other buildings, fences, and graves are found near the church. A south-eastern branch of the fjord extending from Pisigsarfik to Kapisilik occupies the central part of the whole tract and contains several beautiful spots. The Pisigsarfik, i.e. ' (bow) shooting place,' is a mountain with which are connected some traditions concerning the ancient settlers, and the Kapisilik is a small river where the real salmon, which are very rare in Greenland, are found. From this branch there is a passage across a tolerably wide and level lowland to the interior ice-fjord, whose shores are very difficult of access and very little explored. From Kapisilik, a valley about 12 miles long, containing three lakes with traces of inhabitants further than usual from the shore, leads to the Amaraglik-fjord, on whose shore also the remains of a church have been discovered. But, on the whole, the localities mentioned in the ancient records have not been traced with the same degree of probability and distinctness for the Western as for the Eastern Settlement.

Sukkertoppen.—This district comprises the following tract unto 66° 10′ N. lat. Throughout its whole extent the headlands are extraordinarily lofty and precipitous. The mainland as well as some larger islands are studded with inaccessible pinnacled summits furrowed by numerous narrow clefts filled with perpetual ice and snow. No measurements have been taken, but it appears that the height of these mountain chains frequently exceeds 3,000, and sometimes perhaps even attains 4,000 feet, in the immediate vicinity of the sea. The coast of the mainland is broken by three fjords, the Isortok, Kangerdlugsuatsiak, and Kangerdlugsuak or Southern Stream-fjord, which run up the country to a distance of from 40 to 64 miles. Only the second of them produces icebergs. These inlets have been very little explored, and are only known from description of native travellers, and some large maps sketched likewise by natives. According to the information received in this way, it appears that the peninsulas here maintain their elevation towards the interior more than in other fjords, and that not only are valleys or low land rare, but the mountain tops are also covered with more ice and snow here than elsewhere in the interior fjord regions. However, it is difficult to ascertain what belongs to isolated glaciers, and what perhaps may be a part of the inland ice, the border of which is only very little known for this tract.

Trade.—The trade carried on by means of the stations Sukkertoppen, Naparsok, and Kangamiut, during the latest period yielded 92 tuns of oil and 1,000 sealskins, on an average, per annum. The codfish exported from Greenland during the last few years have mostly been purchased here ; it is a chief place for eiderdown, and formerly was for reindeer also.

Census.—In October 1870 the number of inhabitants was 765, distributed in the following places from south to north : Naparsok 81, Sukkertoppen 359, Agpamiut 41, Kangerdluarsuk 54, Timerdlit 45, Kangamiut 197.

Sukkertoppen (65° 25′ N. lat.) is situated upon a tolerably large island, the conical elevations of which present the appearance expressed in its Eskimo name—**manîtsoĸ,** i.e. 'uneven.' The settlement occupies a small peninsula which forms the harbour, and at high-water is divided into three parts ; intercourse can sometimes only be maintained by boats. The building-plots also are very narrow, and surrounded by dark cliffs, which give the spot a sombre appearance on entering the harbour, the rocks at the mouth of the little creek moreover being generally washed by a heavy surf. This is the most populous place in Greenland. Some of its native inhabitants have acquired sufficient skill in building European boats for their cod-fishing. A fine stone-built church stands here, but the missionary resides at Holstenborg. A couple of miles west of the settlement white whales are caught in a very unusual manner, viz. by means of nets in open water, from January to March. Formerly this catch used to yield about 100 white whales every year. Two miles further off is situated the sharp-pointed conical island, Kin of Sal or Umanak, a well known sea-mark.

Naparsok has acquired a sad renown from the famine in the winter of 1856–7. Of the 140 persons who then perished of starvation in South Greenland, the greater part died here and lie buried under the ruins of the huts in which they expired. A rare concurrence of unfavourable circumstances caused this disaster, the communication with neighbouring stations having been cut off and the seal-catch totally failing at the same time. The trader of the place, a European, having consumed his scanty stores by sharing them with the natives, set out for Sukkertoppen in an umiak in the month of March, but no news was received of him before the month of May, when the remains of him and his companions were found upon an island to the north of the latter place. These poor people having been wrecked there had tried to shelter themselves by making a hole in the snow, in which their corpses were found, lacerated and half devoured by bears or foxes.

Kangamiut is an ancient dwelling-place rich in traditions, and was formerly the chief settlement. The sea thereabouts contains an extraordinary abundance of cod-fish, halibut, and sharks. It also appears that the saddle-back seal remains here longer than on other parts of the coast, a favourable catch sometimes being made even in January and February, when the seals have almost disappeared from the southern coast. A few miles to the north is the South Ström-fjord, the mouth of which, on account of the extraordinary violence of current, can only be passed in a boat at the very moment of the turn of the tide. This fjord seems to form a sort of barrier for the passage of a great many saddle-back seals, as they are far more frequently found to the south than to the north of it, and there is some reason to believe that on their migration from south to north a considerable number of them stop here and set out to sea without passing this boundary.

Holstenborg.—This settlement comprises the succeeding tract up to 67° 40′ N. lat., where the Nagsutok or North Ström-fjord forms the boundary between South and North Greenland. This land is indicated by three or four other fjords which do not extend inland more than between 30 or 40 miles, none of them touching the inland ice, which here appears to retreat from the outer shores about 80 miles on an average. Moreover, as far as we are informed, this part of the country is throughout much lower than the former district, the mountains only here and there rising higher than 2,000 feet, and little snow and ice being visible upon them. Probably we have here the most extensive tract of land unbroken by inlets and at the same time free of glaciers, and this is confirmed by the fact that reindeer were formerly most numerous here.

Trade.—The trade now yields about 60 tuns of oil and 400 sealskins yearly on an average, besides whalebone and eiderdown. The trading-posts are Holstenborg, Kerrortusok, Sarfanguak, and Itivdlek.

Census.—In October 1870 the number of inhabitants was 545, distributed among the following places: Itivdlek (southernmost) 48, Sakak 41, Sakardlit 46, Timerdlit 27, Igilorsuatsiak 23, Sarfanguak 31, Umanarsuk 31, Kerrortosuk 129, Holstenborg (northernmost) 168.

Holstenborg (66° 56′ N. lat.) is situated on a projecting peninsula of the mainland, which here rises to a considerable height, but is partly bordered by a strip of flat lowland, and intersected by valleys. The houses, with a church and a missionary dwelling, stand at the mouth of such a valley, somewhat higher above the sea than usual. The blubber store and oil manufactory occupy a separate place at the mouth of the harbour, called Pararsuk, where the captured whales can be towed close to the beach. The harbour is spacious, offering a safe anchorage for ships, and, it is said, a favourable opportunity for repairing them, by means of a sandy beach. It has often been visited by whalers, fishermen, and exploring vessels. On the north side of the harbour the ruins of the original settlement are found, which was founded in 1759. This spot is overgrown by willows, whose luxuriance is exceptional in a spot so near the open sea, but may be explained by the shelter offered by the mountain chain on the north side. Although the whale fishery, formerly so profitable in this place, has now dwindled until it yields only one whale on an average yearly, it is still to be considered one of the chief occupations of the inhabitants of Holstenborg. The settlement is situated just within the arctic circle, the sun being visible for a few days at midnight. Here also we meet with the first sledge-dogs, of which, however, only a few are kept in this place, whereas they are of great importance in all the succeeding more northerly settlements.

Umanarsuk, four miles south of the latter, was formerly a whaling and trading-post. About six miles further to the south-east are the ruins of the former whaling station of Nepisane, mentioned by Egede, and only half a mile from thence another ruin is said to be found, consisting of massive stone walls with two entrances. Some have ascribed this ruin to the ancient Norse, but more likely it may have belonged to the Dutch, and in that case it is the only sign of their having had any establishment on the coast of Greenland.

Egedesminde.—This district extends from the confines of the former station about 60 miles to the north and then about 20 to the east, the outer coast line here suddenly trending in this direction and forming that open space which is known under the name of the Disco Bay. As to the distance of the inland ice from the outer coast and the occurrence of glaciers, this district is almost like the former. The level of the country, however, appears still lower, and it is much more broken up by arms of the sea. The fjords of Nagsutok, Atanek, and Aulatsivik intersect it in many directions, the latter touching the inland ice itself. The interior ramifications of these inlets are only separated from each other by low land and lakes which can be crossed with umiaks, and in this way there is a passage from the south up to Disco Bay through the interior fjord-regions, besides the usual outer route. This is what has caused these tracts to be still more frequented by the natives than those belonging to Holstenborg, and made the hunting grounds of the former the chief rendezvous for the inhabitants of the south and the north. But also the route along the outer shores is everywhere easy and pleasant by umiak or in a common boat. Here no swell from the open sea is to be feared, numerous sounds affording sheltered passages everywhere. At the same time there is an abundance of fish and game ; eggs may be found in most of the islands, and later in the season codfish, halibut, and trout are plentiful.

Trade.—The production of articles for the Trade has greatly decreased, and during the last few years consisted of 74 tuns of oil and 3,400 sealskins yearly, besides eider-down, while at the same time the trading stations were

Egedesminde, Nivak, Hunde (Dog's) Island, Kangatsiak, Iginiarfik, and Agto.

Census.—In October 1870 the population amounted to 1,008, distributed among the following places from south to north: Agto 54, Ikerasak 61, Sagtut 68, Itivdlek 68, Tunungasok 9, Iginiarfik 17, Tasiusarsuk 8, Aulatsivik 17, Niakornarsuk 46, Ikerasarsuk 13, Kangatsiak 50, Kepingasok 34, Kekertarsuatsiak 70, Kangarsutsiak 81, Manermiut 29, Nivak 30, Western Island 38, Itiudlermuit 9, Egedesminde 152, Akunak 28, Maneetsok 42, Hunde Island 84.

Egedesminde is situated upon an island at the entrance to Disco Bay. It is closely surrounded by other islands as well as by narrow sounds and sheltered inlets on all sides. The surface of these islands exhibits nothing but low rounded hills alternating with swampy valleys, and covered only with the usual scanty vegetation of the outer shores. Upon some very low islands in front of the settlement the peculiar peat formation is found which we have described in the section on vegetable products. The settlement has a small church, and a missionary has of late resided there. From thence to the east along the shores of Disco Bay there is generally in winter a regular communication by sledge.

Agto, the southernmost outpost in North Greenland is situated upon an island somewhat less sheltered and even more barren than Egedesminde. A strong current generally makes the ice unsafe thereabouts, and there is but little opportunity for dog-sledging. But the place has been tolerably productive. The surrounding sea is very rich in codfish and halibut; to the south of it walrus are not unfrequent, an island being found there which they are said to visit and land upon. Four miles west of Agto is the island of Rifkol or Umanak, the top of which serves for a sea-mark on account of its height and conical shape.

It is only 850 feet above the level of the sea. From its top the outlines of the island of Disco, at a distance of 82 miles, can be very distinctly recognised.

Christianshaab.—This district comprises the next part of the coast as far as to the Jakobshavn ice-fjord. North of Egedesminde the mainland recedes in forming Disco Bay, and the islands in front of it become rarer, the distance between the inland ice and the outer shores exclusive of Disco varying from 24 to 32 miles for the next 80 miles from south to north. This coast tract is intersected by the ice-fjord and its lateral branches, and partly by crossing the latter, partly by land, it is easy to reach the edge of the interior ice-waste in different places, and even to examine that part of it from which the icebergs issue. Notwithstanding the vicinity of these icy regions, vegetation here assumes a more luxuriant aspect, Disco Bay in some measure bearing the character of a fjord and causing the climate of the eastern shore to be more pleasant. The highest mountains of this part of the mainland measure between 1,200 and 1,400 feet.

Trade.—The trading stations are Christianshaab, Claushavn, Akudlit, and Ikamiut, yielding an annual export of about 110 tuns of oil and 1,700 sealskins.

Census.—In October 1870 the number of inhabitants was 481, distributed among the following places : Ikamiut 102, Akudlit 63, Christianshaab 91 ; and at the mouth of the ice-fjord : Claushavn 127, Igdlumiut 15, Karsomiut 12, Narsarmiut 41, Erke 30.

Christianshaab is situated on the mainland, the houses being hidden behind a point of the latter and some islands which enclose the spacious and sheltered harbour. A valley measuring about 600 or 800 yards in breadth extends on the opposite side of the harbour along the foot of the Kakarsuak hill, on the top of which a beacon is erected at a height of 1,255 feet. Crowberries and blaeberries, which are very abundant in these environs, can be gathered up to the very top of this elevation. The settlement was founded in 1734, and the dwelling-house is probably the same which was inhabited by Hans Egede's son Paul. It stands on a slope at the foot of a hill, which in July is beautifully covered with blue and yellow flowers ; it is built of timber and still habitable. But of late years the settlement has been managed only by an assistant, under the superintendence of the agent of Egedesminde.

The inhabitants of *Claushavn*, together with the other stations nearest to the ice-fjord, derive their chief sustenance from the seal-catch carried on amongst the enormous crowd of icebergs which annually pass through the mouth of the fjord, and a great many of which accumulate by grounding, and remaining for some time in front of it until they are successively lifted by the spring-tides and carried further out to sea. As to the resources thus offered by the ice-fjord and the remarkable action of the large glacier in discharging the bergs, we refer to the preceding sections especially treating of these subjects. The journey from Christianshaab thither, about 20 miles, can be made in winter by land as well as by sea, the route being unusually level.

Jakobshavn.—To this settlement belongs the mainland from the ice-fjord just spoken of to the next ice-fjord, the Torsukatak, including one outpost called Ata, on the inner side of the Arveprins Island, which borders the same ice-fjord. This tract of the mainland offers just the same features as that of the former settlement, being intersected by a northern branch of the ice-tjord and by two smaller fjords.

The *trading stations* are Jakobshavn, Pakitsok, and Ata, which yield an annual produce of about 104 tuns of oil and 900 sealskins.

Census.—In October 1870 the number of inhabitants was 424, distributed among the following places: Jakobshavn 226; and close by it at the mouth of the ice-fjord: Igdlumiut 46, and Kingigtok 37; to the north: Rodebay 36, Pakitsok 25, Ata 24, Arsivik 8, Igdlutuarsuit 36.

Jakobshavn is situated scarcely a mile from the ice-fjord, the houses including stores and dwellings for the officials of the trade stand at the head of a small and narrow harbour, while the seminary, the church, and the house of the physician, are nearer to the outer shore facing Disco Bay. To the north extends a plain, the soil of which is composed of clay and gravel, including marine shells, to a height of ninety feet above the level of the sea. It is interrupted by rocky hills which evidently have been islands when the plain was still submerged. The nearest of them has a straight narrow cliff, the perpendicular walls of which exhibit in a remarkable degree that polished, horizontally striped and furrowed surface which is observed in many other localities of Greenland. A deep and narrow valley, Amituarsuk, filled with numerous fragments of rocks, between which grows a rich vegetation of blaeberries and dwarf birch, separates this hill from the next, called Kakarsuatsiak, on the top of which, at a height of 1,272 feet, a fine view of the ice-fjord can be had. But in order to see the glacier from which the icebergs are detached one has to travel by sledge to about eight miles from Jakobshavn, where at once the whole of these interior ice regions is beautifully displayed to the view. In the immediate neighbourhood of the settlement the mouth of the ice-fjord offers the most attractive scenes.

The houses of Kingigtok are situated scarcely one mile off on the outermost point right opposite to the grounded icebergs, which are so densely packed as to present almost one continuous wall, leaving only a narrow channel along the shore. When regarded from a point above the houses, the kayaks moving about in the open water at first sight look like small seabirds, on account of the delusive appearance of the ice-blocks, the enormous size of which is not duly estimated until objects whose dimensions are well known are seen close to them, so as to admit of their being compared. In the immediate vicinity of Kingigtok a small valley opens towards the fjord, in which are the remains of numerous native houses, called Sermermiut, near to the edge of the water. The soil consisting of gravel and stones, and having been gradually undermined by the sea, presents a wall in which the substratum of the ancient houses is denuded, and shows a remarkable accumulation of relics of the earlier inhabitants. Mould is found to a depth of nearly ten feet, intermixed with numerous remains of Eskimo tools, and containing nothing but materials placed there by human beings, which bear evidence of successive generations having resided here probably for several hundred years. Former houses have several times been levelled and made the foundations for new ones, which supposition is confirmed by fire-places having been discovered at different depths. As far as the author is able to remember, this accumulation greatly surpasses that of Kangek, mentioned before, as well as any other of the same kind in Greenland. Of late years it has yielded a large contribution of stone tools and other relics to archæological collections. On the opposite side of the fjord, at Kaja, similar remains are found of a very ancient hamlet, which have been more closely investigated and described by Nordenskjöld and others, and tend still more to show the great attraction which the ice-fjord always has had for the Eskimo inhabitants of Greenland.

Godhavn.—This district must be considered to comprise the southern and western shores of Disco Island and the

Kronprins Island (Whalefish Island), which are situated in the middle of Disco Bay. On the west side Disco is indented by three fjords, of which the two northernmost have been but little explored, whereas the third and largest, the Disco-fjord, has always been inhabited and often visited by travellers. As far as we are able to judge from what has been ascertained concerning the configuration of Disco, its area may be estimated at nearly 2,000 square miles, of which probably 1,500 are table-land, between 2,000 and 3,000, occasionally upwards of 4,000 feet above the level of the sea, and mostly covered with perpetual snow and ice, while 500 square miles are slopes ending in valleys and low land along the shores.

Trade.—The settlement was originally a chief station for whale fishery, and as such was very profitable during the best period of this trade. In the year 1798 not less than twenty, and in 1799 thirteen whales were caught there. During the years from 1805 to 1809, at Godhavn and Kronprins Island together, fifty whales were caught, or ten per annum. But later on this trade decreased, and has now wholly ceased. The whale fishery carried on by the Royal Trade in 1847 gave two, and in 1851 one 'fish,' whereupon it was abandoned. One or two fish have since been caught by the natives themselves, the necessary requisites having been lent to them for this purpose. For a great many years the settlement did not quite pay the expenses connected with it. The *annual produce* has of late been thirty tuns of oil and four hundred sealskins, on an average, per annum, purchased at the stations of Godhavn, Disco-fjord, and Kronprins Island.

Census.—In October 1870 the number of inhabitants was 245, distributed in the following stations : Godhavn 113 ; three places : Erkigsok 10, Siorak 15, and Kivigtut 22, in the Disco-fjord ; two places upon Kronprins Island—

together 84. The inhabitants of Kronprins Island afterwards removed from thence on account of total impoverishment, and this trading-post is consequently now abandoned.

Godhavn (called *Lievely* by the English whalers) is
situated upon a low peninsula which forms an excellent
harbour, on the opposite side of which a small valley called
Lyngmarken, covered with some willow copse and various
flowers, extends at the base of the precipices which border
the high land. Along the edge of a narrow chasm the
summit of Disco Island is here easily ascended by a few
hours' walk from the settlement. The projecting edge of
the high land just opposite the houses, and distant from
them 3,400 yards, rises 2,300 feet above the level of the
sea, the summit being almost perfectly level. In a distance of one mile from the edge its height rises to
2,400 feet, and the glacier which covers this table-land
originated a little further off in May 1849, but its border could not exactly be ascertained on account of being
levelled with snow which covered the whole surface. The
inspector of the northern districts resides in this place, which
is frequently touched at by foreign vessels, chiefly whalers
and explorers. For the greater part of the year living
there is more dull than at the neighbouring stations, on
account of its isolation. The ice is rarely firm enough for
making excursions to the other settlements around the
Disco Bay without running the risk of its breaking, and
making the return by sledge impossible. The coast of
Disco is very open on both sides. To the west, at a distance of four miles, there are some creeks sheltered by
islands, and forming Fortune Bay harbour, where there
formerly was a whaling station, and where natives have
lived at different times ; but beyond this place there is no
shelter for twenty miles to the entrance of Disco-fjord.
On this route is Uivfak, where the great iron masses were

found, about 20 miles from Godhavn. To the east side of the settlement, not only is there no shelter at all to the mouth of the Waigatt Strait, for a distance of fifty miles, but nearest to Godhavn there is even no footing to be found for five miles along the shore on account of its steepness. At a distance of from twenty to thirty-five miles coal has been found and worked, but caused several disasters and much loss on account of the hazardous navigation.

To Disco-fjord there is a route for sledges by land. The ruins of about 28 houses are found scattered along its shores.

Ritenbenk.—This district is a continuation of that belonging to Jakobshavn, and occupies both sides of the Waigatt Strait to the entrance of Umanak Bay. The east side of this sound is chiefly formed by the Nugsuak peninsula, which is estimated to have the same area as Disco. We have already mentioned the extraordinary elevation of its surface, and of the remarkable vegetation on its northern slope. Most likely its interior exhibits the highest summits of Danish Greenland, approaching 7,000 feet ; it also contains several deep valleys with large lakes. A sledge route 25 miles long leads across the peninsula to the interior of the Umanak-fjord, with one rather steep slope to be passed over in descending to the latter. Both sides of the Waigatt are bordered by high lands between 3,000 and 4,000 feet in height, ending in precipitous walls, the foot of which, especially on the mainland, passes into the gentle slopes along the greater part of the shore. Coalbeds crop out in numerous places on both sides.

Trade.—The trade carried on at the stations Ritenbenk, Kekertak, Sakak, Ujaragsugsuk, and Nugsuak has during the latest period yielded about 116 tuns of oil, and 3,500 sealskins per annum.

Census.—In October 1870 the number of inhabitants

was 447, distributed among the following places: Ritenbenk 92, Kekertak 35, Nouak 40, Ulusat 15, Sakak 85, Ujaragsugsuk 69, Nousak 27, Nugsuak 84.

Ritenbenk is situated upon a small island separated from Arveprins Island by a narrow sound, of which the harbour is the outlet. On the opposite side the Kangek mountain rears its two summits 2,000 and 2,200 feet above the sea. The squalls of southerly wind rushing down from these heights are sometimes dangerous to ships in the harbour. The Arveprins Island can be crossed by sledge in different directions; from the high lands a beautiful view is to be had of the Torsukatak ice-fjord.

Ujaragsugsuk is situated on the shore of Disco. This trading-post has been maintained in order to promote the working of coal in the vicinity, but within these few years two transport boats have been lost there for want of a harbour.

Nugsuak or Noursuak (called Four Islands Point by the English) is situated near the extreme end of the large peninsula of that name. Ten miles south of it issues one of the largest watercourses in Greenland, the Makak river, draining an extensive valley which runs through the peninsula. Upon a point close to the houses stands a remarkable ruin, the only one of ancient origin in North Greenland that bears evidence of having been built by other people than Eskimo. It was originally 10 to 12 feet long and 6 to 8 feet broad inside, the walls being very thick and formed of flat stones gathered in the vicinity. The stones are carefully fitted to one another without any intervening mould. At one end there is a wide entrance. It is usually called the Bear Trap, but its origin and purpose is quite a mystery.

Umanak.—This district comprises the shores surrounding the bay between Nugsuak and Svarte-Huk Point, with its numerous branches. From Kanasut, where the bay begins on the southern side, there are upwards of 100 miles to its south-eastern, and perhaps a little more to its north-eastern termination. About 10 of its branches stretch to the inland ice ; of these branches two are first-rate, and two or three also considerable ice-fjords, all of them uniting in spreading innumerable icebergs over the outer bay at certain times every summer. The mountains on the south side present table-lands between 5,000 and 6,000 feet high near to the shore, and further inland most likely higher. The islands and peninsulas bordering the interior branches of the extensive inlet most frequently rear their tops to a height of between 3,000 and 4,000 feet, and even attain 5,000 to 7,000 feet above the level of the sea, with almost perpendicular walls of a similar height in different places. All that is known of the north-eastern branch is gathered from the imperfect information of native travellers.

Umanak has been the most profitable of all the settle-ments when the number of inhabitants belonging to each of them is taken into account, and scarcely any part of the Green-land sea is more favourable to seal-hunting than Umanak Bay with its ramifications. But, strange to say, the inhabi-tants of its shores at the same time belong to the poorest part of the Greenlanders, both as regards the pitiful state of their houses and their miserable clothing. Many of them resemble the inhabitants of some places in the south which we have already described as representing the utmost degree of impoverishment. Umanak, with its outposts Niakornak, Igdlorsuit, Uvkusigsak, Ikerasak, Sagtorsuak, and Karsok, has of late yielded about 180 tuns of oil and 8,300 sealskins per annum to the Trade.

Census.—In October 1870 the number of inhabitants was 798, distributed among the following places : Umanak 173, Sermiarsut 77, Karsok 32, Ikerasak 110, Tulugak 15, Narsarsuk 11, Umanatsiak 21, Karajak 13, Sagtorsuak 68,

Tugdlitalik 12, Niakornat 85, Uvkusigsak 57, Igdlorsuit 74,
Kugsininguak 21, Kungulertusok 19.

Umanak is situated on an island in the southern part of
the bay, facing the lofty mountains that surround its
interior. The highest point of the little island, which is
only 2 miles distant from the houses, is 3,900 feet above
the level of the sea. Opposite to the settlement, at a
distance of 4 miles, one of the more uncommon bird cliffs,
inhabited by fulmars, presents a perpendicular wall of 3,600
feet in height. To the south, at a distance of between 7
and 12 miles, three clefts are seen filled out with glaciers
issuing from a height of 6,000 feet and descending to the
water's edge or close by it. There is a church in this place,
and a small dwelling for a missionary, but none has resided
there for several years. On November 7 the sun shines
for the last time at Umanak, but continues to light the
mountain tops at noon for 12 days longer, and after having
announced its return in a similar way it again makes its
first appearance on February 2. The only circumstance
that tends to render these dreary months at all supportable
to others than the natives is the sudden change taking
place in December, by which the surrounding sea with all
its numerous ramifications is transformed to one level plain,
from which, with rare interruptions, an easy access can be
gained to every part of its extensive shores until the first
part of May. Even during the darkest period there is
always sufficient daylight for taking a walk across the ice
to the opposite shore of the mainland and back again
with ease, making in all about 10 miles, when the weather
is not too unfavourable. But in the house one is unable
to read by daylight, and especially with a cloudy sky,
and snow lamps have to be kept burning all day. In
weather like this, when one is confined to the narrow
rooms with nothing to vary the monotony of the darkness

that reigns without except the howling of the dogs, in which they all join at intervals, at a sign accidentally given by one of them, Christmas time is of course exceedingly dull to European residents at Umanak, especially to single people. When daylight rapidly increases in February and March there is not only a frequent intercourse with the outposts, but at times visitors also arrive from the neighbouring settlements in the south ; but there is only one sledge-post between Umanak and Upernivik.

Ikerasak is situated 24 miles further up the fjord, and is the furthest outpost towards the great Karajat-glacier which sends forth the greater part of the icebergs encumbering the Umanak-fjord in summer, and rendering the navigation difficult. But the nearer this source of calved ice the more abundant is the catch of seals. This is one of the stations where the ice-nets have especially been made use of. A European appointed here as a trader, and married to a native, carried on the seal-fishery with between 150 and 200 nets, which, during the years 1837 to 1849, on an average yielded from 1,200 to 1,300 seals annually. The same business has been pursued by several other Europeans in North Greenland, and yielded a considerable profit to the Trade, but it has evidently contributed to make the natives whom the net-owners engaged to assist them dependent, and indifferent to their own seal-catching and neglectful of their hunting weapons and other imple-ments, and in this way tended to their impoverishment.

Upernivik.—This northernmost district, extending from the border of the former as far north as the coast, is fre-quented by the natives belonging to the Danish settle-ments in following their hunting and fishing pursuits. This limit may at present be estimated at about 74° N. lat. The peninsula of Svartehuk, constituting its southern part, is very little known, only few Europeans having occasionally set foot on its shores. Its outlines are roughly sketched on the map according to the description of the natives who have crossed it, particularly in the northern part, where people from Umanak and Upernivik used to have their joint hunting grounds, reindeer having formerly been abundant in these regions. The whole peninsula appears to be almost equal in size to that of Nugsuak, but is less elevated, remarkably little encumbered with glaciers, and apparently traversed by several extensive valleys. North of the peninsula the mainland again appears narrow and overflown by the inland ice, which here projects in the shape of the great glacier of Augpadlartok, which discharges numerous bergs of the largest size behind the extensive group of islands which chiefly constitute the district here in question. The highest of these islands is Karsorsuak, the top of which measures 3,400 feet above the level of the sea.

Trade.—The settlement has during the latest years become almost as profitable to the Trade as Umanak, yielding 148 tuns of oil and 6,500 sealskins, on an average, per annum, besides eiderdown, bearskins, and formerly a considerable number of reindeer-skins. The amount of products sold at the different stations in Greenland now almost corresponds to the amount of the seal-catch, and consequently to the quantity of food produced at the same time by the natives for their own consumption, and still more directly to their yearly income in money. But their prosperity and domestic arrangements only badly correspond to these sources of revenue.

Census.—The material condition of the natives belonging to Upernivik seems to be almost as sad as that of their neighbours within the confines of Umanak. There is some reason to believe that the inhabitants of these northernmost settlements are of a duller and slower dis-

position than the rest of the population, and that this
tendency in some measure must be ascribed to their
extraordinary isolation. In October 1870 the number of
inhabitants was 702, distributed among the following
places, all of which, excepting Savernek, at the same
time have been trading-stations: Southern Upernivik 75,
Pröven 112, Karsok 75, Upernivik 88, Savernek 37,
Augpadlartok 80, Kingigtok 111, Kasersuak 57, Tasiusak 67.

Upernivik (72° 48′ N. lat.) is situated upon a small
island, facing the open sea and exposed to its icy winds
and fogs, which in common with the high latitude, and
perhaps the peculiar nature of the rocks, give this settlement a very desolate and dreary appearance. The rocks
exhibit a withered and frequently a yellow and rust-
coloured surface. Of vegetation, only little is to be discovered, with the exception of some green patches near the
houses where the soil has been impregnated with fertilising
matters, whereas large heaps of snow generally have to be
passed in July when coming from the harbour which lies
at some distance. The settlement is furnished with a
church, measuring 25 feet in length and 16 in breadth,
and with a comfortable dwelling for a missionary. A
heavy surf frequently washes over the bare rocks in front
of the houses. In winter the sun is below the horizon for
79 days, of which 39 are darker than the darkest day
at Disco Bay, and during the whole year there is no other
communication with the other settlements than by ship in
summer and one sledge-post in winter. This station is
therefore certainly a place of residence still less attractive
than Umanak.

Tasiusak (73° 24′ N. lat.) is the most northern trading-
post in Greenland. It has for several years been managed
by a Dane, who has his Danish family living with him.

To a European female this indeed seems to be one of the most melancholy places of residence that can be found.

Pröven is furnished with buildings like the principal stations, and managed by an assistant. The environs of this little settlement look pleasanter than those of Upernivik, and still more inviting is the mainland around the neighbouring inlets, which some years ago abounded with reindeer. A little to the north is an extensive fjord, called the Salmon-fjord, leading towards the south-east. From its termination, where pretty willow copses are said to be found, intercourse has formerly been maintained by land with the natives from the Umanak-fjord during the hunting season.

APPENDIX.

—◦◦◦—

I.—*ON THE GLACIERS AND THE ORIGIN OF THE FLOATING ICEBERGS.*

SUPPOSING the whole circumference of Greenland, with the inlets of the sea intersecting the outskirting land included, to amount to 3,400 miles, we must consider 600 of them as merely hypothetical ; 500 have only been sighted from a distance, 1,300 but imperfectly explored, and 1,000 tolerably well known. When we have seen how on the latter tract, or the Danish part of the west coast, the glaciers from which the icebergs detach themselves are hidden behind the headlands, and how little the ice-fjords there have been explored, it is not to be wondered that on the east coast of Greenland, where almost no fjord-head has as yet been visited, hardly any of the glaciers which give rise to the bergs issuing from that side have as yet been discovered. The fjord discovered by the German Arctic Expedition is said to be an ice-fjord ; most likely Scoresby Sound is the mouth of another ; a third one seems to be situated in about 63° 40′ N. lat., and of course there must be several more. But there can be no doubt that the west side of Greenland is far more productive of calved ice than the east side. The bergs from the latter, when drifting towards the south, always coast along the shore without spreading to the east over the Northern Atlantic. If great numbers of them were carried southwards in this way, they could not fail to be noticed south and west of Cape Farewell. But ships rounding this promontory and entering Davis Strait at a distance of 50 miles from the land only meet with a few stragglers, and the number of bergs from the east coast that enter the same sea by following the pack-ice along the shore can, at all events, not be considerable ; the greater part of the bergs which are seen off the South Greenland shores probably issue from the ice-fjords of the same coast. Consequently almost the whole of the bergs which spread over the sea to the latitude of Newfoundland and further, originate from the west side, and there is some reason to believe that the watershed running from south to north through the interior of Greenland is nearer to the east than to the west coast.

The chief mass that constitutes the larger icebergs is a white ice, which, on being closely examined, proves to be thoroughly permeated by very thin longitudinal or lineal air bubbles, which lie parallel to each other, and, according to Helland, diminish its specific gravity from 0·918 to 0·886. A berg consisting merely of such ice would have one-seventh of its bulk above and six-sevenths below the surface of the sea. The white ice is intersected and traversed by straight fissure-shaped streaks of an intensely blue and transparent ice, which on being exposed to heat before melting dissolves into large angular grains. Besides the blue ice, a conglomerate occurs formed of ice-blocks of various size, the interstices having been filled up with snow or crumbled ice. This conglomerate occupies dykes or fissures similar to those already mentioned, but it also forms layers or more considerable parts of the large bergs. Stones and earthy matters are only found in connection with, or imbedded in the conglomerate and the blue ice. Entire bergs are also sometimes formed of these sorts of ice, and from some ice-fjords, especially those which only produce smaller bergs, scarcely anything issues but ice, tinged more or less with blue and intermixed with earthy matters. As regards the question how far icebergs may serve as an explanation of the transference and scattering of erratic blocks, it has been objected that the occurrence of such masses in large icebergs appears to be too rare. On the other hand, it might be asserted that probably these foreign ingredients are chiefly imbedded in the interior of the under part of the large icebergs which is submerged.

The remarkable and highly interesting excursion of Nordenskjöld and Berggren in July 1870, over a part of the inland ice in about 68⅓ N. lat., gave most valuable information respecting its surface, and the rivers and lakes that are to be met with in the icy desert, and especially the peculiar feature of the sudden disappearance of the former in bottomless fissures. The surface was frequently interrupted by basin-formed hollows, the centre of which was occupied by lakes or ponds without any visible outlets, although receiving a supply from numerous rivulets on all sides. The watercourses sometimes proved impassable, causing a great waste of time on account of the circuit that had to be made. The surface of the ice through its whole extent exhibited vertical holes from one to two feet in depth, varying in diameter from a quarter of an inch to a couple of feet, and situated so closely to one another that there was scarcely room left to plant a foot between them. At the bottom of these holes a kind of grey dust or powder was found, which on closer examination proved to consist of a mineral substance. Partly intermixed with this powder and partly dispersed over the whole surface, another powder was discovered, which by help of the microscope was made out to have the structure of vegetable organisms. Berggren has described these remarkable plants under the name of ' Algæ from the inland-ice of Greenland.' He states that several species were found, one of them even pretty abundantly, so as to impart a peculiar colour to more or less extensive patches of the ice, while two of them appeared to be exclusively confined to the mineral powder. We must suppose these foreign matters to be spread over an enormous extent of the icy territory, and their presence is very interesting, not only as proving the existence of organic life upon the ice, but also on account of their powerful action in promoting the melting of it by causing the radiation of the sun's heat. The furthest point reached by the travellers was found to be situated at a height of 2,200 feet above the level of the sea, a distance of 28 miles from the place where they started on the sea-shore, and about 20 miles from the nearest seaward border of the inland ice. On their return they were arrested by a stream flowing between its blue walls with great velocity, which it was quite impossible to cross without a bridge ; but on following its course it suddenly came to a stop, and forming a most magnificent waterfall, fell into a perpendicular hole in the ice. Another smaller stream likewise fell into a beautiful blue-tinted cleft, but a little further on it again reappeared, rising in the shape of a jet of water mingled with air and agitated by the wind.

The whole interior of the country being filled up and levelled to a height of more than 2,000 feet, its ice covering must be impregnated and percolated by water to such a degree as to make it differ essentially from the usual ice-formations on high mountain tops. The crust attaining a thickness of more than 1,000 feet, the changes of temperature in the different seasons must little affect the deeper masses of the ice, the mean temperature of which must exceed that of the air. During the whole summer all the heat cast upon the surface is employed in melting, and, being absorbed by the water, it is carried down in a latent state through the ravines. The cold of the winter, on the other hand, will in some degree be kept off owing to the snowy covering being a bad conductor. Between the uneven surface of the underlying land and the bottom of the ice, as well as throughout the ice itself, we may suppose large reservoirs to exist, containing almost the same quantity of uncongealed water even in the winter. This water percolating the whole body of the ice must in some way or other yield the chief explanation of its extraordinary transference, extending most probably to distances of a couple of hundred miles from the interior towards the ice-fjord. In some cases perhaps the subglacial streams may, even in a slight degree, be considered as lifting the ice so as to facilitate its gliding towards the sea ; but the chief propelling action undoubtedly arises from the water freezing in fissures, perhaps even after having first inundated the surface when its channels and outlets happen to be closed by the movement of the ice. No accumulation of ice, however, will admit of an ice-crust during one winter acquiring such a thickness as that which is caused by reiterated inundations with a thin sheet of water. The ordinary formation and growth of glaciers depend on the quantity of snow annually falling upon the surface, and the rate at which the ice-covering of a lake increases in thickness rapidly diminishes at the time this growth is going on. The brooks of North Greenland offer a striking example of ice forming by irrigation, where their beds are wide and covered with boulders, which is often the case at the mouth of such watercourses. The water generally continues to run beneath the stones for a great part of the winter. Its outlets then may happen to be frozen up, whereupon it rises, inundating the stones and covering them with an ice-crust, which, by successive stopping and overflowing, gains such a thickness that ice is still to be found in these places late in summer, when ice and snow have everywhere else disappeared from the low land. Supposing that the ice which is formed in the central regions of Greenland has to travel to the ice-fjords and issue through them in the shape of bergs, it will not at all events reach them until many years have elapsed. Consequently, during that period, its surface will have been subjected to as many years' reiterated snow and frost, and each period of thawing a certain part of the original ice will disappear in a fluid state towards the sea. Perhaps the final consolidation of by far the greater mass which constitutes the icebergs has taken place nearer to the sea-shore than to the interior, which will facilitate the explanation of its remarkable transference from the distant confines of the tributary basin towards the outlet or ice-fjord. But at all events this transference intimates a sliding of ice along the surface of the whole of the original river basin, which must produce an extraordinary effect in grinding and levelling the inequalities of the ground over which it passes. It appears probable that many isolated rocks or ridges of hills rise from the ground over which the ice has to pass, and for this reason are enveloped in it, rearing their tops into its upper layers. In being demolished they are carried off in the shape of boulders and earthy matters, which are united with the mass and become imbedded in the icebergs; perhaps chiefly in their under parts.

On making inquiries as to the existence of subglacial watercourses running underneath the inland ice into the ice-fjords, the author was informed by the natives of South Greenland that this has always been a well-known fact to them. They say that the more abundant the supply of water, and the more violent its motion is in the streams of fresh water which take the form of wells in the front part of the glacier abutting on the sea, the more effective will the glacier be in producing icebergs. But on account of the glacier being dangerous to approach by sea, the phenomenon can only be observed from some knoll in the vicinity. The surface of the sea close in front of the glacier is kept in continual motion by whirlpools, not unlike those caused by water boiling in a large vessel, or springs issuing from the bottom of a shallow lake. These spots may also be recognised by flocks of sea-birds circling above them, and now and then diving for food. The existence of such freshwater streams in the ice-fjords may also be inferred from the strong seaward current that prevails in them, and without which we could hardly account for their being so regularly cleared of bergs.

The author himself only had in one place an opportunity of observing these submarine wells, viz. at the head of the southern-most branch of the Kvanersok-fjord in 62° N. lat., where he approached the glacier wall to a distance of somewhat more than 1,000 yards, and then landed and ascended a hill. The whirlpool-like movement of the sea occupying a space of upwards of a hundred yards in diameter close in front of the ice was distinctly to be recognised by means of the telescope. The kittywakes swarmed over the spot as they usually do over fishing grounds, and the water of the creek was muddy, although no brooks were observed on the surrounding shores. The native guides asserted that in this branch of the fjord the wells were only just visible, and by far inferior to those of the northern branch, which is more productive of calved ice. However, the quantity of calved ice from the Kvanersok is so inconsiderable compared with that of other fjords, that it hardly deserves the name of an ice-fjord. The remotest branch of the Godthaab-fjord, Kangersunek being a regular ice-fjord, is well known to the natives on account of the reindeer hunt that has been carried on in its environs. An intelligent native who had acquired an exact knowledge of the country, has given a detailed description of the whole border of the inland ice, from 64° to 65° N. lat., illustrated by a map. In two places the ice projects into the sea, discharging bergs, and in both of them enormous wells, indicated at a distance by swarms of birds, are perceptible in front of the ice-wall.

The level of a lake bordering the glacier somewhat up the country rises and falls periodically. While it rises, the move-ment of the nearest submarine wells decreases, and *vice versa* during its fall. Sometimes the water of the lake suddenly and rapidly subsides, while at the same time the springs from the bottom of the sea burst out with violence, and the seaward current of the fjord is perceived to increase even at a distance of 12 miles from the glacier.

Another native has given a similar description, with sketches of the ice-fjords of Sermiliarsuk and Narsalik, situated between 61° and 62° N. lat., the environs of which also at times have frequently been visited by reindeer hunters. As to productiveness the Narsalik must be ranged next to the first-rate ice-fjords. The distance from its mouth to its glacier is about 20 miles. Its interior, though totally inaccessible from the sea, can be approached on both sides from the land. The wells are also here indicated by the swarms of birds and by the whirlpools, which keep some spots free of ice amidst the crowds of bergs which densely fill up the interior of the inlet. On examining the surface of the glacier at a distance of a couple of miles from its outer edge, a basin is discovered in the ice about one mile in diameter, which at times is filled with water and afterwards suddenly emptied, while at the same time a sudden movement is perceived in the fjord, the floating bergs being pushed seaward. The Sermiliarsuk, though less productive, also discharges bergs of a tolerable size ; the same whirlpools have been observed there, and rather far up the country a lake formed by a basin in the inland ice, which at intervals is filled and emptied. The facts here stated evidently hint at the existence of extensive channels in the depth of the ice, which are subjected to continual changes on account of being closed and opened by its movement towards the ice-fjords.

The following notes condensed from Helland's account (Om de iisfyldte Fjorde og de glaciale Dannelser i Nordgrönland) of his valuable researches, and especially of his astonishing and unique surveys of the glaciers which give rise to large icebergs, will serve as a supplement to our statements relative to the inland ice. The breadth of the Jakobshavn ice-fjord, or rather of the glacier occupying it, was 4,500 metres, the dip of the glacier was less than a half degree. Its central part, at distance of 1,000 metres from the side, proceeded at the rate of 20 metres per diem, while at a distance of between 400 and 450 metres, its velocity was 15 metres per diem, and close by the shore only 0·02 metres per diem. The inland ice which projects into the southern branches of the Jakobshavn-fjord, 15 miles from the main glacier, only moves at a rate not surpassing 0·4 to 0·5 metres per diem. The highest iceberg observed at the mouth of the fjord measured 396 feet. The height and extent of the inland ice of Greenland appears to be at variance with the present requirements for the formation of glaciers and perpetual snow in the coast regions, so as to raise some doubt whether the present climate of Greenland would allow of the interior being covered with ice again, if the present inland ice were to disappear. The annual production of the Jakobshavn ice-fjord may be rated at between 2,900 and 5,800 million cubic metres, and that of the Torsukatak at between 1,150 and 2,300 million cubic metres. Finally we have to add, that during Helland's stay at the Jakobshavn glacier, from July 6 in the evening to July 9 in the morning, only one calving of bergs occurred. Without any previous indication, a tremendous roaring noise was heard, while at the same time a white dust was seen to rise, and a large piece of the glacier was detached from its outer edge, which after having rolled for some moments in the water, reared its edge in the air, but almost instantly the pinnacled top of this edge burst asunder and crumbled while falling. The calving having thus commenced, it was instantly followed by a much larger piece being detached, and issuing from the middle part of the glacier at the rate of one metre per second. But the extensive *bouleversements* which now ensued made it impossible to discern the number and size of the larger bergs which were formed out of this portion of the glacier, because clouds of dust now arose in different places, and the floating bergs in the vicinity were also put in motion, rolling and calving. It was more than half an hour before the whole scene again was calm, and the thundering noise which had accompanied the disturbances had subsided. It is also worth noticing that the waters of Tivsarigsok, the small creek of the original fjord, separated from it by the glacier, were considerably affected, and the winter ice that covered it was seen to rise and fall violently. Helland found the same inlet still inhabited by seals, of which one was killed : its stomach contained a specimen of *Gadus agilis.*

In his book, entitled ' The Land of Desolation,' Dr. Hayes has given an interesting and attractive description of a calving which he observed in the Sermitsialik-fjord, south of 61° N. lat. But the dimensions which are given of the iceberg coming into existence

on this occasion appear to be overestimated, if they are founded
upon no exact measurements, because the Sermitsialik belongs to
the least productive fjords, and is hardly considered a real ice-fjord
by people in Greenland. Nor does the author of the present
book agree with the statement of Nordenskjöld (see Admiralty's
' Manual and Instruction for the Arctic Expedition,' 1875, p.
403) that a considerable inclination of the subjacent shore should be a
condition favourable to the formation of large icebergs. On the
contrary, he is almost more inclined to exactly the opposite opinion.

Notwithstanding the insufficiency of our knowledge concerning
the movements of the inland ice and the site of its border throughout many parts of its extent, the intensity of the same movements
is in some measure tolerably perceptible, even to travellers only
passing the outer shores, it being indicated by the quantities of
calved ice issuing from its outlets. The author has tried to trace
all the branches of the inland ice touching the water's edge throughout the whole extent of Danish Greenland on the west coast. In
the following list, the branches are named after the fjords into which
they project or after some other locality of the nearest environs.
The relative force with which they are supposed to be propelled is
indicated by assuming four classes, of which No. 1 corresponds
to first-rate ice-fjords, and No. 4 to those inlets which in Greenland are spoken of as receiving some calved ice but not sufficient
to cause them to be ranged among the ice-fjords. Finally, when
small ' Nunataks ' or insulated portions of ice-free land of less
than 10 miles in breadth divide a branch at its end where it
borders the same inlet, it is generally considered as one glacier,
although in some cases, strictly speaking, it consists of three or
four.

*List of the Glaciers which issue from the inland ice, the supposed
relative force of their movement being indicated by Numbers 1
(the highest) to 4.*

Ilua, Tasermiut, and Sermilik (60° 30′ N. lat.) are doubtful ;
Korok, in Tunugdliarfik, 4 ; Sermilik (north-east of Ikersuak, 61°
10′ N. lat.) 3 ; Kangerdluarsuk, 4 ; Ukevisokak, 4 ; Nuk, 4 (the
latter three along the north-west side of Ikersuak Sound); Sermitsialik, 4 (behind Kagsimiut); one north at Sanerut, 4 ; Ivigtut, 4 ;
Sermiligaitsiak, 3 (61° 30′ N. lat.) ; Narsalik, 2 ; Kuanersok, 4 ;

Kagse, 4 (62° 20′ N. lat.) doubtful ; Tiningnertok, 4 (south of the 'Iceblink,' including one branch still nearer to the latter; Sermilik, 4 (63° 30′ N. lat.) ; Kangersunek, southern 3, and northern 3 (both in the Godthaab-fjord) ; two or three glaciers in about 65½° N. lat. very doubtful ; Kangerdlugsuatsiak, 3 (65° 40′ N. lat.) ; Aulatsivik, southern 4 (67° 50′ N. lat.), and northern 4 (68° 20′ N. lat.) ; Tasiusak comprising Sakardlek and Alangordlek, 4 (southern branch of Jakobshavn-fjord) ; Jakobshavn, 1 ; northern branch of Jak. fj. 4 ; Torsukatak 1 (divided by several Nunataks); Great Karajak, 1 ; Little Karajak, 3 ; Sermilik, 2 (70° 40′ N. lat.); Itivdliarsuk, 2 ; Ingnerit, 2 (71° N. lat.) ; Kangerdluarsuk, 3 (71° 12′ N. lat.) ; Kangerdlugsuak, 3 (71° 18′ N. lat.) ; Umiamako, 1 (71° 24′ N. lat.) ; a few doubtful branches between the latter and the next ; Augpadlartok, 1 (73° N. lat.) ; a few doubtful branches north of the latter.

Glaciers of the Coast regions.—As regards the ice-formations which are quite analogous to those occurring upon high mountain chains in warmer climates, viz., the isolated glaciers or the highland-ice of the coast regions, Helland has also furnished extremely interesting facts which are set forth in his account quoted above. The mountain chain bordering the south side of Umanak Bay at once exhibits the most interesting features relating to the formation of glaciers, so as peculiarly to adapt it to serve as a model of the Greenland coast regions in general as regards this phenomenon. In the winter and spring of 1850 the author surveyed a series of glaciers occupying the clefts of the coast-tract opposite to Umanak Island, and especially noted down and portrayed on the map how far the edges of the glaciers had advanced towards the sea, for the purpose of enabling future observers to make out the changes that might take place in the course of years. In August 1875 Helland surveyed these localities and arrived at the following results.

Tuaparsuit.—The glacier filling the bottom of this valley had maintained almost the same position during twenty-five years, viz. a distance of one mile from the shore.

Sermiarsut is a glacier of extraordinary size, which has formed a morena 600 feet high. The glacier itself, estimated at a thickness of 150 metres, projects to the water's edge, where it forms a steep wall almost three-quarters of a mile in length, while the moraine borders its sides. Apparently it had undergone no alteration ; but of course only the sea must have prevented its growth by wasting its outer edge.

Asakak.—The edge of this glacier was 251 metres distant from the sea in the year 1850. The foremost part of it was now totally covered with stones, which rendered it difficult in some places to discern whether the ground was formed by the glacier or the morena at the side of it. The edge of the glacier was now 500 metres distant from the sea, and consequently it had retired by melting about 250 metres during 25 years.

Umiartorfik comprises two neighbouring glaciers. The north-western and larger one is almost of the same description as Sermiarsut ; the steep wall with which it borders the sea, and which at low water is discovered to rest upon dry ground, seemed to have undergone no alteration. The south-eastern or smaller one was in 1850 about 440 metres distant from the sea, and had now advanced to a distance of 322 metres from it.

Sorkak.—In 1850 the author found this glacier to be most obviously in a state of decrease by melting. Its foremost part was totally covered with stones and earthy matters that had been formerly imbedded in the ice, and the icy substratum did not crop up until some hundred yards from the sea. But the natives related that formerly it had abutted on the sea, and discharged fragments into it. Helland now found that it had again advanced to the water's edge. presenting a wall 25 metres high, and an extensive morena. Near this edge the glacier appeared to have a thickness of 50 metres. Consequently, during a period of perhaps 50 years, this glacier first extended to the sea, then retired several hundred yards from it, and now during the last period of perhaps 20 years has advanced towards it.

Each of the glaciers here mentioned must be supposed to be nourished by the snow and rain falling upon an area of between 20 and 50 square miles, at a height of between 4,000 and 6,000 feet above the level of the sea. On instituting a comparison between the glaciers of Greenland and those of the high lands in warmer climates, and for this purpose choosing the most extensive fields of perpetual snow and ice found in the latter regions, as for instance in the south-eastern part of Iceland and the table-land near Justedal in Norway, it has to be remembered that these snowfields or *mers de glace* have their deflux through a number of branches, or of glaciers more strictly speaking, each with their appertaining watercourses. A study of the movements and changes to which the whole of such an ice-formation is subjected, above all requires it to be considered as divided into parts representing the areas which are drained by each of these branches, or in other words the tributary basins of the glaciers issuing from the common *mer de glace.* These facts being taken duly into account, the glaciers of Umanak, just discovered, undoubtedly may be ranked with the most considerable glaciers known in the other parts of the globe, excepting the glaciers issuing from the inland ice of Greenland. The nature of their changes and movements, which may be studied from their present state, and especially from the moraines piled up on their sides and in front of them, and which now has been so strikingly illustrated by direct experience during a period of 25 years, agrees in the main point with the features of European glaciers which have been the object of profound study and extensive researches. It has been ascertained that their progressive movement is periodical; for a series of years, if it does not wholly cease, it becomes so slow, at least in most of them, that it is unable to compensate for the melting produced by the increasing warmth as they approach the level of the sea, and consequently their foremost part is wasted, and their edge retreats from the shore. But nevertheless, on account of the polar climate, they never withdraw far from the level of the sea, and of course it may happen that the mightiest among them have maintained their position bordering the water's edge at least as far back as we have been able to acquire any information. This instance is represented by two of the glaciers named above. The periodical retreat and progress is most beautifully displayed in the moraines. The ice sliding down from the highland is loaded with gravel and stones, partly spread over its surface, partly imbedded in its layers. On being wasted by melting, it leaves all these transported matters on the ground, whereupon during the period of progress they are pushed forward by the edge of the ice, and piled up in front and on the sides of it. In classifying the fjords which receive calved ice from the inland we have concluded that those of the lowest order, which hardly can be called ice-fjords, may have a tributary basin of 1,500 square miles. From this calculation it may be inferred that a glacier nourished by a surface of between 20 and 50 square miles can make but extremely slow progress. The same conclusion may be drawn from the fact that in most cases the summer warmth of the Greenland climate on the low land is able so far to counterbalance the progress of the glaciers descending from their mountains as to prevent them from reaching the shore. But direct observations illustrating the rate of this progress did not exist before the survey made by Helland in the year 1875.

In his map of North Greenland the author has adopted the name of ' Iis-Ström,' i.e. ice-stream or ice-current, for those outer parts of the inland ice which are moving with greater rapidity towards the ice-fjords than the rest of its outer margin. A cursory glance at a map of Greenland in which the term ' ice-stream ' has been employed in the same way might suggest the idea of a peculiar ice-formation in these spots, thus distinguishing them from the surrounding country, and being recognisable from the configuration of the surface. But on the contrary, it was intended to refer to the analogy of a current of the sea, with a progressive motion limited to certain parts of the apparently uniform mass, the cause of which is not to be guessed from the outer appearance of its surface or environs, as is the case with the ordinary glaciers which descend from mountain tops. We need only remember that the same *mer de glace* which moves with the most extraordinary force towards that branch of the glacier which it ejects in to an ice-fjord, proceeds with no more than $\frac{1}{100}$ of the same speed towards another glacier projecting into a neighbouring inlet, not further off than that both of them, together with their common source—the *mer de glace*—can be overlooked from the same hill of the exterior land. The author must leave it undecided whether a more appropriate term might be chosen than ' ice-stream.' As regards the expression ' ice-fjord,' used especially in speaking of a ' greater ' ice-fjord, it must be granted, that although in Danish Greenland the icebergs always proceed from the interior of inlets, it is not impossible that the inland ice may in some places project as far as the open sea, and discharge icebergs therein, in which case it would be somewhat inappropriate to call such a place an ice-fjord. Perhaps it might have been more correct to adopt such a term as ' iceberg-stream,' thereby denoting a part of the sea which receives icebergs from a glacier and almost continually is crowded with them on their passage in spreading over the ocean.

Some authors, strange to say, still talk of the possibility of finding valleys in the interior of Greenland free from ice and covered with vegetation and even with forests. Referring to what we have stated as to the presence of reindeer and the words of the 'Speculum Regale' on the same subject, we have only to remind the reader that such valleys, surrounded by the inland ice, for want of drainage must necessarily become filled with water and converted into lakes. Another conjecture, somewhat more reasonable, is that of Greenland being now, or not many ages ago having been, intersected by sounds running straight across it. If any sound too narrow and shallow to afford a passage for the calved ice had existed before the ice-period, they would certainly have disappeared by being embodied in the present covering of ice. The possibility of sounds having existed can therefore by no means be denied, but inasmuch as the features of the whole country have in all respects a continental character, it seems that clearly verified facts would be required to induce us to conclusively adopt an opposite opinion. It appears that the origin of the idea of sounds intersecting the interior of Greenland can be traced back to the earliest accounts of rediscovered Greenland, the travellers having perceived that the coast which at first sight offered an appearance of continuity, on closer examination revealed numerous inlets, which they did not succeed in following to their terminations.

Very natural, but at the same time least reasonable, is the application of the same opinion to the ice-fjords in particular, amongst which the Jakobshavn-fjord most frequently has been made an object of it. The ceaseless drift of enormous masses of ice out of an isolated and narrow outlet, whilst none were observed to issue from the other fjords for two or three hundred miles of the adjacent coast-line, would almost appear inconceivable to people who had no clear idea of the existence of the inland ice, without the supposition that some current had conveyed them through a channel from the sea east of Greenland which was well known to be encumbered with ice. As to the traditions of the natives, which are referred to as corroborating the story as to some ancient passage through the country, or the rapid increase of ice-covering, they will, at all events, only be of very limited and indirect historical value, as in all probability they originated in regions inhabited by the Eskimo before they migrated to Green-land, and were merely localised for this country, not to speak of the probability of such traditions being in some cases of European origin.

The ice-fjords of course prove that an enormous surplus of ice is produced in the interior, and that the vast sheet of ice would be liable to expand and spread over the coast regions and their inlets if the ice-fjords did not discharge the surplus. The question whether in reality they are able to perform this service completely, or if, in spite of them, the inland ice slowly encroaches on the regions still free from ice, cannot be decided by means of the observations which hitherto have been made. In some places we know from direct experience that the margin of the inland ice has advanced, and the shores of one ice-fjord of course may be subject to changes and have accidentally passed from an accessible to an inaccessible state since these regions have been inhabited by man. But, on the other hand, the records dating from the time of the ancient Norse give the idea of the conditions having been then the same as now. Perhaps the border of the ice retreats in some places while it advances in others. At any rate, it is remarkable that when the ice had inundated the whole original country, and in this way united the river-beds, its further growth became limited to certain points, and thus, as is now actually known to be the case, little affected the intervals between the ice-fjords.

II.—*METEOROLOGY.*

NUMEROUS registers and notes appertaining to thermometrical and barometrical observations, and to the weather in general, have been received from different stations in Greenland in the course of years. Of these observations some have been taken pretty carefully and even methodically, whereas a great many are, of course, not wholly to be relied on. But inasmuch as the great changeableness of the climate causes one year to differ essentially from another, and requires observations to be carried on for a long series of years in order to give a satisfactory insight into the conditions of the atmosphere, the number of these observations may in some measure make up for their want of accuracy, while at the same time it affords means for controlling them by mutual comparison. Of late the Meteorological Institute of Copenhagen has established stations in Greenland furnished with the necessary instruments, and instructions for more methodical observations.

In the southernmost district observations have been made at three different stations, Frederiksdal, Lichtenau, and Julianehaab, all of them giving nearly the same annual mean temperature of 33·3°. In two other places, Nanortalik and Kagsimiut, observations were also registered, showing respectively one and three degrees lower, but also with less certainty. As to the months and seasons the difference between all these places was found to be greater than those of the whole year, owing to their more or less seaward situation.

The following table has been inserted in order to give a clear view of the range of mean temperature during the different months of the year and in various latitudes. To this end four stations have been selected at a suitable distance from each other, and the observations which happened to be registered at each of them during a course of years have been compiled and calculated so as to derive the most probable means from them. At Upernivik they were continued during the periods from 1832 to 1838, and from 1846 to 1854, making a total of about 14 years. With regard to some months, however, they were very deficient, especially for those of July and August, which can be considered to have been observed only for three or four years. Although the monthly means of the whole year will be found to give a mean of 15·5°, this result, for different reasons, has been corrected to 13·3°. The observations from Jakobshavn comprise the decennium 1840 to 1850, and are by far the most accurate and complete. At Godthaab they date from the periods 1841 to 1846 and 1855 to 1866, in all amounting to 15 years ; omitting, however, for about 6 of them the summer months from June to August. The observations at Lichtenau have been taken during 5 years, from 1841 to 1846. These places may all for the most part be regarded as open coast stations, although they are in some measure sheltered by off-lying islands or headlands. The most sheltered amongst them is Jakobshavn, and a striking abnormality will also be found in comparing the summer months of that place and those of Godthaab, but the author does not venture to decide whether deficiencies of observation may have concurred in causing them.

Monthly mean Temperatures. (*Fahrenheit.*)

	Lichtenau, 60° 31′ N. lat.	Godthaab, 64° 8′ N. lat.	Jakobshavn, 69° 14′ N. lat.	Upernivik, 72° 48′ N. lat.
January . .	22·3	11·8	2·5	÷ 7·1
February . .	24·3	15·6	0·3	÷11·6
March . .	26·4	19·4	8·2	÷ 4·4
April . .	31·5	23·7	18·7	6·6
May . . .	38·8	32·5	32·5	25·0
June . . .	43·7	39·5	41·4	36·9
July . . .	45·7	44·4	45·3	39·9
August . .	44·1	43·3	42·4	37·8
September . .	40·6	36·7	34·7	32·0
October . .	34·0	29·3	25·2	22·1
November . .	26·4	21·7	12·6	10·9
December . .	20·8	15·8	7·5	÷ 1·1
Annual . .	33·2	27·8	22·6	13·3

The author is only in possession of a few abstracts showing the variations of temperature in the different years at the same station, but they will also suffice to illustrate the extraordinary irregularity of the climate in this respect. An earlier period of about 5 years at Godthaab having given 29·0° as the annual mean, the observations continued throughout a later period of about 10 years have led to correct this standard to 27·8°, and of 5 years running we find one with 29·1° and another with 21·1°. This will prove the insufficiency of one year's observation for supplying satisfactory information about the climate of a particular station, one single year probably sometimes differing 10° from another year, and more than 6° from the true annual mean. But still this is nothing in comparison with the variability of the same month in different years, which will be apparent from the following instances :—At Umanak (70° 40′ N. lat.) a series of observations for 10 years show the mean of December to be 17·6° in 1831, but ÷18·9° in 1832 ; of January, 20·8° in 1830, but ÷15·9° in 1835 ; of March, 18·7° in 1840, but ÷16·8° in 1832 ; consequently about 36° of variation for each of these months. At Godthaab during a period of only 5 years we find the mean of December to be 21·2° in one year and 2·3° in another, the mean of February 24·4° in one year, and ÷4·0° in another ; but the summer months only slightly varying, as July from 40·6° to 45·3° and August from 40·6° to 43·2°.

The warm land-wind and the southern wind in some measure seem to depend on each other, the former frequently changing to the latter after having blown for some time, and both of them appearing to serve as substitutes for each other according to locality. Some tracts, principally the interior inlets, are more subject to the land-wind, while in others the southern wind seems to be predominant. The great effect which the land-wind must be supposed to have in tempering the severity of the climate will be apparent from the following table abstracted from observations registered during the 12 years from 1829 to 1841 at Umanak (70° 40′ N. lat.), and showing the mean number of days in each of the seven coldest months on which the land-wind has blown, and the mean temperature of the same days compared with the monthly means.

Strong Wind blowing from E.S.E. in Umanak-fjord.

	Average number of days	Their mean temperature	Monthly mean temperature
October	3	35·4	22·6
November	4	36·5	13·8
December	3	25·2	÷0·2
January	3	26·9	÷6·2
February	2	27·5	÷8·9
March	3	33·2	÷1·3
April	3	35·4	13·8

The local land and sea-winds often appear combined with the other winds. The sea-wind may turn the current of a moderate north wind, and sometimes also of the southern wind, so as to make it follow the direction of an inlet instead of crossing it. The regular sea-wind prevails in summer when the weather is warm in all the fjords, blowing fresh at midday and abating after four o'clock. The land-wind is less regular, prevailing in some fjords much more than in others ; in autumn at times it grows rather tempestuous at the outlets of several of them, while close by on both sides it may be almost calm.

As is the case in all mountainous countries, the direction of the same wind is much affected by special localities. People in Greenland, moreover, frequently confound the true north and the magnetic north. The following table has been abstracted from the above-mentioned registers with a due allowance for these irregularities. As regards the direction, we have only determined the winds by dividing the horizon into four parts conformably to the true north, the first one, N., comprising all the winds between NW. and NE., or, in other words, northerly winds ; the second one, E., all the winds between NE. and SE., or, in other words, easterly winds, and so on ; while finally, C signifies. dead calm. As to their force, six degrees have been adopted, of which O signifies calm or nearly calm, while 5 has been used for reefed topsail-breeze or more. In order to show how long time the different winds have blown, we have divided each season, or 91¼ days, into 1,000 parts, and consequently the numbers indicate the time expressed in such parts.

Average Time in which the different Winds have blown.

	UPERNIVIK				GODTHAAB			
	Winter	Spring	Summer	Autumn	Winter	Spring	Summer	Autumn
N.	255	339	319	288	331	374	303	255
E.	343	231	162	365	384	248	86	336
S.	155	203	280	181	161	217	329	229
W.	18	25	64	44	49	57	151	62
C.	229	202	175	122	75	104	131	118
	1,000	1,000	1,000	1,000	1,000	1,000	1,000	1,000
	(*Force.*)							
0	557	529	400	376	63	91	142	128
1	122	74	98	45	130	194	236	196
2	39	13	31	64	194	210	271	224
3	188	277	353	346	275	244	202	245
4	86	84	110	165	196	165	77	124
5	8	23	8	4	142	96	72	83
	1,000	1,000	1,000	1,000	1,000	1,000	1,000	1,000

Rain and Snow.—As to the annual downpour, we are almost limited to notes about the number of days on which the different kinds of it have been observed at several stations. The variability of the climate is also apparent in a remarkable degree from this part of the meteorological observations. The difference between the quantities of snow falling in different years is astonishing, and sometimes it is poured down at intervals during the course of the whole winter, sometimes the greater part of it falls during a couple of weeks in March and April alone. Some summers are exceedingly dry, while in others, periods of many weeks set in with two days out of three being rain-days, and more or less stormy besides. Mist, which is one of the greatest troubles to travellers on the Greenland sea, greatly depends on localities, decreasing in proportion to the distance from the open sea, and being more common in the south than in the north. It generally sets in with northerly and westerly winds in summer, and does not penetrate far into the country or inlets. The following table shows the average number of days in one place in the north and another in the south, in which the different kinds of downpour have been observed, omitting the mist, and ranging hail in the column for ' mixed.'

Average number of Days with Downpour.

	JAKOBSHAVN			GODTHAAB		
	Rain	Snow	Mixed	Rain	Snow	Mixed
Winter . .	0·5	18·8	0·2	0·4	38·2	4·6
Spring . .	1·5	20·0	1·8	4·8	28·0	3·0
Summer . .	23·2	3·7	4·0	26·5	1·4	2·0
Autumn . .	6·0	15·7	3·8	10·0	15·8	8·0
Annual . .	31·2	58·2	9·8	41·7	83·4	17·6

According to the earlier registers, from which this table has been abstracted, no snow had been observed at Godthaab in July, but afterwards it has been noticed that every two or three years have one day with snow in July. The author has found no notices at all in the earlier registers about the absolute amount of snow and rain calculated as a sheet of fluid water, in all likelihood on account of the difficulty connected with measuring the downpour of snow and distinguishing it from the snowdrift. The only attempt at such observations which he knows to have been formerly made were taken by himself during his stay at Julianehaab. The result was that in a year rain fell on 57 days and snow alone or mixed with rain on 75 days, and that the whole downpour of water from both kinds amounted to 37 inches. If we imagine one half of this water to be snow, making, in its incompact state, tenfold its volume, it would represent a sheet of about 16 feet in thickness. Such a sheet having been submitted to the actions of drifting, thawing, and drying up in the course of the winter, might answer to the appearance of the snow-covering in some years spread over the country at the beginning of May ; but probably this quantity exceeds the true annual mean, and of course such a statement, founded upon observations made in one single year and in one place, is of but little value. In North Greenland the amount of snow annually falling is inferior to that of South Greenland. The observations which of late have been commenced there seem to prove that the climate is very dry, and differs greatly from the estimate just given for Julianehaab.

Changes of Weather.—As to the question about any prevailing law in the succession of changes of weather and their relation to the appearance of the air and the variation of the barometer, only little has been ascertained. At Julianehaab the author arrived at the following conclusions:—In winter and early in spring a rise of the barometer to above 28·90 will most commonly be followed by mild weather, the warm land-wind setting in at the same time. If, after the beginning of this wind or of the change to warmth, the barometer falls, the wind will become more or less tempestuous, and when the barometer is at the lowest point, generally beneath 27·80, the wind will veer through south-west to north, and also from this side blow with a force conformable to the fall of the barometer, which at the same time will rise again. If, on the contrary, after the land-wind has set in, the barometer remains steady, or even rises, it will blow a tolerable breeze, sometimes with intervals of calm, and will at once bring along with it fine weather, commonly with a serene sky for several days even in the depth of winter. In summer this sequence of changes appeared less regular, and the same may be said about the application of it to stations in higher latitudes, principally where the warm land-wind is less common and less distinguished from other winds. However, substituting warmth or southerly wind for the land-wind, the same rule will be more or less distinctly traced also further north. The warm land-wind is generally accompanied by clouds of characteristic oblong forms and often of a deep dark blue colour. In summer the sky may happen to be thus overcast in the most threatening way, an unusual warmth setting in at the same time. But if the barometer then remains steady, at the least above 28·90, the sky will be cleared from the east side without a corresponding wind, and fine warm weather will set in for several days. However, during such fine summer days with the most serene sky, very changeable winds, pretty fresh but always of short duration, often occur from two or three different directions the same day. If in summer, on a fine day, with calm and a clear sky, the barometer suddenly falls, a strong wind from the north is to be expected. As long as an ordinary north wind is blowing, the mountain tops will appear enveloped in clouds, the clearing off of which will accompany the abatement of the wind. If in summer the north wind rises to a gale, it will generally be of no long duration, and after having subsided, it will be followed directly by the opposite wind. Subtile clouds moving in a great height from north to south on a serene sky, generally forebode southern wind. The following table shows the mean height of the barometer at the same four stations as before referred to. The number of days for which observations have been registered are, for Upernivik, 833 ; for Jakobshavn, 3,226 ; for Godthaab, 1,685 ; for Julianehaab, about 600. The observations have been reduced to 32° Fahrenheit. The stations have been all in the immediate vicinity of the shore, hardly more than 50 feet above the level of the sea.

Mean Height of the Barometer.

	Upernivik	Jakobshavn	Godthaab	Julianehaab
Winter . . .	28·61	28·74	28·70	28·61
Spring . . .	28·83	28·95	28·88	28·61
Summer . . .	28·75	28·90	28·86	28·78
Autumn . . .	28·59	28·89	28·84	28·56
Year . . .	28·69	28·87	28·83	28·65

The extremes observed at Jakobshavn were, in winter, 29·99 and 27·34 ; in spring, 30·4 and 27·62 ; in summer, 29·67 and 28·04 ; in autumn, 29·58 and 27·64. At Julianehaab the author once observed 27·04.

NOTES.—In a meeting by which the 'Danish Geographical Society' was opened on December 22, 1876, the director of the Meteorological Institute, Captain Hoffmeyer, gave an interesting lecture on the warm land-wind of Greenland. He explained it as wholly analogous to the 'Föhn' of the Alps. When the barometer is lower in the south than in the north on the west of Greenland, the comparatively warm air over the Atlantic to the east of it will be liable to move towards the west, and in crossing Greenland it will gain more warmth, by sinking down on its west side, than it has lost by rising on the east side. The extraordinary dryness of this wind is explained at the same time.

The temperature of the soil at Godthaab, 4 feet under the ground, only varied between the extremes, 31·5 in March, and 40·1 in September.

III.—*GEOLOGY AND MINERALOGY.*

SINCE the author published his original work our knowledge of the geology of Greenland has been enriched by the researches of several travellers. The English mining engineer, Mr. J. W. Tayler, who explored South Greenland during several years, has given the first exact and detailed intelligence of Ivigtut, and made several discoveries as regards the presence of remarkable minerals in various places. Mr. K. J. V. Steenstrup, Dr. R. Brown, and others surveyed the coal and trap formation in North Greenland. Nordenskjöld brought the first intelligence of large masses of native iron; he and others, before and since, have furnished the materials upon which Professor Oswald Heer founded his valuable investigation of the fossil flora of Greenland. In the following notes we maintain the division into four groups which we have before adopted in the section on the products of the mineral kingdom, although the first and third of them probably ought to be still further divided into several groups. In indicating the localities by the latitude or by mileage, the intention has merely been to facilitate description, for in reality neither the numbers thus given nor the details in general of the maps we possess can lay any claim to that accuracy which such distinct numeric statements might possibly cause the reader to suppose.

I. *The granitic and gneissose group* comprises rocks greatly varying both in composition and appearance. It must be granted that some of them have a decidedly crystalline structure and indications of an igneous origin, while, on the other hand, some of them, occupying, however, only a very limited area, almost in the same degree exhibit the appearance of sedimentary deposits. But nevertheless the geological explorer will find himself highly embarrassed in trying to realise a thorough distinction between primitive and metamorphic rocks, to say nothing of a more

detailed classification. Among the extensive sections exhibited
in the precipitous mountain sides, there is scarcely any in which
no stratification is displayed and no veins or dykes are seen
crossing the strata. On a careful examination, however, the beds
in many places are found to exhibit curvilinear distorted forms,
with a tendency to grow elliptically concentric, bearing no resemblance to deposits successively heaped up over one another, but of
shells or crusts aggregating around the same central body. The
constituent elementary parts of all these rocks are feldspar, quartz,
mica, and hornblende, to which may be added, as subordinate,
but nevertheless exceedingly common, magnetic ironstone and
garnet. In the more extensive crystalline and light-coloured
beds, or massive nodules, feldspar and quartz prevail, while
mica and hornblende constitute the chief ingredients of the
darker and more slaty stripes.

The veins which intersect the layers are most commonly of
the same composition, and especially corresponding to the first-
mentioned kind, with feldspar and quartz prevailing. Such veins,
in forming numerous ramifications and following tortuous lines
in various directions, are widely dispersed almost everywhere,
and in many cases it is difficult to determine whether such
a stripe is to be considered a stratum or a dyke. Consequently they appear to have originated from the strata themselves, fissures having been formed and filled out with ingredients from the strata, either at the time when they were
deposited, but before they had wholly consolidated, or in a later
period. But there are some other dykes which bear evidence of
having originated from fissures, having been filled out with a
matter more distinctly different from the layers, so as to suggest
the idea of its having been produced by a much later igneous
eruption. These more conspicuous dykes, varying in their composition from true basalt or trap, to a sort of porphyritic greenstone
or syenite, form dark and less tortuous, but more extensive bands
across the rocks than the first-named veins. As to their mineralo-
gical character, these supposed eruptive dykes mostly resemble
the great trap formation in North Greenland ; they are very
frequent from the border of the latter down to Cape Farewell, but
always limited to such narrow bands in the older rocks, without
having spread over their surface so as to form mountains by them-

selves like those of the before-mentioned formation in North
Greenland. Notwithstanding the very distinct difference of composition which divides these dykes from the layers intersected by
them, some rocks are met with which form a sort of transition
between both parts. As to their composition the latter bear much
resemblance to the dykes, and they might most properly be
determined as varieties of syenite, but as to their occurrence they
are more analogous to the strata, because of their appearing in
more extensive masses, sometimes constituting entire islands, and
passing gradually into the ordinary stratified gneissose rocks.

The renowned traveller, Charles Giesecke, to whose explorations early in this century the greater part of our information
about the Greenland minerals is due, has described the formation
here in question by distinctly dividing the rocks into the usual
species, as mica-schist, hornblende-schist, granite, syenite, gneiss,
&c. In fact, specimens collected from these mountains of
Greenland commonly answer to these divisions, and consequently
the terms may be made use of for the description, but the author
of the present book is of opinion that in the first place specimens
may be collected which represent a gradual transition from one to
another of the said species, and secondly that none of the latter
can be considered to form a separate formation, the relative age
of which to the others we at present are able to ascertain. Undoubtedly in many instances a single one of them may prevail
over, or occupy a wider extent, but then again they are found
combined and mixed up in different proportions for short distances,
and it must depend on future researches to classify them properly
according to their relative ages and origin. In fact the rocks
which we here comprise under one group exhibit a series of
variations from the most crystalline or the most compact to the
most slaty texture, such as coarse granular granite, syenite,
gneiss, mica-schist, hornblende-schist, schistose quartz, and hornstone, and even clay-slate. The latter, however, is very rare,
apparently confined to some islands in 61° N. lat., while rocks
exactly of the opposite kind, and corresponding to syenite, are
somewhat more amply developed south of them between 60° and
61° N. lat. At any rate the prevalent feature throughout the
coast is gneiss impregnated with hornblende and alternating with
subordinate layers of mica and hornblende-schist containing

garnets, while veins of granite in which magnetic ironstone is disseminated intersect the beds. The more peculiar strata or veins occurring in the same group of rocks are as follows.

Hornblende-schist, containing, besides common hornblende and garnet, different varieties of anthophyllite, actinolite, asbestos, and amianthus, besides magnetic iron-ore and calcareous spar, are frequent.

Dolomite with tremolite, sahlite, and various other minerals, constitute beds of considerable thickness in various places in North Greenland, such as Maneetsok (68° 46′ N. lat.), Nuk (68° 43′ N. lat.), and near to Uvkusigsak (71° N. lat.), but are scarcely to be met with in the south.

Veins of coarse granular granite, either with reddish feldspar—and in this case sometimes containing allanite, zircon, and iron-pyrites, besides magnetite and apatite—or with white feldspar, and then accompanied by tourmaline.

Extensive beds of the soft stone generally denominated pot-stone or steatite, impregnated with, or containing nodules of tremolite and asbestos, and accompanied by several other minerals, are met with in various places, but particularly in South Greenland.

In some places the gneiss beds, as well as the more slaty layers with predominant hornblende and mica, for a considerable extent are rich in disseminated fine-grained sulphuret of iron, and accompanied by graphite. Those tracts generally present an ironshale, mouldering, and barren appearance.

Seams of anthophyllite and actinolite, accompanied by beds of feldspar impregnated with quartz, dichroite, and mica are frequent north of 71° 40′ N. lat.

The cryolite, with the minerals accompanying it, is to be considered neither as a bed nor as a vein or dyke, but as an immense nodule imbedded in one single hollow in a rock of this group. For further details we refer to the description given of it before.

A bed of a peculiar rock composed of eudialyte, sodalite, and hornblende (arfvidsonite) occurs in the interior of the Kangerdluarsuk-fjord (60° 50′ N. lat.) It appears to be much more extensive and less distinctly divided from the surrounding rocks than the cryolite, but has been very insufficiently investigated.

2. *The sandstone of Igaliko*, which hitherto has only been found

to occupy a territory of a few square miles, is very firm and hard, being composed of conglutinated and half-fused quartz particles. Dykes of porphyry traverse it, and it presents the appearance of one of the oldest sedimentary formations, but owing to the total. absence of fossils, it has been impossible to determine the age more accurately.

3. *Trap or basalt connected with beds of sandstone and shale, including coal and other vegetable remains,* occupy an area of about 5,000 square miles, viz. Disco, the outer half of the Nugsuak (Noursoak) peninsula, the Svarte-Huk peninsula, Hare Island, Unknown Island, and a few other adjacent islands, with exception only of the low granitic hills which here and there project from the foot of the cliffs. as at Godhavn for instance. The sandstone rocks have been comprised in one formation with the igneous rocks on account of their making their appearance only as a substratum to the latter, projecting from the foot of the trap rocks, whereas the latter frequently are seen rising immediately from the sea or resting upon granitic rocks without intervening sandstone. The trap beds are mostly horizontal, 50 to 100 feet in thickness, but also dwindling into stripes and vanishing. They are divided from each other, as well as from the common substratum, by sheets of reddish clay or of a sort of trap-tuff or breccia, containing angular fragments of the substratum. This structure causes the abrupt sidewalls of the mountains to appear somewhat terrace-shaped, but gradually sinking into slopes towards their foot. It has been doubted, although the author considers it probable, that sedimentary deposits containing coal also are to be found resting upon trap-beds, or in other words that the vegetation which has given rise to the coal-beds has continued during intervals of the trap eruptions. But at all events the principal sandstone deposits are older than the trap, and have almost entirely been covered by it. As regards the determination of the geological age of the coal-beds by means of the fossil plants accompanying them, a few rolled pieces or erratic blocks have been found on the same shores containing traces of plants, which at first were referred to the old or true carboniferous period, but afterwards proved to be cretaceous. The plants accompanying the coal-beds have been found to belong to two different formations; the upper cretaceous and the lower tertiary groups (Miocene). Of the first, two

subdivisions have been observed, of which the lower contained
fifty-six species of plants, among which nineteen are ferns and
nine cycadeæ. The tertiary group is most beautifully displayed at
Atanekerdluk (mainland, 70° N. lat.), the number of species
determined amounting to 169. The sandstone beds with their
subordinate beds have a thickness of several hundred, rising even
to 2,000, but not exceeding 2,500, feet. In following them along
the shores they are not always found to contain coal-beds, but
always layers of claystone and slate. Large pieces of fossil wood
are scattered over the Asakak-glacier near Umanak. The sides
of the valley, as far from the shore as it has hitherto been explored,
consist only of granitic rocks, for which reason the fossil wood
must have travelled thither from a distance of more than four
miles and a height of at least 2,000 or 3,000 feet. In many
other valleys similar fragments of coal or fossil wood are to be
found among the stones of the river-beds, but the coal-beds which
have chiefly been examined, and in some places made use of, are
all situated in the immediate vicinity of the sea, cropping out in
the outer cliffs or slopes of the hills which form a border from one
to four miles broad along the foot of the trap-rocks. The coal
which has been worked for use contains, on an average—hygro-
scopic water 17, other volatile matter 24, fixed carbon 53, and
ashes 6 per cent. The fossil resin (retinite) is most abundant
in the coals of Hare Island. A sort of clayey ironstone and
pyrites accompany the coals in nodules and very thin stripes.
Magnetic pyrites have been found in much larger nodules in
basalt where sandstone beds were intersected by a basalt dyke,
and had been greatly altered by the action of heat. The strata
of shale or claystone, though generally subordinate to the sandstone, in some localities are more amply developed, so as to constitute the chief mass for an extent of 400 to 500 feet in a vertical
direction. On the mainland in 70° 20′ N. lat. they are of a
reddish colour and hardened, presenting the appearance of having
been acted upon by subterranean combustion. Remains of
shells or mollusca are rather scarce in these deposits, but still they
have been found, mostly belonging to salt-water, but also to freshwater species.

When sighted from a distance the extensive and mostly horizontal trap beds bear much more resemblance to sedimentary or neptunian deposits than to rocks formed by the consolidation of any matter ejected by the action of present volcanoes. The composition of the rocks constituting these extensive strata, however, when closely examined, shows a series of varieties gradually passing from the granular or crystalline to a more compact basaltic texture, with a tendency at the same time to become vesicular or even spongy, so as to assume the appearance of true lava. Their metamorphosing action upon the coal-beds, producing coke, anthracite, and graphite, has been mentioned above. Besides the regular trap-beds, the eruptive mass has formed beds of tuff or breccia as well as dykes and more irregular accumulations of a very distinctly cleaved columnar basalt. The sandstone hills are frequently traversed in many ways by the trap veins, which sometimes even widen into larger masses and appear on the surface as small cliffs along the sea-shore. But it is very curious that apart from the main trap district the same igneous rocks, though so widely spread in the shape of dykes, are rarely met with as eruptions covering parts of the granitic surface. One instance of this kind is met with in 72° 15′ N. lat. on the continent, only a couple of miles from the northern border of the main trap formation. It rises on the top of the granitic hills, is scarcely more than a mile in circumference, and forms a sort of semi-circular ridge around a basin like a crater. The rock is fine-grained basalt, very regularly cleft into small columns. Every heap of *débris* from the trap rocks in general . abounds more or less in amygdaloid specimens, the cavities having been filled up partly with zeolites, partly with different varieties of quartz and carbonate of lime. The latter ingredients are characteristic of the north-western part of the Nugsuak peninsula.

4. *Alluvial Deposits.*—Alternating regular and horizontal beds of sand and clay fill out the bottom of valleys which are not unfrequently met with throughout the coast, but always of a very limited extent. The total area formed by them would be very difficult to calculate, but at any rate it would be quite inconsiderable when compared with that of the trap formation. Where these flat spots are bordered by the sea, they sometimes present steep walls of up to 100 feet in height, the surface rising somewhat higher inland, but scarcely exceeding 200 feet.

In these deposits shells and other fossil remains are very frequent. Collections have been made and classed, which prove the specimens all to belong to still existing species, though some of them may no longer be found in the sea adjacent to the coast where the remains occur. Impressions in clay of small fishes are also found in several places, and are even still formed ; the clay including such organic bodies hardens into rounded nodules of different shapes. The recent marine remains may also probably be found on the surface at greater heights. Finally, we have to add that, besides the regular alluvial beds, accumulations of stones are found which remind us of ancient moraines, and erratic blocks widely scattered are found even upon table-lands at an amazing height, as, for instance, granitic boulders on the top of the trap mountains of Disco. These surprising phenomena connected with the configuration of the land and the features exhibited by the surface of the rocks, have given rise to a series of investigations tending to prove that the inland ice of Greenland formerly extended much further, including the present fjords and bays, and that the alluvial deposits just mentioned were formed when the sea had retired almost to its present confines. It lies beyond the plan of the present book, however, and would, moreover, exceed the ability of its author, to enter on a discussion of these questions. We must, therefore, refer to what has been published by Nordenskjöld, Brown, Steenstrup, Laube, Helland, and others.

Synopsis of the Minerals found in Danish Greenland.

Quartz.—Common quartz sometimes forms considerable layers, *f.i.* about Arsut and Sanerut, and in very large crystals at Ivigtut. Milky quartz with a bluish tint, and smoked topaz, here and there in South Greenland. Of rock crystal no very large crystals are found, excepting in Tunugdliarfik and Igaliko, the largest from thence being 6 inches in length and 4 in breadth. Siliceous sinter is seen in the hot springs of Unartok. Hornstone and jasper occur pretty frequently, and chalcedony in trap, *e.g.* at Niakornak (70° 46′ N. lat.), while moss agate, hyalite, and opal are found on the mainland coast of the Waigatt.

Olivin, scanty in trap.

Felspar, in many varieties, some of which probably are albite.

Crystals, very rare, of orthoclase in talc at Anoritok (70° 48′ N. lat.), of albite at Ekaluit (68° 50′ N. lat.). The felspar of the ordinary syenite is translucent, resembling adularia. Common felspar, white or yellowish, sometimes forms tolerably pure layers, only mixed with some quartz, not unfrequently in the shape of graphic granite. Amazon stone forms a vein in the granite or syenite of Nunarsuit (60° 44′ N. lat.); it is said to be exhausted, but the mineral has also been traced in other places thereabout. A peculiar dark green felspar occurs at Sungausak (68° 21′ N. lat.).

Pumice-stone is found in small rounded pieces, probably coming from the volcanoes of Iceland or Jan Mayen.

Idocrase, in dolomite, Maneetsok (68° 44′ N. lat.).

Staurolite, in slaty talc, in same locality.

Gieseckite, in porphyry, Akuliarusek, near Igaliko.

Nephrite. Specimens resembling this mineral have been found in Disco and several places, but the identity not perfectly ascertained.

Sodalite, crystallised and abundant, with eudialite, between Kangerdluarsuk and Tunugdliarfik (60° 50′ N. lat.).

Eudialite, abundant with the latter, the largest crystals measuring 3 to 4 inches in diameter.

Apophyllite, Disco.

Stilbite, rare and scanty, Disco.

Chabasic, very common, Disco.

Levyne, not unfrequent in North Greenland.

Mesotype, not uncommon in North Greenland, especially in Disco-tjord.

Analcime, near Godhavn, Disco.

Okenite, the most common zeolite in Greenland, occurs in three varieties : compact, radiated, and asbestos-like. The latter especially abundant, and forming veins or layers at Makak (70° 28′ N. lat.).

Sordawalite, in trap veins, South Greenland (?).

Mica is seldom seen in large and regular leaves. A mamillary variety with specular iron, Arsut Island. Crystals very rare, *f.i.* Sagdliarusat (70° 40′ N. lat.), and of a yellow variety in dolomite, Maneetsok (68° 44′ N. lat.).

Chlorite, accompanying copper-ore in Nunarsuit (60° 48′ N. lat.). Probably an ingredient of several soft and slaty rocks of a dark green colour.

Talc, beautiful greenish white, laminated, brought by a native from the South Ström-fjord (about 66° 30′). A compact variety here and there. Probably identical with some varieties of pot-stone, and constituting an ingredient of others.

Serpentine, forming nodules in potstone, and perhaps identical with some of the harder varieties of this mineral, as well as with a green slaty mineral forming considerable veins or layers near Iluilarsuk (61° 48′ N. lat.).

Hornblende. Only seldom a gneissose or granitic rock is found in which this mineral is wanting, while at the same time it forms a chief ingredient of many subordinate strata belonging to these rocks. Perhaps it may be said that its different varieties in some measure occur as a substitute of mica, and that their abundant development is peculiar to the gneissose formation of Greenland. Hornblende-slate, with garnets and *actinolite*, are very common. Here and there they are combined with *asbestos* and *amianthus*, *e.g.* at Karajat and other places near Godthaab ; *tremolite* always accompanies the dolomite in North Greenland ; *anthophyllite* frequently occurs in the environs of Upernivik ; *arfvidsonite* accompanies the eudialyte, and appears in crystals of extraordinary size.

(Ordinary augite in crystallised and distinctly recognisable specimens is hardly known to have been found in Greenland.)

Sahlite, common in the dolomite of North Greenland.

Bronzite and *diallage* here and there, most abundantly in Agto (67° 52′ N. lat.).

Clay occurs only in few varieties, and that of the ordinary kind which forms regular layers in the alluvial formations ; is seldom very pure. Clay-slate mentioned above.

Soap-stone or *steatite* (mentioned above), occurs in different places, especially Karajat (70° 30′ N. lat.), Pakitsok (69° 28′ N. lat.), the environs of Godthaab (most abundantly), Sermesok (61° 12′ N. lat.).

Garnet. Ordinary garnet very common and widely spread, as disseminated in the gneissose rocks and hornblende-slate ; most plentiful and the largest crystals in Agto, Ameralik, and especially Ikatok (62° 40′) ; precious garnet here and there, *f.i.* in Ameralik, Southern Stream-fjord, and especially in Sagdliarusat (70° 40′ N. lat.) ; yellow garnet in small crystals accompanying copper-ore in Nunarsuit.

Dichroite, common in the environs of Upernivik, where it also has been found crystallised, and a great rarity.

Epidote, very common, but only in small portions, and rarely crystallised. It is generally found in a variety of gneiss which has undergone a certain alteration, the felspar having assumed a reddish colour.

Zircon, in violet crystals, generally accompanying allanite wherever this mineral has been found. But elsewhere it occurs only very scantily. In the syenite it has only just been traced, forming small yellow crystals, but it does not constitute a regular ingredient of this rock. A hydrous silicate of zirconia and yttria has been found at Ivigtut.

Beryl, in large crystals with fergusonite, once found near Sardlok (60° 28′ N. lat.).

Tourmaline, not unfrequent as accompanying white felspar. Extraordinarily large crystals have been found imbedded in a layer of mica-slate at Karusulik in Ameralik. The rock from which they have been taken forms a steep wall, which has been hollowed out probably by this operation ; the layer appears almost exhausted, unless blasting should be tried. Large crystals also occur in Sagdliarusat near Umanak.

Saphirin, in mica-schist, near Fiskernæs.

Allanite seems not to be rare, *f.i.* at Nugatsiak (68° 8′ N. lat.) and Inusulik (68° 20′ N. lat.), but most abundantly at Avigait (62° 16′ N. lat.), where also large crystals have been found.

Fergusonite, rare and scanty, Sermesok (60° 12′ N. lat.) and Sardlok (60° 28′ N. lat.).

Tantalite, accompanying the cryolite at Ivigtut. A large amount of beautiful crystals has been collected there, some of them weighing upwards of 3 ounces.

Titanite, in the dolomite of Maneetsok.

Calcareous spar, here and there, very scanty in nodules, thin veins, or layers in the gneissose rocks and in amygdaloids. Any sort of limestone is very rare in Greenland.

Arragonite in large crystals is characteristic of the trap in the environs of Nugsuak.

Dolomite, forming extensive layers in the gneissose formation of North Greenland, already mentioned.

Fluor-spar accompanies the cryolite, and has been got in fine crystals from Kangerdluarsuk and Tunugdliarfik (60° 48′ N. lat.), but elsewhere it appears to be rare.

Cryolite, originally occupying a space about 400 feet long and 100 feet broad in the gneiss at Ivigtut (see previous remarks). The depth of the mass, which probably forms an immense nodule, has not as yet been ascertained. A few years ago the first crystals of it were found.

Alum, in the decayed rocks of Sagdliarusat near Umanak.

Sulphate of iron, in the coals of Kuk near Umanak.

Heavy-spar or *baryta* is very rare in Greenland. The author has seen but one small specimen from the environs of Igaliko.

Sparry iron-ore accompanies the cryolite in large crystals, elsewhere very rare.

Apatite, frequent in granite veins, especially in North Greenland, but only disseminated in small crystals. At Sungausak (68° 21′ N. lat.) crystals were found between 6 and 8 inches in diameter, accompanying green felspar and pyrites.

Magnetic iron-ore, widely spread almost everywhere in grains or small crystals, rarely in layers or merely in nodules a couple of inches in thickness, never in any tolerable quantity.

Specular iron-ore, here and there very scanty as incrustations or small crystals with rock-crystal and calcareous spar.

Brown and red ironstone and *yellow ochre*, here and there, always scanty.

Titaniferous iron-ore, occurrence similar to that of magnetic iron-ore, but much scantier and rather rare, *f.i.* Sagdliarusat, Ikamiut, Narsak.

Tin-stone accompanies the cryolite.

Native silver has been found in small pieces of problematic origin, near Julianehaab; see previous remarks.

Native iron, in loose blocks and imbedded in trap ; see above.

Native copper, traced in the shape of almost microscopical grains in trap, Disco-fjord.

Common pyrites, very frequently met with, but never in large quantities. The finest crystals have been got from Ameralik, and some of extraordinary size accompany the apatite at Sungausak.

Magnetic pyrites. Extraordinary accumulations of this sulphuret of iron have been found in Sagdliarusat, near Umanak, in the gneissose formation, and in Disco imbedded in the sandstone.

In the first place it seems to have given rise to the formation of a peculiar decayed rock rich in sulphates ; whole loose blocks have been found upon the surface, almost wholly consisting of the same mineral, and estimated at a weight of 10,000 pounds. In the second instance, one massive body of it, estimated at about 200 cubic feet, has been found in a basalt dyke which traverses the sandstone of Igdlokunguak in Disco (69° 53′ N. lat.).

Arsenical pyrites, disseminated as pretty large grains in the gneiss of Nanortalik, and accompanying the cryolite.

Variegated copper-ore, scantily here and there disseminated as grains or forming thin layers of a very limited extent, *f.i.* Nunarsuit ; see above.

Copper-pyrites, accompanying the cryolite, elsewhere very rare and scanty.

Galena, accompanying the cryolite ; see above.

Copper-glance occurs like the variegated copper-ore, but still more scantily.

Molybdena, pretty common, but only in small quantities, *f.i.* Narsak, Kangarsuk (61° 28′ N. lat.), Ivigtut.

Blende, very scanty, accompanying the cryolite, one small specimen from the Igaliko-fjord.

Selenide of lead and copper, once found near Godthaab, very scanty.

Graphite, pretty common in two varieties ; the compact graphite originated from coal, and the foliated graphite in the gneiss formation, the latter seldom very pure ; see above.

Native coke, near Umanak ; see previous remarks.

Anthracite, accompanying the compact graphite at Karsok, and forming a layer at Manik (70° 8′ N. lat.).

Coal and *retinite,* abundant in North Greenland ; see previous remarks.

NOTE.—In his descriptions of the Greenland geological formations, Giesecke, as already mentioned, tries to designate all the subordinate rocks of which they are constructed by distinct names according to the geological system and nomenclature of his day. We have asserted that this method is likely to give rise to misapprehensions, because it suggests the idea of distinct and essential differences existing where in reality there are transitions

through innumerable varieties, and where the different composition of the strata does not at all prove an essential difference of
origin. For the same reason his descriptions grow more diffuse
and intricate than necessary. The circumstantiality of the style
in his diary (only existing in manuscript) has been enhanced by a
certain tendency to enumerate as many species of minerals found
in each place as possible, and for this reason to mention mere
traces or indications, and to lay much stress on describing varieties
of the same species. Giesecke being still the chief authority as
regards the mineralogy of Greenland, later accounts of the same
subject have also been encumbered with many details which may
be considered superfluous, and partly give rise to mistakes. We
have here tried to give a succinct view of what appears most important. Several specimens from Greenland which are found in
our collections have not been comprised in the list above on
account of the place where they have been found not having been
sufficiently ascertained, and of others the species has not as yet
been duly determined. Including what, for any of the reasons
here alluded to, may be considered doubtful, the following minerals and localities may still be added to the list above :—

Compact scapolite ; prehnite ; several undetermined zeolites ;
precious serpentine ; krokydolite ; emery ; specular iron in large
crystals from the vicinity of the Iceblink, exactly resembling
that from the island of Elba ; tinstone in the syenite of Frederikshaab ; native silver from a place different from the above-named
but not indicated ; cobalt-ore ; wolfram ; chlorophaite ; diopside ;
phosphate of iron ; lievrite ; wavellite ; native sulphur ; spinel (a
fine crystal from the interior, in about 68° N. lat.) ; gadolinite
and phosphate of lead.

Finally there have of late been discovered :—corundum, troilite,
hisingerite, kryokonite ; and the following found in the cryolite :—
thomsonite, pachnolite, raldtonite, hagemannite, arsuktite, gear-
suktite, ivigtite, wolfram.

A more methodical geological survey of Greenland has recently
been commenced by *K. J. V. Steenstrup*, who already has given
valuable reports on the North Greenland formations, especially the
coalbeds, and on the true nature of the native iron. I am indebted
to him for varied information in writing this Appendix.

IV.—*VOCABULARY OF ESKIMO WORDS AND NAMES.*

In the present additional notes a double aim has been intended, firstly that of giving an idea of the Eskimo language by exemplifying its words and their construction, secondly that of showing as far as possible the correct spelling and the etymology of the most common geographical names, especially those occurring in this book.   In the first respect it forms the continuation of a corresponding brief abstract of the Eskimo grammar given in the Introduction to 'Tales and Traditions of the Eskimo,' to which we must refer those readers who desire more detailed information regarding the remarkable structure of the Eskimo idiom than can be given here.

The language is written with the same letters as the English, only omitting some and adding the letter к, differing from k by its being perfectly guttural, and sounding as something between gh, rk, and rkr.   A few other consonant-sounds are expressed by double letters, especially ss, which is mostly like the French j, and as to the vowels the accents, ' (sharp), ^ (long), and ~ (sharp and long), are used as quite indispensable, and sometimes able to change the sense into the opposite.   As for the rest, the letters are pronounced mostly as in the German, differing from the English especially in the following points : the letter e at the end of a word is never mute, but always to be pronounced ; ai is like y in by; au like ow ; i like i in it ; u like oo; g like g in good ; j like y in yard.

As regards flexion we have only to remark here that the plural is formed by t as final letter, with some modification of the last syllable, and that flexion also substitutes the possessive pronouns by final letters, expressing 'its' or 'his' etc.: which in the Greenlandish grammar have got the name of suffixes.

The peculiar system of constructing words is the most remarkable feature of the Eskimo language. Not considering the inflexions, words are formed of stems which are either primitive or added. The latter can never be used alone, but must be appended to the former singly or followed by more. With regard to their endings both kinds of stems are divided into nominal and verbal. The latter, to become true verbs able to be conjugated, require a particular addition, by means of which in some measure also the former, or the nouns, can be converted into verbs. These additions are in the third person indicative : —poᴋ, —voᴋ, —aoᴋ, or including the object: —pâ, —vâ, —â. For instance, of the verbal stem ajoᴋ is made ajorpoᴋ, he,is bad ; ajorpâ, he is unable to do it, or to subdue him, and of the nominal stem toᴋo, death, is made toᴋuvoᴋ, he is dead, and toᴋupâ, he kills him. The verbal stems in their original form, with their proper endings, are only used as a sort of interjections, in phrases and sometimes in geographical names. A primitive stem, by means of an additional one, is made a compound stem. Sometimes several stems are found bearing a resemblance so as to render it evident that they are related to each other, while nevertheless it is difficult to decide whether they have an independent origin of the same root, or perhaps one of them may be the original, and the others formed out of it by means of some peculiar affixes. A selection of affixes is here premised, especially comprising those occurring in the subsequent list of words and names ; both of which are mainly compiled from Kleinschmidt's Dictionary.

AFFIXES.

In adding the affixes for a stem certain rules have to be observed, some of which here are indicated by signs as follows : (1) signifying that the affix has to be added to the last vowel of the stem, (2) indiscriminately to its final letter, (3) at all events to a consonant, which therefore in some instances has to be inserted, (4) to the root, or an abbreviated form of the stem.

(2) aᴋ, also gaᴋ, raᴋ, offspring or young, also small or inferior.
(1) aᴋ, also gaᴋ, ssaᴋ, (2) taᴋ, substitutes the passive participle.
(1) araᴋ, small, not full grown.
(1) arssuᴋ, not of the common kind.
(4) erpâ or (1) lerpâ, furnishes him with.
(1) erpâ, deprives him of.

(1) **gâ** or **râ**, has it for, uses or regards it as.

(1) **gigpoĸ** or **rigpoĸ**, has or is a fine . . .

(1) **gssaĸ**, future, or intended for.

(1) **giaĸ** or **riaĸ**, requiring to be.

(4) **iaĸ** or (1) **liaĸ**, made, worked.

(4) **iarpoĸ** or (1) **liarpoĸ**, goes or travels to, pursues.

(1) **ínaĸ**, only.

(1) **ípoĸ**, is without.

(1) **juípoĸ**, never.

(1) **ĸarpoĸ**, has . . . ; or there are . . .

(1) **kasik**, bad, disagreeable.

(1) **kípoĸ**, has little or in a small degree . . .

(1) **kerdluk**, having a small or bad.

(1) **ko**, and most frequently the plural **kut**, refuse or remains of . . .

(1) **leĸ** or (3) **dleĸ**, farthest in the direction of.

(1) **lerpoĸ**, begins to.

(1) **lik**, having or provided with.

(3) **dluarpoĸ**, well, sufficiently, duly.

(3) **dluk** or (1) **luk**, sometimes signifying bad, sometimes almost without any sensible signification.

(1) **mineĸ**, part or fragment of.

(2) **mio**, inhabitant of, the plural **miut** frequently in names signifying inhabited place.

(3) **naĸ** or (1) **rnaĸ**, peculiar, not of the common kind.

(2) **narpoĸ**, is able to make or cause one . . .

(2) **neĸ** (to verbal stems) the state or effect of.

(1) **ngilaĸ**, expresses the negation.

(1) **nguaĸ**, plural **nguit**, small or little.

(2) **niarpoĸ**, tries or endeavours to . . .

(3) **pak**, or rather its plural **pait**, many.

(3) **palugpoĸ** or **palârpoĸ**, has the appearance of . . .

(1) **rĸigpoĸ**, again and better, or is clever in . . .

(1) **savoĸ**, will . . . (substituting the future tense).

(2) **siorpoĸ**, goes to look for, is occupied with, or travels in . . .

(3) **ssuaĸ**, large or very . . . (plural **ssuit**).

(2) **taĸ**, belonging to (also substituting the passive participle, *see above*).

(3) **toĸ** or **soĸ**, and (1) **ssoĸ** or **tsoĸ**, being in the state or action of (substituting a nominal participle).

(1) **tsiaĸ** or (3) **atsiaĸ**, tolerable.

(1) **tuaĸ**, the only.

(2) **tuvoĸ** or **suvoĸ**, has many.

(2) **tôĸ** or **sôĸ**, in a high degree, or having much, or large . . .

(3) **useĸ**, an incomplete . . .

(1) **ussaĸ**, something like . . .

(1) **vik** or (3) **fik**, place or time, where or when . . .

WORDS AND NAMES.

In this list the words are ranged according to the stems, the derivative words being grouped under the stems to which they belong. All the geographical names mentioned in this book being embodied in the list, a comparatively great part of the words will be found identical with names. The construction and sense of the derivative words in most cases will be found immediately given by the affixes which are explained above, and for this reason it seemed unnecessary to add a translation of many of the names. It will be seen that the etymology of local names is simpler and more regular in the Eskimo than in more civilised languages. But of course here also we meet with several names of doubtful origin and meaning. Such names are nevertheless appended in order to show how they are supposed to be correctly spelled ; they will be found partly with the stems, being in this case marked (?), partly at the end of the list.

agdlo, breathing-hole ; **agdluitsoᴋ,** from (1) **ípoᴋ** and (1) **tsoᴋ.**
agpa, auk, plural **agpat, agpamiut.**
aipaᴋ, companion, **áipâ,** his or her spouse.
ajorpoᴋ, is bad, **ajúngilaᴋ,** is good.
aᴋigsseᴋ, ptarmigan ; **aᴋigssiaᴋ,** young pt.
ake, opposite, pay, answer ; **akia,** its or his . . .
ako, a smaller part of a larger body, an interval ; **akugdleᴋ,** middlemost, as a name for certain mountains or bays ; **akuliaᴋ,** the part of the nose situated between the eyes ; **akuliarusek,** a frequent name of mountains facing the sea, and enclosed between two branches of it, while connected by a low isthmus with the mainland ; **akungnagpok,** is situated between others ; **akungnak** (?) **akungnât** (?).
alángoᴋ, shady side ; **alangordleᴋ.**
ameᴋ, skin ; **ameraᴋ,** bark of a tree, painting of a surface ; **ameralik.**
amípoᴋ, is narrow ; **amitsuarssuk,** from (1) **tsoᴋ** and (1) **arssuk,** a name for narrow branches of fjords.
anaᴋ, excrement ; **anartussoᴋ,** from (4) **tuvoᴋ** and (1) **ssoᴋ.**
anore, wind ; **anoritôᴋ** ; **anordluítsoᴋ,** where there is no bad wind.
angivoᴋ, is large ; **angisôᴋ, angisôrssuaᴋ.**
angmagssaᴋ, capelin ; **angmagssalik.**
angut, a man or male ; **angutâ,** his father.
anguvoᴋ, catches, reaches ; **angussaᴋ,** captured seal.
arnaᴋ, woman ; plural **arnat.**
arsivoᴋ, has abundance of provisions ; **arsivik.**

at, nether part, only used with suffixes, f.i. **atâ,** its n. p., such as the foot of that mountain.

âtâк, saddleback seal; **âtârssuaк,** full-grown s.

atavoк, is connected with or attached to something; **ataneк,** a name for parts of land connected by narrow isthmus; **atanekerdluk**; **atangmik** (?).

auk, blood; in a more indefinite sense—something dissolved, discontinued, detached and put in motion; **augpalârtoк** or **augpalugtoк,** red; **aulavoк,** moves; **aulatsivik, áupoк,** is melted; **aulisarpoк,** fishes with a line; **aulisagaк,** a fish.

ausiak, spider; plural **ausiait.**

ava, north; **avangnaк,** north wind; with suffix, **avangnâ,** its northern part, or the country north of it; **avangnamiut, avangnardleк,** northernmost.

avataк, hunting bladder; **avatarmiut.**

avigpâ, divides it in two parts; **avigait** (?)

ipeк, dirt; **evkitsoк,** clean (irregularly formed by **kípoк** and **tsoк**).

iga, pot for cooking over other fire than a lamp; **igaleк,** small sideroom to the house-passage, used for a kitchen; **igalíko, igaussaк, igánguaк.**

igípâ, throws it away; and **igípoк,** shoots with firearms; **iginiarfik.**

igdlo, house; **igdlokasik, igdlorssuit, igdlorpait, igdlorssuatsiait, igdlo-tuârssuit** (**tuaк** and **arssuk** in plural); **igdluernerit,** abandoned houses, from (1) **erpâ** and **neк.**

igpiк, a shore forming a steep bank or cliff, and consisting of clay or gravel.

ika, yonder; **ikeк,** a broad and unsheltered bay or inlet which has to be crossed by travellers; **ikerssuaк, ikerasaк,** a sound or open thoroughfare of the sea between land or ice; **ikerasârssuk, ikamiut.**

ikápoк, is shallow; **ikátoк.**

ilimanaк, the verbal root of **ilimanarpoк,** it is expected.

ikípâ, sets fire to it; **ingneк,** plural **ingnerit,** fire.

ilivâ, puts it down or aside, buries him; **iliveк,** a grave.

iluípoк, is entire; **iluileк,** land appearing to be an island, however connected with a larger land; **iluilârssuk.**

ilo or **iluk,** interior; **ilua,** its interior; **iluliaк,** a glacier-fragment or iceberg, plural **ilulissat.**

imaк, contents of a vessel or space, also sea or ocean; **imartuneк,** a spacious inlet with a narrow entrance to it from the sea.

imeк, freshwater; **imerigssoк,** having fine or copious water.

inuk, man, with suffix, **inua,** its owner; **inûvoк,** lives, is born; **inugsuk,** beacon, seamark; **inugsulik.**

ipe, handle; **ipiutaк,** a very narrow isthmus between a peninsula and its mainland.

iso, end; **isua,** its end; **isúnguaк.**

isorpoк, is turbid or muddy; **isortoк,** having muddy water; **isortuarssuk.**

ituípoк, crosses the land or ice from one water to the other; **itivdleк,** low and narrow land to be crossed in bearing the boat in order to make a short cut, or to avoid a dangerous shore; **itivdlermiut, itivdliatsiaк, itivd-liarssuk.**

iviangeĸ, woman's breast; iviangussat, a name for hills with two rounded summits.

ivik, grass; ivigaĸ, plural ivigkat, small grass; ivigtût, plural of ivigtôĸ, rich in grass.

ivnaĸ, a precipice offering no footing; ivnârssuk and ivnârssúnguaĸ, names for high precipitous cliffs.

ĸajaĸ, a kayak or skin canoe; ĸajauvoĸ, perishes in kayak; ĸajâ, his kayak.

ĸak, surface; ĸaersoĸ, from (1) erpâ and (3) soĸ, a rock without vegetation; ĸagdlo or ĸavdlo, eyebrow, and as a name, a cliff encircling a lake; ĸagdlumiut; ĸagsse, an enclosed valley or bay, a meeting-house; ĸagssimiut; ĸagssiarsuk; ĸangataĸ, a cave; ĸârajúgpoĸ, has a rounded surface; ĸârajugtoĸ; ĸáĸaĸ, mountain; ĸáĸarssuaĸ, ĸáĸarssuatsiaĸ.

ĸamutit (plural), sledge.

ĸarajaĸ, a bay tolerably surrounded or sheltered by rocks.

ĸarmaĸ, house wall, plural ĸarmat.

ĸârpâ, makes it burst—(the sea) breaks over it; ĸârusuĸ, a cave; ĸârusulik.

ĸasigiaĸ, a spotted seal (Callocephalus vitulinus); ĸasigiánguit.

ĸaĸorpoĸ, is white; ĸaĸortoĸ, white.

ĸeĸertaĸ, island; ĸeĸertarssuaĸ, ĸeĸertarssuatsiaĸ.

ĸernerpoĸ, is black; ĸernertoĸ, black.

ĸerroĸ, stoneheap; ĸerrortût, ĸerrortussoĸ.

ĸilerpâ, binds it; ĸilerte, or plural ĸilertit, hair-tuft; ĸilertinguit.

ĸimagpâ, leaves it; ĸematulivoĸ, lays in stores; ĸematulivik, depository for provisions.

ĸingâĸ or ĸingartaĸ, the sharp edge of the shinbone; ĸingartarssuit.

ĸingoĸ, head of a bay; with suffix, ĸingua, its head.

ĸiorpâ, clips or cuts it; ĸîoĸe, a name for isolated islands situated far out to sea (?).

ĸipivâ, twists or wrings it; ĸipingassoĸ, distorted.

ĸiporaĸ, furrow, especially on the belly of a whale; ĸiporĸaĸ, humpback-whale; ĸiporĸarmiut.

ĸiteĸ, middle; with suffix, ĸerĸa, its middle; ĸeterdleĸ, middlemost.

ĸivigpoĸ, flees from human society; ĸivigtut.

ĸunguleĸ, scurvy grass (*Cochlearia*); ĸungulertussoĸ.

ĸŭpâ, makes (a room) narrower by removing a wall; ĸôrnoĸ, narrow part of an inlet or river; ĸôroĸ, valley or cleft.

ĸut or ĸule, upper part; ĸulâ, its upper part, the hill which rises above it.

kanajoĸ or kanioĸ, frogfish, plural kanâsut or kanîsut.

kange, what lies farther towards the interior or the central part of a country or a body, to be used with suffix, kangia, what lies east or inward of it; kangigdlît, plural of kangigdleĸ, signifies the same; kangerdluk, a bay or fjord; kangerdluarssuk, kangerdlugssuaĸ, kangerdlugssuatsiaĸ, kangersuneĸ; kangeĸ, or kangâĸ, a very frequent name for projecting and steep promontories; kangínguaĸ, kangâmiut, kangârssuk, kangârssutsiaĸ, kangâtsiaĸ.

kapipâ, makes (any sort of garment) double; **kapiseκ**, outer jacket made of guts; **kapisilik**, a true (scaly) salmon.

kingigpoκ, is elevated above its environs; **kingigtoκ, kingigtorssuaκ**.

kipivâ, cuts it; **kipissaκ**, what is shortened by cutting off a piece; **kipissako** (?).

kit, kitâ, kitdleκ, kigdlît, the opposite of **kange**, etc., seaward or outward, etc.; **kitsigpoκ**, is situated far seaward; **kirsigsat**.

kîvâ, bites or squeezes it; **kigut**, tooth; **kigutilik**, a sperm-whale, also a wolf-fish (Anarrichas lupus).

kuáneκ, the Angelica plant; **kuánersôκ**.

κûk, watercourse, river; **kûngmiut, kûgssineκ**, dried-up river or river-bed; **κûgssinínguaκ, kugssangavoκ**, slopes; **kugssanga** (?).

kujat, south; **kujatâ**, its southern part, or also what lies south of it.

majorpoκ, ascends; **majorκaκ**, a passage to the top of a mountain, which elsewhere is inaccessible.

maκigpoκ, bears a kayak or boat by land ; **maⲧκaκ**, a place where the boat is carried in this way from the sea to a lake.

maneκ, a kind of moss used for torches or to kindle a fire; **manermiut**.

manigpoκ, is even; **manigtoκ**, even; **manïtsoκ**, uneven.

mániκ, egg.

marraκ, clay.

nagtoralik, eagle; **nagtoralínguit.**

nagssuk, horn or antler; **nagssugtôκ.**

nano or **nanoκ**, polar bear; **nanortalik.**

napavoκ, stands upright; **napassoκ.**

nárparpoκ, falls sick; **nápaut**, sickness.

narssaκ, flat land; **narssâraκ, narssalik, narssârssuk.**

natseκ, fjord-seal (*Pagomys fœtidus*); **natsilik.**

neκe, flesh of warm-blooded animals used for food; **nerivok**, eats; **neriavoκ**, is greedy; **neria** (?).

niaκoκ, head; **niaκornaκ**, a rounded rock situated at the end of a low point; **niaκornârssuk.**

nipigpoκ, adheres to something; **nepisa**, lump-fish (Cyclopterus).

nûk, point or cape; **nûgaκ, nûgatsiaκ, nûssaκ, nûgssuaκ.**

nuna, land; **nunataκ**, land encompassed by a glacier or by a glacier and the sea; **nunatarssuaκ, nunarssuit, nunatsiait.**

orpik, a bush or tree, copse, a birch tree.

orssoκ, blubber.

pâκ, entrance; **pâmiut, pâkitsoκ, pârarssuκ.**

pamioκ, a tail; **pamiagdluκ**, tail of a seal.

pe (the richest of all the stems in derivations), thing, property; **pivoκ**, does, gets, happens; **peκarpoκ**, has something; **perκigpoκ**, is healthy; **perdluk**, disaster; **piaraκ**, young; **pilivoκ**, prepares provisions; **piniarpoκ**, provides; **pîpoκ**, is poor.

pisigsârpoκ, practises bow shooting; **pisigsârfik.**

puivok, emerges from the water; **puisse**, a seal; **puisortoκ.**

pôĸ, sack ; pôruseĸ, a sack, to be filled with blubber for winter provision.

sak or sâ and sarĸaĸ, the front, and particularly the sunny side, sâgpâ, faces or turns towards it ; sarĸarmiut, sarĸarssuatsiaĸ, sagdleĸ, plural sagdlît, the foremost (islets) ; sagdliaĸ, sagdliarussat, sãpoĸ, is thin ; sãtoĸ, thin, a slaty stone, the plural sãtut, a name for low and flat islands in front of higher land ; sãtorssuaĸ, sãrdloĸ.

sánerut, the shorter of two pieces crossing each other.

sarfaĸ, current ; sarfánguaĸ.

savik, a knife and iron ; saverneĸ, loss of knife or iron.

sermeĸ, ice formed upon solid objects, glacier ; sermilik, sermiliarssuk, sermitsiaĸ, sermitsialik, sermersôĸ, sermiligaitsiaĸ, sermermiut, sermiarssuit (ssuk ?).

sigssaĸ, shore ; sigssardlugtoĸ, sigssarigsoĸ.

siko, ice formed upon water ; sikuvoĸ, is frozen over.

sioraĸ, sand, plural siorkat.

sordlak, root, especially the eatable root of *Sedum Rhodiola* ; sordlagtôrssuaĸ.

sorĸaĸ, whalebone.

sukaĸ, pillar or beam to support a roof or anything else.

sungaĸ, gall ; sungaussaĸ, similar in colour to gall.

taseĸ, lake or pool ; tasermiut, tasiussaĸ, tasiussârssuĸ, taserssuaĸ.

time, body, central or chief part of something, interior ; timerdleĸ, farthest from the outer shores, or towards the interior, plural timerdlît.

tine, low water, ebb ; tiningnertôĸ, where the water at ebb-tide recedes far from the shore.

tingivoĸ, moves through the air ; tigssalugpoĸ, gushes or wells as a jet ; tigssaluk.

tipik, smell ; tivssarigsoĸ, odorous.

tôrnaĸ, guardian spirit ; tôrnait, their guardian spirits.

torssôĸ, house-passage ; torssukátak, a name for narrow sounds between high cliffs leading into a wider inlet.

tuapak, a boulder or pebble ; plural tuapait, stoneheap on the beach ; tuapagssuit.

tûgdlik, the great northern diver ; tûgdlitalik.

tugpoĸ, strikes again or rests upon something ; tugdlek, nearest to another in a row ; tugdlerúnaĸ (Sedum Rhodiola) ; tungmerak, a step or a spot to get footing ; tungmerardluk.

tulugaĸ, raven.

tunuk or tuno, backside ; tunugdleĸ, hindmost ; tunugdliarfik ; tunungas-soĸ, turned the wrong way, showing its backside.

ujarak, stone ; ujaragssuit, ujaragsugssuk (the suffix sugssuk only known from names).

ukioĸ, winter ; ukîvoĸ, he winters in some place ; ukîssut, used as a name for Danes, viz., strangers who remain in the country for the winter ; ukîvik, ukîvisoĸaĸ, old wintering place.

ulo, woman's knife, also harpoon point ; **ulugssat,** pieces of iron for harpoon points.

ûmavoᴋ, lives, is alive ; **ŭmat,** heart ; **ŭmánaᴋ,** frequently used as a name for islands of a conical or pointed cupola-like shape ; **ŭmánârssuk, umánatsiaᴋ.**

umiaᴋ, open skin-boat ; **umiartorfik, umîvik,** a station for putting up and securing the boat upon land, while going up the country for reindeer ; **umiamako** or **umiamakut** (?).

upernâᴋ, spring, in the North used for summer ; **upernivoᴋ,** stays somewhere with one's tent during spring ; **upernivik.**

ûvoᴋ, has been in or near a fire, is burnt or boiled ; **ûnartoᴋ,** hot.

uvkusik, an obsolete word for a pot, but still used in Labrador ; **uvkusigssaᴋ,** pot-stone.

NAMES OF MORE DOUBTFUL ETYMOLOGY.

agdlumersat, agssakaᴋ, agto, aluk, arsuk, ikigait, nivâk.

V.—*ANTIQUARIAN NOTES.*

THE Runic stone found in the year 1824 in a cairn upon the island Kingigtorsuak, lying in 72° 55′ N. lat., has been read and interpreted by George Stephens as follows :

'*Elling Sigvathson and Baanne Tortarson and Enrithi Osson on the Saturday before Gang-day raised these beacons (land-marks) and ridded (made this clearing)* 235 (=1235).'

Gang-day, Rogation-day or St. Mark's day, is the 25th of April. In 1235 St. Mark's day fell upon Wednesday. The foregoing Saturday was April 21.

The author of this book has been particularly puzzled by the season, it being strange, though not at all impossible, that ships should have reached so high a latitude and their crew landed there so early in the year. But on closer consideration the inscription presents another peculiarity which he thinks may serve as an explanation. Landing on one of the outer islands in 73° N. lat. seems to have been no unusual undertaking for the Norse colonists during their summer expeditions, while on the other hand Runic stones are known to be very rare. There is no probability that the above-named travellers, merely for a joke, should have tried to immortalise their names by such a monument. We may suppose that there existed a peculiar emulation amongst those ancient seafarers in trying to gain their northern fishing and hunting grounds as early in the spring as possible, and that for this reason the exact indication of the day (a runologic rarity) is the main point in the inscription.

Another Runic stone has been found at Igaliko, and its inscription is interpreted :

'*Vigdis M(ar's) d(aughter) rests here. May God gladden her soul!*'

Another gravestone, but bearing only Roman letters, was discovered at Ikigait. The words must be translated, 'Here rests
Hroar Holgrimson.' On the same, moreover, is cut a long cross
bounded by an oval, above which are traces of another inscription,
of which only the word IDUS remains.

Several other tombstones have turned up, with fragments of
inscriptions, crosses, and other figures. A bit of a bell was found
at Igaliko, weighing five pounds and measuring 5½ inches in length
and one inch in breadth. Pieces of bell-metal have been found in
different inhabited places, probably from having been carried about
as curiosities by the later inhabitants. On digging in the interior
of the church of Kagsiarsuk the author found pieces of burnt wood
at a certain depth, containing iron nails and appearing to have
been parts of the roof which, after having tumbled down, had
been covered with stones from the walls of the building.

A few words in the language of the present Greenlanders have
been referred to by Hans Egede, and afterwards by others, as
results of an ancient Norse influence. But the Labrador dictionary
published in 1864 by the Moravian missionaries shows that the
most important of them, viz. **kuánek** (Angelica) and **nisa** (porpoise) are also found in the Labrador dialect, the latter with
exactly the same signification, the former representing another
eatable plant. The rest of these examples are scarcely worth
mentioning, and consequently these supposed remains of the
ancient Norse dwindle to nothing. Kleinschmidt has conjectured
that the name **kalâlek,** by which the present South Greenlanders
but not the North Greenlanders denote their own nation, has originated from a corruption of ' Skræling,' which an Eskimo is liable
to pronounce as sakalâlek.

In researches and discussions concerning the origin of the
Eskimo, and especially the Greenlanders generally, two questions
are confounded, viz., first, in what country the nation has developed
that stage of culture, with all its peculiarities, which afterwards it
has retained almost unaltered, and which so distinctly divides it
from all the neighbouring nations ; and secondly, how from the
country which in this way may be called their cradle, they have
migrated and spread over the vast territories now occupied by
them. The author considers both problems very obscure and

dubious, but in his 'Tales and Traditions' he has stated as his opinion that this cradle-land must be sought in the north-western corner of America, and that the Asiatic side of Behring's Strait was to the original Eskimo one of the first coasts beyond the sea upon which some of them settled. But he does not consider it impossible that from the Asiatic coast, in some way or other, they have emigrated again, spreading over the arctic archipelago. Although it has been proved that Eskimo existed in Greenland towards the year 1000, their comparatively sudden increase on the west coast during the period between the loss of the ancient colonies and the rediscovery by John Davis nevertheless remains mysterious.

VI.—*MISCELLANEOUS NOTES.*

Mortality and sickness, etc.—An abstract has been made of the returns of population from the southernmost part of Greenland to show the causes of deaths.   It comprised a number of 4,770 deaths, occurring during the period from 1782 to 1853, and gave the following numbers for each of the causes mentioned in the statements :

Perished in kayak, 415 ; otherwise drowned, 59 ; frozen to death, 8 ; fallen down from rocks, 19 ; crushed by icebergs, 8 ; murdered, 2 ; from ill-treatment, 2 ; different disastrous accidents, 37 ; poisoned (by putrefied meat), 36 ; disappeared, 5 ; infants overlaid, 16 ; infants otherwise come to an untimely end, 222 ; common diseases of childhood, 407 ; decrepitude, 384 ; complaints of the throat, 21 ; complaints of the chest, 139 ; stitch, 471 ; catarrhal fever (influenza?), sniff, etc., 622 ; inflammatory fever, 95 ; putrid fever, nervous fever, and typhus, 16 ; whooping-cough, 96 ; brain fever, 17, consumption, 230 ; dropsy, 30 ; gout or rheumatism, 3 ; scurvy, 3 ; various complaints in the stomach, 73 ; complaints of the abdomen, 8 ; vomiting, 33 ; diarrhœa, 11 ; vomiting and diarrhœa, 6 ; obstruction, 18 ; rupture, 1 ; calculous disease, 2 ; boils, 50 ; gangrene, 2 ; contusions, 4 ; spitting blood, 84 ; other kinds of bleeding, 48 ; sudden deaths, 12 ; cramp and epilepsy, 86 ; caries, 2 ; swelling, 105 ; mental disease and madness, 3 ; suicide, 3 ; various diseases, 93 ; of epidemics (two great epidemics in 1782 and 1800 are *not comprised* in this list), 98 ; still-born (supposed to have been generally not registered), 16 ; causes not indicated, 449.

In North Greenland kayak disasters are fewer, but deaths by other accidents more frequent, than in the South.   For instance, out of 536 deaths during five of the later years, the following were caused by accidents : perished in kayak, 20 ; drowned otherwise, especially on the ice, 17 ; chance shot, 6 ; frozen to death, 4 ; various accidents, 12.

Boils, which sometimes attain an enormous size, and cutaneous diseases, especially the itch, are very frequent. On the other hand it is remarkable that syphilis had never been heard of amongst the natives until of late years it suddenly appeared in the neighbourhood of Ivigtut, after their females had maintained a most scandalous intercourse during more than ten years with the numerous Europeans of this establishment.

The Moravian community of Frederiksdal has now and then been increased by heathens, immigrants from the East coast ; during the period from 1856 to 1860 their number was stated to have been 50.

Prices of the Greenland wares at the auctions in Copenhagen.— A tun (252 gallons without the cask) of seal-oil was sold at the rate of 21*l.* 18*s.* in the year 1844 ; 23*l.* 9*s.* in 1858 ; 31*l.* 18*s.* in 1864 ; and 27*l.* 8*s.* in 1870. Skins are sorted into three or five classes according to their quality. From 1866 to 1873 saddleback sealskins, No. 1, from 4*s.* 6*d.* to 6*s.* 6*d.* ; No. 2, from 3*s.* 6*d.* to 6*s.* ; ordinary sealskins (Natsek), No. 1 from 1*s.* 9*d.* to 5*s.* ; No. 2 from 6*d.* to 3*s.* ; eiderdown per pound from 14*s.* to 1*l.* 2*s.* Omitting the year 1871, foxskins have obtained : blue, No. 1 from 1*l.* 9*s.* to 2*l.* 13*s.* ; No. 3 from 6*s.* 6*d.* to 10*s.* 6*d.* ; white, No. 1 from 5*s.* 6*d.* to 12*s.* ; No. 2 from 2*s.* 6*d.* to 4*s.* 9*d.* In the year 1871 foxskins reached quite extraordinary prices, viz., for the above-mentioned numbers respectively, 4*l.* 15*s.*, 2*l.* 7*s.*, 1*l.* 2*s.*, and 11*s.*

Navigation.—From 1781 to 1856 the Royal Greenland Board of Trade has sent out 564 expeditions to Greenland, of which 11 were made with vessels to be stationed there, one was obliged to turn back half way, 15 were lost, most of them with all hands on board, but the rest returned safely. From 1857 to 1875 there have been despatched 197 expeditions ; of which, one a vessel to be stationed in Greenland, one turned back half way, and one was wrecked, but without loss of life; 7 of them were obliged to winter in Greenland. Of the expeditions since 1857, 20 have been made with ships which made two voyages in the same summer, and 11 with chartered vessels. The Royal Greenland Board of Trade owns 9 ships, with a tonnage of 2,010 tons. From 1846 to 1875 the average duration of the voyages was as follows :—

	From Copenhagen to		To Copenhagen from	
	South Greenland	Disco Bay	South Greenland	Disco Bay
Better Sailers . .	34 days	40 days	28 days	31 days
Slower Sailers . .	44 ,,	47 ,,	34 ,,	39 ,,

VII.—*SYNOPSIS OF THE GREENLAND FLORA.*

PUBLISHING his Danish edition of 1857, the Author was furnished by Prof. Joh. Lange with an Appendix, containing an enumeration of the species of phanerogamic plants known from Greenland at that time. As a great many new facts have since been brought to light concerning the flora of Greenland, Lange now intends to publish a book on this subject himself. However, he kindly offered previously to give the list here following of the genera with the number of species now known of phanerogams, which shows that the total number of species since 1857 has been enlarged from 320 to 361. As regards the Cryptogamic plants Lange had not as yet made up any lists, especially on account of important additions to our knowledge of this part of the Greenland flora being now expected from the Swedish naturalists Berggren and Friis. For this reason I applied to Dr. Brown, who is known from his own botanical explorations in Greenland, requesting him to give this most necessary supplement to the above-named list by Professor Lange, so that no part of the flora should be wholly wanting. Dr. Brown kindly complied with my desire, but as the mere statement of the numbers of species would be of less value as regards the cryptogams, on account of the present imperfect state of our knowledge about them, we agreed in thinking it more suitable to give this part of the flora more in detail by stating the names of the species, so far as published. For the reasons given, it must of course be very imperfect. However, it may serve to give an idea of the cryptogamic flora of Danish Greenland. Furthermore, Dr. Brown has added, at my request, some general remarks on the Greenland plants from a phyto-geographical point of view.

SUMMARY VIEW OF THE FERNS, FERN-ALLIES, AND
FLOWERING PLANTS.   (PROFESSOR JOH. LANGE.)

I. ACOTYLEDONEÆ.

EQUISETACEÆ (Horse-tail order), 4 sp.

Equisetum . . . . 4 sp.

FILICES (Ferns), 13 sp.

Polypodium	.	. . 3 sp.	Cystopteris	. . .	1 sp.
Aspidium .	.	. . 2 ,,	Woodsia .	. . .	3 ,,
Lastrea	.	. . 2 ,,	Botrychium	. .	2 ,,

ISOËTEÆ (Quillworts), 1 sp.

Isoëtes . . . . 1 sp.

LYCOPODIACEÆ (Club-mosses), 6 sp.

Selaginella. . . . 1 sp. | Lycopodium . . . 5 sp.

II. GYMNOSPERMÆ.

CUPRESSINEÆ, 1 sp.

Juniperus. . . . . 1 sp.

III. MONOCOTYLEDONEÆ.

GRAMINEÆ (Grasses), 44 sp.

Phleum	.	. . 1 sp.	Bromus	. . .	1 sp.
Alopecurus	.	. 2 ,,	Vahlodea .	. .	1 ,,
Anthoxanthum	.	. 1 ,,	Dupontia .	. .	1 ,,
Hierochloe	.	. 1 ,,	Aira (Deschampsia)	.	3 ,,
Agrostis .	.	. 3 ,,	Trisetum .	. .	1 ,,
Calamagrostis	.	. 3 ,,	Catabrosa.	. .	3 ,,
Glyceria .	.	. 7 ,,	Agropyrum	. .	1 ,,
Poa .	.	. 10 ,,	Elymus .	. .	1 ,,
Festuca	.	. 3 ,,	Nardus .	. .	1 ,,

CYPERACEÆ (Sedges), 51 sp.

Eleocharis.	.	. 1 sp.	Kobresia .	. .	1 sp.
Scirpus	.	. 2 ,,	Elyna .	. .	1 ,,
Eriophorum	.	. 2 ,,	Carex .	. .	44 ,,

JUNCACEÆ (Rush order), 15 sp.

Juncus . . . . 9 sp.	Luzula . . . . 6 sp.

JUNCAGINEÆ (Flowering Rush order), 1 sp.

Triglochin . . . . 1 sp.

COLCHICACEÆ (Meadow Saffron order), 1 sp.

Tofieldia . . . . 1 sp.

SMILACEÆ, 1 sp.

Streptopus . . . . 1 sp.

ORCHIDEÆ (Orchid order), 5 sp.

Habenaria. . . . 1 sp.	Listera . . . . 1 sp.
Platanthera . . . 2 ,,	Corallorhiza . . . 1 ,,

NAJADEÆ (the Seawrack order), 5 sp.

Zostera . . . . 1 sp.	Potamogeton . . . 4 sp.

TYPHACEÆ (Bulrush order), 1 sp.

Sparganium . . . . 1 sp.

IV. DICOTYLEDONEÆ.

BETULACEÆ (Birch order), 5 sp.

Alnus . . . . 1 sp.	Betula . . . . 4 sp.

SALICINEÆ (Willow order), 6 sp.

Salix . . . . 6 sp.

SALSOLACEÆ (Saltwort order), 1 sp.

Blitum . . . . 1 sp.

POLYGONEÆ (Dock order), 7 sp.

Koenigia . . . . 1 sp.	Rumex . . . . 3 sp.
Oxyria . . . . 1 ,,	Polygonum . . . 2 ,,

COMPOSITÆ (Daisy and Dandelion order), 22 sp.

Erigeron . . . . 3 sp.	Antennaria . . . 2 sp.
Achillæa . . . . 1 ,,	Gnaphalium . . . 3 ,,
Arnica . . . . 1 ,,	Leontodon. . . . 1 ,,
Matricaria. . . . 1 ,,	Taraxacum . . . 3 ,,
Artemisia . . . . 1 ,,	Hieracium . . . 6 ,,

CAMPANULACEÆ (Harebell order), 2 sp.

Campanula . . . . 2 sp.

RUBIACEÆ (Bedstraw order), 2 sp.

Galium . . . . 2 sp.

GENTIANEÆ (Gentian order), 4 sp.

Gentiana . . . . 3 sp. | Pleurogyne . . . 1 sp.

MENYANTHEÆ, 1 sp.

Menyanthes . . . . 1 sp.

BORAGINEÆ (Borage order), 1 sp.

Stenhammaria . . . . 1 sp.

LABIATÆ (Deadnettle and Thyme order), 1 sp.

Thymus . . . . 1 sp.

SCROPHULARIACEÆ (Snapdragon order), 13 sp.

Limosella .	. . . . 1 sp.	Rhinanthus .	. . 1 sp.
Veronica .	. . . 2 ,,	Euphrasia .	. . 1 ,,
Pedicularis	. . 7 ,,	Bartsia .	. . 1 ,,

LENTIBULARIEÆ (Butterwort order), 2 sp.

Utricularia. . . . 1 sp. | Pinguicula . . . 1 sp.

PLANTAGINEÆ (Ribwort order), 2 sp.

Plantago . . . . 2 sp.

PLUMBAGINEÆ (Sea-pink order), 1 sp.

Armeria . . . . 1 sp.

POLEMONIACEÆ (Jacob's-Ladder order), 1 sp.

Polemonium . . . . 1 sp.

PRIMULACEÆ (Primrose order), 2 sp.

Primula . . . . 2 sp.

DIAPENSIACEÆ (Diapensia order), 1 sp.

Diapensia . . . . 1 sp.

PYROLACEÆ (Winter-Green order), 4 sp.

Pyrola . . . . 4 sp.

VACCINIACEÆ (Whortleberry order), 3 sp.

Vaccinium . . . . 2 sp. | Oxycoccos . . . . 1 sp.

ERICACEÆ (Heath order), 10 sp.

Arctostaphylos . . . 2 sp.	Rhododendron . . . 1 ,,
Cassiope . . . . 2 ,,	Loiseleuria . . . 1 ,,
Phyllodoce . . . 1 ,,	Ledum . . . . 2 ,,
Andromeda . . . 1 ,,	

UMBELLIFERÆ (Hemlock order), 2 sp.

Archangelica . . . 1 sp. | Haloscias . . . . 1 sp.

CORNEÆ (Cornel order), 1 sp.

Cornus . . . . 1 sp.

SAXIFRAGACEÆ (Saxifrage order), 12 sp.

Saxifraga . . . . 12 sp.

CRASSULACEÆ (Stonecrop order), 3 sp.

Sedum . . . . 3 sp.

RANUNCULACEÆ (Buttercup order), 14 sp.

Thalictrum . . . 1 sp.	Ranunculus . . . 10 sp.
Anemone . . . . 1 ,,	Coptis . . . . 1 ,,
Batrachium . . . 1 ,,	

PAPAVERACEÆ (Poppy order), 1 sp.

Papaver . . . . 1 sp.

CRUCIFERÆ (Cress order), 25 sp.

Vesicaria . . . . 1 sp.	Nasturtium . . . 1 sp.
Cochlearia . . . . 2 ,,	Sisymbrium . . . 1 ,,
Draba . . . . 9 ,,	Arabis . . . . 3 ,,
Capsella . . . . 1 ,,	Turritis . . . . 1 ,,
Lepidium (?) . . . 1 ,,	Cardamine . . . 2 ,,
Eutrema . . . . 1 ,,	Hesperis . . . . 1 ,,
Braya (Platypetalum) . . 1 ,,	

VIOLARIEÆ (Violet order), 3 sp.

Viola . . . . 3 sp.

DROSERACEÆ (Sun-dew order), 1 sp.

Parnassia . . . . 1 sp.

PORTULACACEÆ (Purslane order), 1 sp.

Montia . . . . 1 sp.

ALSINACEÆ (Sandwort order), 22 sp.

Sagina	. . . . 5 sp.	Halianthus	. . . 1 sp.
Alsine	. . . . 4 ,,	Stellaria	. . . . 6 ,,
Arenaria	. . . . 2 ,,	Cerastium	. . . . 4 ,,

SILENACEÆ (Campion order), 5 sp.

Silene . . . . 1 sp. | Melandrium (Wahlbergelia) 3 sp.
Viscaria . . . . 1 ,, |

EMPETRACEÆ (Crowberry order), 1 sp.

Empetrum . . . . 1 sp.

ONAGRARIEÆ (Willowherb order), 6 sp.

Chamænerium . . . 2 sp. | Epilobium . . . . 4 sp.

CALLITRICHINEÆ (Callitriche order), 2 sp.

Callitriche . . . . 2 sp.

HIPPURIDEÆ (Marestail order), 1 sp.

Hippuris . . . . 1 sp.

HALORRHAGEÆ (Milfoil order), 1 sp.

Myriophyllum . . . . 1 sp.

POMACEÆ (Apple order), 1 sp.

Sorbus . . . . 1 sp.

ROSACEÆ (Rose order), 16 sp.

Rubus	. . . . 2 sp.	Potentilla	. . . . 8 sp.
Dryas	. . . . 2 ,,	Comarum	. . . . 1 ,,
Sibbaldia	. . . . 1 ,,	Alchemilla	. . . 2 ,,

LEGUMINOSÆ (Pea order), 2 sp.

Vicia . . . . . 1 sp. | Lathyrus . . . . 1 sp.

CATALOGUE OF THE CRYPTOGAMIC PLANTS OF GREENLAND.
(DR. R. BROWN.)

To compile a list even approaching to completeness of the cryptogamic plants of Danish Greenland is in the present state of our knowledge quite impossible. Accordingly, the following lists, which are given as an appendix to the synopsis of the flora, is not presented as such ; though at the same time they will be found to be a tolerably accurate catalogue of the species which have been published as natives of the region this volume is occupied with the description of. (1) The lichens, with three exceptions, are given on the authority of the list prepared by Dr. Lauder Lindsay, of Perth, when studying the lichens discovered by me in Greenland ('Arctic Manual,' p. 284, 'Trans. Linn. Soc.' vol. xxvii. p. 305, 1871, with 5 plates). (2) The list of the mosses and liverworts is founded on the collections made by Dr. Berggren (Nordenskjöld's 'Redogörelse för en Expedition till Grönland år 1870') and the writer ('Arctic Manual,' p. 172). (3) The algæ are enumerated from the collections of Drs. Berggren, Sutherland, and Walker, and my own collections. (4) The short list of fungi is founded on a few collected by Walker, the German Expedition, and the Editor. The list of lichens has been revised by Dr. Lindsay, while Professor Dickie, who originally identified many of the species, has kindly performed the same good office for the catalogue of mosses and algæ. It would have been rash at the present date, and without reference to all his specimens, to have attempted to unravel the synonymy of Giesecke's list. Accordingly, that task I have left for Drs. Friis and Berggren—though I believe the results will not be equal to the labour.

LICHENES (Lichen order), 203 sp.

Ephebe pubescens, L.
Pyrenopsis hæmatopis, Smrf.
Collema melænum, Ach.
C. flaccidum, Ach.
C. saturninum, Dicks.
C. lacerum, Sw.
Calicium furfuraceum, L.

Sphærophoron coralloides, Ach.
S. fragile, L.
Cladonia pyxidata, L.
C. carneola, Fr.
C. verticillata, Hffm.
C. gracilis, L.
C. furcata, Schreb.

Cladonia rangiferina, L.
C. uncialis, L.
C. sylvatica, Hffm.
C. amaurocræa, Flk.
C. cornucopioides, L.
C. bellidiflora, Ach.
C. deformis, L.
C. digitata, L.
C. degenerans, Flk.
C. alcicornis, Flk.
C. squamosa, Hffm.
C. fimbriata, Hffm.
C. cyanipes, Smrf.
Stereocaulon paschale, L.
S. tomentosum, Fr.
S. denudatum, Flk.
Thamnolia vermicularis, Sw.
Usnea melaxantha, Ach.
Alectoria jubata, L.
A. Thulensis, Th. Fr.
A. divergens, Ach.
A. ochroleuca, Ehrh.
Dactylina arctica, Br.
Cetraria aculeata, Ehrh.
C. odontella, Ach.
C. islandica, L.
C. nivalis, L.
C. cucullata, Bell.
C. juniperina, L.
C. sæpincola, Ehrh.
Nephroma arcticum, L.
N. papyraceum, Hffm.
Peltidea aphthosa, Ach.
P. canina, Hffm.
P. rufescens, Fr.
P. scabrosa, Th. Fr.
P. venosa, L.
Solorina crocea, L.
S. saccata, L.
Sticta scrobiculata, Scop.
Parmelia saxatilis, L.
P. physodes, L.
P. encausta, Sm.
P. hyperopta, Ach.
P. olivacea, L.

Parmelia fahlunensis, L.
P. stygia, L.
P. alpicola, Th. Fr.
P. lanata, L.
P. conspersa, Ehrh.
P. centrifuga, L.
P. incurva, Pers.
P. diffusa, Web.
Physcia pulverulenta, Schreb.
P. stellaris, L.
P. cæias, Hffm.
P. obscura, Ehrh.
P. lychnea, Ach.
Umbilicaria pennsylvanica, Hffm.
U. vellea, L.
U. spodochroa, Hffm.
U. anthracina, Wulf.
U. arctica, Ach.
U. hyperborea, Ach.
U. proboscidea, L.
U. flocculosa, Hffm.
U. erosa, Web.
U. polyphylla, L.
U. cylindrica, L.
U. hirsuta, Ach.
Pannaria brunnea, Sw.
P. lepidiota, Th. Fr.
P. Hookeri, Sm.
P. hypnorum, Vahl.
P. muscorum, Ach.
Squamaria saxicola, Poll.
S. chrysoleuca, Sm.
S. straminea, Whlnb.
S. gelida, L.
S. elegans, Link.
S. murorum, Hffm.
S. fulgens, Sw.
S. melanaspis, Ach.
S. geophila, Th. Fr.
Lecanora tartarea, L.
L. parella, L.
L. oculata, Dicks.
L. atra, Huds.
L. subfusca, L.
L. frustulosa, Dicks.

Lecanora epanora, Ach.
L. badia, Ehrh.
L. varia, Ehrh.
L. atro-sulphurea, Whlnb.
L. cenisea, Ach.
L. glaucoma, Ach.
L. bryontha, Ach.
L. peliscypha, Whlnb.
L. molybdina, Whlnb.
L. smaragdula, Whlnb.
L. chlorophana, Whlnb.
L. ventosa, L.
L. nimbosa, Fr.
L. oreina, Ach.
L. turfacea, Whlnb.
L. sophodes, Ach.
L. mniaræa, Ach.
L. exigua, Ach.
L. verrucosa, Ach.
L. calcarea, L.
L. cinerea, L.
L. lacustris, With.
L. ferruginea, Huds.
L. jungermanniæ, Vahl.
L. fusco-lutea, Dicks.
L. cerina, Hedw.
L. aurantiaca, Lightf.
L. crenulata, Th. Fr.
L. vitellina, Ehrh.
L. leucoræa, Ach.
Urceolaria scruposa, L.
Pertusaria paradoxa, Linds.
Lecidea contigua, Hffm.
L. fusco-atra, L.
L. panæola, Ach.
L. spilota, Fr.
L. lapicida, Ach.
L. auriculata, Th. Fr.
L. alpestris, Smrf.
L. arctica, Smrf.
L. agtæa, Smrf.,
L. sabuletorum, Schreb.
L. parasema, Sch.
L. turgidula, Fr.
L. atro-brunnea, Ram.

Lecanora armeniaca, DC.
L. elata, Sch.
L. pallida, Th. Fr.
L. vitellinaria, Nyl.
L. disciformis, Fr.
L. insignis, Næg.
L. myriocarpa, DC.
L. atro-alba, Ach.
L. scabrosa, Ach.
L. urceolata, Th. Fr.
L. coronata, Th. Fr.
L. geminata, Fw.
L. petræa, Wulf.
L. grœnlandica, Linds.
L. geographica, L.
L. globifera, Ach.
L. atro-rufa, Dicks.
L. decipiens, Ehrh.
L. squalida, Ach.
L. candida, Web.
L. obscurata, Smrf.
L. cumulata, Smrf.
L. cinnabarina, Smrf.
L. vernalis, L.
L. cuprea, Smrf.
L. castanea, Hepp.
L. tornœensis, Nyl.
L. fuscescens, Smrf.
L. uliginosa, Schrad.
L. leucoræa, Ach.
L. pezizoidea, Ach.
L. flavo-virescens, Dicks.
L. icmadophila, Ach.
L. sanguineo-atra, Ach.
L. fusco-rubens, Nyl.
L. discoensis, Linds.
L. Campsteriana, Linds.
L. Friesiana, Linds.
L. Egedeana, Linds.
L. subfuscula, Nyl.
Arthonia trabinella, Th. Fr.
Endocarpon miniatum, L.
E. hepaticum, Ach.
E. Dædaleum, Kremp.
E. viride, Ach.

418   *Danish Greenland.*

Verrucaria clopima, Whlnb.
V. maura, Whlnb.
V. ceuthocarpa, Whlnb.
V. epidermidis, Ach.

Verrucaria pygmæa, Körb.
V. tartaricola, Linds.
Pyrenothea grœnlandica, Linds.

To the above list may be added 68 varieties of the species, making in all, according to our present knowledge, 271 species and varieties of the order found in Greenland. From East Greenland, Körber ('Die zweite deutsche Nordpolarfahrt,' vol. ii. pp. 75–82) records 55 species, with the exception of 10 new species, mostly identical with those of West Greenland.

MUSCI (Mosses), and **HEPATICÆ** (Liverworts) sp. 231.

Gymnostomum curvirostrum, Ehrh.
Weissia crispula, Hedw.
W. fugax, Hedw.
W. cirrhata, Hedw.
Cynodontium polycarpum, Ehrh.
C. alpestre, Wahlenb.
C. virens, Hedw.
C. Wahlenbergii, Hedw.
C. gracilescens.
Trematodon brevicollis, Hornsch.
Dicranella crispa, Hedw.
D. Grevilleana, Br. and Sch.
D. subulata, Hedw.
Arctoa fulvella, Br. and Sch.
Dicranum Blyttii, Br. and Sch.
D. squarrosum, Starke.
D. polycarpum, H. and T.
D. cerviculatum, Hedw.
D. virens, Hedw.
D. fragilifolium.
D. arcticum, Sch.
D. elongatum, Schwægr.
D. fuscescens, Turn.
D. scoparium, L.
D. palustre, Lapyl.
Campylopus Schimperi, Milde.
Fissidens osmundioides, Hedw.
F. viridulus, Wahlenb.
Blindia acuta, Dcks.
Pottia Heimii, Hedw.
Anacalypta latifolia, Schwægr.

Didymodon rubellus, Roth.
Distichium capillaceum, L.
D. inclinatum, Hedw.
Ceratodon purpureus, L.
Leptotrichium flexicaule, Schw.
L. glaucescens, Hedw.
Trichostomum rigidulum, Dcks.
Desmatodon latifolius, Hedw.
D. stylylius, Br. and Schw.
D. Laureri, Schultz.
Barbula brevirostris, Br. and Sch.
B. tortuosa, L.
B. fragilis, Wils.
B. mucronifolia, Schwægr.
B. aciphylla, Br. and Sch.
B. ruralis, L.
Grimmia apocarpa, L.
G. contorta, Wahlenb.
G. torquata, Grev.
G. funalis, Schwægr.
G. ovata, W. and M.
G. alpestris, Schl.
G. mollis, Br. and Sch.
G. pulvinata, Hook. and Tayl.
Racomtrium lanuginosum, Hedw.
R. canescens, Hedw.
R. sudeticum, Funk.
R. fasciculare, Schrad.
Amphoridium lapponicum, Br. and Sch.
Ulota Hutchinsiæ, Sm.

Orthotrichum Kelliasii, Müll.
O. Breutelii, Hampe.
O. rupestre, Sch.
Encalypta rhabdocarpa, Schwægr.
Œdipodium Griffithianum, Dcks.
Dissodon splachnoides, Thunb.
Tayloria serrata, Hedw.
Tetraplodon mnioides, L. fil.
Splachnum Wormskjoldii, Horn.
S. vasculosum, L.
Funaria hygrometrica, L.
Leptobryum pyriforme, L.
Webera cucullata, Schwægr.
W. longicolla, Schwartz.
W. cruda, Schreb.
W. annotina, Hedw.
W. nutans, Schreb.
W. Ludwigii, Spreng.
W. albicans, Wahlenb.
Bryum arcticum, R. Br.
B. purpurascens, R. Br.
B. oeneum, Blytt.
B. pendulum, Hornsch.
B. calophyllum, R. Br.
B. alpinum, L.
B. argenteum, L.
B. capillare, L.
B. pseudotriquetrum, Hedw.
B. pallens, Sw.
B. obtusifolium, Lindb.
B. Duvalii, Voet.
B. Wahlenbergii, R. Br.
B. crudum, Schreb.
B. Zierii? Dicks.
B. carneum? R. Br.
B. cæspiticium, Dicks.
Anomobryum concinnatum, Sprner.
Zieria julacea, Sch.
Z. demissa, Hornsch.
Mnium affine, Bland.
M. orthorhynchum, Br. and Sch.
M. subglobosum, Br. and Sch.
M. hymenophyllum, Br. and Sch.
M. hymenophylloides, Hüb.
Cinclidium stygium, Sw.

Catoscopium nigritum, Hedw.
Meesia uliginosa, Hedw.
M. Aristicha.
Paludella squarrosa, L.
Aulacomnium turgidum, Wahl.
A. palustre, L.
Bartramia ithyphylla, Brid.
Philonotis fontana, L.
Conostomum boreale, Sw.
Tortula fallax, Hedw.
Timmia austriaca, Hedw.
T. bavarica, Hessl.
Psilopilum arcticum, Wahlenb.
Pogonatum alpinum, L.
Polytrichum piliferum, Schreb.
P. hyperboreum, R. Br.
P. juniperinum, Hedw.
P. strictum, Menz.
P. commune, L.
Myurella julacea, Vill.
M. apiculata, Hüb.
Pseudoleskea atrovirens. Dcks.
P. catenulata, Brid.
Thuidium abietinum, L.
Pterigynandrum filiforme, Timm.
Climacium dendroides, Hedw.
Orthothecium chryseum, Schwæg.
O. intricatum, Hartm.
O. strictum, Ltz.
Camptothecium nitens, Schreb.
Brachythecium salebrosum, Hoffm.
B. collinum, Schleich.
B. reflexum, W. and M.
B. glaciale, Br. and Sch.
Plagiothecium denticulatum, L.
P. pulchellum, Hedw.
P. Mühlenbeckii, Br. and Sch.
Amblystegium Sprucei, Bruch.
Hypnum Halleri, L. fil.
H. stellatum, Schreb.
H. polygamum, Br. and Sch.
H. Kneiffii, Sch.
H. Nilsoni, Sch.
H. intermedium, Lindb.
H. vernicosum, Lindb.

Hypnum exannulatum, Gümb.
H. fluitans, Hedw.
H. revolvens, Sw.
H. uncinatum, Hedw.
H. filicinum, L.
H. rugosum, Ehrh.
H. callichroum, Brid.
H. Bambergeii, Sch.
H. Heufleri, Jur.
H. alpestre, Sw.
H. norvegicum, Br. and Sch.
H. arcticum, Sommerf.
H. ochraceum, Wils.
H. cordifolium, Hedw.
H. giganteum, Schimp.
H. sarmentosum, Wahlenb.
H. stramineum, Diks.
H. Schreberi, Willd.
H. trifarium, W. and M.
H. turgescens, Sch.
H. badium, Hartm.
H. scorpioides, L.
H. riparium, L.
H. pulchellum, Dicks.
H. molle, Dicks.
H. rutabulum, L.
Hylocomium splendens.
Andræa petrophila, Ehrh.
A. alpestris, Sch.
A. obovata, Thed.
A. Rothii, W. and M.
A. Blyttii, Sch.
A. rupestris, Hedw.
Sphagnum Lindbergii, Sch.
S. subsecundum, Nees.
S. fimbriatum, Wils.
S. rigidum, N. and Hornsch.
S. squarrosum, Pers.
S. teres, Ångstr.
S. acutifolium, Ehrh.

Sphagnum cuspidatum, Ehrh.
Gymnomitrium concinnatum, Corda.
Sarcoscyphus Ehrharti, Corda.
S. sphacelatus, N. v. Es.
Scapania undulata, N. v. Es.
S. uliginosa, N. v. Es.
S. irrigua, N. v. Es.
S. Bartlingii, N. v. Es.
S. compacta, Lindbg.
Jungermannia albicans, L.
J. Taylori, Hook.
J. cordifolia, Hook.
J. ventricosa, Dicks.
J. alpestris, Schleich.
J. minuta, Dicks.
J. attenuata, Lindenb.
J. Flörkii, W. M.
J. quinquedentata, Web.
J. lycopodioides, Wallr.
J. setiformis, Ehrh.
J. bicuspidata, L.
J. divaricata, E. B.
J. islandica, N. v. Es.
J. trichophylla, L.
J. julacea, Lightf.
J. grœnlandica, N. v. Es.
J. albescens, Hook.
J. saxicola, Schradr.
J. laxifolia, Hook.
J. catenulata, Hübner.
J. barbata, Hook.
J. acuta, Lindbg.
Ptilidium ciliare, N. v. Es.
Aneura pinguis, Dam.
Marchantia polymorpha, L.
Sauteria hyalina, Lindb.
S. alpina, N. v. Es.
Hapanthus Flotowianus, N. v. Es.
Alcularia compressa, Hook.
Fimbriaria pilosa, Tayl.

ALGÆ (Seaweeds and their freshwater allies), 90 sp.

Conferva arenosa, Carm.
C. melagonium, Web. a d Mohr.
C. Youngana, Dillw.

Conferva centralis, Lb.
C. rupestris, Kg.
C. bombycina, Ag.

Conferva floccosa, Ag.

C. capillaris, L.

Cladophora arcta, Kutz.

C. Inglefieldii, Dickie.

C. uncialis, Harv.

Prasiola cylindrica, J. Ag.

P. fluvialis, Sommfdt.

Bangia fusco-purpurea, Lyngb.

Porphyra miniata.

P. vulgaris, Ag.

Nostoc sphæricum, Vanch.

Ulothrix mucosa, Thunb.

U. minutula, Kutz.?

Hydrurus pencillatus, Ag.

Oscillaria, sp.?

Microcystis, sp.?

Ulva latissima, L.

U. fusca, Post and Rapr.

Entermorpha clathrata.

E. compressa, L.

E. intestinalis, L.

E. percursa, Hook.

Lyngbya Carmichaelii, Harv.

L. flacca, Harv.

L. speciosa, Carm.

Sphacelaria plumosa, Ag.

S. cirrhata, Ag.

S. arctica, Harv.

Polysiphonia urceolata, Grev.

P. nigrescens, Grev.

Melobesia polymorpha, L.

M. lichenoides, Bost.

Delessaria angustissima, Griff.

D. sinuosa, Lam.

Calliblepharis ciliata, Kutz.

Hypnea purpurascens, Harv.

Euthora cristata, J. Ag.

Rhodophyllis veprecula, J. Ag.

Dumontia filiformis, Grev.

Kallymenia reniformis, Turn.

K. Pennyi, Harv.?

Halosaccion ramentaceum, J. Ag.

Callophyllis laciniata, Kutz.

Rhodymenia palmata.

Ptilota serrata, Kutz.

Callithamnion Rothii, Lyngb.

C. americanum, Harv.

Ceramium rubrum, J. Ag.

Elachista lubrica.

E. fucicola, Fries.

E. flaccida, Aresch.?

Chordaria flagelliformis, Ag.

Myrionema strangulans, Grev.

Cheatopteris plumosa, Ag.

Ectocarpus littoralis, Lyngb.

E. siliculosus, Lyngb.

E. crinitus, Carm.

E. Durkeeï, Harv.

E. Landsburgii, Harv.

Dictyosiphon fœniculaceus, Grev.

Asperococcus Turneri, Hook.

Chorda filum, Ag.

Laminaria fascia, Ag.

L. solindungula, Ag.

L. cuneifolia, J. Ag.

L. longicruris, De la Pyl.

L. atro-fulva, J. Ag.

L. digitata, Lam.?

Saccorhiza dermatodea.

Agarum Turneri, P. and R.

Alaria Pylaii, Grev.

A. Despreauxii, Bory.

Dichloria viridis, Lam.?

Desmarestia aculeata, L.

Fucus nodosus, L.

F. linearis, Fl. Dan.

F. filiformis, J. Ag..

F. divergens, J. Ag.

F. evanescens, J. Ag.

F. medonensis, J. Ag.

F. bursigerus, J. Ag.

F. evanescens grandifrons, J. Ag.

F. vesiculosus, L.

The minute—in most cases microscopic—*Diatomaceæ* and *Desmidiæ* it is impossible in the present state of our knowledge to enumerate. Many are recorded in various works, but until the synonymy of the species is more critically worked out, it would only be risking the perpetuation of errors to repeat the lists here. The following species, which were obtained by Berggren and Nordenskjöld on the inland ice (p. 359) may be here enumerated:— *Pinnularia lata, Navicula sp., Hæmatococcus sanguineus, Pleurococcus vulgaris, Scytonema gracilis,* and *Ancylonema Nordenskjoldii.*

FUNGI (Mushroom and Mould order).

Agaricus vaginatus, Bull.	Hygrophorus virginius, Fr.
A. infundibuliformis, Schæff.	H. coccineus, Fr.
A. brumalis, Fr.	Uromyces intrusa, Lov.
A. furfuraceus, P.	Boletus scaber, Fr.
A. cyathiformis, Bull.	Marasimus arcticus, Berk.

The above list, it is almost needless to say, is exceedingly imperfect, and though Greenland is not well suited for the growth of these plants, many others may be expected to be discovered. For instance, from East Greenland have been recorded *Lycoperdon fuscum* Bon., and *L. bovista* Fr., *Paxillus griseoto-mentosus* Fr. ; *Agaricus simiatus* Fr. ? and a species of *Leptonia, Lactarius,* and *Leucosporus.* The scarcity, as well as the difficulty of preserving them in a state fit for study, will always render our knowledge of Greenland fungi very scanty. We may, however, expect some additions to our list, especially in those families which are parasitic on other plants. As a specimen of those whose presence may be looked for, we may enumerate the following, which were found parasitic on plants collected by the German Expedition to East Greenland (Fuckel, 'Die zweite deutsche Nordpolarfahrt,' vol. ii. pp. 90-969) :—

Melampsora salicina, Tul.	Sphæria arctica, Fuckel.
Pleospora hyperborea, Fuckel.	Ceratostoma foliicolum, Fuckel.
P. arctica, Fuckel.	Cystipora capitata, Fuckel.
P. paucitricha, Fuckel.	Phoma drabæ, Fuckel.
P. herbarium, Tul.	Rhizomorpha arctica, Fuckel.
Sphæria nivalis, Fuckel.	Xylographa arctica, Fuckel.

GENERAL REMARKS ON THE GREENLAND FLORA.
(DR. R. BROWN.)

Sources of our knowledge.—In the works of the early missionaries
are found a few scattered notices of the Greenland plants, but so
fragmentary and incorrect as to be really of very little value. In
the list published by Giesecke in the ' Edinburgh Encyclopædia,'
will be found the earliest authoritative catalogue of the plants of
the Danish possessions. But even this contains many errors,
and as no perfect set of Giesecke's plants are now extant, it
is difficult or impossible always to check his catalogue. The
largest collection of Greenland plants was made by Vahl. This
is now in the herbarium of the Copenhagen Botanic Garden.
Since that date the Danish officers stationed on the coast have
made more or less extensive collections of plants from Cape Farewell to the limits of the trading districts in the north. Among
these may be enumerated the herbarium collected by the author
of this work, and that made by his predecessors, Messrs. Holböll
and Olrik. The surgeons of whalers who have touched here
and there on the coast have also added a little to our knowledge of
the distribution of the species, and the same may be said of the
officers of the different exploring expeditions. The Editor of this
book also made extensive collections in the vicinity of Disco Bay,
and discovered many new species of cryptogamic plants. The
botanists of the two Swedish Expeditions which visited Greenland
likewise made collections which have materially added to our
knowledge. Last of all, Dr. Hooker has summed up our knowledge of the Greenland flora in his memoir on the Distribution of
Arctic Plants, and deduced certain important conclusions which
we briefly summarise in the following introductory remarks. Professor Lange, in the Appendix to 'Grönland geographisk og
statistisk beskrevet,' has digested all our knowledge of the plants
of the Danish possessions up to 1855 in the list there published.
The additions to our knowledge since that period have been
given in the supplement to the ' Flora Danica,' and will be more
fully in the forthcoming flora, of which the synopsis is here given.

Nature of the Greenland flora.—According to Dr. Hooker's investigations the whole number of plants grown within the Arctic circle is about 770.   However, there are many plants not growing within the geographical limit mentioned which are to all intents and purposes as arctic as that north of it.   The plants of South Greenland are examples of this.   When we study the arctic plants of Greenland we find that its flora is decidedly Scandinavian in character.   Almost all the plants are also found in Lapland, and notwithstanding the vicinity of America, few of them belong to the New World.   Asiatic arctic types are equally rare.   Greenland, in other words, forms the western boundary of the European flora. On the east side of Greenland—the portion of the country nearest to Europe—the preponderance of European over American species is even more marked.   This abundance of European types, and absence of American ones, points, among other things, to the long continuance of Davis' Strait and Baffin's Bay as a great gulf separating Greenland from the American continent and continental islands, and to the former connection—within comparatively recent geological times—of Greenland with northern Europe, thus permitting the European flora to travel overland to Greenland.   The Greenland fauna is also essentially of a European and not of an American type.   The East Greenland animals like the East Greenland plants being also more essentially European, the distribution of the musk-ox, lemming, and ermine forming really no exceptions, but only a curious confirmation of this fact.   The sea between Europe and East Greenland is not very deep, and it is probable that the continent or broken archipelago of islands, affording a bridge for the plants and animals to travel over, existed not much later than the tertiary epoch of geologists.   It is also just barely possible that Bear Island, Jan Mayen Island, Iceland, the Faroes, and even Orkney and the Shetland Islands, are remnants of this North Sea 'Atlantis.'   The Greenland flora also differs from that of all other portions of the arctic regions in wanting some extremely common types which advance far north in all other polar districts, and that the general poverty of its flora is more due to the abstraction of arctic types than to a deficiency of temperature is proved by the fact that the southern or extra-arctic portion of Greenland adds few species to its flora. However, we ought to keep the fact in mind, that the southern portion is, for all phyto-geographical purposes, not much less frozen than that lying immediately to the north of it. The plants, moreover, supplied by South Greenland are chiefly Arctic-Scandinavian plants.

Origin of the flora.—Hooker attempts to explain this on the ground that the climate south of Greenland is much more severe than that of any other region outside the arctic circle, and from the distribution of the Greenland flora seeks a confirmation of the Darwinian theory. This, without committing ourselves to the soundness of it, we may explain, premising that owing to the eminence of its author in the botanical world, and its innate attractiveness, it has received considerable attention since it was first promulgated in 1861.

During the ' glacial epoch' the northern plants were driven by the great advancing sheet of ice into all latitudes. On the disappearance of the ice at the close of this period, and the consequent amelioration of the climate, these plants returned, accompanied by the natives of the countries they had been driven into. In Greenland the same circumstances occurred. But as Greenland is a peninsula, the plants were driven into the sea, and therefore on the close of the glacial epoch the aboriginal flora would not return, as elsewhere, accompanied by many strangers. For this reason, therefore, the Greenland flora is poor and unintermixed with many stranger species. There was also on this account no struggle for existence among their progeny, and therefore no selection of better adapted varieties to form in time ' species' peculiar to the country. Dr. Hooker accordingly thinks that Mr. Darwin's theory explains (1) The identity of the Greenland and Lapland floras. (2) Its paucity of species. (3) The fewness of temperate plants in temperate Greenland, and the still fewer plants that area adds to the entire flora of Greenland. (4) The presence of a few of the Greenland and Scandinavian types in enormously remote districts in Alpine localities in Western America and the United States, e.g. *Draba aurea* in Greenland and the Rocky Mountains only, *Potentilla tridentata* in Greenland and Labrador, and *Arenaria grœnlandica* in Greenland and the White Mountains in New Hampshire. Probably these were originally Scandinavian plants, which on the return of the warmer period after the close of the glacial epoch were exterminated in the plains, but remained behind as stragglers on the mountain tops. Finally we may add, as confirmatory of the theory we have explained, that the Scandinavian flora is the only one found in almost every latitude.

Relations of the Greenland flora to the other Arctic floras.— The Greenland flora is poor. It comprises about 361 flowering plants and ferns. Of these, Arctic-Greenland is to be credited with 207 (Monocotyledons 67, Dicotyledons 140). Of these 207, eleven alone are not European. These are *Anemone Richardsonii* (Asiatic) ; *Turritis mollis* (Asiatic) ; *Vesicaria arctica* (American only) ; *Draba aurea* (Rocky Mountains and Labrador only) ; *Arenaria grœnlandica* (mountains of U.S.) ; *Potentilla tridentata* (Labrador only) , *Saxifraga tricuspidata* (Labrador only) ; *Erigeron compositus* (American only) ; *Pedicularis euphrasioides* (Asia). On the other hand, Hooker points out no less than 57 Arctic-Greenland species are absent in Arctic East America, and 36 Arctic-Europe and Greenland species are either absent in all parts of Eastern temperate America, or are extremely local there.

Arctic Eastern America has 165 other species not found in Greenland, and many others on the arctic islands and the west coast of Baffin's Bay, which are not found in West Greenland. According to Buchanan, the south part of East Greenland has no plant which the west coast does not possess. The northern flora of the east coast, on the contrary, is characterised by some peculiarities. The following plants have been found on the northern, but neither on the southern coast of East Greenland nor in West Greenland :—*Ranunculus glacialis* (very doubtful if in West Greenland), *R. auricomus, Dryas octopetala, Saxifraga hieracifolia, S. Hirculus, Pyrola rotundifolia* L., var. *arenaria* Koch., *Polemonium humile, Juncus triglumis,* var. *Copelandi* Buchanan, and *Deschampsia brevifolia* R. Br. (*cœspitosa*). The same may be said in reference to the mammalian fauna. No fewer than 184 of the 349 Arctic East American species (fully one half) are absent from West Greenland, while 105 only are absent from Europe. This makes the meridian of Baffin's Bay very distinct, and marks out Greenland as a subregion of the arctic flora.

Another feature in the Greenland flora—first pointed out by Hooker—is that it wants a vast number of arctic plants which are European. Excluding about 15 which are water plants, or whose range is limited, 230 (all American plants) may be taken. Of these, 56 are found in Iceland, 32 in the antarctic regions, in both Arctic East America and in Europe 57.

Of the Iceland flora, 120 species do not enter Greenland, whereas 50 of the European plants that inhabit Iceland are absent from Greenland. These data, like the others given in the Introduction, are founded on the statements in Hooker's memoin In a few trifling particulars they might now be altered, but as the recent discoveries in no way derange the general conclusion arrived at. it is unnecessary to again recalculate them.

Of *peculiar species* Greenland has almost none among the flowering plants, though many of these have the trivial name *Grœnlandica* attached, e.g. *Ledum grœnlandicum, Stellaria grœn-landica,* &c. These, however, are only varieties of other species, or have been found elsewhere. The following plants are confined in Greenland to the temperate zone, so called :—*Blitum glaucum, Potamogeton marinus, Sparganium minimum.* and *Streptopus am-plexifolium.*

Introduced plants.—These are few, and in almost no instance have been yet naturalised.

The decrease as we go north is rapid, but yet not so rapid as one would suppose, knowing the analogous alpine distribution from the plains to the mountain tops. The alpine and the arctic conditions are, however, different—the long daylight and darkness peculiarly affecting the Greenland flora. In Smith's Sound between 50 and 60 species of flowering plants have been discovered, and the late Arctic Expedition under Sir George Nares discovered on both shores between lats. 82°–83° from 20 to 30 species of flowering plants, including the beautiful *Hesperis Pallasii, Saxifraga flagel-laris,* and *Vesicaria arctica.*

Hypsometrical range of plants.—See p. 65 of this work.

For Danish West Greenland the list of flowering-plants may be said to be almost complete, as there is no great likelihood of any species new to science being added to the flora of this region between Cape Farewell and lat. 73°. Neither is it very probable that Smith's Sound will yield any novelties, the naturalists of the *Alert* and *Discovery* having obtained nothing new among the higher plants. The cryptogamia will, however, repay the investigation of a competent and intelligent worker, even Disco Bay and its shores—one of the best known botanical localities in Greenland—having yielded numerous novelties to investigators who could only devote to botany the leisure of a few months greatly occupied with other work. East Greenland may, however, be expected to yield some plants new to the flora, and possibly even some novelties to science. (Indeed, some of the Disco flowering-plants discovered by the Editor of this book, might in pre-Darwinian days have been accounted ' new species,' but were with greater caution only classed as varieties. See ' Manual and Instructions for the Arctic Expedition, 1875,' p. 256.) On the south coast, Kemisak island, N. lat. 63° 37′, examined by Graah, is the most northern spot the botany of which is tolerably well known. Between Kemisak and Kaiser Franz-Joseph fjord lie nearly nine degrees of almost unsearched territory. It is within this long stretch that the transition between the flora of the southern part and that of the northern part of East Greenland takes place.

VIII.—*SYNOPSIS OF THE GREENLAND FAUNA.*

As an appendix to the Danish edition of 'Grönland geographisk og statistisk beskrevet,' published in 1857, the Author was kindly supplied with valuable contributions illustrating the natural history of Greenland. Professor *J. Reinhardt* supplied catalogues of the mammals, birds, fishes, crustacea, annelidæ, and entozoa ; Professor *J. C. Schjödte* gave a synopsis of the entomology, Dr. *O. A. L. Mörch* furnished a list of the mollusca, and Dr. *Chr. Lütken* one of the echinodermata. These catalogues have since been for the most part revised and supplemented, and in this state they are found embodied in the ' Manual and Instructions for the Arctic Expedition of 1875,' in addition to various articles of great scientific value on the natural history of Greenland by other authors. As, from a physico-geographical point of view, some brief statements concerning the genera and species of the animal as well as the vegetable kingdoms seemed indispensable, the catalogues referred to have been abstracted here again, chiefly after the ' Manual and Instructions,' some of them being revised anew by the original authors, while Professor Reinhardt has assisted me in arranging them. But it will be seen that the plan of the present book required a high degree of compendiousness, and we must refer for further details to the articles on the same subjects by the above-named authors, as well as by *Robert Brown, Alfred Newton, W. Stimpson, W. K. Parker, Rupert Jones,* and others.

I. MAMMALS.

[For further details, see Robert Brown, 'On the Mammalian Fauna of Greenland.']

(Felis domestica, southern stations, scarce.)

1. Canis lupus (*Linn.*), var. alba, only one shot in 1869.
2. —— familiaris (*Linn.*), var. borealis.
3. Vulpes lagopus (*Linn.*), two varieties, blue and white.
4. Ursus maritimus, *Linn.*, white bear.
5. Putorius ermineus (*Linn.*), East Greenland.
6. Odobænus rosmarus (*Linn.*), walrus.
7. Halichœrus grypus (*O. Fabr.*), very doubtful.
8. Phoca vitulina, *Linn.*
9. —— hispida, *Schr.*, Natsek.
10. —— grœnlandica, *Müll.*, saddleback.
11. —— barbata, *O. Fabr.*, thong-seal.
12. Cystophora cristata (*Erxl.*), bladder-nose.
13. Myodes torquatus (*Pall.*), East Greenland.
14. Mus musculus (*Linn.*), Julianehaab.
15. Lepus glacialis, *Leach*, arctic hare.
    (Capra hircus.)
    (Ovis aries.)
16. Ovibos moschatus (*Gmel.*), East Greenland and Smith's Sound.
    (Bos taurus.)
17. Rangifer tarandus (*Linn.*), reindeer.
    (Sus scrofa, Ivigtut, scarce.)
18. Balæna mysticetus, *Linn.*, right whale.
19. Balænoptera antiquorum, *Gray*, big finner.
20. —————— Sibbaldii, *Gray*, Keporkarnak.
21. —————— rostrata (*Müll.*), little finner.
22. Megaptera longimana (*Rud.*), humpback.
23. Catodon macrocephalus (*Linn.*), sperm-whale, very rare.
24. Hyperoodon butzkopf, *Lacép.*, bottle-nose.
25. —————— latifrons (*Gray*), very doubtful.
26. Beluga leucas (*Pall.*), white whale.
27. Monodon monoceros, *Linn.*, narwhal.
28. Globiocephalus melas (*Traill.*), Grinde-Hval.
29. Phocæna communis, *Brookes*, porpoise, Nisa.
30. Delphinus euphrosyne, *Gray* (D. Holböllii), very rare.
31. Lagenorhynchus albirostris, *Gray*, very rare.
32. —————— leucopleurus (*Rasch*), rare.
33. Orca gladiator (*Bonn.*), sword-fish, Ardluk.

II. BIRDS.

[For further details, see Newton's 'Notes,' founded on the list of 1861 by Professor J. Reinhardt, who also has furnished the following list. Those observed very rarely, or as stragglers, are marked with an asterisk.]

1. Haliætus albicilla (*Linn.*), white-tailed eagle.
2. *Pandion haliætus (*Linn.*), osprey.
3. Falco candicans, *Gmel.*, Greenland falcon.
4. —— peregrinus, *Linn.*, peregrine falcon.
5. Nyctea nivea (*Thunb.*), snowy owl.
6. Otus brachyotus (*Gmel.*), scarce.
7. *Picus varius, *Linn.*
8. *Colaptes auratus (*Linn.*), flicker.
9. Chætura pelasgia (*Linn.*), chimney-swift.
10. *Hirundo rufa, *Bp.*
11. *Vireosylva olivacea (*Linn.*), red-eyed fly-catcher.
12. *Empidonax pusilla (*Sw.*), little fly-catcher.
13. *Contopus borealis (*Sw.*), olive-sided fly-catcher.
14. *Dendrœca coronata (*Linn.*), yellow-rumped warbler.
15. *——— virens (*Gm.*), black-throated green warbler.
16. *——— striata (*Forst*), black-polled warbler.
17. *——— Blackburniæ (*Gm.*), orange-throated warbler.
18. *Parula americana (*Linn.*), particoloured warbler.
19. *Heminthophaga rubricapilla (*Wils.*), Nashville warbler.
20. *Geothlypis philadelphia (*Wils.*), mourning warbler.
21. Saxicola œnanthe, *Linn.*, wheatear, Kussagtak.
22. *Troglodytes palustris, *Wils.*
23. *Regulus calendula (*Linn.*).
24. *Turdus migratorius, *Linn.*, American robin.
25. *——— iliacus, *Linn.*, redwing.
26. *——— minor, *Gmel.*
27. *Motacilla alba, *Linn.*, white wagtail.
28. Anthus ludovicianus, *Gmel.*, Pennsylvanian pipit.
29. —— pratensis, *Linn.*, meadow pipit.
30. *Otocorys alpestris (*Linn.*), shore lark.
31. Plectrophanes nivalis (*Linn.*), snow-bunting.
32. ——————— lapponicus (*Linn.*), Narsarmiutak.
33. Zonotrichia leucophrys (*Forst*), white-crowned bunting, scarce.
34. Linota linaria (*Linn.*), mealy redpole, Orpingmiutak.
35. —— canescens *Gould*, Greenland redpole.
35b. rostrata (*Coues*).
36. *Loxia leucoptera, *Gmel.*
37. *Xanthocephalus icterocephalus, *Bp.*

38. *Sturnus vulgaris, *Linn.*, starling.
39. Corvus corax, *Linn.*, raven.
40. Lagopus rupestris (*Gm.*), common ptarmigan.
    (Gallus Gallorum, southernmost stations).
41. *Ortygometra crex, *Linn.*
42. *———— porzana, *Linn.*, spotted rail.
43. *———— carolina, *Linn.*, Carolina rail.
44. *Fulica americana, *Gmel.*, American coot.
45. *Ardea cinerea, *Linn.*, heron.
46. *Botaurus minor (*Gm.*), American bittern.
47. *Hæmatopus ostralegus, *Linn.*, oyster-catcher.
48. Cinclus interpres, *Linn.*, turnstone.
49. Vanellus cristatus, *Mey.*, lapwing.
50. Squatarola helvetica (*Linn.*), grey plover, scarce.
51. Charadrius pluvialis, *Linn.*, golden plover, scarce.
52. ———— virginicus, *Bork.*, American golden plover.
53. ———— hiaticula, *Linn.*, ringed plover.
54. *Totanus flavipes, *Lath.*, yellowshank.
55. Chalidris arenaria, *Linn.*, sanderling, scarce.
56. Phalaropus fulicarius, *Linn.*
57. ———— hyperboreus, *Linn.*, Nalumasortok.
58. *Tringa minutilla, *Vieill.*
59. ———— maritima, *Brünn.*
60. ———— canutus, *Linn.*
61. ———— alpina, *Vieill.*, purple sandpiper, Sarfarsuk.
62. ———— fuscicollis, *Vieill.*
63. *———— maculata, *Vieill.*, scarce.
64. *Macrorhamphus griseus (*Gmel.*), brown snipe.
65. Gallinago media, *Steph.*, common snipe.
66. *Limosa ægocephala (*Linn.*).
67. Numenius phæopus, *Linn.*, whimbrel.
68. ———— hudsonius, *Lath.*, Hudsonian curlew.
69. ———— borealis, *Lath.*, Eskimo curlew.
70. Sterna macroura, *Naum.*, arctic tern.
71 Xema Sabini, *T. Sab.*, Sabine's gull, rare.
72. *Rhodostethia rosea, *Macgill.*, very scarce.
73 Pagophila eburnea, *Gmel.*, ivory gull, Najarsuak.
74. Rissa tridactyla, *Linn.*, kittiwake, Taterak.
75 *Larus argentatus, *Brünn* , herring-gull, scarce.
76. *Larus affinis, *Rhdt.*, doubtful species.
77. *——— chalcopterus, *Licht.*, doubtful species.
78. —— leucopterus, *Fabr.*, Iceland gull, Najanguak.
79. —— glaucus, *Linn.*, burgomaster, Naja.
80. —— marinus, *Linn.*, Najardluk.
81. Stercorarius catarrhactes, *Linn.*, common skua, Jeingak.

82. Stercorarius pomarinus, *Temm.*
83. —————— parasiticus, *Linn.*
84. —————— Buffonii, *Boie.*
85. Procellaria glacialis, *Linn.*, Fulmar or Mallemoke.
86. Puffinus major, *Fabr.*, greater shearwater.
87. —————— Kuhlii, *Boie,* grey shearwater.
88. —————— Anglorum, *Ray,* Mark's shearwater.
89. Thalassidroma Leachii, *Temm.*, fork-tailed petrel.
89b.*—————— pelagica (*Linn.*).
90. —————— Bulweri, *J.* and *S.*
91. Fratercula arctica (*Linn.*), puffin, Kilangak.
92. Uria grylle, *Linn.*, black guillemot or tyste, Serfak.
93. —— Troile, *Linn.*, rare.
94. —— arra, Brünnich's guillemot, auk, Agpa.
95. Arctica alle (*Linn.*), rotge or little auk, Agpaliarsuk.
96. Alca torda, *Linn.*, razor-bill.
97.*—— impennis, *Linn.*
98.*Podiceps Holböllii, *Rhdt.*
99. —————— cornutus (*Gm.*), horned grebe.
100. Colymbus glacialis, *Linn.*, great northern diver, Tugdlik.
101. —————— septentrionalis, *Linn.*, red-throated diver, Karsak.
102.*Sula bassana, *Linn.*, gannet.
103. Graculus carbo, *Linn.*, cormorant, Okaitsok.
104. Mergus serrator, *Linn.*, red-breasted merganser.
105. Clangula islandica, *Gmel.*, Barrow's golden-eye.
106. —————— albeola (*Linn.*).
107. Histrionicus torquatus (*Linn.*), harlequin duck, Tornavi Arsuk.
108. Harelda glacialis (*Linn.*), long-tailed duck, Agdlek.
109.*Fuligula marila (*Linn.*), scaup duck.
110.* —————— affinis, *Eyt.*, American scaup duck.
111.*Œdemia perspicillata (*Linn.*), surf-seater.
112. Somateria mollissima (*Linn.*), eider.
113. —————— spectabilis (*Linn.*), king duck.
114. Anas boschas, *Linn.*, wild duck, Kordlutok.
115. —— acuta, *Linn.*, pintail, Kerdlutor piarsuk.
116.*—— carolinensis, *Gmel.*, American teal.
117.*—— crecca, *Linn.*, teal.
118.*—— penelope, *Linn.*, widgeon.
119. Bernicla Brenta (*Pall.*), Brent goose, Nerdlek:
120. —————— leucopsis (*Bechst.*), bernacle goose.
121.*—————— canadensis (*Linn.*), Canadian goose.
122. Chen hyperboreus (*Pall.*), snow-goose.
123. Anser albifrons, *Gmel.*, Nerdlernak.
124. Cygnus ferus, *Ray,* wild swan, Kugsuk.

III. FISHES.

[The following list must still be regarded as provisional, several species having only been indicated, not described. It is abstracted from the catalogue in the ' Manual,' written by Dr. Lütken, who has in preparation a more complete ichthyology of Greenland.]

1. Gasterosteus aculeatus, *L.*, Kakilisak.
2. Lampris guttatus (*Retz.*).
3. Notacanthus Fabricii (*Rhdt.*).
4. Cottus scorpius, *L.*, Kanajok.
5. —— scorpioides, *Fabr.*, Pukutdlak.
6. Phobetor ventralis (*Val.*) (Cottus gobio, *Fabr.*).
7. Centridermichthys uncinatus (*Rhdt.*).
8. Icelus hamatus, *Kr.*
9. Triglops Pingelii, *Rhdt.*
10. Aspidophorus decagonus, *Schn.*, Kanajordluk.
11. Aspidophoroides monopterygius, *Bl.*
12. —————— —— Olrickii, *Ltk.*
13. Sebastes norvegicus (*Müll.*), Sulugpavak.
14. Himantolophus grœnlandicus, *Rhdt.*
15. Caratias Holbœllii, *Kr.*
16. Oneirodes Eschrichtii, *Ltk.*
17. Cyclopterus lumpus, *L.*, Nepisa.
18. ————— spinosus, *Müll.*, Nepisardluk.
19. Liparis Fabricii, *Kr.*
20. —— arctica, *Gill.*
21. —— Montagui, *Don.*
22. —— lineata, *Kr.*
23. —— tunicata, *Rhdt.*, Apapukutsuk.
24. —— (Careproctus) Reinhardti, *Kr.*
25. Stichæus præcisus (*Kr.*).
26. ———— punctatus, *Fabr.*, Akuliakitsok.
27. Lumpenus aculeatus, *Rhdt.*
28. ———— Fabricii, *Rhdt.*, Tajarnak.
29. ———— medius, *Rhdt.*
30. ———— gracilis, *Rhdt.*
31. Centronotus fasciatus, *Schn.*
32. ————— affinis, *Rhdt.*
33. Lycodes Vahlii, *Rhdt.*, Misarkornak.
34. —— reticulatus, *Rhdt.*, Akuliakitsok.
35. —— seminudus, *Rhdt.*
36. —— perspicillum. *Kr.*
37. —— nebulosus, *Kr.*

38. Anarrichas lupus, *L.*, Kigutilik.
39. ——— denticulatus, *Kr.*
40. ——— minor, *E. Olufs.*, Keerak.
41. ——— latifrons, *Stp. Hallgr.*
42. Bythites fuscus, *Rhdt.*
43. Gymnelis viridis, *Fabr.*
44. Gadus morrhua, *L.*, Sarugdlik.
45. —— ovak, *Rhdt.*, common smaller cod.
46. —— agilis, *Rhdt.*, Misarkornak (G. æglefinus).
47. Merlangus carbonarius (*L.*).
48. Merluccius vulgaris, *Cuv.*, Akuliakitsok.
49. Lota molva (*L.*), Ivigsuak.
50. Brosmius vulgaris, *Cuv.*, Niorpalugak.
51. Motella Reinhardti, *Kr.*
52. ——— ensis, *Rhdt.*
53. ——— argentata, *Rhdt.*
54. Coryphænoides Stroemii (*Rhdt.*).
55. Macrurus rupestris, *Fabr.*
56. ——— trachyrhynchus, *Risso.*
57. Hippoglossus vulgaris, *Fl.*, Netarnak.
58. ——— pinguis (*Fabr.*), Kaleralik.
59. Depranopsetta (Hippoglossoides) platessoides (*Fabr.*).
60. Ammodytes dubius, *Rhdt.* (A. tobianus).
61. Anguilla sp., *Fabr.*, Nimeriak.
62. Clupea harengus, *L.*, Kapisilik.
63–67. Salmo, five species not yet identified.
68. Microstoma grœnlandica, *Rhdt.*
69. Mallotus villosus, *Müll.*, Angmagsak.
70. Scopelus glacialis, *Rhdt.*
71. Stomias ferox, *Rhdt.*
72. Paralepis borealis, *Rhdt.*, Saviliusak.
73. Selachus maximus (*Gunn*).
74. Centroscyllium Fabricii, *Rhdt.*, Kukilik.
75. Somniosus microcephalus (*Schn.*), Ekalugsuak.
76. Raja radiata, *Don.*
77. —— sp., known from some larger eggs.
78. Petromyzon fluviatilis, *L.*
79. Myxine glutinosa, *L.*, Tvik.

IV. MOLLUSCA.

[The following list was prepared in 1877 by Dr. O. A. L. Mörch, to be used here. It comprises only the west coast of Greenland. The asterisk signifies species recorded from Greenland, but not seen by the author himself.]

Class I. **Androgyna.**

Order I. *Geophila*, Fer.—

1. Arion fuscus, *Müll*, probably introduced.
2. Vitrina angelicæ, *Beck*, common chiefly where the Angelica grows.
3. Conulus Fabricii, *Beck*, under mosses, rare.
4. *Hyalinia alliaria, *Miller*, Frederikshaab, *Fabr.*
5. *Helicogena hortensis, *Müll.*, Igaliko, *Wormskiold.*
6. Pupa (Vertigo) Hoppii, *Möll.*, under mosses, rare.
7. Succinea grœnlandica, *Beck*, Kuksuk, &c., common.

Order II. *Hygrophila*, Fer.—

8. Planorbis (Nautilina) arctica, *Beck*, rare.
9. Limnæa (Limnophysa) Vahlii, *Beck*, not rare.
9a. ————————— var. α. Pingelii, *Beck*, in a pond at Nepisetsundet.
9b. ————————— var. β. leucostoma, L. Mölleri, *Beck.*
9c. ————————— var. γ. malleata, rare.
9d. ————————— var. δ. parva, very rare.
10. ————————— Wormskioldii, *Beck*; Arsut, outside a river (Barret).
11. ————————— Holböllii, *Beck*, not common.

Order III. *Ptenoglossata*, Troschel—

12. Menestho albula, *Fabr.*, very rare.
13. Scala grœnlandica, *Perry*, not rare, but local.
14. ——— (Acirsa) borealis, *Beck*; S. Eschrichtii, *Holb.*, on a single spot by Godthaab.
15. Philine granulosa, *Sars*, *Möll.*, 2 spm.
16. ——— punctata, *Möll.* (non Ad.), 2 spm.; B. lineolata, *Couth.*
17. Cylichna alba, *Brown*; B. corticata, *Beck*, common.
18. ——— Reinhardti, *Holb.*, not common.
19. ——— insculpta, *Totten*, rare.
20. Utriculus turritus, *Möll.*, rare.
21. ———— semen, *Reeve*? U. obtusus var., *Friele*, very rare.
22. Diaphana debilis, *Gould*; B. subangulata, *Möll.*, very rare.
23. (Amphisphyra) globosa, *Loven* (Physema?), very rare.
24. ——— ——— expansa, *Jeffr.*, very rare.
25.*———— substriata, *Jeffr.*, 1750 fath., *Jeffr.*
26. Dolabrifera Holböllii, *Bergh.*, unique.

Order IV. *Gymnobranchia*—

27. Dendronotus Reynoldsii, *Couth.*; D. arborescens, *Fabr.*, common.
28. Lamellidoris liturata, *Beck*, common.
29. ——— acutiuscula, *Stp. Möll.*, very rare.

30. Doris (Acanthochila) repanda, *Ald.* and *Hanc.*, rare.
31. Polycera Holböllii (Eupl.), *Möll.*, very rare.
32. —— sp.
33. Proctaporia fusca, *Fabr.*, *Stimps.*
34. Æolis (Coryphella) salmonacea, *Couth.*, not common.
35. —————————— bostoniensis, *Couth.*, var. approximans, Omenak, very rare.
36. Cratena Olrikii, *Mörch*, unique.
37. —— hirsuta, *Bergh.*, unique.
38. Campaspe pusilla, *Bergh.*, unique.
39. Galvina rupium, *Möll.*, very rare.

Order V. *Pellibranchia—*

40. *Limapontia caudata, *Müll.* (*O. Fabr.*).

Order VI. *Pteropoda.—*

41. Clione limacina, *Phipps* (C. borealis, *Brug.*), abundant.
42. Limacina helicina, *Phipps*, abundant.
43. Heterofusus balea, *Möll.*, common.
44. Clione limacina, *Phipps*, abundant.

Class II. **Dioica**, *Latr.*

Order I. *Tænioglossata—*

45. Littorina grœnlandica, *Ch. Mke.*, very common ; var. lævior, L. palliata, *Sag.* ; L. arctica, *Möll.*
46. —— obtusata, *L.*, very rare.
47. Lacuna vincta, *Mtg.* (L. divaricata, *Fabr.*), common.
48. —— crassior, *Mtg.* (L. glacialis, *Möll.*), unique.
49. —— (Temara) pallida, *D. Costa*, very rare.
50. Rissoa (Paludinella) globulus, *Möll.*, rare.
51. —— (Onoba) saxatilis, *Möll.*, very common.
52. ———— castanea, *Möll.*
53.* ———— cimicoides, *Forb.* (*Barret*).
54. ———— scrobiculata, *Möll.*, rare.
55.* ———— arenaria, *Migh.*, 5–35 fath., *Jeffr.*
56. Rissoella eburnea, *Stimps.*, very rare.
57.*Eulima stenostoma, *Jeffr.*, 410 fath.
58.*Aclis Walleri, *Jeffr.*, *Wallich.*
59. Skenea planorbis, *O. Fabr.*, common.
60.*Homologyra rota, *F.* and *H.*, 1622 fath., *Wallich.*
61. Turritella (Tachyrhynchus) erosa, *Couth.*, rare.
62. ——————————— reticulata, *Migh.* and *Ad.* ; T. lactea, *Möll.*, not rare.

438 *Danish Greenland.*

63. Cerithium (Bittium?) arcticum, *Mörch* ; T. costulata, *Möll.*, very rare.
64. Aporrhais occidentalis, *Beck*, a fragment.
65.*———— Serressianus, *Michaud*, 410 fath., *Jeffr.*
66. Onchidiopsis grœnlandicus, *Beck*, very rare.
67. Marsenina grœnlandica, *Möll.*, very rare.
68. ———— micromphala, *Bergh.*, var. præced.?
69. Velutina lanigera, *Möll.*, very rare.
70. ———— haliotoides, *Müll.*, common.
71. ———— (Velutella) flexilis, *Mont.*, unique.
72. ———— (Morvillia) zonata, *Gould* ;
var. grandis, V. canaliculata, *Beck.*
73. Naticea affinis, *Gmel.* ; N. clausa, *S.* and *B.*, not common.
74. ———— (Mamma?) borealis, *Gray* (N. nana, *Möll.*), very rare.
75. ———— (Lunatia) grœnlandica, *Beck*, not common.
76. ———— (Amauropsis) islandica, *Gmel.* ; var. N. fragilis, *Leach*, rare.
77. Amaura candida, *Möll.*, rare.

Order II. *Rhachiglossata—*

78. Tritonium glaciale, *L.*, rare.
79.*———— Hancockii, *Mörch.*
80. ———— scalariforme, *Beck*, not rare.
81. ———— ciliatum, *Fabr.*, rare ; var. lævior.
82. ———— undatum, *L.*, very rare.
83. ———— Terræ Novæ, *Beck*, unique.
84. ———— undulatum, *Möll.*, not rare.
85. ———— grœnlandicum, *Ch.* (B. cyaneum, *Brug.*), very common;
var. α. B. tenebrosum, *Hanc.*
86. ———— perdix, *Beck*, rare (B. Humphreysianum, *Möll.*).
87. ———— hydrophanum, *Hanc.*, 200–300 fath. Pröven, *Olr.*
88. Fusus (Neptunea) despectus, *L.*, very rare ; var. α. F. fornicatus, *Fabr.* ; var. β. F. carinatus, *Lam.*
89. ———— tornatus, *Gould*, unique.
90. ———— (Tritonofusus) Kroyeri, *Möll.*, very rare.
91.*———— fenestratus, *Turt.*, 418 fath., *Jeffr.*
92. ———— latericeus, *Möll.*, very rare.
93. ———— (Sipho) islandicus, *Ch.*, two spm.
94. ———— (Siphonorbis) propinquus, *Ald.*, very rare.
95. ———— Holböllii, *Möll.* (F. tortuosus, *Reeve*), very rare.
96. ———— Pfaffii, *Mörch*, two spm.
97. ———— togatus, *Mörch*, unique.
98. ———— lachesis, *Mörch*, unique.
99. ———— (Volutopsis) norvegicus, *Ch.* ; var. F. Largillier i, *Petit*, two spm.

100. Murex (Trophon) truncatus, *Ström.*, *Jeffr.*, common ;
     var. T. Bamffii, *Don*, rare ;
     var. T. clathratus, *L.* ; T. Gunneri, *Loven*, rare.
101. ——————— craticulatus, *Fabr.*, common.
102. Purpura lapillus, *L.*, on one spot, abundant.
103. Columbella (Astyris) rosacea, *Gould*, common.
104. Volutomitra grœnlandica, *Beck*, not common.

Order III. *Toxoglossata*, Trosch.—

105. Cancellaria (Admete) viridula, *Fabr.* not common.
106. ——————— costellifera, *Sow.*, rare.
107. Pleurotoma (Ischnula) turricula, *Mtg.* ; var. *α*. Defr. nobilis, *Möll.*
     rare ; var. *β*. Defr. scalaris, *Möll.*, rare ;
     var. *γ*. Defr. exarata, *Möll.*, common.
108. ——————— Woodiana, *Möll.*, very rare.
109. ——————— elegans, *Möll.*, very rare.
110.*——————— declivis, *Loven*, 60 fath., *Jeffr.*
111. ——————— pyramidalis, *Ström.* ; P. Vahlii, *Möll.*, common.
112. ——————— cancellata, *Migh.* and *Ad.* ; D. cinerea, *Möll.*, very
     rare ; var. D. Pingelii, *Möll.*
113. ——————— violacea, *Migh.* and *Ad.*, common ; var. *α*. D. cylin-
     dracea, *Möll.* ; var. *β*. spira brevior, P. livida, *Reeve*,
     rare ; var. *γ*. ventricosa, P. Beckii, *Möll.*, rare.
114. ——————— borealis, *Reeve* (P. livida, *Möll.*), rare ; var. *α*. ventri-
     · cosa, D. viridula, *Möll.*, rare.
115.*——————— rubescens, *Jeffr.*, Holsteinb. 10 fath., *Jeffr.*

Class III. **Exocephala**, *Latr.*

Order I. *Rhipidoglossata*, Trosch.—

116. Trochus occidentalis, *Migh.* and *Ad.*, unique.
117. Margarita cinerea, *Couth.*, very common ;
     var. grandis, M. striata, *Brod.* and *Sow.*, very rare.
118. ——————— clathrata, *O. Sars*, var. major, unique.
119. ——————— undulata, *Sow.* and *Brod.*, very common.
120. ——————— grœnlandica, *Ch.* (M. umbilicalis, *Brod.* and *Sow.*), *Jeffr.*,
     not common ; var. minor.
121. ——————— argentata, *Gould* (M. glauca, *Möll.*), very rare.
122. ——————— Vahlii, *Möll.*, rare.
123. ——————— helicina, *Phipps*, *Fabr.*, very common.
124. Mölleria costulata, *Möll.*, Godthaab 60 fath., *Holb.*
125. Scissurella crispata, *Flemg.*, very rare.
126. Cemoria noachina, *L.*, common.

Order II. *Heteroglossata*, Gray—

127. Pilidium rubellum, *Fabr.*, not rare.

128. Lepeta cæca, *Müll.*, common.
129. Tectura testudinalis, *Müll.*, common.
130. Chiton (Tonicia) marmoreus, *Fabr.*, common.
131. —— (Leptochiton) albus, *L.*, *Fabr.*, common.
132. ———————— ruber, *L.*, *Pennt.*, very rare.
133. ——————— cinereus, *L.* (C. asellus, *Ch.*), very rare.
134.*Dentalium striolatum, *Stimps.*, 410–1758 fath., *Jeffr.*
135.* —— candidum, *Jeffr.*, 1100 fath., *Jeffr.*
136.*Siphonodentalium lofotense, *Sars*, 1750 fath., *Jeffr.*

Class IV. **Cephalopoda**, *Cuv.*

137. Octopus grœnlandicus, *Dewhurst*, very rare.
138. Cirroteuthis Muelleri, *Eschr.*, rare.
139. Rossia palpebrosa, *Owen*, very rare.
140. —— Mölleri, *Stp.*, very rare.
141. Sepiola atlantica, *D'Orb.*, *Stp.*, unique.
142. Leachia hyperborea, *Stp.*, unique.
143. Gonatus Fabricii, *Lichtst.*, rare ;
     jun. Onychoteuthis amœna, *Möll.*, common.

Class V. **Acephala**, *Cuv.*

Order I. *Dimya*—

144. Teredo denticulata, *Gray* (T. megotara, *F.* and *H.*), not rare.
145. Mya truncata, *L.*, common ; var. *M.* uddevalensis, *Forb.*
146. —— arenaria, *L.*, very rare.
147. Cyrtodaria siliqua, *Spgl.*, unique.
148. ——— Kurriana, *Dkr.*, Jacobshavn, *Pfaff.*
149. Saxicava arctica, *L.*, very common.
150. Panomya norvegica, *Spgl.*, fossil, *Rink.*
151. Lyonsia arenosa, *Möll.*, local, not abundant.
152. Thracia myopsis, *Beck*, not rare.
153. ——— septentrionalis, *Jeffr.* ; T. truncata, *Migh.* and *Ad.*, unique.
154.*Neæra cuspidata, *Oliv.*, *Wallich.*
155. Tellina (Macoma) calcarea, *Ch.*, common.
156. ——————— mæsta, *Desh.*, very rare.
157. ——————— crassula, *Desh.*, very rare.
158.*——————— inflata, *Stimps.*, 60 fath., *Jeffr.*
159. ——————— tenera, *Leach* (T. grœnlandica, *Beck*), abundant.
160. Venus fluctuosa, *Gould*, Narsalik, very rare.
161. Pisidium Steenbuchii, *Möll.*, in a pond at Baalsrivier.
162. Thyasira Gouldii, *Phil.* (Lucina flexuosa, *Mtg.*?), common.
163.*—— incrassata (Axinus), *Jeffr.*, 1750 fath., *Jeffr.*
164.*—— eumyarius, *Sars*, 1100 fath., *Jeffr.*
165.*—— cycladius (Kellia), *S. Wood*, 1750 fath., *Jeffr.*

166. Montacuta Mölleri, *Holb.*, local. (*Möller, append. n. 7.*)
167.*———— elevata, *Stimps.* ?
168. ———— Dawsoni, *Jeffr.*
169.*———— planulata, *Stimps.* (Kellia rubra, *Gould*).
170.*Kellia symmetros, *Jeffr.*, 1750 fath.
171. Turtonia minuta, *Fabr.*, common.
172. Astarte compressa, *L.* (A. elliptica, *Brown*), very common.
173. ———— crebricostata, *Forbes*, very rare.
174. ———— (Tridonta) semisulcata, *Leach*, rare.
175. ———— (Nicania) striata, *Leach*, very common ;
var. A. globosa, *Möll.*, local.
176. ———————— Banksii, *Leach*, not common.
177.*———————— pulchella, *Jonas* (Warhami, *Hanc.*).
178. Cyprina islandica, *L.*, 3 spm.
179. Cardium ciliatum, *Fabr.* (C. islandicum, *Ch.*), common.
180. ———— elegantulum, *Beck*, rare.
181. ———— (Serripes) groenlandicum, *Ch.*, common ;
var. C. boreale, *Reeve*, unique.
182.*Arca pectunculoides Scacchi, *Wallich.*
182b.*Glomus nitens, *Jeffr.*, 1750 fath.
183.*Limopsis tenella, *Jeffr.*, 1450 fath., *Jeffr.*
184. ————aurita, *Sars*, 1100 fath., *Jeffr.*
184b.*Pecchiolia abyssicola, *Sars*, Baffin's Bay, 336 fath., *Jeffr.*
185. Nucula inflata, *Hancock* (N. tenuis, *Gray*), common ;
var. N. approximata, *Beck.*
186.*———— reticulata, *Jeffr.*, 1100 fath.
187. ———— delphinodonta, *Migh.* and *Ad.* (N. corticata), 100 fath., *Holb.*
188. Nuculana buccata, *Stp.* (N. Jacksonii, *Gould*), common.
189. ———— pernula, *Müll.* (N. macilenta, *Stp.*), very rare.
190. ———— minuta, *Müll.*, very common ; var. Leda complanata, *Müll*
191. ———— (Portlandia) arctica, *Gray*, two spm.
192. ———————— lenticula, *Möll.*, rare.
193.*———————— sericea, *Jeffr.*, 1450 fath., *Jeffr.*
194.*———————— lata, *Jeffr.*, 1750 fath., *Jeffr.*
195.*———————— expansa, *Jeffr.*, 1750 fath., *Jeffr.*
196.*———————— lucida, *Loven*, 410 fath., *Jeffr.*
197.*———————— frigida, *Torell.*, 175 fath., *Jeffr.*
198.*———————— pusio, *Phil.*, 1750 fath., *Jeffr.*
199.*———————— acuminata, *Jeffr.*, 1750 fath., *Jeffr.*
200.*———————— pustulosa, *Jeffr.*, 1450 fath., *Jeffr.*
201. Yoldia limatula ' Say,' *Torell.*, rare.
202. ————hyperborea, *Loven*, common.
203. ———— thraciæformis, *Storer*, 60–70 fath., very rare.
204.*Malletia cuneata, *Jeffr.*, 1750 fath., *Jeffr.*
205.*———— excisa, *Phil.*, 1750 fath., *Jeffr.*

Danish Greenland.

Order II. *Heteromya—*

206. Modiolaria nigra, *Gray*, common.
207. ———— lævigata, *Gray*, very common.
208. ———— corrugata, *Stimps.*, 50–60 fath., *Holb.*
209. ———— faba, *Fabr.*, very common.
210. ———— (Dacrydium) vitrea, *Holb.*, 100 fath., *Holb.*
211. ———— (Crenella) decussata, *Mtg.* ; var. M. cicercula, *Moll.*
212.*Idas argenteus, *Jeffr.*, 1450 fath., *Jeffr.*
213. Mytilus edulis, *L.*, very common.

Order III. *Monomya—*

214. Lima (Limatula) sulculus, *Leach, Loven*, common.
215.*———————— gibba, *Jeffr.*, 1750 fath., *Jeffr.*
216.*———————— ovata, *S. Wood*, 1450 fath., *Jeffr.*
217.*———————— subovata, *Jeffr.*, 1450 fath., *Jeffr.*
218. Pecten islandicus, *Müll.*, common ; var. costis elevatis.
219.*———— grœnlandicus, *Sow.*
220.*———— fragilis, *Jeffr.*, 1750 fath.
221.*———— (Pleuronectia) lucidus, *Jeffr.*, 1450 fath.

BRACHIONOPODA.

222.*Atretia gnomon, *Jeffr.*, 1100 fath., unique, *Jeffr.*
223. Terebratella spitzbergiensis, *Davids.*, very rare.
224. Terebratulina septentrionalis, *Couth.*, unique.
225.*Terebratula cranium, *Müll.*, 100–228 fath., *Wallich.*
226. Rhynchonella psittacea, *Ch.*, common.

V. TUNICATA.
(Chr. Lütken, 1875.)

Ascidiæ simplices—

1. Boltenia Bolteni, *L.*
2. Cynthia crystallina (*Möll.*).
3. ———— rustica (*L.*).
4. ———— pyriformis (*Rthk.*).
5. ———— echinata (*L.*).
6. ———— conchilega (*Möll.*).
7. ———— (Molgula) glutinans (*Möll.*).
8. ———— tuberculum (*Fabr.*).
9. ———— Adolphi, *Kupf.*
10. Phallusia lurida (*Möll.*).
11. ———————— complanata, *Fabr.*
12. Chelyosoma Macleayanum, *Sow., Brod.*
13. Pelonaia sp.

The compound Ascidiæ are rather numerous, but no attempt has been made to identify them.

VI. POLYZOA.

(Chr. Lütken, 1875.)

1. **Cyclostomata—**
    1. Crisia eburnea (*L.*).
    2. Diastopora simplex (*Busk*).
    3. ——.—— hyalina (*Flemg.*).
    4. Mesenteripora mæandrina (*Wood*).
    5. Tubulipora atlantica (*Forb.*).
    6. ———— fimbria (*Lmk.*).
    7. ———— flabellaris (*Fabr.*).
    8. ———— incrassata (*D'Orb.*).
    9. ———— fungia (*Couch*).
    10. ——.—— penicillata (*Fabr.*).
    11. Hornera lichenoides (*Fabr.*).
    12. Discoporella verrucaria (*L.*).
    13. ——.—— hispida (*Fl.*).
    14. Defrancia lucernaria (*Sars*).

2. **Ctenostomata—**
    15. Alcyonidium hirsutum (*Flemg.*).
    16. ———— gelatinosum (*L.*).
    17. ————. hispidum (*Fabr.*).

3. **Chilostomata—**
    18. Cellularia ternata (*Sol.*) (Sertularia reptans, *Fabr.*).
    19. ———— scabra (*v. Ben*) (Sertularia halecina, *Fabr.*).
    20. Gemellaria loricata (*L.*) (Fistulana ramosa, *Fabr.*).
    21. Caberea Ellisii (*Flemg.*).
    22. Bugula Murrayana (*Bean.*).
    23. Flustra chartacea (*Gm.*).
    24. ——— membranacea (*L.*).
    25. .——— papyracea (*Pall.*).
    26. ——— foliacea (*L.*).
    27. Cellaria articulata (*Fabr.*).
    28. Membranipora lineata (*L.*).
    29. ——.——— spinifera (*Johnst.*).
    30. ———.——— Flemingii (*Busk.*).
    31. ——— ——— pilosa (*Linn.*).
    32. Escharipora annulata (*Fabr.*).
    33. Porina Malusii (*Aud.*).
    34. ———ciliata, *Pall.*
    35. Anarthropora monodon (*Busk.*).
    36. Escharella porifera (*Smith*).

37. Escharella palmata (*Sars*).
38. ———— Legentilii (*Aud.*).
39. ———— Jacotini (*Aud.*).
40. ———— auriculata (*Hass.*).
41. ———— Landsborovii (*Johnst.*).
42. ———— linearis (*Hass.*).
43. Mollia hyalina (*L.*) (Cellepora nitida).
44. Myriozoon crustaceum (*Sm.*).
45. ———— subgracile (*D'Orb.*).
46. ———— coarctatum (*Sars*).
47. Lepralia spathulifera (*Sm.*).
48. ———— hippopus (*Sm.*).
49. Porella acutirostris (*Sm.*).
50. ———— lævis (*Flemg.*).
51. Eschara verrucosa (*Busk*).
52. ———— cervicornis (*Pall.*).
53. ———— elegantula (*D'Orb.*).
54. Escharoides Sarsii (*Sm.*).
55. ———— rosacea (*Busk*).
56. Discopora coccinea (*Abdg.*).
57. ———— appensa (*Hass.*).
58. ———— sincera (*Sm.*).
59. ———— Skenei (*Sol.*).
60. Cellepora scabra, *Fabr.*
61. ———— ramulosa (*L.*).
62. Celleporaria incrassata (*Lam.*).
63. Retepora cellulosa (*Linn.*).
64. Loxosoma sp.

VII. INSECTA.

(Abstracted from J. C. Schjödte's list, 1857.)

Eleutherata (Coleoptera)—

1. Nebria nivalis, *Payk.*
2. Patrobus hyperboreus, *Dej.*
3. Bradycellus cognatus, *Gyll.*
4. Bembidium Grapei, *Gyll.*
5. Hydroporus sp.
6. Colymbetes dolabrates, *Payk.*
7. Gyrinus sp.
8. Quedius fulgidus, *Fabr.*
9. Quedius sp.
10. Micralymma brevilingua, *Schjödte.*
11. Anthobium Sorbi, *Gyll.*

12. Staphylinus maxillosus, *L.*
13. ———— fuscipes, *O. Fabr.*
14. ———— Lingnorum, *O. Fabr.*
15. Cistela (Byrrhus) stoica, *O. Fabr.*
16. Simplocaria metallica, *Sturm.*
17. Rhytidosomus scobina, *Schjödte.*
18. Phytonomus sp.
19. Otiorhynchus maurus, *Gyll.*
20. ———— arcticus, *Fab.*
21. Coccinella trifasciata, *Fab.*

Ulonata (Neuroptera parte)—
22. Ephemera culiciformis, *Linn.*

Synistata (Neuroptera parte, et **Trichoptera)**—
23. Hemerobius obscurus, *Zett.*
24. Phryganea grisea, *Linn.*
25. ———— interrogationis, *Zett.*

Piezata (Hymenoptera)—
26. Nematus ventralis, *Dahlb.*
27. Bombus hyperboreus, *Schönh.* (Apis alpina).
28. ———— balteatus, *Dahlb.*
29. Cryptus arcticus, *Schjödte.*
30. ———— Fabricii, *Schjödte.*

Glossata (Lepidoptera)—
31. Argynnis chariclea, *Herbst.* (Papilio Tullia).
32. Chionobes Balder, *Boisd.*
33. ———— Bore, *Hübn.*
34. Colias Boothii, *Curtis.*
35. Agrotis quadrangula, *Zett.*
36. ———— rava, *Herr.*
37. ———— islandica, *Staudinger.*
38. ———— Drewsenii, *Staudinger.*
39. Noctua Westermanni, *Staudinger.*
40. Hadena exulis, *Lefeb.*
41. ———— Sommeri, *Lefeb.*
42. ———— grœnlandica, *Zett.*
43. ———— picticollis, *Zett.*
44. Aplecta occulta, *Rossi,* var. implicata.
45. Plusia gamma, *L.*
46. ———— interrogationis, *L.*
47. ———— parilis, *Hübn.*

48. Plusia diasema, *Dalm.*
49. Anarta algida, *Lefeb.* (Phalæna myrtillo).
50. —— amissa, *Lefeb.*
51. —— leucocycla, *Staudinger.*
52. —— vidua, *Hübn.*, var. lapponica.
53. Phæsyle polaria, *Boisd.*
54. Cidaria brumata, *Linn.*
55. Botys hybridalis, *Hybn.*
56. Teras indecorana, *Zett.*
57. Endorea centuriella, *Schifferm.*
58. Pempelia carbonariella, *Fischer von Roeslerst.*
59. Plutella senilella, *Zetterstedt.*

Antliata (Diptera)—

60. Chironomus polaris, *Kirby.*
61. —— turpis, *Zett.*
62. —— frigidus, *Zett.*
63. —— variabilis, *Stæger.*
64. —— basalis, *Stæg.*
65. —— byssinus, *Meigen.*
66. —— anterrimus, *Meig.*
67. —— picipes, *Meig.*
68. Diamesa Waltlii, *Meig.*
69. Tanypus crassinervis, *Zett.*
70. —— tectipennis, *Zett.*
71. —— tibialis, *Stæg.*
72. Ceratopogon sordidellus, *Zett.*
73. Tipula arctica, *Curtis.*
74. Erioptera fuscipennis, *Zett.*
75. Trichocera maculipennis, *Meig.* (Tipula regelationis).
76. Boletina grœnlandica, *Stæg.*
77. Sciara iridipennis, *Zett.*
78. Simulia vittata, *Zett.* (Culex reptans).
79. Rhamphomya nigrita, *Zett.* (Empis borealis).
80. Dolichopus grœnlandicus, *Zett.*
81. Helophilus grœnlandicus (Tabanus), *O. Fabr.*
82. Syrphus topiarius, *Meig.*
83. Sphærophoria strigata, *Stæg.*
84. Sarcophaga mortuorum, *Linn.*
85. Musca erythrocephala, *Meig.*
86. —— grœnlandica, *Zett.*
87. Anthomyia dentipes, *Fabr.*
88. —— irritans, *Fallen.*
89. —— frontata, *Zett.*
90. —— trigonifera, *Zett.*

91. Anthomyia arctica, *Zett.*
92. ———— triangulifera, *Zett.*
93. ———— scatophagina, *Zett.*
94. ———— striolata, *Fall.*
95. ——·—— rufipes, *Meig.*
96. ——·—— ciliata, *Fabr.*
97. Scatophaga squalida, *Meig.*
98. ——·———— littorea, *Fall.*
99. ————————— fucorum, *Fall.*
100. Cordylura hæmorrhoidalis, *Meig.*
101. Helomyza tibialis, *Zett.*
102. ———— geniculata, *Zett.*
103. Piophila casei, *Linn.*
104. ———— pilosa, *Linn.*
105. Ephydra stagnalis, *Fall.*
106. Notiphila vitipennis, *Zett.*
107. Phytomyzon obscurella, *Fall.*

Suctoria—

108. Pulex irritans (?), *L.*, on the hare only.

Rhyncota—

109. Heterogaster grœnlandicus, *Zett.*
110. Cicada lividella, *Zett.*
111. Aphis punctipennis, *Zett.*
112. Dorthesia chiton, *Zett.*

Siphunculata —

113. Pediculus humanus, *L.*
        Birds' lice—
114. ———— strigis.
115. ———— corvi.
116. ———— clangulæ.
117. ———— gryllæ.
118. ———— bassani.
119. ———— lari.
120. ———·—— tringæ.
121. ———— hiaticulæ.
122. ———— lagopi.

Mallophaga—

123. Trichodectes (?) canis, *De Geer.*

Thysanuara—

124. Podura sp.

VIII. ARACHNIDÆ.

(From J. C. Schjödte's list in 1857.)

Araneæ—

1. Lycosa saccata (*Fabr.*).
2. Attus spp.

Opiliones—

3. Phalangium opilio (?) *L.*, Niutouk.

Acari (*Fabr.*)—

4. Bdella, etc., spp.
5. Acarus siro, itch-mite.
6. ———— cadaverum, in dried fish especially.
7. ———— holosericeus.
8. ———— aquaticus.
9. ———— muscorum.
10. ———— gymnopterorum.
11. ———— coleoptratorum.
12. ———— longicornis.
13. ———— littoralis.

IX. CRUSTACEA.

(From Reinhardt's list in 1857, revised by Lütken in 1875.)

Decapoda—

1. Chionocœtes phalangium (*Fabr.*), Agsagiarsuk.
2. Hyas aranea (*Linn.*), Agsagiak.
3. ——— coarctata (*Leach*).
4. Pagurus pubescens, *Kr.*
5. Crangon boreas (*Phipps*) (Cancer homaroides).
6. Sabinea septemcarinata (*Sab.*).
7. Argis lar (*Owen*).
8. Hippolyte Fabricii, *Kr.*
9a. ———— Gaimardii, *M. Edw.*
9b. (———— gibba, *Kr.*)
10. ———— incerta, *Buchh.*
11. ———— spinus (*Sow.*).
12. ——— macilenta, *Kr.*
13a. ——— Phippsii, *Kr.*
13b. ———— turgida, *Kr.*
14a. ———— polaris (*Sa'.*).
14b. (———— borealis, *Owen.*)

15. Hippolyte aculeata (*Fabr.*).
16. —————— microceras, *Kr.*
17. —————— Panschii, *Buchh.*
18. Pandalus borealis, *Kr.*
19. —————— annulicornis (*Leach*).
20. Pasiphaë tarda, *Kr.*
21. —————— glacialis, *Buchh.*
22. Sergestes arcticus, *Kr.*
23. Thysanopoda inermis, *Kr.*
24. —————— norvegica, *Sars.*
25. —————— longicaudata, *Kr.*
26. —————— Raschii, *Sars.*
27. Mysis oculata, *Fabr.*
28. —— latitans, *Kr.*
29. —— arctica, *Kr.*

Cumacea—

30a. Diastylis Edwardsii (*Kr.*).
30b. (—————— brevirostris (*Kr.*)).
31a. —————— Rathkii (*Kr.*).
31b. (—————— angulata (*Kr.*)).
32. —————— resima (*Kr.*).
33. Leucon nasica, *Kr.*
34. Eudorella deformis (*Kr.*).

Isopoda—

35. Arcturus Baffini (*Sab.*).
36. Idothea Sabini, *Kr.*
37. —————— nodulosa, *Kr.*
38. Oniscus sp. (O. asellus, *Fabr.*).
39. Asellus grœnlandicus, *Kr.*
40. Henopomus tricornis, *Kr.*
41. Jæra nivalis, *Kr.* (Oniscus marinus, *Fabr.*).
42. Munna Fabricii, *Kr.*
43. Anceus elongatus, *Kr.*
44. Praniza Reinhardti, *Kr.*
45. Æga psora (*L.*).
46. —— arctica, *Ltk.*
47. —— crenulata, *Ltk.*
48. Bopyrus hippolytes, *Kr.*
49. —————— abdominalis, *Kr.*
50. Dajus mysidis, *Kr.*
51. Leptophryxus mysidis, *Buchholz.*

Amphipoda (Læmipoda)—

52. Pontoporeia femorata, *Kr.*

53. Opis typica, *Kr.*
54. Lysiamassa gryllus (*Mandt*).
55. Socarnes Vahlii (*Rhdt.*).
56. Anonyx lagena (*Rhdt.*).
57. —— gulosus (*Kr.*).
58. Aristias tumidus (*Kr.*).
59. Hippomedon abyssi (*Goës*).
60. —— Holböllii (*Kr.*).
61. Orchomene minuta (*Kr.*).
62. Onisimus Edwardsii (*Kr.*).
63. ——— plautus (*Kr.*).
64. —— littoralis (*Kr.*).
65. Cyphocaris anonyx, *Ltk.*
66. Stegocephalus ampulla (*Phipps*).
67. Metopa Bruzelii (*Goës*).
68. —— clypeata (*Kr.*).
69. —— glacialis (*Kr.*).
70. Syrrhoë crenulata, *Goës.*
71. Odius carinatus (*Sp. Bate.*).
72. Vertumnus cristatus (*Owen*).
73. ——— serratus (*Fabr.*).
74. —— inflatus (*Kr.*).
75. Paramphitoë glabra, *Boeck.*
76. ——— panopla (*Kr.*).
77. ——— bicuspis (*Rhdt.*).
78. ——— pulchella (*Kr.*).
79. Atylus carinatus (*Fabr.*).
80. —— Smithi (*Goës*).
81. Pontogeneia crenulata (*Rhdt.*).
82. Tritropis fragilis (*Goës*).
83. ——— aculeata (*Lepechin.*).
84. Calliopus læviusculus (*Kr.*).
85. Amphithopsis longimana, *Bk.*
86. Cleïppides tricuspis (*Kr.*).
87. Halirages fulvocinctus (*Sars*).
88. Paramphitoë (?) megalops (*Buchh.*).
89. Acanthozone cuspidata (*Lep.*).
90. Œdicerus saginatus, *Kr.*
91. ——— lynceus, *Sars.*
92. ——— borealis, *Bk.*
93. Monoculodes affinis (*Bruz.*).
94. ——— norvegicus, *Boeck.*
95. ——— latimanus (*Goës*).
96. ——— borealis, *Bk.*
97. Tiron acanthurus, *Lillj.*

98. Harpina plumosa (*Kr.*).
99. Phoxus Holböllii, *Kr.*
100. Haploöps tubicola (*Lilljeborg*).
101. Ampelisca Eschrichtii, *Kr.*
102. Byblis Gaimardi (*Kr.*).
103. Pardalisca cuspidata, *Kr.*
104. Eusirus cuspidatus, *Kr.*
105. Melita dentata (*Kr.*).
106. Gammarus locusta (*Linn.*).
107. Gammaracanthus loricatus (*Sabine.*).
108. Amathilla Sabini (*Leach*).
109. ———— pinguis (*Kr.*).
110. Autonoë macronyx (*Lillieb.*).
111. Protomedeia fasciata, *Kr.*
112. Photis Reinhardti, *Kr.*
113. Podocerus anguipes (*Kr.*).
114. ———— latipes (*Kr.*).
115. Siphonocætes typicus, *Kr.*
116. Glauconome leucopis, *Kr.*
117. Themisto libellula (*Mandt.*).
118. ————bispinosa, *Boeck.*
119. Parathemisto compressa (*Goës*).
120. Hyperia medusarum (*Müll.*).
121. Tauria medusarum (*Fabr.*).
122. Dulichia spinosissima, *Kr.*
123. Caprella septentrionalis, *Kr.*
124. Cercops Holböllii, *Kr.*
125. Ægina longicornis, *Kr.*
126. ———— echinata, *Boeck.*
127. Cyamus mysticeti, *Ltk.* (on the right whale).
128. ———— boopis, *Ltk.* (Oniscus ceti, *Fabr.*).
129. ———— monodontis, *Ltk.*
130. ———— nodosus, *Ltk.*

Phyllopoda et Cladocera—

131. Apus glacialis, *Kr.*
132. Branchipus paludosus (*Müll.*).
133. Nebalia bipes (*Fabr.*).
134. Daphnia rectispina, *Kr.*
135. Lynceus sp. (L. lamellatus *Kr.* ?)

Ostracoda—

136. Cypridina sp. ? (C. excisa ?)
137. Cythere limicola (*Norman*).
138. ———— angulata ? (*G. O. Sars*).

139. Cythere tuberculata (*Sars*).
140. ——— abyssicola (*Sars*).
141. ——— septentrionalis, *Brady*.
142. ——— costata, *Brady*.
143. ——— lutea, *Müller*.
144. ——— emarginata, *Sars*.
145. ——— Finmarchica, *Sars*.
146. Cytheridea papillosa, *Bosquet.*
147. ——— pulchra, *Brady*.
148. ——— oryza, *Brady*.
149. ——— punctillata, *Brady*.
150. Cytheropteron latissimum, *Norman.*
151. Bythocythere simplex, *Norman.*

Copepoda—

152. Pontia (Anomalocera) Pattersonii (*Templ.*).
153. Diaptomus castor, *Jur.*
154. Harpacticus chelifer (*Müll.*).
155. Tisbe furcata (*Baird*).
156. Cleta minuticornis (*Müll.*).
157. Zaus spinosus, *Claus.*
158. ——— ovalis (*Goodsir*).
159. Thorellia brunnea, *Boek.*
160. Calanus hyperboreus, *Kr.*
  (——— quinqueannulatus, *Kr.*)
  (——— spitzbergensis, *Kr.*)
161. Calanus caudatus, *Kr.*
162. Canthocamptus hippolytes, *Kr.*
163. Thersites gasterostei (*Kr.*).
164. Lernæopoda elongata (*Grant*) (on the shark's eye).
165. ——— carpionis, *Kr.* (on the salmon).
166. ——— sebastis, *Kr.*
167. Brachiella rostrata, *Kr.* (on the hippoglossus).
168. Anchorella uncinata (*Müll.*) (on Gadus morrhua).
169. ——— agilis, *Kr.* (on Gadus agilis).
170. ——— stichæi, *Kr.*
171. Lesteira lumpi, *Kr.* (on Cyclopterus lumpus).
172. Diocus gobinus (*Müll.*) (on Phobetor ventralis).
173. Chondracanthus radiatus (*Müll.*) (on Macrurus rupestris).
174. ——— nodosus (*Müll.*) (on Sebastes norvegicus).
175. ——— cornutus (*Müll.*) (on Pleuronectidæ).
176. Tanypleurus alcicornis, *Stp. et Ltk.* (on Cyclopterus spinosus).
177. Herpyllobius arcticus, *Stp. et Ltk.* (on Chætopodous annulata).
178. Caligus (Lepeophtheirus) hippoglossi, *Kr.*
179. ——— robustus, *Kr.* (on Raja radiata).

180. Dinematura ferox, *Kr.* (on the shark).
181. Peniculus clavatus (*Müll.*) (on Sebastes norv.).
182. Hæmobaphes cyclopterina (*Müll.*) (on several fishes).
183. Lernæa branchialis, *L.* (on Gadus spp.).
184. Psilomallus hippolytes, *Kr.*

Cirripedia—
185. Peltogaster paguri, *Rathke* (on Pagurus).
186. Sylon sp. (on Hippolyte sp.)
187. Balanus porcatus (*Da Costa*).
188. ———— balanoides (*Linn.*).
189. ———— crenatus, *Brug.*
190. Coronula diadema (*Linn.*) (on the humpback whale).
191. Conchoderma auritum (*Linn.*).

APPENDIX.

Pycnogonida—
192. Nymphon grossipes (*Linn.*), Niutok.
193. ———— mixtum, *Kr.*
194. ———— longitarse, *Kr.*
195. ———— hirtum, *Fabr.*
196. ———— brevitarse, *Kr.*
197. Eurycyde hispida (*Kr.*).
198. Pallene spinipes (*Fabr.*).
199. ———— intermedia, *Kr.*
200. ———— discoidea, *Kr.*
201. Endeïs proboscidea (*Sab.*).
202. Phoxichilidium femoratum (*Rathke*).

X. ANNULATA.

(Revised by Chr. Lütken, 1875.)

Euphrosynidæ—
1. Euphrosyne borealis, *Œrstd.*

Polynoidæ—
2. Lepidonotus squamatus (*L.*).
3. Nychia cirrosa (*Pall.*).
4. ———— Amondseni, *Mlgr.*
5. Eunoa Œrstedii, *Mlgr.*
6. ———— nodosa (*Sars*).
7. Lagisca rarispina (*Sars*).
8. Harmothoë imbricata (*L.*).
9. Antinoë Sarsii, *Kindbg.* (grœnlandica, *Mlmgr.*).

Sigalionidæ—

    10. Pholoë minuta (*Fabr.*).

Nephtydidæ—

    11. Nephtys ciliata (*Müll.*).
    12. ———— lactea, *Malmgr.*
    13. ———— cæca (*Fabr.*).
    14. ———— longisetosa, *Œrstd.*

Phyllodocidæ—

    15. Phyllodoce citrina, *Mlgr.*
    16. ———— grœnlandica, *Œrsted.*
    17. ———— Rinki, *Mlgr.*
    18. ———— Luetkeni, *Malmgr.*
    19. ———— incisa, *Œrsted.*
    20. Eulalia viridis (*Müll.*).
    21. ———— problema, *Malmgren.*
    22. Eteone longa (*Fabr.*), Sangiak.
    23. ———— cylindrica, *Œrsted.*
    24. ———— flava (*Fabr.*), Sangiarak.

Hesionidæ—

    25. Castalia aphroditoides (*Fabr.*).
    26. ———————— rosea (*Fabr.*).

Syllidæ—

    27. Autolytus longisetosus, *Œrsted*, Igdlolualik.
    28. ———— Alexandri (*Malmgr.*).
    29. ———— incertus, *Mlgr.*
    30. Syllis incisa (*Fabr.*), Sangiak.
    31. ———— Fabricii, *Malmgr.*, Sangiarak.
    32. Chætosyllis Œrstedi, *Malmgr.*?

Nereidæ—

    33. Nereis zonata, *Malmgr.*, Sangiak.
    34. Eunereis (Heteronereis) paradoxa (*Œrsted*).
    35. Nereis pelagica, *Linn.*, Sangiarsuak.
    36. Heteronereis grandifolia (*Rathke*).

Lumbrinereidæ—

    37. Lumbrinereis fragilis (*Müll.*).

Eunicideæ—

    38. Nothria conchylega (*Sars*).

Glyceridæ—

    39. Glycera capitata, *Œrsted*, Pulateriak.

    40. —— setosa, *Œrsted*.

Ariciidæ—

    41. Scoloplos armiger (*Müll.*).

    42. Naidonereis quadricuspidata (*Fabr.*).

Opheliidæ—

    43. Ammotrypane aulogaster, *Rathke*.

    44. Ophelia limacina (*Rathke*).

    45. Travisia Forbesi, *Johnst.*

Scalibregmidæ—

    46. Scalibregma inflatum, *Rathke*.

Te'ethusæ—

    47. Arenicola marina (*Linn.*).

Sphærodoridæ—

    48. Ephesia gracilis, *Rathke*.

Chloræmidæ—

    49. Trophonia plumosa (*Müll.*).

    50. Flabelligera affinis, *Sars*.

    51. Brada villosa (*Rathke*).

    52. —— granulata, *Malmgr*.

Sternaspidæ—

    53. Sternaspis fossor, *Stimpson*.

Chætopteridæ—

    54. Spiochætopterus typicus, *Sars*.

Spionidæ—

    55. Scolecolepis cirrata (*Sars*).

    56. Spio filicornis (*Fabr.*), Igdlolualik.

    57. —————— seticornis, *Fabr*.

    58. Spiophanes Kroyeri, *Grube*.

    59. Leipoceras uviferum, *Möb*.

Cirratulidæ—

    60. Cirratulus cirratus (*Müll.*).

Halelminthidæ—

    61. Notomastus latericeus, *Sars*.

    62. Capitella capitata (*Fabr.*).

Maldanidæ—

63. Nicomache lumbricalis (*Fabr.*).
64. Axiothea catenata, *Mlgr.*

Ammocharidæ—

65. Ammochares assimilis, *Sars.*
66. Myriochele Heeri, *Mlgr.*

Amphictenidæ—

67. Cistenides granulata (*L.*).
68. ———— hyperborea, *Malmgr.*

Ampharetidæ—

69. Ampharete Grubei, *Mlgr.*
70. ———— Goësi, *Mlgr.*
71. Amphicteis Gunneri (*Sars*).
72. Sabellides borealis, *Sars.*
73. Melinna cristata (*Sars*).
74. Lysippe labiata, *Mlgr.*

Terebellidæ—

75. Amphitrite cirrata, *Müll.*
76. ———— grœnlandica, *Mlgr.*
77. Nicolea arctica, *Mlgr.*
78. Scione lobata, *Mlgr.*
79. Axionice flexuosa (*Grube*).
80. Leæna abranchiata, *Mlgr.*
81. Thelepus cincinnatus (*Fabr.*).
82. Leucariste albicans, *Mlgr.*
83. Ereutho Smitti, *Mlgr.*
84. Artacama proboscidea, *Mlgr.*
85. Trichobranchus glacialis, *Mlgr.*
86. Terebellides Strömii, *Sars.*

Sabellidæ—

87. Laonome? (Sabella) Fabricii (*Kr.*).
88. Patamilla reniformis (*Müll.*).
89. Euchone analis (*Kr.*).
90. ———— tuberculosa, *Kr.*
91. Dasychone infarcta, *Kr.*
92. Chone infundibuliformis, *Kr.*
93. Amphicora Fabricii (*Müll.*).
94. Sabella crassicornis, *Sars.*

Eriographididæ—

95. Myxicola Steenstrupii, *Kr.*

Serpulidæ—
96. Hydroides norvegica, *Gunn.*
97. Spirorbis verruca *(Fabr.)*.
98. ———— quadrangularis, *Stimps.*
99. ———— borealis, *Daud.*
100. ———— spirillum, *L.*
101. ———— lucidus *(Mont.)*.
102. ———— vitreus *(Fabr.)*.
103. ———— cancellatus *(Fabr.)*.
104. Protula media, *Stimps.*

Tomopteridæ—
105. Tomopteris septentrionalis, *Stp.*

Lumbricidæ—
106. Lumbricus sp. (terrestris), *Fabr.* (?).
107. ———— (?) rivalis, *Fabr.*
108. Euchytræus vermicularis *(Müll.)* (?).
109. Sænuris lineatus *(Müll.)* (?).
110. Clitellio arenarius *(Müll.)*.
111. ———— minutus *(Müll.)*.
112. Opsonais marina *(Fabr.)*.

Hirudinidæ—
113. Platybdella versipellis *(Diesing)*.
114. ———— Fabricii, *Malm.*
115. ———— Olriki, *Malm.* (from Hyas aranea).
116. ———— affinis, *Malm.* (from Phobetor).
117. Udonella sp. (on Caligus hippoglossi).

Echiuridæ—
118. Echiurus forcipatus *(Fabr.)*.

Priapulidæ—
119. Priapulus caudatus *(Lmk.)*.
120. ———— glandifer *(Ehlers)*.

Sipunculidæ—
121. Phaseolosoma Œrstedii, *Keferst.*
122. ———— boreale, *Keferst.*

Myzostomidæ—
123. Myzostoma gigas, *Ltk.* (on Antedon Eschrichtii).

Chætognatha—
124. Sagitta sp.

Turbellaria (Planariæ and **Nemerteæ)—**

125. Monocelis subulata (*Fabr.*).
126. Planaria lactea, *Müll.*
127. Amphiporus grœnlandicus, *Œrstd.*
128. Omatoplea rubra (*Müll.*).
129. Polystemma roseum (*Müll.*).
130. Tetrastemma grœnlandicum, *Dies.*
131. Notospermum viride (*Müll.*).
132. Meckelia fusca (*Fabr.*).
———— angulata (*Müll.*).

XI. ENTOZOA.

[With an indication of the animals in which they are found.]

(Revised by Chr. Lütken, 1875.)

Cæstoida—

1. Tænia pectinata, *Goeze* (hare).
2. ——— expansa, *Rud.* (reindeer and musk ox).
3. ——— cœnurus, *Küch.* (fox).
4. ——— armillaris, *Rud.* (Uria Brünnichii).
5. ——— sternina, *Kr.* (Sterna macroura).
6. ——— larina, *Kr.* (Larus).
7. ——— micracantha, *Kr.* (Larus).
8. ——— campylacantha, *Kr.* (Uria grylle).
9. ——— microrhyncha, *Kr.* (Charadrius hiaticula).
10. ——— clavigera, *Kr.* (Strepsilas interpres).
11. ——— retirostris, *Cr.* (S. interpres).
12. ——— megalorhyncha, *Kr.* (Tringa maritima).
13. ——— teres, *Kr.* (Somateria, Larus).
    (——— malleus, *Goeze* (formæ monstrosæ).)
14. ——— minuta, *Kr.* (Phalaropus).
15. ——— microsoma, *Cr.* (Somateria, Larus).
16. ——— fusus, *Kr.* (Larus).
17. ——— brachyphallos, *Kr.* (Tringa maritima).
18. ——— grœnlandica, *Kr.* (Harelda glacialis).
19. ——— fallax, *Kr.* (Somateria mollissima).
20. ——— borealis, *Kr.* (Emberiza nivalis).
21. ——— trigonocephala, *Kr.* (Saxicola œnanthe).
22. Bothriocephalus cordatus, *Leuckart* (man, dog, seals).
23. ————————— variabilis, *Kr.* (Phoca vitulina).
24. ————————— lanceolatus, *Kr.* (Ph. barbata).
25. ————————— phocarum (*Fabr.*) (several seals).
26. ————————— fasciatus, *Kr.* (Phoca hispida).
27. ————————— elegans, *Kr.* (Cystophora cristata).

28. Bothriocephalus similis, *Kr.* (Canis lagopus).
29. ——————— ditremus, *Cr.* ? (Colymbus septentrionalis).
30. ——————— rugosus, *Rud.* ? (Gadus uvak).
31. —— —————— punctatus, *Rud.* (Cottus scorpius).
32. ——————— crassipes, *Rud.* ? (Cottus, Gadus, Beluga).
33. ——————— proboscideus, *Rud.* (Salmo carpio).
34. —— —— ——— macrocephalus, *Rud.* (several birds).
35. Octobothrium rostellatum, *Dies.* (Sebastes norv.).
36. Fasciola intestinalis, *L.* (Gasterosteus, Mergus, Larus).
37. Anthobothrium perfectum, *Rud.* (Somniosus microc.).
38. Diplocotyle Olrikii, *Kr.* (Salmo).

Trematoda—

39. Distomum hepaticum, *L.* (sheep, imported ?).
40. ———— seriale (*Rud.*) (Salmo alpinus).
41. Onchocotyle borealis, *Van Ben.* (shark, on the gills).
42. Phylline hippoglossi (*Fabr.*) (Hippoglossus vulg.).

Nematoda—

43. Ascaris mystax, *Zed.* (Canis lagopus).
44. ———— vermicularis, *L.* (man).
45. ———— lumbricoides, *L.* (man).
46. ———— osculata, *Rud.* (Phoca grœnlandica).
47. ———— gasterostei, *Rud.* (Gasterosteus acul.).
48. ———— rajæ, *Fabr.* (Raja radiata).
49. Eustrongylus gigas, *Rud.* (dog).
50. Liorhynchus gracilescens, *Rud.* (Phoca barbata).
51. Ophiostomum dispar, *Rud.* (Phoca grœnl. and hispida).
52. Agomonema commune (*Desl.*).
53. Nematoideum alcæ picæ, *Rud.*
54. Dubium gasterostei aculeati, *Rud.*

Acanthocephala—

55. Echinorhynchus strumosus, *Rud.* (several seals).
56. ——————— acus, *Rud.* (Gadus, Hippoglossus).
57. ——————— polymorphus, *Br.* (Somateria, Harelda).
58. ——————— porrigens, *Rud.* (Balænoptera gigas).
59. ——————— hystrix, *Br.* (Graculus, Mergus serrator).
60. ——————— inflatus, *Cr.* (Charadrius hiaticula).
61. ——————— micracanthus, *Rud.* (Saxicola œnanthe).
62. ——————— pleuronectis platessoides, *Rud.*
(Besides several undetermined species in fishes.)

XII. ECHINODERMATA.

(Revised by Chr. Lütken, 1875.)

Holothuridæ—

1. Cucumaria frondosa (*Gunn*).
2. ———— calcigera, *Ag.* (C. Koreni, *Ltk.*).
3. ———— minuta, *Fabr.* (Œnus Ayresii, *Stimps.*).
4. Orcula Barthii, *Tr.*
5. Psolus phantapus, *Str.*
6. ———— Fabricii (*D. K.*) (Cuvieria F.)
7. Chiridota læve, *Fabr.*
8. Myriotrochus Rinkii, *Steenstrup.*
9. Eupyrgus scaber, *Ltk.*

Echinida—

10. Toxopneustes Drœbachiensis (*Müll.*).

Asterida—

11. Asterias polaris, *M. Tr.*
12. ———— grœnlandica, *Stp.*
13. ———— stellionura, *Val.*
14. ———— albula, *Stimps.* (A. problema).
15. ———— (Stichaster) rosea,. *M. Tr.*
16. Cribella sanguinolenta (*Müll.*).
17. Solaster papposus (*L.*).
18. ———— endeca, *L.*
19. Pteraster militaris (*Müll.*).
20. Ctenodiscus crispatus (*Retz*).
21. Archaster tenuispinus (*D. K.*).

Ophiuridæ—

22. Ophioscolex glacialis, *M. Tr.*
23. Ophioglypha Sarsii (*Ltk.*).
24. ———— robusta, *Ayr.* (Ophiura squamosa, *Ltk.*).
25. ———— nodosa (*Ltk.*).
26. ———— Stuwitzii (*Ltk.*).
27. Ophiocten sericeum (*Forb.*) (Oph. Kroyeri, *Ltk.*).
28. Ophiopus arcticus, *Lgn.*
29. Ophiopholis aculeata (*Müll.*) (Ophiolepis scolopendrica, *M. T.*).
30. Amphiura Sundevalli, *M. Tr.* (A. Holbœlli, *Ltk.*).
31. Ophiacantha spinulosa, *M. Tr.*
32. Asterophyton eucnemis, *M. Tr.*
33. ———— Agassizii, *Stimps.*

Crinoida—

34. Antedon Eschrichtii (*M. Tr.*).

XIII. ANTHOZOA.

Polyactinia (Actinida)—

   1. Actinia crassicornis, *Fabr.*
   2. ——— spectabilis, *Fabr.*
   3. ——— nodosa, *Fabr.*
   4. ——— intestinalis, *Fabr.*
   5–6. Edwardsia spp. 2.
   7–8. Peachia spp. 2 (?).

Antipatharia—

   9. Antipathes arctica, *Ltk.*

Octactinia (Alcyonaria)—

   10. Ammothea arctica, *Ltk.*
   11. Umbellula Linddahlii, *Köll.* (U. miniacea et pallida).

Calycozoa—

   12. Lucernaria auricula, *Fabr.*
   13. ——— quadricornis, *Müll.*
   14. ——— octoradiata (*Lmk.*).
   15. ——— convolvulus, *Johnst.*

XIV. ACALEPHÆ.

(By Chr. Lütken, 1875.)

Ctenophora (Beroidæ)—

   1. Mertensia ovum (*Fabr.*).
   2. Pleurobrachia rhododactyla, *Ag.*
   3. Idya cucumis (*Fabr.*).

Discophora, Hydrozoa—

   4. Aurelia flavidula, *Per. Les.* (Medusa aurita, *Fabr.*).
   5. Cyanea arctica, *Per. Les.* (M. capillata, *Fabr.*)
   6. Charybdea hyacinthina (*Fabr.*).
   7. Trachymene digitalis (*Fabr.*).
   8. Hydra sp., a fresh-water polyp.
   9. Hydractinia echinata (*Fl.*).
   10. Syncoryne mirabilis, *Ag.*
   11. Coryne sp. (Fistulana muscoides, *Fabr.*).
   12. ——— Hydra ramosa, *Fabr.*
   13. Myriophela phrygia (*Fabr.*).
   14. Tubularia indivisa, *L.*

15. Monocaulis grœnlandica, *Allm.*
16. Melicertum campanula (*Fabr.*).
17. Eudendrium sp. (Sertularia volubilis, *Fabr.*).
18. Bougainvillia superciliaris, *Ag.*
19. Stomobrachium tentaculatum, *Ag.*
20. Tiaropis diademata, *Ag.*
21. Campanularia verticillata, *L.*
22. Lafoëa fruticosa, *Sars.*
23. Cuspidella sp.
24. Salacia abietina, *Sars* (Gramonaria robusta, *Stimps.*).
25. Eucope diaphana, *Ag.*
26. Zygodactyla grœnlandica (*Per. Les.*) (Medusa æquoria, *Fabr.*).
27. Halecium muricatum, *Ell. Soll.*
28. Sertularia pumila, *L.* (S. thuja, *Fabr.*).
29. ———— abietina, *L.*
30. ———— fastigiata, *Fabr.*
31. ———— rugosa, *L.*
32. ———— polyzonias, *L.* (S. ciliata, *Fabr.*).
33. ———— tricuspidata (*Alder.*).

XV. SPONGIOZOA.

(From a catalogue by Dr. Chr. Lütken, founded on specimens in the Museum of Copenhagen and those discovered by the German expedition to East Greenland, and determined by Oscar Schmidt and E. Haeckel.)

1. Filifera sp. (Hircinia variabilis).
2. Cacospongia sp.
3. Chalinula ovulum, *O. S.*
4. Reniera sp.
5. Amorphina genitrix, *O. S.*
6. Eumastia sitiens, *O. S.*
7. Suberites Luetkenii, *O. S.*
8. ———— arciger, *O. S.*
9. Thecophora semisuberites, *O. S.*
10. Isodictya fimbriata, *Bbnk.*
11. ———— infundibuliformis, *Bbnk.*
12. Desmacidon anceps, *O. S.*
13. Esperia intermedia, *O. S.*
14. ———— fabricans, *O. S.*
15. Geodia simplex, *O. S.*
16. Halisarca Dujardinii, *Johnst.*
17. Ascaltis Lamarckii, *H.*
18. Ascortis Fabricii (*O. S.*).

19. Ascortis corallorhiza, *H.*
20. Ascandra reticulum (*O. S.*).
21. Leucandra Egedii (*O. S.*).
22. ———— ananas (*Mont.*) (Sycinula penicillata, *O. S.*).
23. ———— stilifera (*O.S.*).
24. Sycaltis glacialis, *H.*
25. Sycandra ciliata (*Fabr.*).
26. ———— arctica, *H.*
27. ———— compressa (*Fabr.*).
28. ———— utriculus (*O. S.*).

INDEX.